MALACHI
The Divine Messenger

SOCIETY
OF BIBLICAL
LITERATURE

DISSERTATION SERIES

J. J. M. Roberts, Old Testament Editor
Charles Talbert, New Testament Editor

Number 98

MALACHI

by
Beth Glazier-McDonald

Beth Glazier-McDonald

MALACHI
The Divine Messenger

Scholars Press
Atlanta, Georgia

MALACHI
The Divine Messenger

Beth Glazier-McDonald

Ph.D., 1983
The University of Chicago

Advisor:
Gösta W. Ahlström

Library of Congress Cataloging-in-Publication Data

Glazier-McDonald, Beth, 1952–
    Malachi, the divine messenger.

    (Dissertation series ; no. 98)
    Originally presented as the author's thesis
(Ph.D.—University of Chicago, 1983)
    Bibliography: p.
    1. Bible. O.T. Malachi—Commentaries.
I. Title. II. Series: Dissertation series
(Society of Biblical Literature) ; no. 98.
BS1675.3.G53   1986   224'.99077   86-27961
ISBN 1-55540-093-0 (alk. paper)
ISBN 1-55540-094-9 (pbk. : alk. paper)

Printed in the United States of America
on acid-free paper

TABLE OF CONTENTS

ACKNOWLEDGMENTS

It is impossible to mention all of those who had a part in stimulating my interest in biblical studies or in the present project, but I would like to acknowledge my indebtedness to G. W. Ahlström, who taught me to view the Old Testament through new eyes, whose advice was invaluable in untangling snarls and clarifying the flow of the argument, and whose friendship and encouragement I deeply appreciate.

Most of all, I am grateful to my husband John for his love, his encouragement, and his repeated exhortations to finish this project before we both slip over the hill; to my parents whose confidence in me has always exceeded my own; and to Samuel (born November 23, 1980) who willingly shared his infancy with Malachi.

INTRODUCTION

The three, short chapters of the book of Malachi have, unlike the majority of prophetic texts, elicited no great scholarly debate. Indeed, as Th. Chary remarked, there is almost total unanimity among exegetes.[1] That statement however, should not be deemed a positive assessment of recent scholarship on Malachi. As early as 1898, C. C. Torrey urged that more attention be paid to the prophet and particularly to the historical conditions that he brings to light.[2] Nevertheless, in the plethora of commentaries and articles that have appeared since that time, old material was simply garbed in new language with few new insights offered. Indeed, in this case, scholarly unanimity reveals not primary exegetical excellence, but indifference. Exactly why commentators had, and continue to have, a low view of the substance and style of Malachi's message cannot be stated unequivocally. Part of the negative appraisal may well be due to the book's extreme brevity, but part of it is also due to a pejorative view of post-exilic religious developments—a view which reveals a scholarly prejudice towards the relative significance of the reestablished temple cult and the realigned priestly hierarchy. Moreover, an imbalanced, monolithic view of prophecy has evolved in which the "Classical" prophets have become the yardstick against which all prophecy is measured. As a result, Malachi, as a representative of the prophetic tradition, is often seen only as a side eddy, a pale shadow of the "great" figures who preceded him. He has lost his originality; he is depicted as colorless and his message as "a monument of the degeneracy of Hebrew prophecy, the product of an age whose religious teachers could only imitate but not attain

---

[1] Th. Chary, *Les prophètes et le culte à partir de l'exil* (Tournai: Desclee, 1955) 160.

[2] C. C. Torrey, "The Prophet Malachi," *JBL* 17 (1898) 1.

to the spiritual fervor of the old prophets."[3] In the same vein, E. Hammershaimb is typical:

> The essential point in the old prophecies of doom was that they set up moral obligations in sharp opposition to the false cult of the people and linked the two together. In Malachi they are no longer connected, and his ethical admonitions sound like cliches merely, pale reminiscences of the older prophets of doom.[4]

What scholars have failed to realize is that the central issue both for Malachi and for the "classical" prophets, was the honor of Yahweh. Indeed, this above all else is what unites Israel's prophets. Although Malachi may indeed be a "minor" prophet, he deserves better treatment than he has often received from critics who fail to recognize his devotion to Yahweh's honor and his concern to bring traditional themes and genres to bear on the needs of his own generation.

This attempt to point out the shortcomings of past scholarship is not meant to imply that there have been no penetrating studies of the book of Malachi. On the contrary, works by A. von Bulmerincq, A. van Hoonacker, Wilhelm Rudolph, and Th. Chary among others, have definitively answered questions ranging from authorship and date to the prophecy's form and meaning.[5] Nevertheless, there are substantive issues, particularly those relating to the prophecy's internal dynamics (poetry versus prose), its unity, and its historical context, that remain unresolved.

It is widely agreed that the contents of the prophecy fall into six clearly marked sections that, generally speaking, imitate the form of an oral debate. Each unit is introduced by a statement of

---

[3] Ibid., 15.

[4] E. Hammershaimb, *Some Aspects of Old Testament Prophecy from Isaiah to Malachi* (Copenhagen: Rosenkilde og Bagger, 1966) 109. Note also, R. E. Clements, *Prophecy and Tradition, Growing Points in Theology* (Atlanta: John Knox, 1975), who concerns himself almost exclusively with the "classical" figures drawing little or no attention to Joel, Nahum, Habakkuk, Zechariah or Malachi.

[5] Cf. especially, A. von Bulmerincq's monumental two-volume commentary, *Der Prophet Maleachi* (2 vols.; Tartu: J. G. Krüger, 1926–1932); cf. also A. van Hoonacker, *Les douze petits prophètes* (Paris: Gabalda, 1908) 693–741; Wilhelm Rudolph, *Haggai-Sacharja—Maleachi* (KAT 13/4; Gütersloh: Gütersloher Verlagshaus Gerd Mohn, 1976) 247–97; Chary, 160f.

Yahweh or the prophet which is then challenged by the priests or people and finally defended by Yahweh himself in words of reproach or doom. It is also generally conceded that the work is prose and not poetry. Indeed, J. M. P. Smith went so far as to say that "if Malachi is to be regarded as poetical, either in form or content, distinctions between poetry and prose must be abandoned."[6] Others however, admit that certain verses exhibit the rhythm and parallelism consonant with a definition of poetry.[7] Because there is so little discussion on the matter, it is difficult to state unequivocally why poetic content is denied. It may be that the outward configuration of the prophecy influenced the decision; the idea that dialogue in general, and the debate form employed here, in particular, are not poetical by definition.[8] If, however, it is posited that the oracle units were not written down at the time of delivery, but at some time shortly after the fact, then the possibility that the author chose the verse form as his vehicle of expression cannot be denied.

The critic of style must begin by listening to the voice of the poet. That is, he begins as a reader. As a critic, he is concerned with what happens to language at the artist's hand, with the distinctive form imposed upon language in the poem. The style of each poet represents a selection from the available resources, concentrated and given dramatic significance in relation to a unique vision of human experience. What must be stressed is that as the material of art changes and, consequently, artists seek out new techniques to transform experience and feeling into these symbolic forms, criticism must shift its emphasis and sometimes the objects of its inquiry. Unfortunately, this has not happened in the biblical field. It is almost as if poetic forms are expected to remain static. What was normative for tenth century poetry should also be normative for fifth. However, neither poetry nor

---

[6] J. M. P. Smith, *Malachi* (ICC; Edinburgh: T. & T. Clark, 1912) 5.

[7] Cf. von Bulmerincq, 1: 419-22. G. L. Robinson, *The Twelve Minor Prophets* (New York: George H. Doran, 1926), remarked that only Mal 1:11; 3:1, 6, 10; 4:1 had poetic qualities, 160.

[8] *Webster's New World Dictionary of the American Language* (Cleveland and New York: World, 1968) defines a poem as "an arrangement of words in verse; especially, a rhythmical composition, sometimes rhymed, expressing facts, ideas or emotions in a style more concentrated, imaginative, and powerful than ordinary speech," 1128.

language as a whole remains constant. Poetry may be influenced by the phonological developments of language, by the pressure of prose style,[9] or, as in this case, by the structure of the prophecy itself. Consequently, that Malachi's style is not the same as that employed by other prophets or by the authors of the Psalms, to name but two examples, should not be a stumbling block in the way of viewing the work as poetry. Indeed, the theory that all poetry must be equally rich in sound is unjust, as is the statement that fifth century poetic material reveals "a disintegration of the earlier pure forms."[10] What is necessary is to exploit the tension created by the regularity of the "ideal" pattern and the irregularity of the syntax of the poem or group of poems in question. What must be recognized is that it is the theme itself that brings about the choice of conventions (parallelism, assonance, etc.) the poet employs in his composition; what is more, theme dictates what variations should be made on those conventions. Consequently, the criteria by which we decide what is or is not poetry must be enlarged to include these factors. Indeed, it is only by subscribing to a more flexible definition of poetry and acknowledging the powerful influences exerted on form by changing historical circumstances and ongoing linguistic developments that we can learn more about the body of Israel's poetry and, therefore, speak of its development rather than its "disintegration."

In the following section the composition of each of Malachi's oracle units will be reviewed by analyzing their internal structure. The prosodic units will be diagrammed by assigning a letter to each significant element in a colon. Parallel elements in succeeding cola will receive the same letter but with a subscript. Each section will, thereby, be shown to develop a tightly knit unit of thought held together by parallelism, repetition of grammatical elements, assonance, and similar poetic devices. Such a descriptive literary analysis will also reveal the strong imprint of the prophecy's form on the poetry's style.

J. M. P. Smith remarked that "the essential unity of Malachi has never been called into question."[11] However, that assertion is

---

[9] Paul D. Hanson, *The Dawn of Apocalyptic* (Philadelphia: Fortress, 1975) 56.

[10] Ibid., 47. Stephen A. Geller remarked that "the canons of classical parallelism . . . are considerably decayed in late verse," *Parallelism in Early Biblical Poetry* (HSM 20; Missoula: Scholars, 1979) 3, n. 7.

[11] J. M. P. Smith, 3. See also, Ernst Sellin and George Fohrer, *Introduction to the Old Testament* (Nashville: Abingdon, 1968) 469-70 and Otto Eissfeldt, *The Old Testament: An Introduction* (New York: Harper and Row, 1965) 442.

belied by the relatively large number of verses that are considered
to be later additions. Exegetes generally excise either parts of all
of Mal 1:11-14; 2:7; 2:11-12; 2:15-16 and 3:22-24, to mention but
a few examples.[12] The grounds for these deletions are not well
documented, especially with regard to 3:22-24, usually understood
as a colophon to the prophetic canon. However, for other verses,
reasons range from *metri causa* to the assertion that the verse in
question either has only narrow connections with what precedes
or follows, is totally superfluous, or does not fit into the historical
context.[13]

Although a descriptive literary analysis will serve to defend
the prophecy as a poetic composition, it will be of only partial
help in defending its integrity. Those verses excised *metri causa*
or because of their supposed tenuous relation to the context in
which they appear can be shown, through such an analysis, to be
very much a part of the original prophecy. However, a defense of
those verses whose secondary status is argued from history requires
both knowledge of the events of the Persian period and an
understanding of the community situation revealed by Malachi's
artistry. Unfortunately, to move from a literary analysis to an
historical inquiry involves an element of speculation and one that
is increased not only by the precarious state of our knowledge
about Judah in the fifth century B.C., but also by the fact that
Malachi offers no reference points for concrete dating. It is
evident, on the one hand, that decreased information tends to
produce intemperate claims that the material at our disposal
cannot substantiate and, on the other, that the attempt to maintain
neutrality produces results that are just as levelling. Although
this method is a balancing act between two extremes, it is recommended by other concerns.

All too often it has been the case that scholars have compart-
mentalized history; that is, they have brought to their study of
Malachi preconceived ideas about what could or could not have
happened in the period and so forced the prophecy to conform to
a false chronology. The major consequence of this prejudgment
is that much that is original to Malachi is excised as secondary in
an attempt to resolve the dissonance produced between the new
ideas introduced by the prophet and the old presuppositions

---

[12] von Bulmerincq, 1.357f. provides a comprehensive list of those verses that
scholars consider secondary. More recent commentaries still excise the same verses.
[13] Ibid., 357f.

brought by scholars to their investigation.[14] This is particularly
the case in those sections banning intermarriage (Mal 2:11-12)
and stressing the importance of the law (תורה) as a community
guide (Mal 2:7, 3:22). Moreover, it is precisely these verses that
make it very clear that the yardstick against which the genuineness
of Malachi's prophecy is measured is the work of Nehemiah and
Ezra. For example, J. Morgenstern asserted that Mal 2:11-12
could not refer to intermarriage because opposition "arose only
with Ezra and Nehemiah in the spirit of Jewish particularism and
isolationism."[15] Similarly, Eissfeldt maintained that those verses
were a later interpolation "reflecting the campaign carried on by
Ezra and Nehemiah."[16]

It is axiomatic that a prophet must be understood, not only
against the background of the historical, political and religious
circumstances in which he was active, but also in relation to the
society in which he lived and for which his message was proclaimed. However, taken alone that principle is still insufficient
to formulate a well-rounded picture. At the same time a prophet
must be permitted to speak out in his own terms, thereby
providing a check against arbitrary, and oftentimes subjective,
interpretations of history. This is precisely what previous investi-
gations of Malachi have failed to do. Giving Malachi the chance
to speak out will not substantially alter our conception of history,
nor will it answer all the remaining questions of fact, of motiva-
tion and of influence, but it will complement the material we
posses and shed welcome light on an otherwise dark period.

It is in the light of the above situation that a new attempt is
undertaken to assess the book of Malachi. Briefly restated, the
goals of this investigation are: to defend a poetic interpretation
of the prophecy, to investigate the claims for unity or non-unity,
and to encourage an interpretation which will throw greater light
on the history of post-exilic Judah. Finally, it must be asserted
that these aims are interwoven. Indeed, it is only when the
prophecy is viewed as a unity that we can determine what type of
text it is (genre), why it was composed (intention) and above all,
from what sort of situation it arose (setting).

---

[14] The failure to recognize Malachi's originality may also, in part, stem from
a scholarly reluctance to concede innovations to a prophet who is considered, for
the most part, to have been anonymous (cf. below, p. 27f.).

[15] J. Morgenstern, "Jerusalem-485 B.C.," *HUCA* 28 (1957) 21.

[16] Eissfeldt, 597.

CHAPTER I

THE PERSIAN PERIOD: AN OVERVIEW

For slightly over two centuries (539 B.C.–333 B.C.) the Persians were the masters of the Near East and they governed by a subtle mixture of firmness, finesse and conciliation. They came both as liberators who engendered hope and as subjugators who demanded compliance. They ushered in an era of relative peace conducive to growth and an innovative economic policy that created a new class of rich and an even greater one of poor.

The intent here is not to present a comprehensive review of the period's history, but to offer a descriptive analysis of the origins of the Persian empire, its administrative machinery, its economic advances and its latent defects. For it is Persian rule which provides the backdrop against which Malachi, a subject of the Persian king just like the rest of his Judean contemporaries, must be viewed.

The foundations of the empire were laid by Cyrus (550–530 B.C.);[1] its borders were further extended by Cambyses (530–522 B.C.) and its greatness climaxed with Darius (522–486 B.C.). The Persians introduced a new type of political structure. The Assyro-Babylonian military empire had collapsed, overwhelmed by the hatred of many people for its cruelties. After a short interval, in the sixth century B.C., even more lands from the Nile to the Oxus were absorbed into the Achaemenid Persian empire, which united in peaceful interchange the many peoples from the Aegean to the Indus. The formation of the empire was due, in part, to a

---

[1] According to Herodotus (I 214) his reign began as early as 558 B.C., G. Bauchanan Gray, "The Foundation and Extension of the Persian Empire," *CAH* 4 (ed. J. B. Bury, S. A. Cook, and F. E. Adcock; Cambridge: Cambridge University, 1926) 6.

formidable armament, but even more to new principles. Unlike the cold cruelty of the Assyrians, the Persians were careful to avoid violent breaches with old local traditions. Rather, they left the subject peoples their liberty, tolerated their religions and administered them in a spirit which identified their welfare with that of the whole empire. That the Achaemenids did not need to resort to the earlier harsh Assyrian practices may be partially due to the fact that the people had by now learned something about how to live in an international society. Moreover, the resistance they offered "was less general and obstinate than that offered to other conquerors."[2]

Cyrus had an idea that was at once political and religious; to return the peoples' gods to them. Indeed, it is clear that "Cyrus obtained the throne and the empire of Babylon with the acquiescence, not to say on the invitation of a large part of the population."[3] He presented himself as a liberator by reversing the policies of Nabonidus, and as a legitimate successor to the crown by accepting the throne as a gift from their own god, Marduk.[4] Moreover, "as lord of Babylonia, he not only became master of its dependencies [Phoenicia and Syria-Palestine],"[5] but he also acquired a gateway to other countries of the west: Egypt and Greece.

An empire may be gained by conquest, but to be maintained it requires a pervasive administrative machinery. The vast size of the Persian empire, the considerable number of people and the languages they spoke necessitated the rapid development of a bureaucracy. The process was set in motion by Cyrus and Cambyses but fully matured under the aegis of Darius when the years of constant conquest had ended.

Administration begins at the top and the Achaemenids were rapidly evolving a tradition of absolute monarchy based upon three political axioms. First, the monarchy must be universal—at least it must embrace all civilized lands in its part of the world, in which a rival power might spring up—for only with such universality could peace be assured among the various peoples.

[2] Ibid., 15.
[3] Ibid., 12.
[4] R. Ghirshman, *Iran* (Paris: Payot, 1951; reprint ed., New York: Penguin Books, 1978) 132.
[5] Ibid., 132.

Second, the monarch must be personally unassailable, exempt from anyone's admonition or criticism (*lèse majesté*). Finally, the monarch must be surrounded by an aristocratic professional staff heading the bureaucracy, who (though themselves subject to the king's will) inturn were in a sufficiently exalted position to be able to govern in a relatively detached spirit of *noblesse oblige*.

In the eyes of the Achaemenids, royalty was of divine essence and each king was considered, in effect, as having been chosen by Ahura-Mazda, the supreme god.[6] Indeed, it was due to divine aid that kings triumphed over their enemies.[7] In Persia itself, religion and politics were inextricably linked, and this principle was extended to embrace the conquered countries where kings sought to obtain the religious consecration of their domination.[8] Cyrus was called to the throne of Babylon by Marduk while Cambyses and Darius took the title "son of Re" as though the Egyptian deity himself had elevated them to the throne.[9] It was the type of policy that was destined to win the people's sympathy and fidelity.

Just as the king was the head of state, so Persians were the ruling class within it. Indeed, the chief officials were usually chosen from among noble families or from the royal family itself.[10] It was the instability of the empire, the tendency of the conquered to reassert their independence that necessitated Persian involvement in all aspects of governance since "they [i.e., the Persians] alone could be counted on to remain loyal to the king."[11]

Surrounded though he was by counsellors and other bureaucrats, the king simply could not be expected to keep tabs on all the activities in such an extensive realm. As a result, more manageable units of government were created by dividing the empire into

---

[6] Note Darius' words in the Behistun inscription: "By the grace of Ahura-Mazda I am king," G. B. Gray and M. Cary, "The Reign of Darius," *CAH* 4 (ed. J. B. Bury, S. A. Cook, and F. E. Adcock; Cambridge: Cambridge University, 1926) 185.

[7] Roland G. Kent, "A New Inscription of Xerxes," *Language* 9 (1933) 37–38.

[8] Gray and Cary, 185.

[9] Roland de Vaux, "Les décrets de Cyrus et de Darius sur la reconstruction du temple," *RB* 46 (1937) 35ff.

[10] M. J. Dresden, "Persia," *IDB* 3 (ed. George Arthur Buttrick; Nashville: Abingdon, 1962) 742.

[11] Ghirshman, 142.

twenty provinces or satrapies. Although it is certain that both Cyrus and Cambyses created some satrapies, it was "Darius who established them throughout the empire,"[12] each under the governance of a satrap or "protector of the realm."[13] Further, each satrapy was split into smaller districts headed by subordinate governors (also called satraps).[14]

The satrap was his province's civil and judiciary authority. His duties included controlling local finances, securing the requisite levy for the armed forces,[15] and maintaining good relations with the neighboring provinces.[16] However, his power was subject to certain restrictions. He could not send expeditions against neighboring peoples who were not part of the empire,[17] nor was he permitted to enter into an important domestic affair without first consulting the court.[18]

In order to ensure further that power was not concentrated in the hands of one man, additional checks and balances were imposed upon the satrap. Beside him the king placed a military commander and a secretary of state.[19] In this way the king armed himself against the continual danger of seeing the governor of a distant satrapy evade the orders of the central authority and pursue schemes to achieve independence on his own. This triad of officials—satrap, secretary and general—was independent of one another, each taking his orders directly from the court.[20] The checks and balances did not stop there. In addition to the secretary who supplied the court with information, the satrapies were covered by an elaborate police network whose officials were known as "the ears of the king."[21] They were charged with inspecting all of the areas of the kingdom and reporting back to the king.

---

[12] Ghirshman, 144.

[13] Gray and Cary, 194.

[14] Ibid., 194.

[15] Ibid., 198.

[16] Ibid., 197.

[17] Eduard Meyer, *Geschichte des Altertums* (7 vols.; 2d ed.; Stuttgart: J. G. Cotta'sche, 1928–1939), 4/1.49.

[18] Cf. here, Ezra 3:8; 4:1; 5:6; 6:1 where Tattenai, the governor of Abar-Nahra seeks directives from the court regarding the rebuilding of the Jerusalem temple.

[19] Ghirshman, 144.

[20] An impressive line of communication was built into the Persian road system to facilitate the movement of royal dispatches, Gray and Cary, 193.

[21] Ghirshman, 144.

Moreover, they were followed by soldiers whose duty it was to protect them and "to render effective help if needed."[22]

One of the satrap's chief obligations was the collection of the tribute, a fixed yearly sum paid partly in kind and partly in money. From Herodotus (III, 89) we learn that it was Darius who first introduced contributions in the form of tribute.[23] To ensure fairness, he studied the productive capacity of each province, taking into account the fertility of the soil and the productive capacity of the individual.[24] The annual tribute paid by the fifth satrapy, which included Judah (Herodotus III, 91),[25] amounted to 350 talents.[26]

The tribute, however, was not the only financial burden imposed upon the satrapies. Ezra mentions several other forms of taxation, specifically, the impost (בלו, Ezra 4:13) and the toll (הלך, Ezra 4:13).[27] It is also probable that there was a fixed annual land tax (Neh 5:4).[28] Furthermore, money and contributions in kind were required for the support of the army, the king's households, the satraps and the sub-satraps. For example, Babylon had to provide for the royal court four months each year,[29] and Nehemiah reports (5:14) that even a small province like Judah had to feed the one hundred and fifty people who daily dined at the governor's table. It has been established that the value of these contributions and charges amounted to "two or three times as much as the fixed money tax."[30]

A. T. Olmstead remarked that "rarely among ancient monarchs do we find a ruler who so thoroughly understood that the

---

[22] Ibid., 144.

[23] A. T. Olmstead, *History of the Persian Empire* (Chicago: The University of Chicago, 1948) 185.

[24] Meyer, 4/1.78ff.

[25] Judah was called a מדינה, a territory of jurisdiction. "The term is used in Imperial Aramaic to designate a large or small province," Geo Widengren, "The Persian Period," in *Israelite and Judean History* (ed. J. H. Hayes and J. M. Miller; Philadelphia: Westminster, 1977) 510.

[26] Olmstead, 293.

[27] בלו—impost, tax paid in kind to support the provincial administration; הלך—tax imposed on travellers for the construction and maintenance of roads, cf. Widengren, p. 527; Franz Rosenthal, ed., *An Aramaic Handbook* (2 vols.; Wiesbaden: Otto Harrassowitz, 1967), 1/2.19,23.

[28] Gray and Cary, 199.

[29] Meyer, 4/1.81.

[30] Gray and Cary, 200.

successful state must rest on a sound economic foundation."[31]
That ruler was Darius. Not only did he initiate the tribute which
caused 'tons' of precious metal to flow into government coffers,
but he also introduced a uniform system of weights and measures
and standardized the monetary unit.[32] The relative peace, which
was one of the positive aspects of Persian domination, gave an
unprecedented impetus to the economic life of the empire. An
excellent road system and increased security facilitated the development of internal trade, and foreign commerce, too, was stimu-
lated.[33] However, trade and sales were heavily taxed.[34] Moreover,
the government kept a tight rein on the money supply, coining
very little of the vast amount of gold and silver that entered the
treasury,[35] thereby rapidly draining the empire of cash. Because
the demand for products grew, credit was necessary in order to
continue business. This and the fact that taxes had to be paid in
silver, produced successively increased borrowing that led more
and more often to default, confiscation and even enslavement
(cf. Neh 5:4).[36] The inflationary spiral soon became an insidious
disease that contributed to resentment and social instability.[37]

In principle, the fiscal innovations begun by Cyrus (economic
organization on the national level, uniform tax system, standardized weights and measures, fixed coinage) were a positive
inducement to economic growth and development. However, the
administration's apparent greed, which led to overtaxation and to
tight money policy, condemned it to failure from the start.
Although government coffers were overflowing, "little of the vast
sum was ever returned to the satrapies."[38]

Although it would be inaccurate and unjust to regard the
Achaemenids as conquerors imposing themselves on subject
peoples of whom they demanded only blind obedience to their
victorious might, the fact remains that imperialism underlay all

---

[31] Olmstead, 185.
[32] Ibid.
[33] Ghirshman, 185–86.
[34] Ibid., 187.
[35] Olmstead, 298.
[36] Ibid.
[37] Widengren, 524.
[38] Olmstead, 297–98.

their policies.[39] The large amount of autonomy granted to the satrapies by the Persians, and the astute policies whereby ancient cultures and religious associations were preserved, tend to obscure their obvious political motives. The situation of Judah provides an excellent example. When Cyrus permitted the Jews to return to Jerusalem and rebuild the temple, it was not the goodness of his heart that prompted his action. Rather, it was the fact that "Palestine was a road that led to Egypt, as yet unconquered."[40] Further, when Egypt was incorporated into the empire,[41] it was imperative to possess safe lines of communication with the Persian garrison there because of Egypt's instability.[42] Again, Judah was of strategic importance.

That the administrative tactics of the Persians were, on the whole, more humane than those of the preceding and succeeding empires[43] cannot be denied. However, that perception has encouraged the tendency to overstate their achievements and play down the empire's latent defects. Although the Persians inaugurated an era of peace and prosperity, it is also the case that their economic policy very nearly broke the backs of their constituents. Moreover, the fact that provinces rebelled against the Persian domination,[44] reveals the inherent disaffection toward foreign rule. Indeed, no matter how progressive or how placating the system, it cannot be denied that self-determination, the independence to pursue courses of their own choosing, is the predilection of all people, and especially those forced to live under foreign rule.

[39] Ghirshman, 203.

[40] Ibid., 132.

[41] Cambyses conquered Egypt in 525 B.C., Widengren, 522.

[42] Olmstead, 308; Widengren, 529.

[43] Ghirshman, 127.

[44] For example, Egypt rebelled in 486 B.C. (Olmstead, 228) and Babylon in 482 B.C. (Olmstead, 236).

CHAPTER II

THE DATE OF MALACHI

The themes with which Malachi deals and the images he paints make it abundantly clear that he is a child of the Persian period. Not only has the temple been rebuilt (Mal 1:10; 3:1, 10), but public worship is again carried on in it. At the same time, however, there was a loss of earlier religious enthusiasm. The return from Babylon brought with it none of the ideal glories promised by Deutero-Isaiah, and the completion of the temple was followed by disillusionment over the anticipated prosperity announced by Hag (cf. 1:7f, 2:7f) and Zech (1:7; 2:8). Unlike other prophets who complain that the people put their trust in sacrifice to the detriment of righteousness and mercy (cf. Isa 1:11; Hos 6:6; Amos 5:21-24), Malachi deplores Israel's parsimony both in the performance of temple worship (Mal 1:6-8, 12-14) and the payment of tithes (Mal 3:8-9). To the prophet, these deficiencies signify contempt for Yahweh. It is more likely, however, that poor harvests (Mal 3:11), trouble from neighbors (Neh 4:2f, Ezra 7:7f) and the general poverty induced by the Persian economic policy (cf. Neh 5) were the factors directly responsible for such behavior. Cultic indifference (Mal 1:13), moral laxity (Mal 3:5), and scepticism regarding divine justice (Mal 2:17; 3:13f) were only secondary manifestations.

Two other factors evidence the fact that Malachi belongs within the Persian period. As proof of Yahweh's love for his people, the prophet does not call to mind the destruction of the oppressive Babylonian empire or the return of the people to their land. Rather, his love is demonstrated by the humiliation and devastation that is heaped upon Edom, Israel's mortal enemy

(Mal 1:2-5).[1] Moreover, according to Malachi, Judah is administered by a *peḥâ* (Mal 1:8), a term used in the Persian period "to designate the governor of a small satrapy or province."[2]

Although the materials for a confident conclusion about the exact date of Malachi do not exist, a comparison of the terms in which Malachi speaks with the conditions of Judah in the Persian period leaves no doubt that his prophecy, generally speaking, belongs to the age of Nehemiah and Ezra.[3] According to Malachi, the priesthood was lax (Mal 1:6f), mixed marriages were prevalent (Mal 2:10-16), the people were remiss in the payment of tithes (Mal 3:8) and there was a distinct lack of social justice (Mal 3:5). These abuses, especially the latter three, are just those which Nehemiah and Ezra set about to reform (cf. Neh 5:1-13; 10:33f; 13:1-3, 23f; Ezra 9-10). However, this is not to assert that Malachi's work was exactly contemporaneous with that of either Nehemiah or Ezra. It is extremely unlikely that Malachi was active during the time that Nehemiah was in Jerusalem since Mal 1:8 implies that the *peḥâ* was accustomed to receive gifts from the population (cf. also Neh 5:15). Nehemiah, however, tells us that he refused to avail himself of the privilege (Neh 5:14, 18).[4]

Similarly, it is improbable that Malachi prophesied during the interval that separated Nehemiah's second visit to Jerusalem (ca. 433-430 B.C.)[5] from Ezra's arrival in the city (397 B.C.).[6] The people's derelict attitude toward the payment of tithes and other sacred dues (Neh 10:32-39, 13:23-31) impelled Nehemiah to institute a commission during his second visit. Headed by four "faithful" men, its duty was to administer the temple treasury (Neh 13:10f).[7] From Ezra 8:33, it is apparent that when he was active in Jerusalem, a similar commission was in effect and

---

[1] A. van Hoonacker, *Les douze petits prophètes* (Paris: Gabalda, 1908) 695.

[2] Geo Widengren, "The Persian Period," in *Israelite and Judean History* (ed. J. H. Hayes and J. M. Miller; Philadelphia: Westminster, 1977) 510.

[3] For the controversial chronology of Nehemiah and Ezra, see Widengren, 503-9, and H. H. Rowley, *The Servant of the Lord* (2nd ed. rev.; Oxford: Basil Blackwell, 1965) 137-68. I follow both of these scholars in dating Nehemiah's activity (445 B.C.) prior to Ezra's (397 B.C.).

[4] van Hoonacker, 697.

[5] Widengren, 532.

[6] Rowley, 167-68.

[7] A. van Hoonacker, "Notes sur l'histoire de la restauration juive après l'exile de Babylone," *RB* 10 (1901) 182f.

exercising its function. Malachi, however, makes no reference to any such commission.

All three men—Malachi, Nehemiah and Ezra—were confronted by the problem of mixed marriages, and each struggled to abolish them, even resorting to some strong-armed tactics (cf. Mal 2:12; Neh 13:23f). However, it was Ezra's radical reform, demanding not only the dissolution of such marriages, but also the prohibition against any further intermarriage in the future, that definitely curtailed, or even ended, the abuse (cf. Ezra 9-10).[8] Consequently, Malachi cannot be dated after Ezra (i.e., after 397 B.C.).

It is the opinion of a majority of scholars that Malachi belongs in the period between 470 B.C. and 450 B.C., before Nehemiah's arrival.[9] This coincides with the reigns of Xerxes (485-65 B.C.) and Artaxerxes I (465-25 B.C.). The most precise dating of the prophecy was presented by A. von Bulmerincq. He meticulously studied each of the oracle units, and assigned to each a time not only by year, but by season as well.[10] Insofar as he considered that the oracles were composed between 485 B.C. and 445 B.C., he is in agreement with normal dating of the book. However, Malachi itself, by its very vagueness, simply cannot support the definiteness of von Bulmerincq's dating.[11]

Proposing an alternate view, O. Holtzmann attempted to attribute the work to the first half of the third century B.C. by relating "those who fear Yahweh" (Mal 3:16) to the Hasideans of I Macc 2:42.[12] Because this involves an unnecessarily subtle interpretation of the evidence we possess, it too is best disregarded.

[8] Cf. here Rowley, 162 and Widengren, 536.

[9] Cf. van Hoonacker, 699; S. R. Driver, *The Minor Prophets*, (New York: Oxford University American Branch, Henry Frowde, 1906) 292; Ernst Sellin and George Fohrer, *Introduction to the Old Testament* (Nashville: Abingdon, 1968) 470; Otto Eissfeldt, *The Old Testament: An Introduction* (New York: Harper and Row, 1965) 442; Th. Chary, *Les prophètes et le culte à partir de l'exil* (Tournai: Desclée, 1955) 161; Rex Mason, *The Books of Haggai, Zechariah and Malachi* (Cambridge: Cambridge University, 1977) 137-39.

[10] A. von Bulmerincq, *Der Prophet Maleachi* (2 vols.; Tartu: J. G. Krüger, 1926-1932), 1.140.

[11] von Bulmerincq considered Malachi to be one of Ezra's assistants and maintained that Ezra was the "messenger" mentioned in Mal 3:1, 2.336. This view cannot be maintained if only because Ezra must be dated after Nehemiah.

[12] O. Holtzmann, "Der Prophet Maleachi und der Ursprung des Pharisäerbundes," *ARW* 29 (1931) 1-21.

A date shortly before Nehemiah's arrival suits Malachi with regard to the content of his message (i.e., 470-450 B.C.). To further narrow these limits is precarious because Malachi offers no reference points for concrete dating. Nevertheless, the poor economic circumstances to which both Malachi and Nehemiah attest appear to have become prevalent during the reign of Artaxerxes I (465-25 B.C.).[13] As a result, it is likely that Malachi was active some time after 460 B.C.[14]

Depression and discontent were the prevailing feelings in Malachi's day. Expectations of plenty had been aroused but remained unrealized. In the cultic sphere the situation culminated in the mere perfunctory performance of duty. Yahweh's altar was disdained (Mal 1:6-8, 13), vows were carelessly fulfilled (Mal 1:14) and justice was perverted (Mal 2:6-9; 3:5). As a prophet, Malachi was very involved in, and concerned about, the community in which he lived. Consequently, he was under no illusions as to the degeneracy of religion in his day and the moral laxity abroad among his people. More than other prophets, Malachi exposes the priests and people to themselves. He interprets their thoughts, puts them in abrupt, naked language and pictures them as demurring to every charge brought against them. Pitiless though he was in his indictment of the evils around him, he nevertheless held out the challenge of a bright hope for the future. When the priests were purified, Israel's sacrifices would again be accepted (Mal 3:3-4), and when the full tithe filled the storehouse, the envious admiration of the nations would ensue (Mal 3:10b, 12). The wicked in the community would be exterminated and the righteous vindicated (Mal 3:16f). It was Malachi's aim to recall the people to moral and religious earnestness. However, although he insisted upon the importance of maintaining the purity of worship, he was no formalist. Certainly, man's observance or neglect of his ritual obligations is a measure of his regard for Yahweh. Yet what Malachi demands is not the fulfillment of these rules for their own sake, but the interior dispositions (reverence, faithfulness) that find outward expression in them. Indeed, he

[13] R. Ghirshman, *Iran* (Paris: Payot, 1951; reprint ed., New York: Penguin Books, 1978) 195; A. T. Olmstead, *History of the Persian Empire* (Chicago: The University of Chicago, 1948) 297f.

[14] This date allows time for economic conditions to further deteriorate after the accession of Artaxerxes I.

enforces the claims of the law, but only insofar as its forms are an expression of that spirit.

Malachi was a man of incisive moral force, contending boldly and independently against the abuses of his time. He found it necessary to impose a degree of discipline upon a demoralized people who found life in Judah to be in total opposition to what the promises of Haggai and Zechariah had said it would be. As a result, the people were in danger of losing everything distinctive about themselves and their religion. This stress on discipline implies a degree of separation (cf. Mal 2:10-16), and it is the latter, the separation, which is usually described as a major tenet of post-exilic Judaism. Thus we see Malachi as one of the major contributors to the formation of normative Judaism.

CHAPTER III

THE FORM OF THE PROPHECY

Commentators generally point out that what is distinctive about Malachi's prophecy is the "catechetical" format.[1] Indeed, the question and answer schema employed by the prophet in order to articulate his message is particularly striking because of its rationalized, didactic cast. It is a pattern that is strictly adhered to in each of the six oracle units comprising the prophecy (cf. Mal 1:2-5; 1:6-2:9; 2:10-16; 2:17-3:5; 3:6-12; 3:13-21), and serves to make crystal clear exactly what the people's failure is, and why they continue to experience the curses threatened for covenant breakers.

The most comprehensive analysis of the form of Malachi's prophecy was presented by E. Pfeiffer.[2] He characterized the six sections as "Disputationsworte" or "speeches of disputation" and detailed the tripartite arrangement of each. The oracle units begin with a general statement of truth spoken by Yahweh or the prophet. Following C. H. Cornill, Pfeiffer labelled these opening remarks "positive affirmations" (cf. a "hingestellte Behauptung").[3] They appear both as simple statements of fact (Mal 1:2) and as rhetorical questions (Mal 1:6; 2:10). These declarations induce objections on the part of the hearers that assume the form of short inquiries (cf. Mal 1:2b; 1:7; 3:8). Finally, the "positive affirmation" is exhaustively substantiated by illustrations and citations of fact.[4]

---

[1] S. R. Driver, *The Minor Prophets* (New York: Oxford University, American Branch, Henry Frowde, 1906) 298.

[2] Egon Pfeiffer, "Die Disputationsworte im Buche Maleachi (Ein Beitrag zur formgeschichtlichen Struktur)," *EvTh* 19 (1959) 546-68.

[3] Hans Jochen Boecker, "Bemerkungen zur formgeschichtlichen Terminologie des Buches Maleachi," *ZAW* 78 (1966) 80.

[4] Pfeiffer, 554f.

The beauty of this schema inheres both in its compactness and in its movement. Indeed, Malachi manipulated the form with remarkable skill. There is no excess verbiage; rather each element of the dispute flows naturally into the succeeding one, furnishing the whole with an aura of spontaneity. This can best be appreciated by means of an example. In the first oracle unit, Mal 1:2–5, the "hingestellte Behauptung" appears as a self-assertion of Yahweh about his behaviour: אהבתי אתכם, "I have loved you" (Mal 1:2a). The onlookers rapidly counter: במה אהבתנו, "How have you loved us?" (Mal 1:2b). In what follows, vv. 3–4, Yahweh proves his love for his people Israel by evoking the picture of Edom's demise. He says: "Was not Esau Jacob's brother? Yet I loved Jacob; but Esau I hated. And I turned his mountains into a waste and his inheritance over to the jackals of the wilderness." Though Edom says, "We have been beaten down, but we will rebuild the ruins;" thus says Yahweh of Hosts: "They may build but I will tear down. And they will be called 'the territory of wickedness' and 'the people whom Yahweh eternally cursed'." The unit climaxes with the statement that when the people fully comprehend what Yahweh has accomplished they will recognize not only his solicitude but the full extent of his greatness (Mal 1:5): ועיניכם תראינה ואתם תאמרו יגדל יהוה מעל לגבול ישראל.

H.-J. Boecker, while approving Pfeiffer's results, nevertheless takes issue with his terminology and proposes labelling the oracle units "Diskussionsworte oder Streitsgespräche" rather than "Disputationsworte."[5] Moreover, he remarks that many scholars use the terms "Diskussionsworte" and "Disputationsworte" indiscriminately.[6] Therefore, he intended the change to be a conceptual clarification. According to Boecker, "eine 'Behauptung' formuliert eine, these über die dann 'disputiert' wird."[7] However, he says that since Mal 3:13a, for example, is not a "positive affirmation," what follows cannot be a dispute. Moreover, he considers the dispute form to be at home in academic circles, since the term is defined in the most recent *Duden-Lexikon* as a "gelehrtes Streitsgespräche."[8] However, his criticism is unwarranted. An "affirmation" is a positive declaration, an assertion that something is

---

[5] Boecker, 80.
[6] Ibid., 79.
[7] Ibid.
[8] Ibid.

true.[9] This definition suits all of Malachi's opening statements, be they like 1:2, "I have loved you," or like Mal 3:13, "Your words have been all too strong against me." Furthermore, to label the oracle units "Diskussionsworte" is to misconstrue the scope of the sections and their force. A discussion implies talking about something in a deliberative fashion with varying opinions offered constructively and, usually, amicably, in order to settle an issue or decide upon a course of action.[10] On the other hand, a dispute implies an argument in which there is a clash of opposing opinions, often presented in a heated manner.[11] And this is precisely the picture that Malachi paints of the situation. He is not relating the amicable proceedings of a meeting between god and man. Rather, he presents a study in contrasts between the way Yahweh insists that Israel should act and the manner in which she conducts herself in reality,[12] and between the way Yahweh acts and the manner in which the people perceive his actions. The whole tenor of the work recommends the application of the label "Disputationsworte."

Malachi was not the first to employ this question and answer schema. Indeed, numerous examples are scattered throughout the Old Testament, cf. Deut 29:23f; 1 Kgs 9:8-9; Amos 5:18; Jer 13:12f; 15:1f; 22:8-9; Hag 1:9f; 2:10f; Ezek 11:2f; 18:19; Isa 49:11; 50:1f. However, there are both qualitative and quantitative differences in Malachi's treatment of the form. Although the questions in the instances cited above and in Malachi's prophecy are posed in the same staccato manner (cf. Jer 23:33—מה־משא יהוה; and Mal 1:2—במה אהבתנו), in Malachi, the answers receive a much more detailed elaboration. Further, the concise statement of fact that precedes each question is peculiar to Malachi's style, and it is precisely in these introductory remarks, according to J. A. Fischer, that the essentials of the prophet's teaching are to be found.[13]

---

[9] *Webster's Third New International Dictionary of the English Language,* unabridged (Springfield, Mass.: G. & C. Merriam Co., 1976), 35.

[10] Ibid., 648.

[11] Ibid., 655.

[12] James A. Fischer, "Notes on the Literary Form and Message of Malachi," *CBQ* 34 (1972) 318.

[13] Ibid., 317. Fischer isolates the essentials of Malachi's teaching from the introductory remarks as follows: (1) Yahweh loves Jacob; (2) he is Israel's father; (3) he is the father of all Israelites; (4) he wants honesty not words; (5) he is faithful to his word; (6) he wants honesty not words.

Finally, the question and answer schema is more pervasive in Malachi than in other Old Testament works.

Some scholars consider the question and answer schema to be a literary convention while others regard it as the proceedings of real life confrontations. For example, J. Wellhausen insisted that "die Form der Rede und Gegenrede wiederhold sich öfters; die Diskussion ist natürlich nur schriftstellerisch Form . . ."[14] However, E. von Waldow remarked that "die Disputationsworte . . . wohl keine literarische Imitationen, sondern eher wirkliche und echte Disputationen sein werden."[15] To determine whether the body of question and answer schemata as a whole is the product of real life incidents or of literary ingenuity is impossible. Each schema must be so specified on the basis of the context in which it exists. For example, in the case of a group of schemata which have the style of a third person recitation, it is almost certain that we are dealing with a literary convention. A future situation is envisioned when people will pass by a place, see the destruction that has been visited upon it and ask why such a thing happened. Jeremiah 22:8-9 is a prime example of this:[16]

ועברו גוים רבים על העיר הזאת ואמרו איש אל־רעהו
על־מה עשה יהוה ככה לעיר הגדולה הזאת: ואמרו על
אשר עזבו את־ברית יהוה אלהיהם וישתחוו לאלהים
אחרים ויעבדום

Unfortunately, with Malachi, the answer is not quite as cut and dry. Indeed, to state definitively that the prophet was relating a series of actual confrontations is to go beyond the evidence we possess.

Nevertheless, his style is certainly reportorial. Moreover, no future situation is posited; rather, Malachi appears to be confronting immediate community circumstances. It must be stressed that prophets were not backstage artists. They functioned squarely

---

[14] J. Wellhausen, *Die kleinen Propheten übersetzt und erklärt* (Berlin: Georg Reimer, 1892) 203f; cf. also J. A. Fischer, 316 and B. O. Long, "Two Question and Answer Schemata in the Prophets," *JBL* 90 (1971) 131.

[15] H. E. v. Waldow, *Anlass und Hintergrund der Verkündigen des Deuterojesaja (Diss. Theol., Bonn, 1953)*, 28-36; cf. also Pfeiffer, 546f and Gerhard Wallis, "Wesen und Struktur der Botschaft Maleachis," *Das Ferne und Nahe Wort* (BZAW 105; Berlin: Alfred Töpelmann, 1967) 232.

[16] Cf. also Deut 29:23-27 and 1 Kgs 9:8-9.

in the public arena. Prophecy was not only the response of the prophet to the questions posed by his society and time; it was also the questioning of that society by its incisive prophetic critique. Indeed, in the final analysis, prophecy was always a questioning and being questioned. And this is precisely what we see in Malachi. The question and answer schema embodies the essence of prophecy and enables us to see the prophetic process at work.

Involved in his community and obviously distressed by what he saw, Malachi confronted his contemporaries. And they, in turn, disillusioned, bitter, and sceptical reacted by questioning everything he said. Recalling the community situation described in the previous chapter, such a scenario is highly plausible. The didactic cast, the patterned similarity, the structural coordination and integration visible throughout the work should not stand in the way of perceiving it as the account of an actual confrontation or series of confrontations. Rather, these factors may indicate only that the prophecy was written down and edited some time after the fact.

CHAPTER IV

MALACHI 1:1

מַשָּׂא דְבַר־יְהוָה אֶל־יִשְׂרָאֵל בְּיַד מַלְאָכִי[1]

The burden of Yahweh's word, directed to Israel by Malachi.

Malachi's prophecy opens with a word cluster—מַשָּׂא דְבַר־
יְהוָה—that occurs only two more times in the Old Testament, in
Zech 9:1 and 12:1. Based on this evidence, scholars have concluded that the phrase was employed by the redactor of the Book
of the Twelve Prophets to introduce three anonymous
oracles, two of which were appended to Zechariah in the course
of transmission, and one which somehow achieved independent
status—Malachi.[2] However, can it be assumed that, simply
because the same word cluster appears three times, it must follow
that the three oracles were anonymous and were quite arbitrarily
assigned their present places in the canon? A. van Hoonacker
remarked that there is no need to attribute the superscription of
Zech 9:1; 12:1 and Mal 1:1 to a single hand. "Nothing opposes
the hypothesis that Mal 1:1 was formulated as an imitation of
the others."[3] Although a step in the right direction, if only
because his suggestion admits that the passages may have had a
history independent of one another, the issue is far more complex
than that.

---

[1] The Hebrew text here and in all succeeding instances is taken from the
Biblica Hebraica Stuttgartensia (ed. K. Ellinger and W. Rudolph; Stuttgart:
Deutsche Bibelstiftung, 1967–77).

[2] Ernst Sellin and George Fohrer, *Introduction to the Old Testament*
(Nashville: Abingdon, 1968) 469 and Otto Eissfeldt, *The Old Testament: An
Introduction* (New York: Harper and Row, 1965) 440.

[3] A. van Hoonacker, *Les douze petits prophètes* (Paris: Gabalda, 1908) 705.

Each of the three passages begins with מַשָּׂא, a word which requires further explanation. Both BDB and KB define מַשָּׂא as an "utterance" or an "oracle."[4] Similarly, the RSV, NAB and NEB utilize the translation, "oracle."[5] In his commentary on Jeremiah 23:33f, K. H. Graf defended the translation of מַשָּׂא as "Ausspruch."[6] He analogized that just as משא פנים (2 Chr 19:7) is derived from נשא פנים, and just as משא נפש (Ezek 24:25) is derived from נשא נפש, so too משא קול, "lifting up of the voice," an "utterance" can be deduced from נשא קול, "to lift up the voice."[7] However, the noun phrase משא קול is unattested. Moreover, the pattern naśā° plus object is generally qualified by another verb. For example, the expression, "to lift up the eyes," נשא עינים, is usually followed by the verb "to see" (cf. Gen 24:63; 33:1; 43:29; Exod 43:10; Judg 19:17). Similarly, a verb of saying generally follows "to lift up the voice," נשא קול (cf. Gen 21:26; Judg 21:2; 1 Sam 11:4; 2 Sam 13:36; Isa 24:14; Job 2:2).[8]

Concurring with the translation "Ausspruch," Sellin labelled the combination משא דבר-יהוה "eine unnatürliche Tautologie."[9] Naturally, if מַשָּׂא is rendered "Ausspruch," the expression is tautological. However, מַשָּׂא is a maqtal form of the stem נָשָׂא, "to lift up, bear, carry, take." Accordingly, a noun derived from that stem means "a load, burden, lifting."[10] And indeed, Sellin's tautological difficulty disappears if מַשָּׂא is so translated. H. S. Gehman averred that the rendering "burden" is the best translation "since it represents literally the Hebrew word and at the same time allows us to read into the word all that is implied in the Hebrew."[11] מַשָּׂא, as used in prophecy, often carries with it ideas of judgment and catastrophe and suggests "sublime

[4] Cf. BDB, 672; KB, 570.

[5] Cf. also, Eissfeldt, 460.

[6] K. H. Graf, *Der Prophet Jeremia erklärt* (Leipzig: T. O. Weigel, 1862) 315.

[7] Ibid.

[8] It should be noted that although the expression נתן קול appears frequently (cf. Jer 4:16; 22:20; 51:16; Lam 2:17, no one asserts that מתן means "utterance."

[9] Ernst Sellin, *Das Zwölfprophetenbuch übersetzt und erklärt* (KAT 12/2 Leipzig: A Deichertsche, 1930), 547.

[10] Cf. BDB, 669f.

[11] Henry S. Gehman, "The 'Burden' of the Prophets," *JQR* 31 (1940) 110. The author lists all the prophetic passages where מַשָּׂא means "burden." Included are Isa 13:1; 14:28; 15:1; 17:1; 19:1; 21:1; 21:11; 21:13; 22:1; 23:1; 30:6; Ezek 12:1f; Nah 1:1; Hab 1:1; Zech 9:1; 12:1; Mal 1:1; Jer 23:33, 116f.

ominousness.''[12] Gehman maintains that "if burden is understood in this sense, as a technical term, it is decidedly preferable to 'oracle' or 'prophetic utterance,' terms which do not have the same connotation and do not carry the ominous import of 'burden.' ''[13]

If the three oracles in which the word cluster appears are examined, striking differences become apparent. Indeed, elements of similarity are only superficial. Each begins with the phrase משא דבר־יהוה, and each contains some foreshadowing of impending calamity, punishment or judgment which Gehman contends is inherent in the oracle by virtue of the word מַשָּׂא.[14] However, there the similarities cease. Zechariah 9 begins:

משא
דבר־יהוה בארץ חדרך
ודמשק מנחתו
כי ליהוה עין אדם
וכל שבטי ישראל

In this case, with the exception of the word מַשָּׂא, the verse does not appear to be a superscription at all, but is part of a larger poetic oracle. The form employed here closely approximates Isaiah's oracles against the nations (Isa 13:1; 15:1; 17:1; 19:1; 21:1; 21:11; 22:1; 23:1; 30:6).[15] By contrast, the entire first half of Zech 12:1—מַשָּׂא דְבַר־יהוה עַל־יִשְׂרָאֵל—functions as a superscription. Numerous prophetic parallels are extant in which the content of the oracle is expressed by means of the preposition עַל ('on,' 'concerning') (cf. Jer 14:1; 46:1; 1 Kgs 16:1).[16] However, Mal 1:1 differs from both, sharing characteristic features with other prophetic passages. First of all, the addressee is specified by the preposition אֶל ('to,' 'for'), cf. Hag 1:1; Zech 4:6. Further, the role of the prophet is characterized by means of בְּיַד (by) (cf. Jer 50:1; Hag 1:1; 1:3; 2:1; 1 Chr 11:3; 2 Chr 29:25; 35:6). Finally, it is

---

[12] Ibid., 110.

[13] Ibid.

[14] Ibid., 110f.

[15] Note here especially Isa 15:1; 17:1; 19:1; 21:1 etc., where each verse is prefaced by מַשָּׂא and the name of a country, city or place. As in the Zechariah passage, the remainder of the verse begins the oracle in poetic form.

[16] Note that the Jeremiah passages also contain the phrase דבר־יהוה.

precisely in Jer 50:1 and Hag 1:1 that the closest parallels to
Mal 1:1 as a whole are found:

Jer 50:1	הדבר אשר דבר יהוה אל־בבל אל־ארץ כשדים
	ביד ירמיהו הנביא
Hag 1:1	היה דבר־יהוה ביד־חגי הנביא אל־זרבבל . . .
	ואל־יהושע
Mal 1:1	משא דבר־יהוה אל־ישראל ביד מלאכי

The above is meant to establish that features occurring in
the heading of Malachi are consistent with those found in other
prophetic literature. Therefore, the hypothesis that the three
passages: Mal 1:1; Zech 9:1 and 12:1, had a history independent
of one another should be given more weight than the insistence
that they share a common origin by virture of a surface resemblance. Moreover, it is generally posited that the three oracles
were anonymous. However, the problem of the authorship of the
book of Malachi deserves separate study; its answer should not
be concluded on the basis of an alleged similarity to the two
Zechariah passages.

The evidence from the versions and the philological difficulty
of taking the noun מַלְאָכִי as a proper name, coupled with the
lack of historical information about such a personage, have
convinced the majority of scholars that the word refers not to a
person but is an appellative.[17] According to G. L. Robinson, the
best explanation of "Malachi" is "to take it as adjectival and
equivalent to the Latin *Angelicus*, signifying one charged with a
mission, message, hence a missionary."[18] Similarly, it is quite
apparent from LXX and Targum renderings that they did not
consider 'Malachi' a proper name. The Septuagint translates
בְּיַד מַלְאָכִי with ἐν χειρὶ αγγέλου αὐτοῦ,[19] and the Targum adds the

---

[17] Rex Mason, *The Books of Haggai, Zechariah and Malachi* (Cambridge:
Cambridge University, 1977) 135–36; Gerhard Wallis, "Wesen und Struktur der
Botschaft Maleachis," *Das Ferne und Nahe Wort* (BZAW 105; Berlin: Alfred
Topelmann, 1967) 230; G. A. Smith, *The Book of the Twelve Prophets* (2 vols.;
New York: A. C. Armstrong and Son, 1899), 2.331; Eissfeldt, 441.

[18] G. L. Robinson, *The Twelve Minor Prophets* (New York: George H.
Doran, 1926) 158.

[19] According to W. Rudolph and A. van Hoonacker, the third person suffix
was employed on stylistic ground to conform to the requirements of the clause,

clause, "whose name was Ezra the Scribe."[20] The Babylonian
Talmud (Meg 15a) and Jerome share this tradition. There is,
however, another facet to the problem. The current thesis is
typified by C. C. Torrey's position. "It may be assumed that the
prophecy is anonymous, the proper name 'Malachi' having
originated as a misinterpretation of the word in 3:1, aided perhaps by Haggai 1:13,"[21] (ויאמר חגי מלאך יהוה). According to
Sellin, it was the redactor who identified the "messenger of
Yahweh" encountered in 3:1 with the author of the book and
who, consequently introduced the word into the superscription.[22]

W. Rudolph remarks that this complicated construction
rests on the assumption that מַלְאָכִי, 'my messenger,' or 'my
angel' cannot be a proper name "because no father would so
name his son."[23] This is correct. However, the linguistic premises
for repudiating the formation as inconsistent with a contracted
Hebrew name pattern are inconclusive, cf. מַלְאָכִיָּה . Indeed, the
parallels between אֲבִי (2 Kgs 18:2) and אֲבִיָּה (2 Chr 29:1); אֻרִי
(1 Kgs 4:19) and אוּרִיָּה (1 Chr 11:41); פַּלְטִי (1 Sam 25:44) and
פַּלְטִיאֵל (2 Sam 3:15) cannot be denied. Although the form מַלְאָכִיָּה
is unattested, the name could have been borne by a man just as
was פְּנִיאֵל (1 Chr 8:25).[24] Many scholars, however, reject מַלְאָכִיָּה
as a proper name because no father would name his son
'Messenger of Yahweh',[25] or 'Yahweh is Messenger,'[26] since it
rests with "Yahweh alone to invest a man with the function
expressed by a like title."[27] Moreover, this title, "as a personal
denomination, is reserved in the Old Testament for a super-
human figure."[28] However, according to von Orelli, it is possible
that the man did not bear this name from birth, but only from

cf. Wilhelm Rudolph, *Haggai-Sacharja-Maleachi* (KAT 13/4; Gütersloh: Gütersloher Verlagshaus Gerd Mohn, 1976) 247; van Hoonacker, 705.

[20] Rudolph, 247.
[21] C. C. Torrey, "The Prophet Malachi," *JBL* 17 (1898) 1.
[22] Sellin and Fohrer, 469. Cf. also Eissfeldt, 441 and Mason, 136.
[23] Rudolph, 247; van Hoonacker, 705.
[24] van Hoonacker, 705.
[25] Ibid.
[26] G. Johannes Botterweck, "Jacob habe ich lieb—Esau hasse ich," *Bibel und Leben* 1 (1960) 28; G. A. Smith, 331.
[27] van Hoonacker, 705 and cf. Rudolph, 247.
[28] van Hoonacker, 705.

his call to be a prophet.[29] Furthermore, Rudolph has defended the interpretation of מַלְאָכִיָּה (מַלְאָכִי) as a proper name by construing it is a genitival relationship (cf. Obadiah, Abdiel), rather than as subject and predicate and finds no serious philological evidence against it.[30] מַלְאָכִיָּה would, thereby, be translated "messenger of" or "from Yahweh" in the sense of "sent by Yahweh."[31]

The assumption that the appellative 'my messenger' was a late editor's attempt to equate the author of the book with the promised messenger of Mal 3:1 carries with it definite interpretational implications. Indeed, such an identification wrecks havoc with the book's message, furnishing the text with a confused, almost unintelligible meaning, especially since the role of the messenger in Mal 3:1 is characterized as a future one. Furthermore, the appellative interpretation blatantly controverts the final two verses (3:23-24) which still envision a messenger who will effect a restoration some time in the future. In spite of the difficulties associated with the book's authorship, many commentators agree that the style of the prophecy, its historical descriptiveness and its theological content all point to a genuine prophetic figure. Finally, it is indeed the case that מַלְאָכִי was understood by the Masoretic tradition as a proper name.[32]

[29] C. von Orelli, *The Twelve Minor Prophets* (Edinburgh: T. & T. Clark, 1893) 382; cf. also G. L. Robinson, 157.

[30] Rudolph, 247.

[31] Ibid. It should be emphasized however, that although this formation is plausible, we have no empirical evidence for proper names including the element "messenger."

[32] von Orelli, 382-83.

CHAPTER V

MALACHI 1:2-5[1]

A^2	B^2		²אהבתי אתכם אמר יהוה	
B_1	$A_1{}^2$		ואמרתם במה אהבתנו	
			הלוא־אח עשו ליעקב² נאם־יהוה	
A	B		ואהב את־יעקב	
B_1	A_1		³ואת־עשו שנאתי	
A	B	C	ואשים את־הריו שממה	
	B_1	$C_1{}^2$	ואת־נחלתו לתנות מדבר	
Z	A^2		⁴כי־תאמר אדום רששנו	a
	C^2	D	ונשוב ונבנה חרבות	b
	$A_1{}^4$		כה אמר יהוה צבאות	c
	$C_1{}^2$	$B_1{}^2$	המה יבנו ואני אהרוס	d
	A^2	B^2	וקראו להם גבול רשעה	e
		$B_1{}^4$	והעם אשר־זעם יהוה עד־עולם	f
$AB\|\|A_1B_1$			⁵ועיניכם תראינה ואתם תאמרו	
			יגדל יהוה מעל לגבול ישראל	

[1] In analyzing the internal structure, I have diagrammed the prosodic units by assigning a letter to each grammatical element or cluster of elements. In the latter case, the number of elements included is indicated by a superscript, e.g., A^2. Parallel elements in succeeding lines receive the same letter but with a subscript, e.g., A_1. Such a notational methodology is recommended by the length of many of the lines of the prophecy. Assigning to each element a different letter obscures the parallelism. Note, for example, that although Mal 1:2a–b may be diagrammed ABCD//C₁EA₁, the chiastic arrangement becomes very much clearer when related elements are grouped together: A^2 (I loved you), B^2 (says Yahweh) //$B_1{}^2$ (But you say), $A_1{}^2$ (How have you loved us?).

[2] Mal 1:2c–3a may also be viewed as a tricolon (macro-structure ABB) with the first two lines bound together by the repetitive parallelism of יַעֲקֹב.

1:2   *"I have loved you," says Yahweh.*
      Yet you say: "How have you loved us?"
      "Was not Esau Jacob's brother?" oracle of Yahweh.
      "Yet I loved Jacob;
1:3   *but Esau I hated.*
      Therefore, I turned his mountains into a waste
      and his inheritance over to the jackals of the wilderness."
1:4   *Though Edom says: "We have been beaten down,*
               but we will rebuild the ruins;"
      Thus says Yahweh of Hosts:
           "They may build, but I will tear down.
      They will be called 'territory of wickedness'
      and 'the people whom Yahweh eternally cursed.'
1:5   *Then your own eyes will see, and you yourselves will say,*
      "Yahweh is great beyond the territory of Israel."

Content and Structure

The poetry of this short section is interesting because of its irregularity; the interplay between tight parallelism and non-parallel units, between symmetry and asymmetry. The challenge is thus one of discerning just what links these two diverse modes of expression. In the case of 1:2-1:3a, the solution is patent. Two couplets, each chiastically parallel,[3] are interrupted by the rhetorical question (2c)—"Was not Esau Jacob's brother?" With the preceding couplet (1:2a, b), this rhetorical question shares a common length, while the following couplet takes up its key words, עֵשָׂו, יַעֲקֹב. Similarly, with 1:5, another non-parallel unit, the same solution can be applied. As the climax of the section, the result of Yahweh's actions on his people's behalf, it flows naturally from the preceding verses. Moreover, 1:5a, which contains a distinct caesura with good internal parallelism (A:B//A:B), shares a key word with the entire oracle, a form of the verb אמר, cf. 1:2a, b; 1:4a, c. Finally, the total lack of parallelism in 1:5b serves a creative function for it reinforces the sentiment of the verse, the greatness of Yahweh that knows no bounds.[4]

---

[3] Note that the key word in each couple is אהב, "to love."
[4] Note the recurrence of this sentiment in 1:11 and 1:14.

Text and Commentary

[1:3]—C. C. Torrey maintained that the translation of תַּנּוֹת as 'jackals' is "condemned both by its form and by the verb שִׂים, whose meaning here is already determined by the first clause of the half-verse."[5] Consequently, he adopted, with corrections, the reading proposed by Stade and Nowack: נְוֹת (נְאוֹת) מִדְבָּר "dom-iciliè ou les prairies du desert."[6] Viewing the לת of לְתַנּוֹת as a dittography from נַחֲלָתוֹ, he further emended the text to read simply נְוֹת מִדְבָּר.[7] Van Hoonacker was convinced that תַּנּוֹת could not refer to an animal since the construction of the couplet requires תַּנּוֹת מִדְבָּר "to characterize the state to which Yahweh reduced Edom's territory."[8] Therefore, he accepted Torrey's recon-struction, maintaining that his suggestion created excellent paral-lelism between שְׁמָמָה and נְוֹת מִדְבָּר neither being introduced by a lamed.[9]

By contrast, A. von Bulmerincq maintained that the paral-lelism between שְׁמָמָה and מִדְבָּר נְאוֹת was tenuous at best. His proposed reading לִמְעוֹן תַּנִּים (a jackals' lair) was based on passages like Jer 9:10 (cf. also Jer 10:22; 49:33) where the phrase is parallel to שְׁמָמָה.[10] He further defended his use of מָעוֹן by referring to the LXX and Peshitta translations, both of which employ a term meaning "dwelling, habitation" (cf. δώματα; ܐܗܪ). Similarly, he maintained that the use of the masculine plural תַּנִּים was justified in view of the renderings of the Vulgate (dracones) and Aquila (εἰς σειρῆνας).[11]

Both of these suggested reconstructions require comment, especially because the MT, as it stands, although difficult, is not unintelligible. Torrey's hypothesis rests on the assumption that the verb שִׂים cannot have two different meanings in the same verse. Indeed, if the meaning remains constant, the sense of the second clause is distorted, "And I made his inheritance jackals of

---

[5] C. C. Torrey, "The Prophet Malachi," *JBL* 17 (1898) 2.

[6] A. van Hoonacker, *Les douze petits prophètes* (Paris: Gabalda, 1908) 706.

[7] Torrey, 2, n. 5.

[8] van Hoonacker, 706.

[9] Ibid., 707.

[10] A. von Bulmerincq, *Der Prophet Maleachi* (2 vols.; Tartu: J. G. Krüger, 1926–1932), 2.27.

[11] Ibid.

the wilderness," and emendation is necessary to restore balance. However, usage should not be anticipated, but should be defined on the basis of context. In this case, the lamed before תַּנּוֹת presages a change in meaning, a further qualification of the verb that translates "to turn into" into "to turn over to" (i.e., "to give to").[12] Such an interpretation is doubly beneficial: it requires no textual emendation and it clearly expresses the destructive sentiment of the verse—"I turned his mountains into a waste and his inheritance over to the jackals of the wilderness."

However, it must be admitted that it is the form of 'jackals,' תַּנּוֹת, that has caused many to view the text as corrupt.[13] The usual plural of תַּן is תַּנִּים (cf. Isa 13:22; Jer 9:10), although תַּנִּין does occur in Lam 4:3. Nevertheless, those who choose to accept the LXX and Peshitta readings (δώματα; ܐܘܢܐ), and thereby emend the MT to נְוֹת damage the sense of the text. Indeed, 'wilderness habitations' are contrary to the implied complete devastation. Furthermore, the word נָוֶה (cs. נְוֹת; נְאוֹת) means "pasture, meadow"[14] and has the overwhelmingly positive connotation of fertility, bounty (cf. Pss 23:2; 65:13; Joel 2:22, Zeph 2:6). It is the word נָוֶה that means a "habitation,"[15] and therefore corresponds to δώματα, ܐܘܢܐ. Moreover, three codices of the LXX (א. A. B.) end the verse with εἰς δώματα ἐρήμου, where δώματα comes from δόμα, meaning "gift"[16] and not from δῶμα, "chief room, house,"[17] To speculate on the reasons behind the rendering δόματα ἐρήμου is dangerous because of the lack of information. However, it may be that the irregular plural of תַּן confused translators and led them to view תַּנּוֹת as a miswriting of מַתָּנוֹת, "gifts."[18] Although the sense of δόματα ἐρήμου, "wilderness gifts," "gifts to the wilderness," fits the tenor of the verse better than "wilderness habitations," it is still the case that תַּנּוֹת מִדְבָּר best suits the context. The feminine plural termination (תַּנּוֹת) may perhaps have been employed under the influence of the

[12] BDB, 942-64.
[13] Cf. Torrey, 2, n. 5; van Hoonacker, 706; Ernst Sellin, *Das Zwölfprophetenbuch übersetzt und erklärt* (KAT 12/2; Leipzig: A. Deichertsche, 1930) 593.
[14] BDB, 627.
[15] Ibid.
[16] LSJ, 444.
[17] Ibid., 464.
[18] Cf. Gen 25:6 where the LXX uses δόματα to translate מַתָּנוֹת.

preceding feminine nouns, שְׁמָמָה and נַחֲלָה. Jackals are often mentioned as haunting deserted sites (cf. Isa 13:22; 43:13; Jer 9:11; 10:22; 49:33; 51:37). Indeed, the jackal is actuality and symbol. It represents the threat, constantly in the wings, waiting to pounce and tear.

[1:5]—The more usual meaning of the verb זָעַם is "to be indignant," cf. Arab. غَمَّ تَزَّ: "groaned, roared (camel); spoke angrily (man)," [19] and Ps 7:12; Isa 66:14; Zech 1:12. Nevertheless, it is used in the sense of "to curse" in Num 23:7f where it is parallel to אָקֹב and אָרָה, and in Prov 24:24 where it is parallel to יִקְּבֻהוּ. Both Marti and Sievers considered the following עַד־עוֹלָם a later addition and, therefore, omitted it.[20] However, there are no grounds for such a deletion, especially since the verse refers to a curse pronounced on Edom. One of the characteristics of a curse is its unqualified and irrevocable execution and it is this characteristic to which the עַד־עוֹלָם alludes.

Discussion

In the first oracle unit, the reference is to Jacob and Esau, not as individuals, but as symbols of the nations descended from them. In fact, it is these nations to which the prophet really refers (cf. Obad 6, where Esau stands for Edom, just as Jacob often stands for Israel, Cf. Num 24:5; Isa 10:21; 14:1; Obad 10). Edom was not just any people. Geographically she was Israel's neighbor and, according to tradition, both were sprung from the same womb; they were twins, (Gen 25:22f). Because of this close relationship, similar treatment by Yahweh might have been expected. In point of fact, however, while Yahweh loved Jacob, he did not care for Esau, and Malachi refers to some recent desolation of Edom's territory as proof of that statement. The habitual antagonism between the two nations found release through many outlets: through war, mutual recriminations and jealousy (cf. Amos 1:11; Obad 10-14; Ezek 35:3, 10, 12, 13; Ps 137:7; Jer 49:7-12; Lam 4:21f; Isa 34; 63:1-6). Malachi's appeal to a disaster which had recently befallen Edom, as evidence of Yahweh's love for Israel, was thus one eminently suited to evoke an immediate response in the hearts of his contemporaries.

[19] BDB, 276.
[20] Sellin, 593.

The lack of definite historical information about a catastrophe that badly ravaged Edom but stopped before Judah, has led scholars to treat these verses figuratively, primarily as a metaphor of the gratuitous nature of the predilection of which Jacob is the object. For example, Rex Mason maintains that the main emphasis of these verses is on Yahweh's freedom to select and reject; "they are an idiomatic way of expressing the fact that Jacob and not Esau was chosen."[21] G. Wallis linked 1:2-5 with 2:10ff and suggested that the prophet was opposing fraternization between the two countries. "Under the guise of 'we all have one father and one god created us' (2:10), the boundaries between holy and unholy have become obscured. . . . This section, therefore, is aimed not so much at Edom itself as at a liberal, pro-Edom trend in Jacob."[22]

However, it must be asked whether figurative explanations of the oracle unit constitute the only interpretive course open to the investigator. In the first place, Malachi's language is not metaphorical. In the crucial verse, 1:3, his words are unmistakably clear. Second, a pairing of biblical and extra-biblical sources permits another picture to emerge. The Old Testament confronts the scholar with a group of prophecies that presage Edom's demise, cf. Obad 1f; Ezek 25:12f; Jer 49:7f; Joel 4:19. Indeed, the country will become a desolate wilderness "for the violence done to the people of Judah," (Joel 4:19). With Malachi, however, it is no longer a question of a coming destruction. According to 1:3, Edom already has been destroyed. Therefore, it may be posited that, in the period separating the last of the above-mentioned prophecies and Malachi,[23] something happened to Edom. However, just what occurred and who was responsible must still be determined.

According to Jacob M. Myers, Edom was crushed by the migrations of nomadic Arab tribes, specifically the Qedarites and

---

[21] Rex Mason, *The Books of Haggai, Zechariah and Malachi* (Cambridge: Cambridge University, 1977) 141. For variations on this theme, see Sellin, 592 and Torrey, 2.

[22] Gerhard Wallis, "Wesen und Struktur der Botschaft Maleachis," *Das Ferne und Nahe Wort* (BZAW 105; Berlin: Alfred Topëlmann, 1967) 233f.

[23] Perhaps the time between 515 b.c. and 460 b.c. is indicated. According to G. W. Ahlström, Joel is to be dated to the period between 515 b.c. and 500 b.c., cf. *Joel and the Temple Cult of Jerusalem* (SVT 21; Leiden: Brill, 1971) 111-29.

the Dedanites.[24] Starcky posits a northern Arabian alliance under the suzerainty of the "king of Qedar."[25] Similarly, John Bright states that following the Babylonian downfall, the Arabs descended upon Edom with devastating effects.[26] However, to the contrary, J. R. Bartlett maintains that all these pictures of a nomadic Arab occupation are "the correlative of an over-simplified view of the absence of sedentary occupation in Edom between the Edomites and the Nabataeans," a view propounded by Nelson Glueck.[27] Excavations from Umm el-biyarah, Tawilan and Buseirah show continuity in settlement through the seventh century.[28] Moreover, continuous settlement coupled with continuity in language and script appears to be the case through the Persian period at Buseirah, Tel el-kheleifah and Petra.[29] Glueck himself remarks that "almost invariably where there was an Edomite settlement it was followed by a Nabataean one."[30] Furthermore, Bartlett rejects the hypothesis of Qedarite dominance in the region stating that it rests on the very uncertain identification of Geshem the Arab, Nehemiah's southern enemy (cf. Neh 2:10; 6:1f), Gashmu, father of Qainu, king of Qedar (cf. bowl found at Tell el-maskūta) and Gashm son of Shahr (Lihyanite inscription JS 349).[31] Finally, although references from the time of Ashurbanipal (ca. 650 B.C.) suggest that the Qedarites may have ranged as far south as Edom, there is no evidence that they attempted to settle there.[32]

A further option remains. In the Old Testament, the Qedarites are closely linked with the Nebaioth (Isa 60:7; Gen 25:73). Although the Qedarites are not associated with Edom, the Nebaioth are, cf. Gen 28:9; 36:3. Because the Nabataeans followed the Edomites, scholars have often flirted with the temptation to link the Nebaioth and the Nabataeans. Unfortunately, such an

[24] Jacob M. Myers, "Some Considerations Bearing on the Date of Joel," *ZAW* 74 (1962) 187.

[25] Jean Starcky, "The Nabataeans: A Historical Sketch," *BA* 18 (1955) 86.

[26] J. Bright, *Jeremiah* (AB; New York: Doubleday & Co., 1965) 332.

[27] J. R. Bartlett, "From Edomites to Nabataeans: A Study in Continuity," *PEQ* 111 (1979) 53.

[28] Ibid., 54.

[29] Ibid., 54–56.

[30] Nelson Glueck, "Explorations in Eastern Palestine," *AASOR* 15 (1935) 61, 72.

[31] Bartlett, 61.

[32] Ibid., 62.

association has been firmly opposed on linguistic grounds.[33] However, E. C. Broome recently challenged previous reconstructions and maintained that the Naba(i)ati, who were Assyrian enemies in the mid-seventh century, the Nebaioth of the Old Testament and the Nabayat, a name found on mid-sixth century graffiti near Tēmaᵓ in northern Arabia, are all related; indeed, they are identical to the Nabaṭu, the Nabataeans of the fourth and subsequent centuries.[34] He asserted that this name, be it written Naba(i)ati, Nabayat, or Nebaioth, was foreign to those who recorded it, a critical linguistic datum, since such names tend to "pass into general currency altered to fit the phonological patterns and structures of the language acquiring them."[35] Consequently, because Assyrian had no diphthongs, the name would enter their language as Nabaᵓati. Arabic, however, would receive it with a "y" sound since a long "a" in the second syllable diphthongalizes upon entrance into that language.[36] Further, Broome remarked that the evidence we possess makes it highly probable that the original pronunciation of the name was Nabātu.[37] This is very close to the Assyrian rendering, a fact that should not be too surprising, since they had direct contact with these people and recorded their encounters in annals. Therefore, according to Broome, the Assyrians should be viewed as the best authorities on pronunciation.[38] At the same time, it is also plausible that the Nabataeans themselves pronounced their name with stress on the ultima—Nabaṭú. The shift in stress, which occurred under the influence of Aramaic, the language of their inscriptions, was the cause of the pharyngalization that led to the change from t > ṭ, from Nabātu to Nabaṭú.[39]

Because of the highly convincing nature of Broome's reconstruction, the problem of the relationship among the Nabaᵓati-Nebaioth-Nabataeans is removed from the linguistic sphere and thus becomes a question of geography and history. The Old

[33] Cf. Starcky, 85f.

[34] E. C. Broome, "Nabaiati, Nebaioth and the Nabataeans: The Linguistic Problem," *JSS* 18 (1973) 1–16.

[35] Ibid., 12.

[36] Broome, 13. Broome notes that the Arabic form of the name was taken over into Hebrew, 10.

[37] Ibid., 15.

[38] Ibid., 10–11.

[39] Ibid., 14–15.

Testament supports a southerly position for the Nebaioth, who were linked by marriage to the Edomites, Gen 28:9; 36:3. Bartlett maintains that the area of Nebaioth-Nabataean occupation was "bounded by the mountains of Edom to the west, the Hisma plateau to the SW, Teima to the south, the Najūd to the east and Wadi Sirhan to the NE."[40] As political authority decayed in Edom with the fall of their monarchy, increasing numbers of Nabataeans were able to extend their pasturage westward to include large tracts of Edomite land and eventually to "surround and take over the small communities located by the springs."[41] Whether or not they pushed the Edomites out is unclear but present information suggests that they intermarried with those who remained in the land after others went to Judah.[42]

Exactly when the Edomite monarchy came to an end is still disputed. Although many scholars assume that Nebuchadnezzar was responsible,[43] the fact that Edom supported the Babylonian king when he attacked Jerusalem makes it unlikely (cf. Ps 137:7; Ezek 33:15; Obad 10-14). John Lindsay suggests that Edom's pro-Babylonian stance was economically motivated by the desire to "control the trade route to Philistia and the Mediterranean port of Gaza."[44] With tacit Babylonian consent, they were able to make inroads into Judean territory. The seals found at Kheleifah, level IV, confirm that Edom still possessed its territory west of the Arabah through the mid sixth century B.C.[45] This leads Lindsay to conclude that her independence was lost during the reign of king Nabonidus, the last Babylonian monarch (559-39 B.C.).[46] The Neo-Babylonian empire depended on trade. King Nabonidus spent much time in western Arabia trying to gain control of Arabian trade and commerce along the famous 'incense route' between Tēmaʾ and Yathrib (modern Medina).[47] Cuneiform sources report that prior to advancing on Tēmaʾ itself, it

[40] Bartlett, 65.

[41] Ibid.

[42] Iain Browning, *Petra* (London: Chatto & Windus, 1974) 29.

[43] Bartlett, 57.

[44] John Lindsay, "The Babylonian Kings and Edom, 605-550 B.C.," *PEQ* 108 (1976) 36.

[45] Ibid., 31.

[46] Ibid., 32.

[47] Browning, 32.

was necessary to subdue a certain city whose name ended in -*dummu*.[48] Two possibilities for identification exist: (1) Dumah, which has been identified with Arabic Dûmet ej-jendel (spelled "*Adummatu*" or "*Adumu*" in Assyrian royal inscriptions),[49] and (2) Edom (Akk. "*Udumu*"). Lindsay believes that a siege of Dûmet ej-jendel would have been out of the question because Nabonidus ostensibly followed the main trade route to Tēmaᵓ that "went south from Syria through Edom,"[50] and because the "distance across the waterless desert from Edom to Tēmaᵓ would make any diversion of the Babylonian troops such as to siege Dûmet ej-jendel,"[51] too great a risk. Edom, however, is a distinct possibility. It was on the route that Nabonidus followed and if it is agreed that control of Arabian trade was his goal, the city of Elath, then in Edomite hands and "a key link in the chain of marts between south Arabia and the Mediterranean would have to be taken."[52] According to Lindsay, "there is room on the inscription for the name of a city," and indeed, "Elath may be the missing town name before Adummu."[53] Moreover, Lindsay assumes that "an attempt by Babylonian forces to seize Elath would deal first with Edomite centers of strength in the rear."[54] Although there is no information that permits the conclusion that Nabonidus indulged in destruction of the territory and deportation of the population, some destruction and death were the inevitable results of such campaigns.

Nabonidus' campaigns in Edom and in the surrounding area had two major consequences. They disrupted the life of sedentary Edom and probably brought about its monarchy's downfall and with it the unity that is associated with a strong leader. Further, it was perhaps because of all this Babylonian military activity, the goal of which was to secure the trade routes, that local nomadic groups felt that it was time to move on. Both Pliny and Diodorus attest to the fact that the Nabataeans augmented their living as shepherds with frequent bouts of

---

[48] Cf. *ANET*, 305-7; 312-15.
[49] Lindsay, 33.
[50] Ibid., 34.
[51] Ibid.
[52] Ibid., 36.
[53] Ibid., 33, 36.
[54] Ibid., 36.

caravan raiding or piracy.[55] Consequently, with the tightening up of Babylonian security, life became more difficult and the greener pastures of Edom beckoned invitingly. It is probable that Nabataean immigration further increased shortly thereafter. For when Babylon fell, the Persian victors did not immediately extend their interests in that direction.[56] Interestingly enough, Malachi asserted that Edom's heritage was "given over to the 'jackals' of the wilderness," 1:4. Whether that refers specifically to the Nabataeans is, of course, open to speculation, but it certainly fits in well with their predatory role.

That the Nabataean settlement in Edom was a protracted affair, accomplished without any sudden expulsion of the remaining native inhabitants, is strongly indicated by the evidence we possess. Indeed, to state that the Edomites fled before the mass movement of a particular group is to deny that intermittent but stepped-up infiltration of desert dwellers could have produced the same results over a longer period. Indeed, this appears to be the type of circumstance to which Malachi attests. Physically Edom's territory was destroyed (1:3), while the constant influx of people with a different life style no doubt undermined their remaining strength and unity, ultimately forcing many to seek new homes. Although they desired to rebuild the ruins of their land, as Malachi reports (1:4), lack of manpower and economic wherewithal would doom their efforts to failure.

Based on all the information, another reconstruction of events is possible. Whether Mal 1:3 refers to Nabonidus' campaigns or to the results of the Nabataean incursions is unclear. As mentioned previously, however, there are no indications that Nabonidus devastated Edom. The major consequences of his

[55] Philip C. Hammond, *The Nabataeans—Their History, Culture and Archaeology* (Studies in Mediterranean Archaeology 27; Gothenburg, Sweden: Paul Astroms, 1973) 12.

[56] Another period of increased Nabataean immigration may have been the time after Cambyses' death in 522 B.C. His successor, Darius, had to contend with Gaumata, a pretender to the throne, and numerous revolts among the subject peoples, including the Babylonians and the Egyptians. This required dispatching additional armies to the warring fronts which may have left Edom unprotected thereby facilitating Nabataean movement. Note the similar conditions in the period of Xerxes accession, 486 B.C. It appears that periods of accession had an unsettling effect on the empire as a whole, cf. A. T. Olmstead, *History of the Persian Empire* (Chicago: The University of Chicago, 1948) 110, 234-37.

campaigns appear to have been political instability, disunity and the loss of economic strongholds, e.g., Elath. Therefore, it may have been the Nabataeans who ruined the land. However, that is not to say that they entered Edom intent upon destruction. In the nearly one hundred years that elapsed between Nabonidus' campaigns and Malachi's prophecy, two processes may have been at work. First, it is possible that as more and more Nabataeans entered Edom extending their pasturage, their grazing herds destroyed previously arable land.[57] Second, it is also conceivable that, as their numbers grew and they pushed further and further into the country, they surrounded and took over Edomite communities located by water sources. Being nomads and having little use for permanent structures, they permitted these places to deteriorate. Although the information in Malachi does not allow definitive conclusions to be drawn, such a scenario is not incompatible with his prophecy. Indeed, 1:3 might be translated: "Therefore I turned his mountains into a waste by giving his inheritance over to the jackals of the wilderness."[58]

Such a chronology of events not only enlightens a previously dark historical picture, but it enables Nabataean inroads into Edom to be put into perspective. Certainly, the Nabataeans, with their nomadic background did not establish Petra as a trading capital overnight. Indeed, it is probable that for some time after their arrival in Edom they continued to live as shepherds. Sedentarization is a lengthy process. It is, therefore, likely that it was in the two and one-half centuries between Nabonidus' campaigns and 312 B.C., when the Nabataeans were definitely established at Petra, that this accommodation to a new way of life evolved.

[57] Hammond, 13.

[58] If Joel's message stems from the time around 500 B.C., his prophecy mentioning a future destruction of Edom is not out of place, cf. above, note #23. Although Malachi's prophecy certainly reveals that Edom's territory was devastated, the reasons given for that destruction are "theological." Indeed, be the facts of history what they may, Malachi intends his hearers to understand that it was all the work of Yahweh on Israel's behalf. Nevertheless, that does not mean that the information within his prophecy is incompatible with an historical interpretation.

CHAPTER VI

MALACHI 1:6–2:9

$ABCA_1C_1$	^{6}בן יכבד אב ועבד אדניו
C^3DB	ואם־אב אני איה כבודי
$C_1{}^3DB_1$	ואם אדונים אני איה מוראי^1
$A^3B^2B_1{}^2$	אמר יהוה צבאות לכם הכהנים בוזי שמי
$A_1B_{11}3$	ואמרתם במה בזינו את־שמך
CD^2E^2	^{7}מגישים על־מזבחי לחם מגאל
$A_1B_{111}{}^2$	ואמרתם במה גאלנוך
$C_1D_1{}^2E_1{}^2$	באמרכם שלחן יהוה נבזה הוא^2
$A^2BC\ DE$	^{8}וכי־תגשון עור לזבח אין רע
$A^2B_1B_{11}DE$	וכי תגישו פסח וחלה אין רע
A^2B	הקריבהו נא לפחתך
$C(Z)C_1{}^2$	הירצך או הישא פניך אמר יהוה צבאות
$(Z)A_1{}^2B^2C_{11}$	^{9}ועתה חלו־נא פני־אל ויחננו
DEF	מידכם היתה זאת
$C_{111}{}^3$	הישא מכם פנים אמר יהוה צבאות
A^4B	^{10}מי גם־בכם ויסגר דלתים
$A_1{}^2B_1{}^2$	ולא־תאירו מזבחי חנם
A^3B	אין־לי חפץ בכם אמר יהוה צבאות
$CA_1{}^2B_1$	ומנחה לא־ארצה מידכם
$(Z)A^2A_1{}^2$	^{11}כי ממזרח־שמש ועד־מבואו
BCD	גדול שמי בגוים
$A_{11}{}^2EFG$	ובכל־מקום מקטר מגש לשמי
$E_1{}^2$	ומנחה טהורה

^{1} These three lines may also be viewed as a tri-colon (macro-structure ABB) all bound together by the repetitive parallelism of אב and אדון. Note that in 1:6c, אדונים refers to Yahweh and is a *pluralis majestaticus*.

^{2} The macrostructure of this verse is AABAB.

Notation	Hebrew
$(Z)BCD$	כי־גדול שמי בגוים אמר יהוה צבאות
ABC	^{12}ואתם מחללים אותו
DE^2F^2	באמרכם שלחן אדני מגאל הוא
$E_1F_1E_{11}$	וניבו נבזה אכלו
AB^2	^{13}ואמרתם הנה מתלאה
A_1B_1	והפחתם אותו אמר יהוה צבאות
$A_{11}C + C + C$	והבאתם גזול ואת־הפסח ואת־החולה
$A_{11}C_1$	והבאתם את־המנחה
$DC_{11}E$	הארצה אותה מידכם אמר יהוה
$ABCDE$	^{14}וארור נוכל ויש בעדרו זכר
$B_1B_{11}E_1F$	ונדר וזבח משחת לאדני
$(Z)A^3$	כי מלך גדול אני אמר יהוה צבאות
$A_1{}^2B$	ושמי נורא בגוים
	$^{2:1}$ועתה אליכם המצוה הזאת הכהנים
$A^2B\|\|A^2B_1{}^3$	^{2}אם־לא תשמעו ואם־לא תשימו על־לב
CDE	לתת כבוד לשמי אמר יהוה צבאות
FGH	ושלחתי בכם את־המארה
F_1H_1	וארותי את־ברכותיכם
$F_1{}^2$	וגם ארותיה
$(Z)A_1B_1{}^3$	כי אינכם שמים על־לב
A^2B^2	^{3}הנני גער לכם את־הזרע
A_1D^3	וזריתי פרש על־פניכם
$C_1{}^2$	פרש חגיכם
D^2C_{11}	ונשא אתכם אליו
	^{4}וידעתם כי שלחתי אליכם את המצוה הזאת
	להיות בריתי את־לוי אמר יהוה צבאות
$ABCDD_1$	^{5}בריתי היתה אתו החיים והשלום
$E (=E + D)\ CD_{11}F$	ואתנם־לו מורא וייראני^3
$F_1{}^4$	ומפני שמי נחת הוא
A^2BC	^{6}תורת אמת היתה בפיהו
$A_1B_1{}^2C_1$	ועולה לא־נמצא בשפתיו
$A + AB^2$	בשלום ובמישור הלך אתי
$B_1{}^2A_1$	ורבים השיב מעון
$(Z)A^2B^2$	^{7}כי־שפתי כהן ישמרו־דעת
$B_1{}^2A_1$	ותורה יבקשו מפיהו
$(Z)CD^2C$	כי מלאך יהוה־צבאות הוא
A^2B^2	^{8}ואתם סרתם מן־הדרך
A_1C^2	הכשלתם רבים בתורה

^{3} אָתֶּן־לוֹ: I gave = E + these = D = life and peace, 2:5a, + to him = C.

$A_{11}D^2$	שחתם ברית הלוי אמר יהוה צבאות
A^3BC	9וגם־אני נתתי אתכם נבזים
C_1D^2	ושפלים לכל־העם
A^2B^2C	כפי אשר אינכם שמרים את־דרכי
$B_1{}^2C_1$	ונשאים פנים בתורה

(1:6) *"A son honors his father, and a servant his master;*
therefore, if I am a father, where is the honor due to me?
And if I am a master, where is the reverence due to me?"
says Yahweh of hosts to you, "O Priests, to you who
despise my name."
But you say, "How have we despised your name?"

(1:7) *By offering polluted bread on my altar.*
Yet you say, "How have we polluted you?"
By saying, "Yahweh's table is contemptible."

(1:8) *"And when you bring a blind animal to sacrifice,*
[declaring it] 'not bad!'
And when you bring the lame and the sick,
[declaring it] 'not bad!'
Present that to your governor!
Will he be pleased with you or even gracious
toward you?" says Yahweh of hosts.

(1:9) *"And now, appease God that he might show us favor.*
Since all this was your doing,
should he be gracious to you?" Says Yahweh of hosts.

(1:10) *"Would that there were one among you who would shut*
the doors
that you might not enkindle my altar in vain."
"I have no delight in you," says Yahweh of hosts,
"nor will I accept an offering from your hand."

(1:11) *"For from the rising of the sun to its setting,*
my name will be great among the nations.
And in every place burnt sacrifice will be offered
to my name;
indeed, a pure offering.
For my name will be great among the nations,"
says Yahweh of hosts.

(1:12) *"But you defile it*
by saying, 'The table of the Lord is polluted
and its fruit—its food—is despicable.'

(1:13) *And you say, 'What a pain!'*
    And you sniff at it," says Yahweh of hosts:
    "When you bring that which is mutilated, the lame
        and the sick.
    Thus you bring the offering.
    Should I accept it from you?" says Yahweh.
(1:14) *"Accursed is the cheat who has a male in his flock,*
    but who, having made a vow, then sacrifices a
        spoiled thing to the Lord."
    "For I am a great king," says Yahweh of hosts,
    "and my name is awesome among the nations."
(2:1) *Now, O Priests, this commandment is directed to you.*
(2:2) *"If you do not listen and if you do not direct*
        your mind
    to give honor to my name," says Yahweh of hosts,
    "then I will send out the curse against you;
    and I will put a ban on your produce.
    Indeed, I have banned it already
    because you are not so directing your mind.
(2:3) *Indeed I am restraining the seed to your disadvantage.*
    And I will smear dung on your faces
    —the dung of your feasts—
    and you will be carried away together with it.
(2:4) *And thereby you shall know that I sent this commandment*
        to you
    so that my covenant with Levi may hold," says Yahweh
        of hosts.
(2:5) *"My covenant has been with him—a covenant of life*
        and peace.
    I gave these to him and reverence (I asked from him)
        and he revered me,
    And before my name he stood in awe.
(2:6) *True instruction was in his mouth*
    and unrighteousness was not found on his lips.
    He walked with me in integrity and justice
    and turned many away from iniquity.
(2:7) *For the lips of the priest should guard knowledge*
    and they should seek instruction from his mouth,
    because he is the messenger of Yahweh of hosts.
(2:8) *But as for you, you turned aside from the way.*
    You caused many to stumble through your instruction.

You corrupted the Levitical covenant,"
says Yahweh of hosts.
(2:9) *"And indeed, I have made you both despised*
       and abased before all the people,
       because you do not guard my ways
       nor do you have consideration with regard to the
          instruction."

Content and Structure

The second oracle unit, 1:6–2:9, is directed to the priests, who enjoyed a special relationship with Yahweh (2:5). It is a powerful indictment of their negligence and the resultant profanation of the cult. Cultic activity was the focal point around which the religion revolved. The praxis, the administration of the cultic establishment, the vested interests of the clergy and the celebration of the festivals, were not devoid of intrinsic importance, but were the index of religion as it was practiced in the life of the society. Because the maintenance of holiness and the keeping of the law were essential to the survival of the community, the priests were necessary to the people. But often they perceived themselves as a privileged class who, by virtue of their birth, were entitled to service from the people. They tended to accept the honors appertaining to their position while inwardly mocking the cultic practices it was their duty to perform. It is precisely this to which Malachi refers. The priests are accused of having a poor interior disposition (1:13) and of offering sacrifices of inferior quality (1:8, 1:13). They are thereby guilty, not only of profaning the cult directed to Yahweh (1:7), but of misleading the people who came to them for guidance (2:8–9).

This section is emotion-ridden and the question and answer schema is the perfect vehicle to convey the tensions that arise from heightened feelings of anger, bitterness and disbelief. The oracle unit opens with a "hingestellte Behauptung," i.e., a positive assertion, stating two principles to which everyone will assent: "A son should honor his father (אב) and a servant his master (אדון)," 1:6a. Closely related to this is the indisputable fact that Yahweh is Israel's father (cf. Exod 4:22f; Deut 32:5–6, 18–19; Isa 1:2; 43:6; 63:16; Jer 2:4; Hos 11:1) and her master, lord (cf. Exod 3:12; 9:1; Lev 25:55; 1 Sam 3:9; 1 Kgs 8:66; Zeph 3:9).

These premises should lead the hearers to the obvious conclusion
that Yahweh as father and master deserves both respect from his
children and deference from those who serve him. But such
correct responses are not forthcoming from the priests, a group
sharing in a special relationship with Yahweh; a group whom
he calls "despisers of my name," בּוֹזֵי שְׁמִי (1:6). Immediately on
the defensive, the priests raise a double objection. They protest
the assertion that they have nothing but contempt for Yahweh's
name, בַּמֶּה בָזִינוּ אֶת־שְׁמֶךָ (1:6e). When Yahweh counters by declar-
ing that they show their disrespect by bringing "polluted bread,"
לֶחֶם מְגֹאָל, to his altar, the priests object to the implication that
they thereby treat him unworthily, בַּמֶּה גֵאַלְנוּךָ (1:7a, b). In what
follows, 1:7c-14, Yahweh razes their objections by citations of
fact and illustrations of their disreputable conduct.

Because of the unusual length of this oracle unit, E. Sellin
divided it into two independent sections: 1:6-14 and 2:1-9.[4]
However, the numerous parallels linking 1:6-14 and 2:1-9
militate against any such division. On the contrary, it is evident
that the entire oracle is a unit composed of two *Gattungen*: a
speech of condemnation (1:6-14) and a speech of punishment
(2:1-9). Indeed, just as a verdict of guilt requires a corresponding
sentence, so too 1:6-14 is incomplete without 2:1-9. The speech
of punishment functions here as does 1:5 in the first oracle
unit. In each case, specific deeds evoke specific responses. In
1:5, Yahweh's hostile actions against Edom inspire a positive
response on his people's part; they come to recognize his greatness.
In 2:1-9, the priests' total lack of respect for Yahweh and
their slovenly cultic performance elicit a negative reaction from
Yahweh. Their culpability is declared (1:6-14), and punishment
is set (2:1-9); they are cursed.

The poetic texture of this section is a combination of the
symmetrical and the asymmetrical, the terse and the verbose.
Coupled with the conventions used by the prophet, these features
are apt vehicles to convey a sense of mounting tension. Indeed,
the entire oracle unit is held together by the tension of opposites.
It is a study in contrasts between the reverence that Yahweh
deserves and the contempt with which he is treated (1:6f); between

---

[4] Ernst Sellin, *Das Zwölfprophetenbuch übersetzt und erklärt* (KAT 12/2;
Leipzig: A. Deichertsche, 1930) 593, 598.

the cult as it will be and the cult as it is (1:11f), between the ideal priest and the priest in reality (2:6-8). This buildup of tension can be seen most clearly in the constant repetition of forms of בָּזָה "to despise, to hold in contempt" (1:6d, e; 1:7; 1:12c; 2:9a and cf. its synonym גָּאַלII, 1.7a, b; 1:12b) and its opposite כִּבֵּד, "to honor" (1:6; 2:2), two words around which both speech and counterspeech revolve. Although Yahweh is deserving of honor, the priests stand accused of treating his name with contempt (1:6). Further, that they regard it as of little consequence whether or not the sacrificial ritual is properly performed is evidenced by the fact that they consider both Yahweh's table and the food on it to be contemptible (נִבְזֶה, niphal participle), 1:7, 12. What becomes overwhelmingly obvious as Yahweh enumerates the priests' faults in the accomplishment of their duties, is that every offense against his will implies a בזה, a "despising" of him. The tension is finally resolved through punishment. Just as the priests profaned the altar, so now they will be profaned, becoming victims of the very disrespect that they had shown to Yahweh, 2:9.[5]

Complementing the tension aroused by repetition of key words, is the tension expressed through the use of extended parallelism. This is clearly visible in 1:6, 7, 12, where Yahweh and the priests debate the charges of misconduct.

לכם הכהנים בוזי שמי	(1:6d)
ואתם מחללים אתו	(1:12a)
ואמרתם במה בזינו את־שמך	(1:6e)
ואמרתם במה גאלנוך	(1:7b)
מגישים על־מזבחי לכם מגאל	(1:7a)
באמרכם שלחן יהוה נבזה הוא	(1:7d)
באמרכם שלחן יהוה מגאל הוא	(1:12b)

Here the use of extended parallelism, coupled with extensive word repetition, increases the force of each utterance and the severity of each offense. Other instances of extended parallelism include Mal 1:8-10, 2:6-8 and 2:2-3, 3:9-11. These verses will be fully discussed in the text notes.

---

[5] Key word repetition is also effective where the acceptability-unacceptability of offerings is debated, cf. רצה (1:8, 10, 13); נשא פנים (1:8, 9).

Text and Commentary

[1:6]—This verse abounds in ʾaleph-alliteration. It occurs twelve times: twice in 1:6a, eight times in 1:6b, c, and one time each in 1:6d and e. Together with the sound repetition at the end of words (1:6b, c—כבודי, אני, מוראי, אני) it functions as an intensifier. It forces the issue to the forefront of the hearer's consciousness.

On the basis of the renderings of Codex Sinaiticus (φοβηθήσεται) and St. Jerome (timebit), most scholars fill out the MT of 1:6a by supplying the verb יִירָא: בן יכבד אב ועבד יירא אדניו, A son honors his father and a servant fears his master."[6] Although this addition provides 1:6aβ with a complement to every word in 1:6a, its insertion into the text must be questioned. The Peshitta and two codices of the LXX (Vaticanus and Alexandrinus) translate the MT faithfully. Moreover, the construction employed in 1:6a, in which two parallel lines forming a couplet are governed by the same verb, is a frequent poetic device. This is the case, for example, in Pss 78:43 and 114:4:

אשר־שם במצרים אתותיו ומופתיו בשדה־צען
ההרים רקדו כאילים גבעות כבני־צאן[7]

In both of these instances, when the verb is mentally transferred from line A of the couplet to line B, the result is two complete sentences. Structurally, therefore, the addition of יִירָא in 1:6a is unnecessary. Similarly, the semantic affinity that exists between ירא and כבד obviates the necessity of introducing יִירָא into the text. כָּבֵד means "to honor, revere" and implies regarding someone or something with great respect, admiration, awe and deference. יָרֵא means "to fear, revere" and implies respectful dread, awe and reverence.[8] Although these two words are not

[6] Cf. Sellin, 593; A. van Hoonacker, *Les douze petits prophètes* (Paris: Gabalda, 1908) 708; Wilhelm Rudolph, *Haggai, Sacharja-Maleachi* (KAT 13/4; Gütersloh: Gütersloher Verlagshaus Gerd Mohn, 1976) 251.

[7] Cf. also Gen 49:11; Deut 32:10, 13; 33:17; Judg 5:26; 2 Sam 18:42; Hab 3:3, 11; Pss 29:6; 114:2. Note S. Geller's discussion of "deletion" in *Parallelism in Early Biblical Poetry* (HSM 20; Missoula: Scholars, 1979) 299f.

[8] Note that H. Ringgren remarks that "the fear of God means reverence before God, the religious attitude in general," *Israelite Religion* (Philadelphia: Fortress, 1966) 127.

totally synonymous and, therefore, cannot be interchanged in all instances, they both share connotations of respect and awe. Consequently, when the meaning of ירא is not limited to reactions of fear and dread, כבד may be considered an appropriate variant. This is the case in 1:6a. Here כבד with its nuances of "to revere" (respect, combined with love) and "to defer to" (courteous regard for a superior) aptly describes, not only the relationship between a father and son, but between a master and his servant.

Although יִרְאָ is unnecessary in 1:6a, מוֹרָאִי, a masculine noun derived from ירא, is an integral part of 1:6c. Indeed, the sentence is structurally incomplete without it. Certainly כְּבוֹדִי could have been repeated, but enhanced rhetorical effect is gained from variational repetition and therefore, מוֹרָאִי, which belongs to the same semantic paradigm, was used instead. This too, is a common feature of Hebrew poetry, cf. Gen 4:23; 49:11, 17; Num 23:21a; Judg 5:26; 2 Sam 22:14.

[1:7]—This verse begins to detail the scandalous conditions in which the priests offer sacrifice.

מִזְבְּחִי, "my altar," is parallel to שֻׁלְחַן יהוה, "the table of Yahweh," cf. Ezek 41:22.[9] The types of offerings the priests bring (נגש) to Yahweh's altar are described as לֶחֶם מְגֹאָל. לֶחֶם refers to "offerings" in general; they are the bread or food of Yahweh. This designation is used most frequently by the Priestly writers and Ezekiel; (Lev 3:11, 16; 21:6, 8, 17, 21, 22:25; 23:17; Num 28:2, 24; Ezek 16:19; 44:17). מְגֹאָל is the pual participle of גאלII and means "polluted, desecrated, defiled, stained." Exactly what types of polluted offerings are brought to Yahweh are detailed in 1:8.

Many commentators emend גֵּאַלְנוּךָ (piel pf. of גָּאַל) in 1:7b to גֵּאַלְנוּהוּ on the basis of the LXX, ἐν τινι ἠλισγήσαμεν αὐτους (= ἄρτους = לֶחֶם).[10] Such a change is unnecessary. The 2m.s. suffix refers to Yahweh. The lines from 1:6e through 1:7c contain a double question-and-answer sequence that is parallel in all respects (1:6e//1:7b; 1:7a//1:7c). When the priests ask Yahweh how they have despised him, בַּמֶּה בָזִינוּ אֶת־שְׁמֶךָ (1:6e), he recalls the inferior quality of their offerings (1:7a). When the question is posed a second time, בַּמֶּה גֵּאַלְנוּךָ (1:7b), Yahweh responds by

[9] Rudolph, 261; van Hoonacker, 708; Roland de Vaux, *Ancient Israel* (2 vols.; New York: McGraw Hill, 1965), 2. 413.
[10] van Hoonacker, 709; G. Johannes Botterweck, "Jacob habe ich lieb-Esau hasse ich," *Bibel und Leben* 1 (1960) 100.

citing their low regard for his altar (1:7c). The intent of the priests' queries is not to question the fact that they offer polluted sacrifices, but to question how such offerings pollute Yahweh. The answer appears in Yahweh's responses. Because the cult is directed to him, any offense against that cult represents a direct affront to Yahweh himself.

[1:8–10: Overview]—1:8a, b introduces a progression of ironies. Yahweh begins by enumerating the poor-quality sacrifices offered to him (1:8a, b). He then suggests to the priests that they bring those types of animals to their פֶּחָה, their governor, for use at his table (1:8c). Finally, he asks them whether the governor will be pleased with such an array of gifts, הֲיִרְצְךָ א הֲיִשָּׂא, פָנֶיךָ (1:8d). The questions are rhetorical. Indeed, the fact that the query is posed twice, in two different ways, emphasizes the assurance of a negative reception.[11]

The progression continues in 1:9. This verse is not a call for penitence;[12] it is an ironic challenge directed to the priests. They are invited to entreat God's favor, to appease him, חלו־נא פני־אל (1:9a). Just as in 1:8d, however, the rhetorical question posed in 1:9c (הישא מכם פנים) makes it abundantly clear that their efforts will be of no avail and that they have no one to blame but themselves for their failure, מידכם היתה זאת, (1:9b). Not only does 1:9 add another link to the chain of ironies, but it brings the progression full circle—from Yahweh to man and back to Yahweh again. In 1:8a, b Yahweh enumerates the types of sacrificial animals that the priests bring to him. Whether he will accept or reject them is not stated, but the verses that follow leave the answer in no doubt. The very fact that man (the governor) refuses the offerings (1:8c, d), precludes their acceptance by Yahweh. They will certainly not appease him (1:9). Indeed, 1:10 expresses this in absolute terms: אין־לי חפץ בכם, מנחה לא־ארצה מידכם. It is more than a savage denunciation of the temple worship as performed by the priests; it is the enunciation of a wish that such service would cease altogether (1:10a). In

---

[11] Note that van Hoonacker, 709, emends the text on the basis of the LXX (εἰ προσδέξεται αὐτό = the offering) to הֲיִרְצֵהוּ, "will he accept it = the offering." Such a change is unnecessary. It is not a question of the inferior quality of the offerings. That has already been established. Rather, it is a question of how the governor will react to emissaries bearing such gifts.

[12] Sellin notes that this is Wellhausen's interpretation, 595.

his vehement and radical rejection of the cult, Malachi is in line with the cultic polemic of the pre-exilic prophets who reject the cult because the people have rejected the *mišpaṭ* and *ṣĕdāqāh* of Yahweh; they do not "follow the right cultic way,"[13] (cf. Amos 5:21f; Hos 6:6; Mic 6:6f; Isa 1:11f; Jer 7:21f). As Mal 1:11 and 3:3-4 demonstrate, it is not the sacrificial system in itself that is denounced. What Malachi decries is the service of Yahweh that consists of improper offerings and the irreverent priestly service that simply goes through the motions without the proper interior disposition (cf. 1:7-8, 12-13).[14]

Adding piquancy to and complementing the progression of ironies, is the multiplication of synonyms. The first group of such words include [נגש] (1:8a, b—תַּגִּישׁוּ, hiphil imperfect) and קָרֵב (1:8c—הַקְרִיבֵהוּ, hiphil imperative) meaning—"to bring, to present" an offering[15] (cf. Lev 2:8 where the terms are parallel). As 1:8d implies, the rationale behind proffering these offerings is to secure the good will of the presentee. Therefore, parallel to these two verbs is חַלּוּ־נָא in 1:9a (piel impv., חָלָה), "appease, mollify."[16] The use of חָנַן (1:9a) "show favor, be gracious to,"[17] and נָשָׂא פָנִים (1:9c) "be gracious to, favorably inclined toward,"[18] makes it abundantly clear that the goal of "appeasing, softening" Yahweh is to induce him to show favor and to secure his good will. Moreover, it is precisely the aspect of finding favor or acceptance through the actions described by these verbs ([נגש], קרב, חלה) that circumscribes the second group of synonyms, cf. רָצָה (1:8d—הֲיִרְצְךָ, qal impf., "to be pleased with, accept favorably"[19]) and נָשָׂא פָנִים (1:8d—הֲיִשָּׂא פָנֶיךָ; 1:9c—הֲיִשָּׂא מִכֶּם פָנִים, qal impf., "to lift up the face, be gracious to"). While the above three occurrences imply that the offerer will be unable to "find favor" when what is offered is inferior and when he is incapaci-

---

[13] Ahlström, *Joel and the Temple Cult of Jerusalem* (SVT 21; Leiden: Brill, 1971) 47.

[14] Note that according to Mal 3:4, the cleansing of the priesthood on Yahweh's day will result in its rededication to Yahweh and in the reorientation of the cult; sacrifices will be offered with the proper intent (בצדקה).

[15] BDB, 621 (נגש) and 897-98 (קרב).

[16] Ibid., 318.

[17] Ibid., 335.

[18] Ibid., 670.

[19] Ibid., 953.

tated by an irreverent interior disposition, the two occurrences in
1:10 categorically affirm the unacceptability of the offerer, cf. אֵין־לִי
חֵפֶץ בָּכֶם "I have no pleasure in you" (חֵפֶץ, n.m., delight,
pleasure)[20] and מִנְחָה לֹא־אֶרְצֶה מִיֶּדְכֶם, "I will not favorably receive
any sacrifice from you."

[1:8]—In 1:8a, b the לֶחֶם מְגֹאָל (1:7a), the polluted offerings,
are specified as those that are blind (עִוֵּר), lame (פִּסֵּחַ), and sick,
weak (חֹלֶה). The law requires that all sacrificial victims be free
of blemish, sound in every particular—תָּמִים, cf. Exod 12:5;
Lev 22:18f; Num 6:14; 19:2; Deut 15:21; 17:1. Unlike animals that
are פִּסֵּחַ and עִוֵּר, those that are חֹלֶה are not listed among the
beasts unsuitable for sacrifice. Nevertheless, their inclusion is
implicit. The verb חָלָה means "to be sick, weak, defective."[21]
Therefore, animals that are חֹלֶה (qal active participle) are imperfect in some way. חֹלֶה may be considered a synonym of מוּם,
"blemish, defect."[22] According to Lev 22:20, no blemished animal
may be brought as a sacrifice, כל אשר־בו מום לא תקריבו כי־לא לרצון
יהוה לכם (cf. also Deut 15:21).

The literal translation of אֵין רָע is "there is not evil (in it); it
is no evil." However, the rendering "not bad" best captures the
priests' negative attitude toward the cult. According to Yahweh,
it is with this phrase that they declare that lame, blind and sick
animals are perfectly acceptable offerings; they are "not bad."
Indeed, because the priests consider Yahweh's altar to be beneath
contempt (1:7c), surely the quality of victims offered upon it is
of no consequence.

[1:9]—The use of two forms of the verb חָלָה, "to be weak":
חֹלֶה (1:8b, qal act. participle) and חַלּוּ (1:9a, piel impv.) adds
another ironic twist to this section. In 1:8b, the priests sacrifice
'weak' victims to Yahweh; in 1:9a, they endeavor to make
Yahweh 'weak,' to soften him. The phrase חַלָּה פְּנֵי־אֵל, "to entreat
the favor (face) of god," is found many times throughout the OT
(cf. Exod 32:11; 1 Sam 13:2; 1 Kgs 13:6; 2 Kgs 13:4; Jer 26:19;
Zech 7:2).

Van Hoonacker offers two explanations for the first person
plural suffix on יְחָנֵּנוּ (חָנַן, qal impf., "show favor to, be gracious

[20] Ibid., 343.
[21] Ibid., 317.
[22] Ibid., 548.

to,''[23] cf. Pss 67:2; 123:2). He considers it very likely that this
suffix refers to the priests themselves.[24] This implies that a group
of priests is being asked to intercede for all of them: "Entreat
god's favor that he might be gracious unto all of us." In view of
the fact that one of the chief tasks of the priests was to appease
the deity and thereby induce him to show his favor (cf. Zech 7:2),
this interpretation must be given weight. Moreover, that such
entreaties could be made on one's own behalf, is attested in
2 Kgs 13:4. Van Hoonacker also suggests that the plural suffix
may refer to the people. The priests were intercessors, mediators,
between Yahweh and the community at large.[25] This interpretation is similar to that of E. Sellin, who states, "Es liegt kein
Grund zu Bedenken gegen das וְיָחָנֵּנוּ vor, der Ausruf erklärt sich
als feststehender liturgischer Anruf an die Priester."[26] In this
case, therefore, the people ask the priests to entreat Yahweh's
favor so that he might show them favor. Although the image of
the priest calling out to Yahweh on their behalf is a striking
one, a reference to the people is out of place here, coming as it
does in the midst of a section that vehemently proclaims the
priests' guilt. Nevertheless, it is possible that both suggestions
may be combined by an ironic twist. A common liturgical
formula was used (חלו־נא פני־אל ויחננו) but the referent was
changed from the people to the priests themselves. Despite their
function as appeasers of Yahweh and despite the quantity of
practice the priests have had as such, in view of the severity of
their offenses, no amount of entreaty will be able to gain his
favor this time.

The literal rendering of מידכם היתה זאת הישא מכם פנים
(1:9b, c) is, "This was from your hand. Will he lift up your
face?" A translation that more strongly exposes the priests' guilt
is, "Since all this was your doing (the inadequate interior disposition which reveals itself in cultic inadequacies), should he
be gracious to you?"

[1:10]—The combination of מִי and an imperfect expresses a
wish (Oh that . . . , Would that . . .). The particle גַּם as an adverb

[23] Ibid., 336.
[24] van Hoonacker, 709–10.
[25] Ibid., 709.
[26] Sellin, 595.

denoting addition also serves to introduce intensive clauses. Its force does not only affect the word that immediately follows but frequently extends to include the whole of the following sentence, cf. "Would that there was one among you and would that he might shut the doors."[27]

דְּלָתַיִם: dual of דֶּלֶת (n.f.), cf. Deut 3:5; Josh 2:19; Isa 26:20; Zech 11:1. Malachi is apparently referring to some sort of enclosure that surrounded the temple precinct. According to 1 Kgs 6:36; 7:12, the inner court in which the first temple stood (in contrast to the great court [1 Kgs 7:12] which included the temple and the palace) was encircled by שלשה טורים גזית וטור כרתת ארזים, "three courses of hewn-stone and a course of hewn cedar beams." Similarly Ezekiel, who envisioned a temple in a restored Jerusalem (Ezek 40-44), contemplated a structure that would stand in a court enclosed by two walls, the gates of which would be guarded to prevent entry by foreigners. Although this temple was never built, Ezekiel did see the Solomonic temple and arranged his idealized sanctuary along its lines.[28] Because the second temple (completed ca. 515 B.C.) appears to have followed the basic plan of the first,[29] it may be that its area too, was demarcated by some sort of encircling structure, entry to which was gained through doors.

In front of the temple, but within the inner court, stood an altar made of bronze that was used for sacrifice (cf. 1 Kgs 8:64; 9:25; 2 Kgs 16:14). Although this altar was destroyed in 587 B.C. according to Ezra 3:1-6, its rebuilding was the first task of the returned exiles. This is probably the altar to which Malachi refers in 1:10b, וְלֹא־תָאִירוּ מִזְבְּחִי חִנָּם. תָאִירוּ is a hiphil imperfect (2 m. pl.) of אור, "to light, light up,"[30] cf. Isa 27:2. In Mal 1:10b, אור implies starting up the altar fires.

[1:11]—The phrase מִמִּזְרַח־שֶׁמֶשׁ וְעַד־מְבוֹאוֹ (cf. Pss 50:1; 113:3; Isa 45:6; 59:19) is a merismus indicating totality of place. It is paralleled by וּבְכָל־מָקוֹם in 1:11c.

The unusual construction מקטר מגש לשמי ומנחה טהורה has been the subject of much scholarly discussion and many attempts

[27] GKC, #153, 483.

[28] de Vaux, 2.323.

[29] Ibid., 324. Note that the second temple was probably not as grand as the first, cf. Ezek 3:14; 6:4; Hag 2:3.

[30] BDB, 21.

have been made to remove perceived textual difficulties. Indeed, the most vexing problem for the translator has been the hophal participles. D. H. Müller considered it highly unlikely that two participles with the same form would be juxtaposed, the one having a nominal value and the other a verbal. Therefore, he placed a waw between מֻקְטָר and מֻגָּשׁ and deleted מִנְחָה טְהוֹרָה.[31] Other commentators have considered one of the participles to be superfluous. Wellhausen excised מֻגָּשׁ while Nowack, Marti[32] and von Bulmerincq[33] deleted מֻקְטָר. Because the LXX θυμίαμα προσάγεται suggests the interpolation of מֻקְטָר as a noun, "incense," Lagrange, van Hoonacker and Chary repointed the consonants to read מְקַטֵּר.[34] Sellin averred that nothing need be deleted or repointed. The best reading was to be obtained by slightly rearranging the word order of the text: מֻקְטָר לִשְׁמִי וּמֻגָּשׁ מִנְחָה טְהוֹרָה, "Und an allerlei Orten wird meinem Namen geopfert // und dargebracht rein Opfergabe."[35] Finally, F. Horst and K. Elliger excised the entire verse as an intrusion from another source.[36] The grounds for this deletion were not entirely textual. Both men contended that the universalistic sentiments echoed here were at variance with the particularist stance of the prophet (cf. 1:2-5).[37]

Despite all the attempts to emend this line, it is possible to retain the MT exactly as its stands. The hophal participles can be taken as a substantive (מֻקְטָר, cf. 1:14 where מָשְׁחָת a hophal

---

[31] D. H. Müller, "Discours de Malachie sur les rites des sacrifices," *RB* 5 (1896) 536.

[32] Noted by van Hoonacker, 711.

[33] A. von Bulmerincq, *Der Prophet Maleachi* (2 vols.; Tartu: J. G. Krüger, 1926-1932), 2.118.

[34] M.-J. Lagrange, "Notes sur les prophéties messianiques des derniers prophètes," *RB* 15 (1906) 80; van Hoonacker, 711; Th. Chary, *Les prophètes et le culte à partir de l'exil* (Tournai: Desclée, 1955) 179.

[35] Sellin, 596.

[36] Friedrich Horst, *Die Zwölf kleinen Propheten: Nahum bis Maleachi* (HAT, 3rd Aufl; Tubingen: J. C. B. Mohr, 1964) 265-67; K. Elliger, *Das Buch der Zwölf kleinen Propheten* II (ATD; Göttingen: Vandenhoect & Ruprecht, 1951) 187-88.

[37] Whether the universalistic sentiments of this verse are at variance with Malachi's particularistic stance (cf. 1:2-5; 2:10-16) must be questioned. By nature, Israelite prophecy is particularistic. It is Israel-centered whether the prophets rebuke the people, predict their downfall or proclaim their salvation. Malachi

participle appears as a noun, "a blemished animal") and a verb
(מַגִּשׁ) respectively. The use of two participles to form a subject-
verb relationship is found in Isa 21:2.[38] In Malachi, the verb
[נגשׁ] is employed five times in the sense of "to bring an offering,"
cf. 1:7; 1:8 (2x): 2:12; 3:3. מֻקְטָר can easily be understood as a
general term for that which is sacrificed since verbs derived from
the stem *QTR* indicate the rising of the smoke of sacrifice
(Lev 1:9f; 2:11; 6:15; 8:21; 9:13f, 17, 20; Num 5:26). A translation
based on this analysis would render מֻקְטָר as "burnt sacrifice,"
i.e., that which man lets go up in smoke,[39] and מֻגָּשׁ as "is
offered." The phrase מִנְחָה טְהוֹרָה qualifies the מֻקְטָר. It describes
the sacrifice as physically, ceremonially pure, cf. Lev 14:4; 20:25.[40]
Further, טְהוֹרָה may also describe the "pure" intent with which
the sacrifice is offered. The parallels between this verse and Mal
3:2-4, where the purification of the priesthood is pictured as
resulting in their offering proper sacrifices in Jerusalem, are
striking, cf. טהר ,[נגשׁ] ,מִנְחָה.

גדול שמי בגוים appears to be a refrain. It occurs twice in this
verse and is paralleled in 1:14 by וּשְׁמִי נוֹרָא בַגּוֹיִם. Whether these
lines have a present or a future orientation will be discussed in
what follows.

Difficult textually, this verse has also been subjected to many
interpretations. The four most prevalent exegetical options are
that 1:11 refers to the worship of Yahweh by the diaspora community,[41] to the worship of Yahweh by proselytes,[42] to the

---

envisions a time when all nations will acknowledge Yahweh's greatness; they
will worship him. Although universal, it may be asked whether it is possible to
view this idea as an extension of particularism. When the nations join themselves
to Yahweh, they will all be his people, cf. Zech 2:15, and will all share in the
status and privileges of Israel.

[38] Martin Rehm, "Das Opfer der Völker nach Mal. 1:11," *Lex Tua Veritas:
Festschrift für Hubert Junker* (Trier: Paulinus, 1961) 194, n. 6.

[39] Ibid., 196.

[40] This construction is paralleled by phrases in Mal 1:7-8 where improper
offerings are first called לֶחֶם מְגֹאָל (1:7) and are further described in 1:8 as those
that are פִּסֵּחַ, עִוֵּר and חֹלֶה.

[41] J. M. P. Smith, *Malachi* (ICC; Edinburgh: T & T Clark, 1912) 30f.
B. Duhm, "Anmerkungen zu den Zwölf Propheten," *ZAW* 31 (1911) 179f;
von Bulmerincq, 2.105f.

[42] C. von Orelli, *The Twelve Minor Prophets* (Edinburgh: T. & T. Clark,
1893) 389.

contemporary worship of Yahweh by the nations,[43] or to the
future worship of Yahweh by the nations (גּוֹיִם).[44]

J. M. P. Smith,[45] B. Duhm[46] and von Bulmerincq[47] maintain
that this verse refers to the Jews of the diaspora who, scattered
throughout the world, rendered a more acceptable service to
Yahweh than did the careless priests in the Jerusalem temple.
Through them was Yahweh's name magnified among the
nations. Sellin[48] and others[49] reject this interpretation stating
that the only natural explanation for גָּדוֹל בַּגּוֹיִם is not that the
nations know about Yahweh, but that the "heathens" themselves
revere, worship him. Von Orelli suggests that what Malachi had
in mind were Jewish proselytes among the nations who proved
more zealous than the inhabitants of Jerusalem.[50] Because,
according to the laws in Deuteronomy, sacrifice could be offered
in Jerusalem only, cf. Deut 12:5-14,[51] the offerings of these
proselytes are understood in the spiritual sense of praise and
prayer.[52] But there is nothing in the passage to suggest such
usage. Indeed, the root *QTR*, "to go up in smoke," assumes real
sacrifice. Moreover, the fact that Mal 1:11 implies that large
numbers of people in all corners of the world sacrifice to Yahweh
militates against this interpretation, especially since almost
nothing is known about a vast movement of proselytism in this
period.[53]

The view that this verse reflects Malachi's conviction that
the gods of the nations were only so many different names for
Yahweh, and that the nations were, therefore, in reality wor-

[43] C. C. Torrey, "The Prophet Malachi," *JBL* 17 (1898) 3; G. A. Smith, *The Book of the Twelve Prophets* (2 vols; New York: A. C. Armstrong, 1899) 2.359; S. R. Driver, *The Minor Prophets* (New York: Oxford University, American Branch, Henry Frowde, 1906) 304; G. L. Robinson, *The Twelve Minor Prophets* (New York: George H. Doran, 1926) 166-67.

[44] Rehm, 193-208; van Hoonacker, 712f; Chary, 183.

[45] J. M. P. Smith, 30f.

[46] Duhm, 179f.

[47] von Bulmerincq, 2.105f.

[48] Sellin, 596.

[49] Rehm, 198.

[50] von Orelli, 389.

[51] Rudolph, 263.

[52] Cf. von Orelli, 389.

[53] Cf. Sellin, 596.

shipping Yahweh, finds many supporters.[54] J. Lindblom asserts that the reference here is

> . . . to the monotheistic tendency of pagan religions during the Persian period. Worship of only one god, of the most high god, of the god of heaven was widespread. This tendency was observed by Malachi and he identified the worship of this god with the worship of Yahweh, the god of Israel, regarded as the god of the universe.[55]

Thus the implied contrast in Mal 1:11 is between the present cultic indifference of the priests of Jerusalem and the present religious earnestness of the nations. There are two principle reasons behind the widespread acceptance of this interpretation. On the one hand, it is assumed that since no verb is expressed in the Hebrew it can only be rendered, "my name is great among the nations."[56] Moreover, inasmuch as the verses before and after 1:11 refer to conditions existing in Malachi's own time, so must verse 11.[57] On the other hand, the closeness of the relationships between the Persian authorities and Judean leaders (Sheshbazzar, Zerubbabel, Nehemiah, Ezra) during the Persian period coupled with the openness of Persian rule which facilitated the dissemination of new ideas, has led scholars to ascribe Persian influence to the post-exilic religious phenomena. Therefore, the universal worship of one god apparent in this verse is considered to be a direct outgrowth of Persian religious tendencies, tendencies bequeathed to the nations under her hegemony.[58]

Vigorously opposing this view, van Hoonacker wonders how Malachi, who attached such great importance to ritual sacrifices, and who appeared so severe with regard to the negligence of the priests, could consider as sufficient compensation for the suppression of the cult of Yahweh at Jerusalem, the cult of the nations directed to the supreme deity.[59] Indeed, Malachi's

---

[54] Cf. above, note 43.

[55] J. Lindblom, *Prophecy in Ancient Israel* (Philadelphia: Fortress, 1962) 406.

[56] Cf. Driver, 305.

[57] Cf. Rudolph, 260 and Raymond S. Foster, *The Restoration of Israel* (London: Darton, Longman and Todd, 1970) 160.

[58] Cf. Chary, 181, 186.

[59] van Hoonacker, 712.

negative attitude toward the Edomites, 1:2-5, and his condemnation of the abominations committed in Jerusalem, 2:10-16 (intermarriage, idolatry), "preclude a positive assessment of heathen
religion" on his part.[60] Both van Hoonacker and M. Rehm assert
that verse 11 cannot be understood except as a characteristic of
the divine cult proper to the messianic age.[61] R. Pautrel states
that the cult presupposed by Mal 1:11 "ne deviendra possible
que par la substitution d'une loi nouvelle à l'ancienne, disons
au temps de l'ère messianique."[62]

Several arguments can be mustered in support of the premise
that this verse is oriented toward the future. Mal 1:11 begins
with a phrase, ממזרח־שמש ועד־מבואו, "From the rising of the
sun to its setting" (cf. Phoenician Karatepe, 1:4-5, llmṣ' šmš wᶜd
mb'y)[63] that is often found in contexts which look to a future
demonstration of Yahweh's power and greatness to the whole
world (Isa 45:6; 59:19; Pss 50:1; 113:3). Moreover, the note of
universality that is so striking in this verse (גָּדוֹל שְׁמִי בַגּוֹיִם cf. its
parallel in 1:14 וּשְׁמִי נוֹרָא בַגּוֹיִם), belongs to the essential content
of prophetic "eschatology"[64] (Isa 2:2f; 11:10f; 42:1-9; 45:1f, 14f,
22f; Mic 4:1ff; Zeph 3:8-9; Hag 2:7; Zech 8:20f; 14:16). In the
prophetic vision, a time will come when Yahweh will be acknowl-
edged as king (Mal 1:14; Zech 14:16; Pss 95-99) when the nations
will join themselves to Yahweh (cf. Isa 14:1; Zech 2:15), and
when they will seek him in Jerusalem and entreat his favor
(Mic 4:1f; Isa 2:3f; Isa 11:9, 42:4; 51:4; Jer 3:17; Zech 8:22. The
universal character of Malachi's eschatology is based on his faith
in the sublimity of Yahweh as god of the world, of all peoples,
(cf. 1:5; 1:11, 14) and his conviction that all that flouts this divine
majesty is subject to judgment (cf. 2:1-9). The images that he
paints are not foreign to Yahwism, but are part and parcel of the
traditions he received from his predecessors. To simply assert
that Persian universalistic ideas have influenced the text is not
satisfactory; it begs the question and overstates our knowledge of

[60] Rehm, 201.

[61] van Hoonacker, 713 and Rehm, 205.

[62] R. Pautrel, "Malachie," in *Dictionnaire de la Bible, Supplément* (Tome 5;
ed. F. G. Vigouroux and L. Pirot; Paris: Librairie Letouzey et Ané, 1957) 744.

[63] Cf. H. Donner-W. Rollig, *Kanaanäische und Aramäische Inschriften* (3
vols.; Weisbaden: Otto Harrassowitz, 1966), 1.5.

[64] For a definition of prophetic eschatology, cf. J. Lindblom, 360f and Paul
Hanson, *The Dawn of Apocalyptic* (Philadelphia: Fortress, 1975) 11-12.

the nature and growth of Persian religion. Iranian texts and other evidence are not simple to interpret, and the relation between older Persian religion and the religion that was influenced by Zoroaster is a complex one.[65] Moreover, because universalistic ideas can be traced far back in OT thought, there is no necessity to postulate borrowing from the Persians.

It has been stated that noun-clauses, because of their verbless state, can describe only present conditions (cf. p. 59). On the contrary, the temporal reference of such clauses must be inferred from the context.[66] Because the themes of this verse are futuristic, the noun-clauses within it may be said to point to a future fulfillment. Indeed, it is not unusual for a participle, when it is the predicate of a noun-clause, to announce future actions or events, especially if it is intended to announce the event as imminent, or at least near at hand and sure to happen (1 Kgs 2:2; 2 Kgs 4:16; Isa 3:1; 7:14; Jer 30:10; Zech 2:13; 3:8).[67] Therefore, the noun-clauses in this verse may be translated, "My name will be great among the nations" (גָּדוֹל שְׁמִי בַּגּוֹיִם), and "Burnt sacrifice will be offered to my name" (מֻקְטָר מֻגָּשׁ לִשְׁמִי).

Malachi describes the future in absolute terms. It is the ideal, the inverse of the present. Prevailing conditions will be transformed and a new order will come into existence. Sacrifices will not cease but the manner in which they are offered and those who offer them will be changed. A pure sacrifice will replace the impure and Yahweh will be worshiped throughout the world and not solely in Jerusalem. And it is in the name of this pure sacrifice that Malachi judges current temple practice.

[1:12]—This verse is parallel to 1:6e, 1:7c and provides a vivid contrast to the pure worship described in 1:11 (cf. 1:12a— באמרכם שלחן אדני—1:12b; בוזי שמי 1:6e // אתם מחללים אותו = שם הוא מגאל // 1:7c—באמרכם שלחן יהוה נבזה הוא). Together with 1:13-14, this verse resumes the documentation of the priests' guilt.

לחלל את־השם, "to defile the name" is frequently used by the Priestly circle and Ezekiel, cf. Lev 18:21; 19:12; 20:3; 21:16; 22:2; Ezek 20:39; 36:20f; 39:7.

---

[65] Donald E. Gowan, *Bridge Between the Testaments* (Pittsburgh: Pickwick, 1976) 64.

[66] GKC, #114f, 453.

[67] Ibid., #116p, 359-60.

נִיב—n. m. fruit, cf. Isa 57:19 (נוב: qal, to bear fruit). Both Driver and Rudolph consider נִיבוֹ to be a garbled dittography from נִבְזֶה and therefore, delete it.[68] Van Hoonacker, however, thinks it probable that the original line read נִיבוֹ נִבְזֶה. Consequently, he deletes אָכְלוֹ as an explanatory gloss.[69] According to Sellin, the symmetry of this verse recommends the reading הוּא וְנִיבוֹ נִבְזֶה, he (it) and its fruit are contemptuous. Further, he contends that אָכְלוֹ is a miswriting of כֻּלּוֹ, "er und seine Frucht ist verächtlich ganz und gar."[70]

Despite the many attempts to emend the text, it is possible to retain this line intact. In 1:12b, the שֻׁלְחַן אֲדֹנָי, the table of the Lord, is described as polluted (מְגֹאָל), and it is polluted precisely because of the contemptible food offered upon it (1:12c). Simply because two synonymous words appear in the same line, it does not follow that one of them must be superfluous. The fact is that Malachi delights in the piling up of synonyms for emphasis, cf. 1:8-10. Both נִיבוֹ and אָכְלוֹ are parallel to לֶחֶם, "bread, offerings" in 1:7, and all are parallel to מִנְחָה in 1:10. They are the offerings brought to Yahweh's altar, cf. 1:7, 12. Finally, the principle of the *lectio difficilior,* "the more difficult reading," should be abandoned only when the consonantal text makes no rational sense. In this line, וְנִיבוֹ נִבְזֶה אָכְלוֹ, "its fruit, its food, is despicable," constitutes the more difficult reading. The fact that no major translation difficulties are posed by the line obviates the necessity of viewing either נִיבוֹ as a dittography or אָכְלוֹ as an explanatory gloss.

[1:13]—מַתְּלָאָה - מָה -what + תְּלָאָה, n.f., weariness, hardship, cf. לָאָה, "to be weary, impatient."[71] According to GKC, "the form מה (followed by a *Dageš forte conjunc.*) . . . may be explained from the rapid utterance of the interrogative in connexion with the following word. Most probably, however, the Dageš forte is rather due to the assimilation of an originally audible ה(מה)."[72]

מַתְּלָאָה is an expression of boredom, disgust; "What a pain!" As a consequence of the boredom they feel, the priests scorn to fill their office.

[68] Driver, 308; Rudolph, 251.
[69] van Hoonacker, 714.
[70] Sellin, 597.
[71] BDB, 521.
[72] GKC #37, 113.

גָּזוּל is a qal. passive participle of גָּזַל, "to tear away, seize,
rob," cf. Arab. جَزَلَ—"to cut in two."[73] On analogy to 1:8,
Wellhausen, Nowack and Marti replace גָּזוּל with אֶת־הַעִוֵּר, the
blind.[74] Rudolph retains גָּזוּל but suggests that the simple translation, "that which was robbed," is too ambiguous since a priest
would be unable to recognize a pilfered animal. Therefore, he
recommends the translation, "that which was torn off (by
beasts)," cf. Mic 3:2, גזלי עורם מעליהם.[75] Since such animals
could not be eaten by men, cf. Lev 7:24; 17:15; 22:8; Ezek 4:14;
44:31 (טְרֵפָה), it is extremely unlikely that they would be acceptable to Yahweh. Moreover, the damage resulting to the animal
from seizure by beasts would be just as obvious to the priest as is
lameness or blindness. Van Hoonacker retains גָּזוּל but adds
אֶת־ה.[76] This is unnecessary, cf. the similar construction in
1:8b—תַּגִּישׁוּ פִּסֵּחַ וְחֹלֶה.

[1:14]—Malachi here extends the divine curse to include
the laity. The cheater (נוֹכֵל) among them is one who has (יֵשׁ)
a male animal (זָכָר) in his herd that corresponds to all the
cultic demands, and who promises (נֹדֵר) it as an offering, but
who, when the time comes to honor the vow (cf. Num 30:3;
Deut 23:22-24), substitutes an inferior piece (מָשְׁחָת), cf. Lev 27:10.
E. Sellin contends that this verse "mit dem eigentlichen Thema
des Propheten, der Polemik gegen die Priester, hat . . . nichts zu
tun."[77] This interpretation is, however, extremely shortsighted.
The priests are implicated by the very fact that the people commit
such misdeeds. Indeed, even if the priests do not condone their
actions, neither do they make any effort to curtail them. This
verse details one further instance of the priests' total disregard
for Yahweh and the cult. It amply reinforces their nonchalant
attitude, cf. אֵין רָע, 1:8 and מַתְּלָאָה, 1:13.

נוֹכֵל is a qal active participle from נָכַל, "to be crafty, deceitful,"[78] hence, "a cheat."

According to Lev 1:2f, an unblemished, sound male, a
זָכָר תָּמִים, was the sacrificial victim *par excellence*. Since an
adjective describing the quality of the male beast (זָכָר) does not

[73] Rudolph, 260.
[74] This is noted by van Hoonacker, 715.
[75] Rudolph, 264.
[76] van Hoonacker, 715.
[77] Sellin, 597-98.
[78] BDB, 647.

appear in 1:14, Rudolph adds the qualifier זָכֶה, "pure, clean," a word which he contends was omitted through *homoioarkton*.[79] Because, however, the attitude of soundness, completeness (תמים) is implicit in the antithesis with מָשְׁחָת (1:14b), "a blemished, corrupt animal" (hophal participle, שחת, cf. Lev 22:25), such an addition is unnecessary.

The two previous announcements of the greatness of Yahweh (1:5, 11) culminate in 1:14c, d with the statement that he is a great king, מֶלֶךְ גָּדוֹל, and inspires awe among the nations, וּשְׁמִי נוֹרָא בַגּוֹיִם (cf. Jer 10:10; Zech 14:9, 16, 17; Pss 47:3, 8; 95:3; 98:6).

[2.1]—With this verse, the speech of punishment begins. וְעַתָּה is a word of transition. The priests' guilt has been established and now (וְעַתָּה) they must accept the consequences. וְעַתָּה is similarly used to introduce a punishment in Hos 5:7, 8:8, 13.

מִצְוָה is a feminine noun meaning "order, command, commandment."[80] Van Hoonacker translates מִצְוָה with "verdict, decree"[81] and Sellin, with "strafbeschluss, Strafurteil,"[82] cf. Hos 5:1. In an extended discussion, von Blumerincq remarks that מִצְוָה

> kann auch jede sonstige göttliche Willensäusserung, die das Handeln des Menschen normiert, bezeichnen, z.B. 1 Sam. 13:13; 2 Kön. 13:21. So wird das Wort auch hier zu verstehen sein, und zwar genauer im Sinne von Rechts-und Urteilsspruch = מִשְׁפָּט (Dt. 17:11; 1 Kön. 3:28; 20:40).[83]

Von Bulmerincq also notes those places where מִצְוָה and מִשְׁפָּט appear in proximity to one another (Deut 5:28; 6:1; 8:11; 11:1; Num 36:13).[84] In this verse the sense of מִצְוָה seems to embrace both command and sentence, decision of judgment. In 2:2b, the priests are ordered to give honor to Yahweh, לָתֵת כָּבוֹד לִשְׁמִי (cf. also 1:6). If they do not, a curse will be their sentence. Indeed the command is swallowed up by the sentence since, according

[79] Rudolph, 260.
[80] BDB, 846.
[81] van Hoonacker, 716.
[82] Sellin, 598.
[83] von Bulmerincq, 2.173.
[84] Ibid., 173.

to 2:2e, they have already been punished for non-compliance with Yahweh's demand. The same structure is apparent in Lev 26:14f and Deut 28:15f where failure to obey Yahweh's command (מִצְוָה) will result in severe punishment.

[2:2-3]—All the priestly faults enumerated thus far find a common denominator here. Because they do not give proper respect to Yahweh (cf. also 1:6), punishment is unavoidable.

The difficulties associated with these two verses are manifold. They include textual problems and interpretational uncertainty. These problems cannot be solved one by one, line by line. Since 2:2-3 are closely connected, each exegete who attempts to resolve a difficulty must carefully gauge how the proposed solution will affect what follows. Failure to do this dissolves the links and thereby lessens the effectiveness of the utterance as a whole.

Although scholars routinely discuss what 'blessings' are meant in 2:2d, וארותי את־ברכותיכם, the meaning of ארר (וְאָרוֹתִי, qal perfect) is taken for granted. It is translated 'to curse.' H. Brichto contends that while the English term 'curse' "has a broad connotation ranging from a simple synonym for misfortune to a condition of unrelieved hopelessness brought on by supernatural forces, magical or divine,"[85] the contexts in which the Hebrew ʾrr occur, demonstrate conclusively that "the word has its own specific denotation."[86] Etymologically, the Hebrew stem ʾrr is related to Akkadian arāru, "to ban, block off."[87] Consequently, Brichto defines ארר as, "to curse from the operational point of view." It is the imposition of a "ban or barrier, a paralysis on movement or other capabilities."[88]

Von Orelli and Driver define the blessings (בְּרָכוֹת) of the priest as those boons that Yahweh conferred on the tribe, i.e., life and peace, 1:5.[89] Hitzig suggests that they are the revenues of which the priests are the beneficiaries.[90] Rudolph, van Hoonacker and von Bulmerincq add that these blessings are not only

---

[85] Herbert Chanan Brichto, *The Problem of "Curse" in the Hebrew Bible* (Philadelphia: Society of Biblical Literature and Exegesis, 1963) 82.

[86] Ibid., 86.

[87] Ibid., 17, and cf. "Arāru" in *CAD* 1/2, 234-36.

[88] Brichto, 216-17.

[89] von Orelli, 392; Driver, 308.

[90] This is noted by van Hoonacker, 717.

material but include the priests' privileged position.[91] One
further definition of "blessing" remains to be expounded. Because
the concept of blessing includes both the direct and indirect
yield of the ground (cf. Gen 26:12; Lev 25:21; Deut 12:15; 14:24;
Hag 2:19; Pss 65:11; 132:15; Mal 3:10), blessings may be synonymous with fertility.[92] Indeed, if בְּרָכוֹת are understood as the
earth's produce (cf. 2:3 הנני גער לכם את־הזרע), and if ארר is
translated "to ban, block off," the entire line yields excellent
sense. As in Gen 3:17f, the blessing of fecundity is denied to man
by a divinely imposed curse. The threat is that the conditions
requisite for fertility will be withheld from man by a מְאֵרָה, a
spell (2:2c), unless proper respect is accorded to Yahweh (2:2a).
The fact that fertility has already been diminished (2:2e) indicates
that the ban is effective.

Parallel to this line is 2:3a, הנני גער לכם את־הזרע "I am
restraining the seed to your disadvantage," (cf. 2:2) וְאָרוֹתִי // (2:3)
לָכֶם אֶת־הַזֶּרַע // (2:3) אֶת־בִּרְכוֹתֵיכֶם (2:2); הִנְנִי גֹעֵר. Although the
R.V., A.V. and the RSV consistently translate גָּעַר, "to rebuke,"[93]
A. A. Macintosh questions whether 'rebuke' in the sense of
moral censure, reprimand, covers every usage of גָּעַר in the OT.[94]
He suggests that גָּעַר originally described those physical reactions
coincident with passionate anger, and he notes 2 Sam 22:16
where גערה is parallel to words denoting bodily expression of
wrath, cf. נִשְׁמַת רוּחַ אַפּוֹ.[95] When Yahweh is the subject of the
verb, it conveys the further sense of the effective working out of
his anger.[96] He verifies this latter sense by reference to a number
of passages where the root describes an operative curse and the
attendant deprivation or destruction, cf. Deut 28:20 where מגערת
is parallel to ארר and מארה, and Nah 1:4 where גער has the sense
of "to curse" the sea; it is dried up.[97] In Zech 3:2, the Satan is not
morally reprimanded. Here גער (יגער) denotes that his power is
restrained, held back. Similarly, in Mal 3:11, the אֹכֵל (the

[91] Rudolph, 265; von Bulmerincq, 2.179f, and van Hoonacker, 717.

[92] For a discussion of בְּרָכָה, see J. Scharbert, "ברך brk; ברכה berakhah,"
TDOT 2.279-307.

[93] Cf. also BDB, 172.

[94] A. A. Macintosh, "A Consideration of Hebrew גער," VT 19 (1969) 470, 473.

[95] Ibid., 473.

[96] Ibid.

[97] Ibid., 473-74.

devourer, the personification of agricultural disaster) is driven back (וְגָעַרְתִּי לָכֶם בָּאֹכֵל). In these examples, Yahweh's anger effects the paralysis of a curse in its objects. This is precisely the sense of 2:3a. In answer to the unworthy actions of the priests, Yahweh's anger is given full rein. He restrains (גער) the seed (זרע) so that the fields will not yield produce from which the priests might benefit, cf. also 2:2d.

This interpretation is vigorously opposed by W. Rudolph[98] who contends that restraining the seed (2:2d; 2:3a) would strike everyone and not just the priests who would thereby lose their emolument.[99] Therefore, he maintains that the בְּרָכוֹת that are cursed in 2:2d refer both to the material benefits the priests garner and to their privileged position in society.[100] Moreover, on the basis of the LXX, ἰδοὺ ἐγὼ ἀφορίζω ὑμῖν τὸν ὦμον, and the Vulgate, ecce ego proiiciam vobis brachium, Rudolph emends the MT of 2:3a to—הנני גדע לכם את־הזרע.[101] According to 1 Sam 2:31, cutting off the arm (גדע את־הזרע) implies the loss of the priestly office. Just as once the Elides (1 Sam 2:31) were deprived of their priestly dignity and replaced by the Zadokites, so shall the priesthood of the Jerusalem temple be displaced.[102] In this way, Rudolph creates parallelism between 2:2d and 2:3a. What is cursed is the priests' privileged position; they will be cut off from their office. But, the price of this conformity is too high since it requires the replacement of the MT of 2:3a. Further, the statement that barring fertility is inappropriate because it would affect the innocent congregation is shortsighted. As evidenced by 1:14, the people were not blameless. The cultic irregularities of

---

[98] Rudolph, 260f.

[99] Ibid., 260. He further maintains, p. 260, that if זֶרַע means "posterity," the verb גָּעַר is too weak (i.e., I am threatening your seed = with childlessness, child mortality). Moreover, the LXX never translates גָּעַר, rebuke, with ἀφορίζω. However that may be, since, as mentioned, זֶרַע is parallel to בְּרְכוֹתֵיכֶם, "produce," the translation 'posterity' is inappropriate. In addition, Macintosh, p. 477, maintains that if גָּעַר implies that a ban was placed on the crops, ἀφορίζω may be an appropriate translation, cf. Luke 6:22, where it is used in association with curses (ἀφορίζω: "Mark off by boundaries, banish, set apart, cast out, excommunicate,") cf. LSJ, 292.

[100] Rudolph, 265.

[101] Rudolph, 265 and cf. Sellin, 55; Botterweck, 105. Van Hoonacker notes that Wellhausen, Nowack and Marti also emend on the basis of the Greek, 718.

[102] Botterweck, 105.

which they stand accused are expanded in 3:6–12, a section that is parallel to 1:6–2:9. Just as the priests scant Yahweh by offering inferior sacrifices and by having a nonchalant attitude toward him, so too, the people scant him by failing to pay tithes and other contributions, cf. 3:8d. As a result, the whole nation is cursed, בַּמְּאֵרָה אַתֶּם נֵאָרִים (3:9a, cf. 2:2). From Mal 3:10 it is evident that the curse resulted in decreased fertility. The people are told that if they bring the whole tithe to the storehouse, Yahweh will open the doors of heaven (אֲרֻבּוֹת הַשָּׁמַיִם, cf. Gen 7:11) and pour out a blessing = fertility (בְּרָכָה, 3:10). What comes through clearly in this passage is that the blessings of 2:2d (cf. also זֶרַע = the potential blessing of fertility, 2:3a) which come under the מְאֵרָה of the deity, are identical with the בְּרָכָה of 3:10. Both are synonymous with the rains required to fructify the soil.

פֶּרֶשׁ n. m. offal as ripped out in preparing the victim;[103] it is the entrails together with their contents that are removed prior to sacrifice.[104] According to Lev 4:11f; 8:17; 16:27, the פֶּרֶשׁ is taken outside the camp and burned. It is those parts of the victim that are rejected. As a consequence of offering animals inappropriate for sacrifice to Yahweh, he will spread offal (dung = פֶּרֶשׁ) on the faces of the priests, the dung of their festal sacrifices, and they will be assimilated to it, cf. 2:3d. This constitutes an act destined to severely humiliate the priests, cf. Nah 3:6.

וְנָשָׂא אֶתְכֶם אֵלָיו: Although the subject of נשא is not stated, on analogy to constructions like וְקָרְאוּ לָהֶם (1:4), where the subject of the verb is not made explicit (they will call them = they will be called), the sentence may be translated as a passive: one will carry you away to it = you will be carried away to it.[105]

[2:4]—This verse is non-poetic and is parallel to 2:1, another non-poetic verse. The command, מִצְוָה, issued here is the same as that expressed in 2:2—לָתֵת כָּבוֹד לִשְׁמִי. If the priests follow the מִצְוָה, the covenant with Levi will continue (לִהְיוֹת בְּרִיתִי אֶת־לֵוִי). Most scholars contend that this covenant is presupposed

103 BDB, 831.
104 Rudolph, 265.
105 GKC #144f, g, 460. Cf. Gen 29:2; 26:18; 35:1; 1 Sam 38:16; 1 Kgs 12:1.

in Deut 33:8–11.[106] This aspect will be further discussed in the next section.

לִהְיוֹת: Sellin maintains that originally the text read לְחָתֵת (hiphil inf. cs., חתת, cf. Isa 9:3, "to break, shatter"). He contends that since the thought of a broken levitical covenant was abhorrent to later generations, the text was changed and לִהְיוֹת, "to be, to continue," was inserted.[107] Rex Mason translates, "My covenant with Levi falls to the ground." He suggests that because of their unfaithfulness, the priests lost their special privileges.[108] Similarly, Th. Chary translates "pour que ne subsiste plus mon alliance, mĕhĕyôt berîtî."[109] To the contrary, Ringgren states that

> characteristic examples illustrating the meaning "exist, be present" (היה) frequently involve the infinitive construct (146x). It refers predominantly to an enduring state or process lying in the future (92x). However, it can also indicate the continuance of an action (cf. 1 Sam. 19:8, "and the war continued") or a condition (cf. Mal. 2:4, "that my covenant with Levi may hold").[110]

Because it is evident from 3:1–5 that Yahweh does not intend to abrogate his relationship with the priests (the process of purification will begin with them), the translation "that my covenant with Levi may hold" must be considered superior.

This is the first instance of covenant abuse related by Malachi. Here the priests are guilty not only of acting contrary to covenantal stipulations, but of failing to return to Yahweh, to reform their ways when they are confronted with their misdeeds. As a result, Yahweh is forced to act. He creates by his judgment (2:1–9) the event of the return to him (3:1–5). Punishment, then, is not merely a penalty for a covenant breach, but is also a necessary preparation for future renewal, cf. 3:3.

[106] Rudolph, 267.
[107] Cf. Sellin, 599.
[108] Rex Mason, *The Books of Haggai, Zechariah and Malachi* (Cambridge: Cambridge University, 1977) 147.
[109] Chary, 167.
[110] Ringgren, "היה hayah," TDOT, 3.37. Cf. also Driver, 307.

[2:5]—The terms of the covenant with Levi are here described. It involves mutual obligations: Yahweh, on his part, bestows life and peace on the priests, and they, on their part, conduct themselves with "reverence," מוֹרָא (n.m. from יָרֵא), toward him.

נִחַת is the niphal perfect of חָתַת, "to be shattered, dismayed, in awe of." [111] It is parallel to וַיִּירָאֵנִי, 2:5b, "and he feared, revered me."

[2:6-8]—Like 1:6, 7, 12 and 1:8-10, these lines are an example of Malachi's use of extended parallelism. They contrast the past, faultless service of the priest (2:6) and the priest as he should be (2:7) with the present manifestations of priestly decadence (2:8).

תּוֹרָה: n.f. direction, instruction, law:[112] תּוֹרָה was originally the giving of an instruction or a decision on what was right or wrong in the cultic sphere. It included rules of practical conduct, decisions on what was sacred or profane, clean or unclean, cf. Lev 6:2, 7; 10:10-11; Ezek 2:26; 44:23; Hag 2:11-13.[113] As used by Malachi, תּוֹרָה (2:6, 8) appears to refer to religious teachings in a broader sense. It is not merely instruction regarding ceremonial requirements, but guidance into the right way of life, cf. 2:6 וְרַבִּים הֵשִׁיב מֵעָוֹן.[114] In this sense, תּוֹרָה may be parallel to דַּעַת (2:7), "knowledge with moral quality, the ability to discern between right and wrong,"[115] cf. Gen 2:9, 17 and cf. also Hos 4:6 where תּוֹרָה and דַּעַת are parallel. The priests were not the only deliverers of תּוֹרָה. According to Isa 9:14 and Zech 7:12, it was also a prophetic function. Prophets were men of the דָּבָר, the word. They were Yahweh's spokesmen, inspired to give a particular message in definite circumstances and were, thus, men through whom Yahweh's will was revealed.

---

[111] BDB, 369.

[112] תּוֹרָה is derived from ירה I, "To cast, throw"; in the hiph., "to shoot." G. W. Ahlström remarks: "That this verb in the hiph. may have developed the meaning "to instruct" is not impossible to believe. An oracle is thought of as giving the will of the deity. Therefore, all oracles show 'the way of the god'; they are his law," *Joel and the Temple Cult*, 99 n.1.

[113] Joachim Begrich, "Die priesterliche Tora," *Werden und Wesen des Alten Testaments* (BZAW 66; Berlin: Alfred Töpelmann, 1936) 64.

[114] Aelred Cody, *A History of Old Testament Priesthood* (An Bib 35; Rome: Pontifical Biblical Institute, 1969) 123.

[115] BDB, 395.

The possibility that the תּוֹרָה of the priests was written down should not be dismissed. According to Hos 8:12f, some תּוֹרָה, at least, was written down. In Deut 31:9, it is the written law which Moses entrusts to the priests, cf. also Jer 2:8. תּוֹרָה includes not only tradition formed in the past, but also responses made to newly presented problems of law, ethics, ritual and morality. Because the solutions to these complex problems were sought in the nucleus of previously formed law and tradition, recourse to a compendium of precedents is not inconceivable.

הָלַךְ אִתִּי[116] וּבְמִישׁוֹר בְּשָׁלוֹם: In an Akkadian text it is said of an official that *qirbi ekurrātišu šalmeš littalakuma lišallimma parṣišu* (cf. *CAD* A, 325b). M. Weinfeld suggests the translation, "Let him serve perfectly in his sanctuaries and duly perform his rites," and contends that "this description corresponds in sentiment and terminology with that of the ideal priest in Mal. 2:6," cf. הָלַךְ אִתִּי = Akk. *ittallaku;* bešalom = šalmeš).[117] הָלַךְ אִתִּי means "to walk with" and implies intimate companionship with god and faithfulness to him.[118] According to Weinfeld, הָלַךְ אִתִּי + שָׁלוֹם is equivalent to the Akkadian *ittallaku šalmeš* and implies "loyal and faithful service."[119] The root *šlm* conveys the idea of perfection; "In the cultic sphere it indicates the correct performance of rites and in the moral sphere it indicates integrity and goodness," cf. Ps 37:37 where it is parallel to תֹם and יָשָׁר.[120] Weinfeld translates 2:6, "He served me with integrity and equity."[121]

מַלְאַךְ יהוה: The priest is here designated the intermediary *par excellence* between Yahweh and the people. In Malachi's scheme, he takes the place of the prophet for whom this title was previously reserved (cf. Hag 1:13; Isa 44:26; 2 Chr 36:15-16).

After the defeat of 587 B.C., Israelite society underwent a restructuring. The community was fragmented and governance was distrupted; the Davidic line no longer exerted control.

---

[116] Note that ישר means "to be smooth, straight, right." The noun מִישׁוֹר (m.) means "uprightness."

[117] Moshe Weinfeld, *Deuteronomy and the Deuteronomic School* (Oxford: Clarendon, 1972) 76.

[118] Ibid., 76.

[119] Ibid.

[120] Ibid.

[121] Ibid.

Concomitant with these disruptions in Israelite life, there appears to have been a diminuation of the prophetic role in society.[122] This may have resulted from the fact that the traditional loci for prophetic performance disappeared since a close association between prophet and monarchic institutions was no longer possible. Indeed, "the changes in political structures introduced by the Persian empire helped to diminish the role of the prophet in society."[123] To this it may be added that the prophets came to be regarded as disreputable figures unworthy of the people's trust (cf. Jer 23:33f; Ezek 13:10-12, 17-19, 22; Zech 13:2-6). Consequently, in the post-exilic period, their authority was superceded by that of the priests, a group whose epistemologies were based on much less subjective factors than that of prophecy. Malachi's translation of the role of intermediary *par excellence* from the prophet to the priest may have stemmed from an awareness on his part of the decline of prophetic influence. Prophecy was no longer an effective vehicle for mediating the divine will.[124]

וְאַתֶּם should be translated, "But as for you." The pronoun is emphatic to heighten the stark contrast between the ideal (2:6) and the actual (2:7).

[2:9]—This verse concludes the second oracle unit and enunciates the priests' punishment. Just as they despised Yahweh by despising his altar (1:7, 12), so now they will be despised (נִבְזִים, niphal participle of בָּזָה).

The priests are guilty of not keeping the ways of Yahweh and of not considering the תּוֹרָה. These abuses are paralleled by the reproaches directed to the priests in 2:8, cf. 2:8a—ואתם סרתם // הכשלתם רבים בתורה—2:9 // אינכם שמרים את־דרכי, 2:8b // מן־הדרך אינכם נשאים פנים בתורה—2:9.

---

[122] Prophecy however, did not disappear. There were prophets after Malachi; some of them are mentioned in Nehemiah (6:7, 14), and others were doubtless active in that and even later periods.

[123] Robert P. Carroll, *When Prophecy Failed* (New York: Seabury, 1979) 204-5.

[124] Note that Malachi himself was embroiled in disputes with his contemporaries. It may be that the prophet's own recognition of the diminution of prophecy's influence, coupled with his close ties to the priesthood (cf. his obvious devotion to cult and priestly purity) led him to emphasize the mediating function of the priests.

אֵינְכֶם does double duty here, negating both שֹׁמְרִים and נֹשְׂאִים.[125] נָשָׂא פָנִים means "to regard, consider," cf. Prov 6:35. That the priests failed to consider the תּוֹרָה suggests that, when making decisions, they resorted not to legal precedent but looked to themselves only. By giving incorrect instruction, they caused the people to stumble, 2:8.

Discussion

It is an exegetical commonplace that Malachi, in spite of his cultic interest, is not at all familiar with the Priestly writings. O. Eissfeldt's remark is typical: "The influence of the Priestly code is not yet to be discerned, for it is clearly Deuteronomy which ranks as the final authoritative law, and its language has also, in fact, influenced Malachi."[126] Von Bulmerincq and Th. Chary concede that while the prophet was aware of and utilized expressions from within the P corpus, the quantity of Deuteronomic words and phrases in the prophecy is more copious and indeed, striking.[127] To illustrate this point, both men catalogued the expressions from each source. Although it cannot be denied that those from the Deuteronomic are more numerous than those from the Priestly, in point of fact, the difference is slight.[128] Consequently, these lists disprove the long propounded scholarly theory that Malachi had little or no contact with P. Indeed, priestly influence may be discerned in such words and phrases as לֶחֶם—1:7, bread, offering (Lev 3:11, 16; 21:6, 8, 17, 21, 22; 22:25; Num 28:2, 24), קָרַב לִי (hiphil)—1:8, to present, offer (Lev 3:3, 7, 9, 14; 7:8, 16; Num 29:13, 36); חִלֵּל אֶת־הַשֵּׁם—1:12, to defile the name (Lev 18:21; 19:12; 20:3; 21:6; 22:2, 32), זָכָר—1:14, male animal (Gen 6:19; 7:3, 9, 16; Exod 12:5; Lev 1:3, 10, 3:1, 6; 4:23; 22:19), פֶּרֶשׁ—2:3, offal, dung (Exod 29:14;

[125] Cf. van Hoonacker, 720 and Sellin, 601.
[126] Otto Eissfeldt, *The Old Testament: An Introduction* (New York: Harper and Row, 1965) 443. Cf. also Ernst Sellin & George Fohrer, *Introduction to the Old Testament* (Nashville: Abingdon, 1968) 470; James Swetnam, S. J., "Malachi 1, 11: An Interpretation," *CBQ* 31 (1969) 203; D. O. Procksch, *Die kleinen prophetischen Schriften nach dem Exil* (Stuttgart: Vereinsbuchhandlung, 1916) 60; G. A. Smith, 348.
[127] von Bulmerincq, 1.436f and Chary, 173f.
[128] von Bulmerincq, 1.436f.

Lev 4:11; 8:17; 16:27; Num 19:5) and אֲרֻבּוֹת הַשָּׁמַיִם—3:10, the window of heaven (Gen 7:11; 8:2).[129]

The theory that Malachi was uninfluenced by the P writings is rooted in the peculiar sensitivity to chronological order that dominated the Wellhausen school and its followers and precluded an investigation of the alternative possibility that the documents (P and D) might have existed concurrently. The result of the evolutionary presuppositions of the Wellhausen school was an oversimplification of the religious development of Israel. It was assumed that primitive ideas were early and more advanced conceptions late. Hence, all biblical data was arranged to fit into that evolutionary mold. Once it was affirmed that the P source reflected and dealt with the post-exilic situation in Palestine,[130] and once it was assumed that the legislation therein was revealed by Ezra,[131] the idea that Malachi, who preceded the scribe,[132] could have had any knowledge of its contents, was unthinkable. Although the shortcomings of the Wellhausen documentary hypothesis are widely recognized today,[133] it is evident that the theory still exerts an enormous pull on scholarship. Rather than recognize the numerous points of intersection between Malachi and P, scholars force the prophecy to conform to a Deuteronomic mold. This is best illustrated by Mal 2:4-5, two verses which describe a covenant between Yahweh and the Levites. Scholars posit that because Malachi makes no distinction between priests and Levites (cf. 1:5-2:9, 3:3), the separation of the priests into higher and lower clerical orders was not yet carried out. Indeed, they contend that the natural conclusion to draw from the reference by Malachi to Levi, is that "the prophet is in the same tradition as Deuteronomy according to which Levites and Priests were virtually synonymous."[134] Consequently, the majority of scholars contend that Mal 2:4-5 is based on the covenant men-

---

[129] Other occurrences will be listed as they appear.

[130] Julius Wellhausen, *Prolegomena to the History of Ancient Israel* (Gloucester, Mass.: Peter Smith, 1973) 123, 497.

[131] Ibid., 8, 497.

[132] Cf. Ch. III.

[133] R. Abba, "Priests and Levites," *IDB* 3 (ed. George Arthur Buttrick; Nashville, Abingdon, 1952) 886.

[134] L. H. Brockington, "Malachi," *Peake's Commentary on the Bible* (ed. M. Black; Edinburgh: Thomas Nelson and Sons, 1962) 657.

tioned in Deut 33:10.[135] That some consider the levitical covenant
in Malachi to be presupposed in Jer 33:20[136] may be viewed as an
extension of the scholarly predilection for Deuteronomy. According to J. Philip Hyatt, Jeremiah "was acquainted with the
original addition of Deuteronomy" and his book "has received
expansion and redaction at the hands of the 'Deuteronomic'
editors.[137] Because it is thought to be post-Deuteronomic, the
covenant of perpetual priesthood mentioned in Num 25:12f is
quickly dismissed from consideration.

Although Deuteronomy canonized the idea that membership
in the tribe of Levi gave a man the right to function as a priest,
if he so chose, a distinction does exist therein between priests
and Levites. This is recognized by S. R. Driver who concedes
that

> ... in P the priests constitute a fixed minority of the
> entire tribe, viz. the descendants of Aaron, in D they are a
> fluctuating minority of the entire tribe, viz. those
> members of the tribe who are officiating for the time at
> the central sanctuary.[138]

Similarly, A. Cody states that "priests in Deuteronomy are not
really equated with, or equivalent to Levites."[139] "In the Deuteronomic code, 'Levite' still has a purely ethnic, tribal sense and
'priest' has a functional sense."[140] The evidence from Ezra and
Nehemiah shows that Levites were present, along with priests at
the time of the restoration, and the distinction between the two
groups appears to be well-established. According to J. Pedersen,
the classification of the temple staff was "rooted in tradition."[141]

---

[135] Cf. Horst, 260-61; R. C. Dentan, "Malachi," *IB* 6 (ed. George Arthur
Buttrick; New York: Abingdon, 1956) 1131f; J. M. P. Smith, 38; Rudolph, 267;
Brockington, 657; von Bulmerincq, 2.212.

[136] Mason, 147.

[137] J. Philip Hyatt, "Jeremiah and Deuteronomy," *JNES* 1 (1942) 158f; cf.
also Sellin and Fohrer, 295; Eissfeldt, 352f.

[138] S. R. Driver, *A Critical and Exegetical Commentary on Deuteronomy*
(3rd ed.; Edinburgh, T. & T. Clark, 1902) 219.

[139] Cody, 127.

[140] Ibid., 129.

[141] Johannes Pedersen, *Israel Its Life and Culture* (4 vols.; London: Oxford
University, 1973), 3.183.

"The records of the return show that the division was already an accomplished fact among the families in exile, and since it cannot, of course, have been introduced at a time when there was no temple cult, and when they were, moreover, in a strange country, it must be based on an early tradition from the monarchical period." [142] Pedersen maintains that,

> . . . the history of Josiah tells of a special increase in the lower priesthood. Of course, a lower priesthood existed at the royal temple even before that time. Ezekiel's classification of the priests forms the basis for the ordering of the temple service and even . . . for the arrangement of the temple. It may, therefore, be taken for granted that his rules are based on traditions from the monarchical period. It accords with this that the division between priests and Levites was maintained among those who lived in Babylonia, as we can see from accounts of their return. It was necessary for the service of the temple that both orders should return home. This must be because the temple tradition required it. [143]

If it is admitted that the division of priests into higher and lower orders was not a post-Malachi development, but evolved in the period of the monarchy and is visible in the subtle distinctions between priests and Levites in Deuteronomy, then some other reason must be found to explain Malachi's apparent lack of distinction between the two groups.

Although Deuteronomy insinuated that all priests ought to be Levites, until the exile, the non-levitical and non-Israelite Zadokites provided the priesthood of the Jerusalem temple. [144] Aelred Cody maintains that "Ezekiel 40–48 shows an important gain for the Deuteronomic code's idea that all priests are to be levites; the Zadokites themselves are called 'Levitical' priests (43:19; 44:15) and are included among the 'sons of Levi' (40:46)." [145] "These texts," he says, "reveal that before the end of the exile, Zadokite circles were themselves capitulating to the

---

[142] Ibid., 185.
[143] Ibid., 181.
[144] de Vaux, 2.394.
[145] Cody, 166.

pressure of current ideals of value judgments and admitting that ideally they should be levites."[146] Pedersen contends that "the unity of the priesthood aimed at by the gathering of them under the tribe of Levi, was accomplished at the restitution after the exile."[147] He remarks that although this unification was not "so systematically carried through as the proposals of Deuteronomy and Ezekiel would seem to imply,[148] in post-exilic times the entire priesthood was subsumed under one genealogy with Levi as its first ancestor, the priests proper being sons of Aaron, 'the Levite' *par excellence,* cf. Exod 4:14-16.[149] The Zadokites traced their lineage through Eleazar, the son of Aaron (1 Chr 5:27f, 24:1f), and Aaronic priests of the house of Abiathar traced their descent through Ithamar, another of Aaron's sons.[150] Thus, 'levite' became a generic name, and the 'sons of Aaron' who belonged, in toto, to the tribe of Levi could surely be called, in that sense, levites or levitical priests. This development may account for Malachi's lack of distinction between priests and Levites. Since, in the post-exilic period, all priests had to claim levitical descent, the terms 'priest' and 'Levite' were virtually interchangeable.

Before this information can be applied more specifically to the Malachi passage, it must be determined which, if any, of the three previously mentioned "covenants" (cf. Deut 33:8f; Jer 33:20f; Num 25:10f) is presupposed in Malachi 2:4-5. Because scholars routinely agree that Malachi, like Deuteronomy, makes no distinction between priests and Levites (cf. p. 74), there is no question in their minds but that Mal 2:4-5 is based on Deut 33:9—שָׁמְרוּ אִמְרָתֶךָ וּבְרִיתְךָ יִנְצֹרוּ, "They observed your word and guarded your covenant." Although W. Rudolph recognizes that by Malachi's time a division of the clerical orders had long been in effect, he contends, nevertheless, that Mal 2:4f is rooted in Deut 33:8f.[151] He maintains that because the prophet is referring to the time of Moses, a time when such separation had not yet

[146] Ibid., 166.
[147] Pedersen, 3.183.
[148] Ibid., 186.
[149] Ibid.
[150] For more detailed reconstructions of this process, see Abba, 885 and de Vaux, 2.390f.
[151] Rudolph, 267.

occurred, he employed the terminology of that time and subsumed all the priests under the name 'Levi' (*primus inter
pares*).[152]

A closer look at the Deuteronomy passage reveals that Levi
was the recipient of a blessing which accorded to him the priestly
privileges of the Urim and Thummim, v. 8, of teaching ordinances and law, v. 10, and of offering sacrifice on the altar, v. 10.
Certain events which lie in the past, because they evidently serve
to provide Levi with legitimate authority to perform this important office, are now recalled in the saying, cf. Exod 17:1-7; 32:26-
29; Num 20:1-13. Indeed, it may be that the past actions of the
Levites provided the basis for a covenant with Yahweh, v. 10.
Because of their zeal for and their loyalty to him (cf. Exod
32:26f), they were accorded priestly privileges. However that
may be, the request to appoint Levi to the office of the priest, the
eagerness to make him play a full cultic role and the desire to
keep his enemies at bay, discernible in these verses, may suggest
that at the time these verses were written,[153] the office, in the case
of Levi, was neither well-established nor secure.

When this passage and Mal 2:4f are examined together, little
is found to recommend dependence of one on the other. The
only word that they have in common is בְּרִית. Moreover, while
the 'covenant' of Deut 33:9 is nebulous, the one in Malachi is
detailed, describing the grades of mutual obligation and dependence between the parties involved (2:5).

It is also claimed that the covenant with Levi is presupposed
in Jer 33:17f.[154] Of the Levites, it is said that they will never lack
a man to offer burnt sacrifices, to burn cereal offerings and to
make sacrifices before Yahweh forever, v. 18. Jeremiah insists
that a covenant was concluded with the Levites in their priestly
function just as a covenant was made with David in the royal
function. The passage may date from a time when the priesthood
had assumed an importance for the life of the nation equal to or
even surpassing that of kingship. This situation was not verified

---

[152] Ibid.

[153] Cody believes that Deut 33:9b-10 stems from the eighth century B.C.,
p. 120. Cross and Freedman consider it a late composition, cf. F. M. Cross and
D. N. Freedman, "The Blessing of Moses," *JBL* 67 (1948) 191-210.

[154] Mason, 147.

before the exile, but it was afterwards, particularly after hopes for a Davidic restoration were dashed with the passing of Zerubbabel.[155] As Nötscher observes, it appears from the author's tone that he is encouraging those who had already been disillusioned with the priesthood.[156] This passage may perhaps be a culmination of the disillusionment with the priesthood (Zadokite?) that is reflected in the post-exilic prophets and in Chronicles, possibly from the time of Nehemiah and Ezra.[157] If this is the case, the prophecy belongs temporally and conceptually alongside Malachi and cannot be assumed to provide the basis for 2:4-5.

According to Number 25:1f, when the Israelites were living at Shittim they allowed themselves to be seduced by Moabite women and began to sacrifice to their god, Baal-Peor. Yahweh was angered and public execution of the guilty was scheduled. Zimri, a Simeonite, came to the slaughter with his Moabite woman, v. 14. Both were killed by Phinehas, the son of Eleazar, the son of Aaron and thus was the slaughter of Israel checked. Because he turned Yahweh's anger by his zeal, Phinehas was promised an everlasting covenant of priesthood, הנני נתן לו את־ ברית שלום והיתה לו ולזרעו אחריו ברית כהנת עולם vv. 12-13. When this passage is set beside Malachi 2:4, 5, the correspondences are too striking to be dismissed.

(1)	להיות בריתי את־לוי		הנני נתן לו את־בריתי
(2)	בריתי היתה אתו	repetition	היתה לו. . . ברית
(3)	בריתי (ברית) החיים והשלום		בריתי (ברית) שלום[158]
(4)	ברית החיים		ברית כהנת עולם

In Malachi, Yahweh promises the Levites life and peace and they, in return, promise to revere him. In the Numbers passage, Phinehas is accorded an eternal (עוֹלָם) covenant of peace (שָׁלוֹם). Just as the Levites revere Yahweh (2:5), so too, Phinehas, by his

[155] Most scholars regard this passage as an addition because its language is late and it is missing in the Greek, cf. W. Rudolph, Der Prophet Jeremia (HZAT; Göttingen: Vandenhoeck & Ruprecht, 1958) 201 and F. Giesebrecht, Das Buch Jeremia (HKzAT; Göttingen: Vandenhoeck & Ruprecht, 1970) 186.

[156] Friedrich Nötscher, Das Buch Jeremias (HSAT; Bonn: Peter Hanstein, 1934) 248-50.

[157] Cf. Rudolph, Der Prophet Jeremia, 201f and de Vaux, 2.390-94.

[158] בְּרִיתִי שָׁלוֹם is an ellipsis for בְּרִיתִי בְּרִית שָׁלוֹם.

actions, demonstrates his reverence. Indeed, based on the similarities of language and construction, it may be posited that
Mal 2:4-5 is based on Num 25:12f. That Malachi calls this
covenant Levitical rather than Aaronic (via Phinehas) stems
from the aforementioned subordination of the priesthood to the
house of Levi. Because of this development, the covenant concluded with Phinehas became the common property of the
"levitical" priesthood and Phinehas became "le lévite, generale-
ment admis comme ancêtre et modèle idéal du sacerdoce officiant
du temps de Malachie." [159]

Finally, it must be stated that a distinction between priest
and Levite is apparent in this oracle unit. It is not a distinction
of function but of attitude. Malachi has constructed a "levite-
cohen" model in which the "levite" personifies the ancient and
idealized priestly class while the "*cohen*" characterizes the present
degenerate clergy. The use of כֹּהֵן in 2:7 does not destroy this
model. When Malachi asserts that שִׂפְתֵי כֹהֵן יִשְׁמְרוּ־דַעַת "the lips
of the priest should guard knowledge," he is subtly affirming
that the priests of his own day do not. Similarly, the use of בְּנֵי־לֵוִי
in 3:3 is not destructive. Through purification the levitical ideal
will be attained once again.

---

[159] J. Halévy, "Le prophète Malachie," *RS* 17 (1909) 20. It is interesting to
note that in Num 25:1f., Phinehas is commended for combatting idolatrous
practices: illicit sexual relationships and worship of other gods. It is precisely
these two practices that Malachi condemns in the next oracle unit, 2:10-16.

CHAPTER VII

MALACHI 2:10–16

AB^2C	^{10}הלוא אב אחד לכלנו
$AB_1{}^2C$	הלוא אל אחד בראנו
A_1D^3	מדוע נבגד איש באחיו
D_1E^2	לחלל ברית אבתינו
$\overline{ABA_1{}^2B_1{}^2}$	^{11}בגדה יהודה ותועבה נעשתה בישראל ובירושלם
$(Z)A_{11}B$	כי חלל יהודה
C^4	קדש יהוה אשר אהב
$A_{111}C_1{}^3$	ובעל בת־אל נכר
$\overline{A^2B^3}$	^{12}יכרת יהוה לאיש אשר יעשנה
$B_1 + B_1D^2$	ער וענה מאהלי יעקב
B_{11} _____	ומגיש מנחה ליהוה צבאות
$\overline{A^2B}$	^{13}וזאת שנית תעשו
B_1CD^2	כסות דמעה את־מזבח יהוה
$C_1 + C_{11}$ _____	בכי ואנקה
$\overline{A^3B^2}$	מאין עוד פנות אל־המנחה
$A_1B_1{}^2$	ולקחת רצון מידכם
$\overline{A\ B^2}$	^{14}ואמרתם על־מה
$B_1{}^2CD^2$	על כי־יהוה העיד בינך
D^3	ובין אשת נעוריך
$E\ F^2\ D_1$	אשר אתה בגדתה בה
$\overline{D_{11}{}^2D_{11}{}^2}$	והיא חברתך ואשת בריתך
$\overline{ABCD^3}$	^{15}ולא־אחד עשה ושאר רוח לו
$A_1B_1C_1$	ומה האחד מבקש
D_1 _____	זרע אלהים
AB	ונשמרתם ברוחכם
$\overline{B_1{}^2A_1{}^2}$	ובאשת נעוריך אל־יבגד
$(Z)\ AB\ C^4$	^{16}כי־שנא שלח אמר יהוה אלהי ישראל
B_1DE^2	וכסה חמס על־לבושו

$C_1{}^3$ אמר יהוה צבאות
A B   ונשמרתם ברוחכם
$A_1{}^2$ ולא תבגדו

(2:10) *Have we not all one father?*
        Has not one God created us?
        Why then do we act faithlessly
            every man against his brother,
        violating the covenant of our fathers?
(2:11) *Judah has acted faithlessly, and an abomination has been*
            committed in Israel and in Jerusalem.
        For Judah has profaned the sanctuary of Yahweh
            which he loves,
        and has married the daughter of a foreign god.
(2:12) *May Yahweh cut off the man who does this-*
        the aroused one and the lover-from the tents of Jacob,
        and the one who brings near an offering to Yahweh of
            Hosts.
(2:13) *And this moreover you do:*
        You cover Yahweh's altar with tears,
            weeping and groaning.
        Thus, there will no longer be a turning to the offering,
            or a taking of favor from your hand.
(2:14) *Yet you say, "Wherefore?"*
        Because Yahweh bears witness between you
            and the wife of your youth,
        with whom you have dealt deceitfully,
        although she was your companion, and the wife of
            your covenant.
(2:15) *And not one does it and has a remnant of spirit.*
        And what is that one seeking—a seed of God?
        Therefore, take heed to your spirit,
        and do not act faithlessly with the wife of your youth.
(2:16) *"For one who divorces because of aversion,"*
            says Yahweh, the God of Israel,
        "thereby covers his garment with violence," says Yahweh
            of Hosts.
        Therefore, take heed to your spirit
        and do not act faithlessly.

Content and Structure

In this the third oracle unit, Malachi once again turns to the people (cf. 1:2-5), and confronts them with a double abuse that has social and religious consequences: marriage with foreign women and divorce of legitimate wives. It is no coincidence that Mal 1:6-2:9 and 2:10-16 are juxtaposed. In each oracle unit a covenant is corrupted (2:8—שחתם ברית הלוי) or desecrated (2:10—לחלל ברית אבתינו) by the actions of the group addressed (priests, 1:6-2:9; people, 2:10-16).

This section opens with a "hingestellte Behauptung," a positive affirmation, in the guise of two questions: הלוא אב אחד לכלנו // הלוא אל אחד בראנו, "Do we not all have one father? Has not one god created us?" (2:10). That they must both be answered with an unqualified 'yes' is undeniable. Indeed, the paternity of Yahweh has already been stressed (1:6; cf. Exod 4:22; Num 11:12; Deut 32:6, 18; Isa 63:16; 64:8; 67:4). Similarly that he created the people is incontrovertible (cf. Gen 1:27; 5:2; 6:7; Isa 42:5; 45:12, 18). Thus, it should follow that all his children, as brothers, display affection and act without treachery in their dealings with one another. That this response is not forthcoming from the people is made abundantly clear in what follows, 2:10c, d-13. The people have desecrated the covenant concluded long ago with their forefathers by marrying foreign women (2:11) and by attaching themselves to the cults of their new wives (2:13a-c). As a result of this double estrangement (from their own people and cult), Yahweh refuses to accept their offerings (2:13d, e; cf. 1:10). In their obtuseness, the people question Yahweh, asking him wherein they have incurred his displeasure, 2:14—עַל־מָה. Yahweh answers, not by a reiteration of the previous offenses, but by citing another related abuse. The people betray (בָּגַד) the wives of their youth (2:14) by divorcing them (2:16). The consequences of their actions (intermarriage, apostasy, divorce) are two. Not only will they be cut off socially and cultically from their people and god (2:13), but their new marriage will be unproductive; their seed will never germinate (2:15).

Of the poetic devices employed in this oracle unit, key word repetition and the resultant parallelism are the most striking (cf. also 1:6-2:9). The verb בָּגַד, "to betray, act faithlessly," is used five times, above all in the specific connotation of marital impropriety (2:10, 11; 2:14, 15, 16). There is a four-fold use of אֶחָד, "one" (2:10—2x; 2:15—2x).[1] Other repeated words include בְּרִית, "covenant" (2:10, 14); חִלֵּל, "to defile, pollute" (2:10, 11); מִנְחָה, "offering" (2:12, 13) and רוּחַ, "breath, spirit" (2:15—2x; 2:16).

Alliteration, another common poetic device, is in evidence throughout this section, cf. 2:10—וּבָעַל; 2:11—אֵל אֶחָד, אָב אֶחָד; 2:14—בָּגַדְתָּה בָּהּ, מַגִּישׁ מִנְחָה, עֵר וְעֹנֶה; 2:12—בַּת־אֵל, cf. also 1:6. Alliteration, like other features of rhetoric, is used to greatest effect in variation and in combination with other types of literary artifice. As in the second oracle unit (1:6-2:9), the alliteration in 2:10-16 is complemented by sound repetition at the end of words (terminal rhyme), cf. 2:10—בָּגְדָה יְהוּדָה; 2:11—אֲבֹתֵינוּ, בְּרָאָנוּ, לְכֻלָּנוּ; 2:14—בָּגַדְתָּה בָּהּ; תּוֹעֵבָה נֶעֶשְׂתָה.[2] These conventions are all sug-gestive of ideas, images and emotions; they function as ligatures, binding the unit into a coherent whole.[3]

Text and Commentary

[2:10]—בָּרָא-qal perfect, "to create." This verb is used exclu-sively to denote divine creation and appears predominantly in the qal (38x), cf. Gen 1:27; 5:1-2; 6:7; Deut 4:32.[4] In Isa 45:12, Yahweh "made" (עָשָׂה) the earth, but "created" (בָּרָא) man; he created (בָּרָא) Israel as a people (Isa 43:1, 7, 15; Mal 2:10).

בָּגַד: this verb expresses the unstable relationship of men to existing, established regulations and can be translated, "to act faithlessly." The treacherous acts of man (2:10-16) stand in direct contrast to Yahweh's faithfulness and trustworthiness (3:6). More precisely, בָּגַד denotes the faithlessness of the people to their covenant responsibilities (2:10), and is often a synonym of verbs like חָטָא, "to sin."[5] In 1 Sam 14:33, it is evident that

---

[1] The parallelism between these two verses will be discussed in the commentary on 2:15, cf. pp. 103-9.

[2] Cf. J. J. Gluck, "Assonance in Ancient Hebrew Poetry," *De Fructu Oris Sui*, Essays in Honor of Adrianus van Selms (Ed. I. H. Eybers, F. C. Fensham et al.; Pretoria Oriental Series, 9; Leiden: Brill, 1971) 83.

[3] P. P. Saydon, "Assonance in Hebrew as a Means of Expressing Emphasis," *Bib* 36 (1955) 37.

[4] H. Ringgren, "בָּרָא, bārā³," *TDOT* 2.246.

[5] Hans-Jurgen Zobel, "בָּגַד, bāghadh; בֶּגֶד, beghedh," *TDOT* 1.471.

sinning against Yahweh (חטא ליהוה) by violating his ordinances, is equivalent to a בֶּגֶד, a treacherous act, against him.[6] In Ps 78:57, the people commit treacherous acts when they do not observe (לֹא שָׁמַר) Yahweh's testimonies (cf. Ps 119:58). The expression בָּגְדוּ בִי in Hos 6:7 is used in connection with the people's transgression (עָבַר) of the covenant (בְּרִית), i.e., their relationship to Yahweh.[7]

The verb בָּגַד also denotes faithlessness in marriage, deserting one's legal partner and cementing a relationship with someone else. The object of this faithless behavior or betrayal can be the wife (Exod 21:8; Mal 2:14), the husband (Jer 3:20) or Yahweh (Jer 9:1). Finally, apostasy, turning away from Yahweh to worship other gods, constitutes a בֶּגֶד against him. This is evident from Hos 5:7 where the faithless acts of the people against Yahweh are compared with the birth of illegitimate children (בָּנִים זָרִים). Indeed, it is a characteristic of this prophet that he describes apostasy as adultery; Israel has forsaken Yahweh and given herself to Baal.[8] Jeremiah says that Judah has dealt treacherously with its god. She has forsaken him and has no fear of him (3:21). Just as a woman is faithless to her lover, so Israel is faithless to Yahweh, אכן בגדה אשה מרעה כן בגדתם בי בית ישראל, 3:20. She exchanged him for idols and that which is worthless (3:9).

All three of these nuances of בָּגַד, covenant faithlessness, marital faithlessness and faithlessness to Yahweh and his cult, are clearly present in Mal 2:10-16, and are closely interrelated. That the use of בָּגַד in 2:10-16 denotes faithlessness to covenant responsibilities in general, is evidenced by the parallel phrase לחלל ברית אבתינו, "to profane the covenant of our fathers," 2:10d. As will be discussed more fully below, one of the stipulations of that covenant was that the Israelites limit their contacts with the people around them by agreeing not to marry them. Thus, they minimized the risk of being lured away from Yahweh to follow other gods (cf. Exod 34:10f; Deut 7:1f). The two other uses of בָּגַד in this oracle unit, although still circumscribed by their relationship to covenant faithlessness, are more specific in their thrust.

[6] Cf. Lev 19:26 and the prohibition against eating blood, דם.
[7] Hans Walter Wolff, *Hosea* (Philadelphia: Fortress, 1974) 121.
[8] Ibid., 100-101.

Malachi asserts that intermarriage not only profanes the covenant, but also constitutes an act of betrayal of Judean wives (2:14-16). It is a בֶּגֶד, a violation of the bond which unites the members of the nation among themselves and with Yahweh in the same family. Moreover, by marrying a בַּת־אֵל נֵכָר, a daughter of a foreign god, the men combine worship of Yahweh with worship of the gods of their wives (2:13). This, too, is a בֶּגֶד, a turning away from Yahweh.

The expression חִלֵּל בְּרִית means "to profane, violate" a covenant.[9] It is also found in Ps 89:35.[10] In this verse, Mal 2:10, חִלֵּל בְּרִית is parallel to בָּגַד, "to act treacherously." The same ideas are connected in Hos 6:7 where the verb בָּגַד is parallel to the phrase עָבַר בְּרִית, "to trespass or transgress a covenant."[11]

בְּרִית אֲבֹתֵינוּ, "The covenant of our fathers": Malachi is not announcing the universal thought that all men are brothers. The reference to "the covenant with the fathers" makes it clear that he is thinking only of Judah. It was the 'Exodus' election which provided the most solid content for the faith of Israel in its pre-exilic period (cf. Exod 20:2; Lev 25:35; Deut 5:6). In the course of time, however, the patriarchal election came to prominence. Van Seters contends that the shift from the Exodus to the Patriarchal election is evident in 2 Isa (cf. 41:8f). Just as God called Abraham from a distant land and brought him to Canaan, so too he will bring back the exiles.[12] Van Seters remarks that for Deuteronomy, Jeremiah and Ezekiel, the land promise theme was closely connected with the conditional covenant contracted in the wilderness, disobedience to which would result in forfeiture.[13] Because "the exile was proof that the covenantal relationship was broken and with it the claim to the land," the resultant crisis of faith and identity could be overcome

[9] *Gesenius' Hebrew and Chaldee Lexicon* (Grand Rapids, Michigan: William B. Eerdmans, 1949) 281.

[10] G. W. Ahlström, *Psalm 89: Eine Liturgie aus dem Ritual des leidenden Königs* (Lund: C. W. K. Gleerups, 1959) 126-27, 133.

[11] Other expressions for breaking a covenant include: הפר (פרר) ברית, "to break a covenant," Gen 17:14; Lev 26:15; Deut 31:16, 20; עזב ברית, "to forsake a covenant," Deut 29:24; Jer 22:9; מאס, בזה ברית, "to despise a covenant," 2 Kgs 17:15; 1 Sam 33:8.

[12] John Van Seters, *Abraham in History and Tradition* (New Haven: Yale University, 1975) 265.

[13] Ibid., 265.

only by "associating the land promise not with the 'fathers' of the Exodus but with the forefathers" long before it, to whom the promise was unconditional (cf. Gen 15:9-10, 17-21).[14] Connected with Yahweh's promise of the land to Abraham is his promise of numerous progeny, Gen 12:1-3. According to Van Seters, this too, can be best understood in the context of the exile.[15] For Deuteronomy, the number of people in the land was of secondary importance. What counted was their loyalty to Yahweh (cf. Deut 11:26-28; 28).[16] Only with the threat of extinction during the exilic period do numbers become important (cf. Gen 12:1-3; 22:17; Jer 30:19; Isa 51:1-2; 54:3). Further, he asserts that "concern with ethnic descent and racial purity becomes increasingly important in the exilic and post-exilic periods because it goes hand in hand with the patriarchal promise."[17] In Gen 24:2-8, emphasis is placed on the antagonism between Abraham and the indigenous population with regard to the question of intermarriage. "The inference in 24:7 is that for the patriarchs (Israel) to intermarry with Canaanites would be a rejection of God's promise to give all the land of the Canaanites to them."[18] Deuteronomy also stresses nonintermarriage because it leads to apostasy and breech of the covenant (cf. Deut 7:1f). No covenants are to be made with the people of the nations; they are to be exterminated. The focus of the Yahwist in the Genesis narratives, however, is different. According to Van Seters, he is not averse to covenants with local authorities, cf. Gen 21:22-4; 26:26-31.[19] Moreover, apostasy is not an issue. What is at stake is the preservation of the racial purity of the descendants of Abraham "so that the land promise, which has become the covenant between Yahweh and Israel through Abraham (15:7-21), can be upheld."[20]

Van Seters remarks that the covenant shift from the Exodus fathers to the Patriarchs was complete by the time of the Chronicler and is evident in the covenant with the fathers mentioned

[14] Ibid.
[15] Ibid., 272.
[16] Ibid., 273.
[17] Ibid., 277.
[18] Ibid.
[19] Ibid.
[20] Ibid.

in Neh 9:7-8 (this he connects with Gen 15).[21] Therefore, it is
probable that had Van Seters considered this Malachi passage, he
would have connected the phrase "the covenant of our fathers"
in Mal 2:10, with the promises made to Abraham. Indeed, because
of Van Seters' treatment of the covenant shift and the intermarriage theme in Gen 24:2f, it is tempting to link the covenant
mentioned in Malachi with that of the patriarchs. Nevertheless,
his contention that apostasy was no longer a factor inherent in
the Gen 24 stand against intermarriage, blunts the edge of his
argument.[22] Whether he means that apostasy and syncretism
were no longer issues of the exilic and post-exilic cults, is not
made clear. However, as G. W. Ahlström remarks, "it is too
often taken for granted that in the post-exilic time, there was no
room for worship of any god other than Yahweh."[23] What is
undeniable is that in Mal 2:10-16, the prime pitfall of intermarriage is not the loss of ethnic purity, but the resultant
incorporation into the Yahweh cult of the cultic rites of other
gods (cf. 2:13). The connection between intermarriage and
apostasy is made explicit in the covenants detailed in Exod
34:10f and Deut 7:1f. In both, Israel agrees to the stipulation not
to intermarry since the marriage of an Israelite male to a foreign
woman results in a turning away from Yahweh to follow her
gods (cf. Exod 34:16: וְהִזְנוּ אֶת־בָּנֶיךָ אַחֲרֵי אֱלֹהֵיהֶן; Deut 7:4: כִּי־יָסִיר
אֶת־בִּנְךָ מֵאַחֲרַי וְעָבְדוּ אֱלֹהִים אֲחֵרִים). To state unequivocally to
which of these two covenants Malachi had recourse, is impossible. Both are connected with the Exodus theme, both are related
to the giving of the law and both make similar statements about
the negative impact of intercourse with foreigners. However, the
language of Malachi approximates neither. Nevertheless, his use
of the phrase "covenant of the fathers," and his clear allusion
to the stipulation that Israel not marry foreigners indicates
that he was aware of a covenant tradition like the one concluded with the Exodus fathers, Exod 34 and Deut 7. His
reference to it here may have been calculated to remind his
contemporaries of their obligations, and to bring home strongly
the enormity of their offense.

[21] Ibid., 264, n. 41.

[22] Ibid., 277.

[23] G. W. Ahlström, *Joel and the Temple Cult of Jerusalem* (SVT 21; Leiden:
Brill, 1971) 27.

[2:11]—In this verse as in 2:10, בָּגַד and חִלֵּל are parallel: בָּגְדָה יְהוּדָה, 2:11a // חִלֵּל יְהוּדָה, 2:11c. The most interesting aspect of this parallelism is the gender shift from feminine, בָּגְדָה יְהוּדָה (2:11a) to masculine, חִלֵּל יְהוּדָה (2:11c). In the first instance (2:11a), Judah as the name of the country, is regarded as a feminine substantive.[24] When, however, the same noun refers to the people within the nation, as in 2:11c, it is construed as masculine.[25] The feminine-masculine shift here functions as an indicator of totality. It stresses the enormity of the people's offense by enunciating that betrayal is practiced everywhere in the country, 2:11a, and profanation by every one of its inhabitants, 2:11c. Between the two occurrences of Judah (2:11a, c), the phrase בְּיִשְׂרָאֵל וּבִירוּשָׁלָם is found, 2:11b. Not content with the general "everywhere and everyone," the prophet moves directly to the center and specifically implicates the cult congregation. As G. A. Danell remarks, "the cult congregation in the Jerusalem temple has always been called Israel."[26] Similarly, G. W. Ahlström concludes that "Israel refers primarily to the cult congregation of the Jerusalem temple, since people and cult are often synonymous" (cf. Joel 2:17; 4:2; Zeph 3:14).[27] Indeed, it may be said that it is in Jerusalem that the true Israel can (or should) be found.[28] Malachi's attack makes it clear that this is not the case. By embracing non-Yahwistic rituals the people have defiled Yahweh's temple (קֹדֶשׁ). Therefore, their sacrifices will no longer be accepted (2:13) and they will be cultically and socially cut off (2:12). This verse details one more instance of the prophet's preoccupation with a pure Yahweh cult (cf. 1:6-2:9).

תּוֹעֵבָה, is a feminine noun from the root תָּעַב, "an abomination, something abominable."[29] Gesenius remarks that it is "especially used of things which are made impure and illicit by the decrees of religion."[30] תּוֹעֵבָה "always seems to refer to cultic

[24] GKC, #122h, 391.

[25] Ibid., #122i, 391.

[26] G. A. Danell, *Studies in the Name of Israel in the Old Testament* (Uppsala: Appelbergs boktryckeryi-a.-b., 1946) 99.

[27] Ahlström, *Joel*, 26.

[28] D. Jones, "The Traditio of the Oracles of Isaiah of Jerusalem," *ZAW* 67 (1955) 239.

[29] *Gesenius' Hebrew and Chaldee Lexicon*, 859.

[30] Ibid.

irregularities."[31] It is the word employed to "designate a rite or phenomenon as non-Yahwistic, i.e., belonging to another deity" (cf. Deut 7:25f; 13:15; 32:16; Isa 1:13; 44:19; Jer 6:5; 16:18; Ezek 8:6; 11:18).[32] According to P. Humbert, תּוֹעֵבָה expresses the intransigence of Yahwism.[33] It can refer to serving gods other than Yahweh (Deut 13:15; 17:4), making idols (27:15), Canaanite rites (12:31) or to sacral prostitution (23:10). It is a theological formula "servant essentiellement à la réaction antipaganisante et à la défense rigoriste de la pureté du cult Yahviste."[34] In this verse, 2:11, it is evident that the תּוֹעֵבָה is intermarriage (2:11d, cf. also Ezra 9:1, 11, 14). What is more, the commission of the תּוֹעֵבָה profanes Yahweh's temple (קֹדֶשׁ).[35] As T. Chary observes, "le temple est si parfaitement planté au milieu de la vie religieuse qu'il est directement affecté par l'infidélité."[36] He states, however, that because the idea of a ritual profanation of the temple by intermarriage is so novel, many scholars prefer to translate קֹדֶשׁ with "chose consacrée," i.e., the holy community.[37] Nevertheless, it must be stressed that intermarriage is banned precisely "a cause de la contamination religieuse qui en résultait" (cf. Deut 7:1f; Exod 34:15-16; Num 25:1-5).[38] The connection between idolatrous practices and defiling Yahweh's sanctuary is made explicit in Lev 20:2f. The man who gives his seed to Molech will be stoned to death.[39] He will be cut off (כָּרַת מִן, cf. Mal 2:12) from his

---

[31] Donald E. Gowan, "Prophets, Deuteronomy and the Syncretistic Cult in Israel," *Transitions in Biblical Scholarship* VI (Ed. J. Coert Rylaarsdam; Chicago: The University of Chicago, 1968) 107.

[32] Ahlström, *Joel*, 27.

[33] P. Humbert, "Le substantif to ᶜēbā et le verbe tᶜb dans l'Ancien Testament," *ZAW* 72 (1960) 224. He maintains that "l'allusion deutéronomique à la to ᶜēbā est fréquemment et expressément formulée en fonction de la ségrégation d'Israël d'avec les peuples cananéens," 225.

[34] Ibid., 224.

[35] For the combination of עָשָׂה + תּוֹעֵבָה, "to commit an abomination," cf. Deut 13:15; 17:14; Ezek 16:15; 18:12; 33:26.

[36] Th. Chary, *Les prophètes et le culte à partir de l'exil* (Tournai: Desclée, 1954) 163.

[37] Ibid., 164, cf. A. van Hoonacker, *Les douze petits prophètes* (Paris: Gabalda, 1908) 723; Ernst Sellin, *Das Zwölfprophetenbuch übersetzt und erklärt* (KAT 12/2; Leipzig: A Deichertsche, 1930) 603.

[38] Chary, 163.

[39] Cf. Martin Noth, *Leviticus* (OTL; Philadelphia: Westminster, 1977) 147f.

people because he defiled Yahweh's sanctuary (מִקְדָּשִׁי, 20:3).
Indeed, all who go a whoring (זָנָה) after Molech will be cut off,
(20:5). In Ezekiel, the contamination of the temple is linked
directly to the commission of תּוֹעֵבוֹת, abominations. According
to P. Humbert, "dans Ezéchiel on la regard [the תּוֹעֵבָה] essentiellement sous l'angle de la violation de l'ordre sacre, cultuel par-
ticulièrement, de la souillure du sanctuaire par example."[40] The
idols in the temple (8:10), women weeping for Tammuz (8:14)
and men worshiping the sun (8:16) are all called תּוֹעֵבוֹת גְּדֹלוֹת
and all defile Yahweh's temple (מִקְדָּשׁ, cf. also Ezek 5:11; 23:36,
38; 44:6, 7, 13). Finally, of the nearly 310 occurrences of קֹדֶשׁ,
"holiness, sacredness, apartness, a holy thing,"[41] eighty-two bear
the concrete sense of "temple, sanctuary" (cf. Exod 28:43; 29:30;
35:19; 39:1; Pss 20:3; 150:1; Ezek 42:14; 44:19, 27). Therefore, it
cannot be argued that the profanation of the sanctuary through
intermarriage is a novel idea. Further, the belief that unaccept-
able practices in the religious sphere defile Yahweh's temple
harmonizes well with Malachi's stand on cultic matters. He was
a ritual formalist interested, above all, in a pure Yahweh cult, a
cult properly performed (cf. 1:6-2:9).

"To take a wife" is expressed by the verb בָּעַל, the root
meaning of which is "to become master" (Deut 21:12; 24:1).[42]
Just as the unmarried woman was under the authority of her
father, so the married woman was under the authority of her
husband and was one of his "possessions" (cf. Exod 20:17). The
husband was, in every respect, the dominant partner. He was his
wife's lord (בָּעַל) and he was to rule over her (cf. Gen 3:16).[43] In
the context of this oracle unit, it is probable that בעל has an
additional connotation. Not only does a man marry a foreign
woman, he also marries her god; that is, he is wedded to her cult
and her god becomes his lord, master (בעל).

בַּת־אֵל נֵכָר: "The daughter of a foreign god." The phrase
אֵל נֵכָר, "foreign god," occurs in Deut 32:12; Ps 81:10 (cf. אֱלֹהֵי
נֵכָר, "foreign gods," Gen 35:2, 4; Deut 31:16; Josh 24:20, 23;

[40] Humbert, 230.
[41] *Gesenius' Hebrew and Chaldee Lexicon,* 725.
[42] Ibid., 130.
[43] J. C. de Moor, "בַּעַל baᶜal," *TDOT* 2.182.

Judg 10:16; 1 Sam 7:3; Jer 5:19). The combination בַּת־אֵל נֵכָר has
constituted an interpretive crux. Some scholars like von Bulmerincq, van Hoonacker, Chary, J. M. P. Smith and E.
Sellin translate literally, "the daughter of a foreign god" = a foreign
woman.[44] Others, like G. W. Ahlström, C. C. Torrey, F. F.
Hvidberg and A. Isaksson[45] contend that had the prophet "meant
simply to designate foreign women, he would have used the
phrase נָשִׁים נָכְרִיּוֹת (1 Kgs 11:1, 8; Ezra 10:2; Neh 13:26), since
an ordinary woman is never called a daughter of god. The
latter expression connotes something special," i.e., a goddess.[46]
Although the implications of these renderings will be discussed
below (pp. 113f.), two arguments may be adduced here in favor
of a literal translation. The point that "daughter of a foreign
god" can only mean "goddess" is not well taken. By the same
reasoning, "the children of Yahweh" (Deut 14:1; 32:19; Hos 1:1;
Isa 1:2) would be gods, although the term is indisputably applied
to Israelites. Similarly, in Num 21:29, the Moabites are called
sons and daughters of the god Chemosh. Although worshipers
of the Moabite god, they themselves are not gods.[47]

Second, it is highly probable that בַּת in 2:11 is antithetically
parallel to אָב in 2:10. It is made very clear in 2:10 that Yahweh is
the father of all Judeans and they, by analogy, are his children.
As a non-Judean, therefore, the בַּת of 2:11, is not his daughter.
Significantly, the entire phrase בַּת־אֵל נֵכָר may be antithetically
parallel to 2:10a, b. Not only is Yahweh their father (אָב), he is
also their god (אֵל). Indeed, as the אֵל אֶחָד , one (only) god, of his
people, he stands in opposition to the אֵל נֵכָר, the foreign god of
2:11. Finally, the sentence בָּעַל בַּת־אֵל נֵכָר graphically demonstrates the consequences of intermarriage. By marrying a foreign
woman, her god and cult are allied with that of Yahweh
and, as a result, his paternity, his creative effort as אֵל on

---

[44] Cf. Sellin, 603; Chary, 163; van Hoonacker, 723; J. M. P. Smith, *Malachi*
(ICC; Edinburgh: T. & T. Clark, 1912) 52f.

[45] Cf. Ahlström, *Joel*, 49; Abel Isaksson, *Marriage and Ministry in the New
Temple* (Lund: C. W. K. Gleerup, 1965) 31; C. C. Torrey, "The Prophecy of
Malachi," *JBL* 17 (1898) 4f; F. F. Hvidberg, *Weeping and Laughter in the Old
Testament* (Leiden: Brill, 1962) 120f.

[46] Ahlström, *Joel*, 49.

[47] A. von Bulmerincq remarks that בַּת־אֵל נֵכָר is poetic while נָשִׁים נָכְרִיּוֹת is
prosaic, *Der Prophet Maleachi* (2 vols.; Tartu: J. G. Krüger, 1926–1932), 2.259.

Israel's behalf is obscured, even rejected or usurped. The use of
נָשִׁים נָכְרִיּוֹת to denote foreign women lacks the power to evoke all
these associations. It may be for this reason that the prophet
substituted בַּת־אֵל נֵכָר.

[2:12]—יַכְרֵת is a hiphil jussive from כָּרַת, "to cut off."[48] The
phrase כָּרַת מֵאֹהֶל, "to cut off from the tent," appears only
here, but note the parallel נָסַח מֵאֹהֶל (Ps 52:7) and נָתַק מֵאֹהֶל
(Job 18:14). The combination of מִן + כָּרַת, "to cut off from" is a
frequently used expression in the O.T. (cf. Isa 9:13; וַיַּכְרֵת יהוה
מִיִּשְׂרָאֵל רֹאשׁ וְזָנָב and Lev 17:10; 20:3, 5, 6; Amos 1:5, 8; Nah 2:14;
Zeph 1:3).

אָהֳלֵי יַעֲקֹב—the tents, dwelling of Jacob: "the dwelling places
of a whole people are summed up as their ʾohalim, "tents,"
cf. Hos 4:20; Jer 30:18; Zech 12:7; Ps 78:55."[49] Since tents and
their inhabitants form a unit, the phrase "tents of Jacob" may
mean the Judean community.[50] More specifically, it may designate the cult community.[51] As mentioned previously, Israel refers
to the cult community of the Jerusalem temple (cf. p. 89f.). Significantly, Israel is often found in parallelism with Jacob, יַעֲקֹב,
(cf. Num 24:5: אֹהָלֶיךָ יַעֲקֹב // מִשְׁכְּנֹתֶיךָ יִשְׂרָאֵל, and Deut 33:10;
Isa 14:1; Ps 14:7). Isa 43:22f is especially instructive. The subject
is Israel's worship in its entirety, and the charge that the prophet
makes is a tremendous one. Jacob and Israel are condemned
for participating in an improperly conceived cult. Indeed, instead
of serving Yahweh with their sacrifices, Yahweh was made
to serve them 43:22-24). As a result, "Jacob was destroyed
and Israel reviled" (43:28).[52] Throughout Isaiah chapters 43,
44 and 48, Yahweh's cult community, pre-exilic and exilic, is
called יַעֲקֹב // יִשְׂרָאֵל. That יַעֲקֹב may be equated with the cult
community in Mal 2:12 is evidenced by its proximity to יִשְׂרָאֵל in
2:11 and by the cultic concerns of the oracle unit. The sense of
2:12 is that the man who intermarries (לָאִישׁ אֲשֶׁר יַעֲשֶׂנָּה) will be
cultically excommunicated for his offense against Yahweh.

[48] BDB, 504.
[49] Klaus Koch, "אֹהֶל ʾōhel," TDOT 2.121.
[50] Ibid.
[51] Note that אֹהֶל can also refer to a temple, cf. Ahlström, Joel, 86, n. 1. It is
significant that as yet there was no differentiation between the secular and cultic
community. It was the same because it was the deity's community.
[52] Claus Westermann, Isaiah 40-66 (OTL; Philadelphia: Westminster, 1969)
116f.

Against van Hoonacker, לְאִישׁ should not be translated "to, for the man."[53] According to Gesenius: "Another solecism of the later period is the introduction of the object by the preposition ל as sometimes in Ethiopic and very commonly in Aramaic"[54] (cf. Num 10:25; 2 Sam 3:30; Isa 11:9; Jer 40:2; Ps 69:6; 73:18; Ezra 8:16; 1 Chr 29:22). Therefore, 2:12 should be translated, "May Yahweh cut off the man who does this . . . from the tents of Jacob."

עֵר וְעֹנֶה: The phrase עֵר וְעֹנֶה has always been a riddle. Wellhausen's argument in favor of עֵד וְעֹנֶה is ingenious, but not convincing.[55] In the first place, the definite technical meaning which he claims for עֵד וְעֹנֶה, "Kläger" and "Vertheidiger," cannot be deduced from actual Hebrew usage. עֵד is a witness; whether for or against is always determined by the context.[56] The verb עָנָה, as a legal term is also used both ways, and more frequently for accusing than for defending.[57] Moreover, according to Torrey, it does not appear that the prophet is speaking of a legal tribunal. "The ᶜed and ᶜoneh are to be cut off, not from the judgment seat, but 'from the dwellings of Jacob'."[58] The equivalence of the terms עֵד and עֹנֶה led van Hoonacker to posit that two synonyms were used to accentuate the force of the expression.[59] Therefore, עֵד וְעֹנֶה, was the defense that the prophet wished to see suppressed with regard to the one who committed the abuse. He coordinated מַגִּישׁ with עֵד וְעֹנֶה, translated it 'cult minister,' cf. 3:3, and suggested that the person was deprived of all aid—legal and cultic—before Yahweh.[60]

Keeping the MT intact, many scholars consider עֵר וְעֹנֶה to be an alliterative proverbial expression describing an entire body, everyone. Driver translated the phrase, "him that waketh and

---

[53] Cf. van Hoonacker, where he translates, "Puisse Jahvé, pour l'homme qui fait cela, supprimer . . . ," 724.

[54] GKC, #117n, 366.

[55] J. Wellhausen, *Die kleinen Propheten übersetzt und erklärt* (Berlin: George Reimer, 1892) 237. His reading is based on the LXX ἕως καὶ ταπεινωθῇ which suggests עֵד וְעֹנֶה.

[56] "To bear witness against," cf. 1 Kgs 21:10, 13; "To bear witness for," cf. Isa 43:9, 10: 44:8, 9; Job 29:11; Lam 2:13.

[57] "To accuse," cf. Exod 20:16; Num 35:30; Deut 19:18; 2 Sam 1:16; "To defend," cf. Gen 30:33; 1 Sam 12:3.

[58] Torrey, 5, n. 12.

[59] van Hoonacker, 724.

[60] Ibid.

him that answereth," i.e., everyone,[61] and von Orelli, "he that calls and he that makes reply," i.e., all active in the house.[62] Von Orelli also maintained that the clause מַגִּישׁ מִנְחָה "applies specifically to the priest whose every sin is double because of his near relation to the Lord (3:3)."[63] W. Rudolph suggested that עֵר was a substantive from the verb עיר, "to protect" (cf. Deut 32:11; Job 8:6), therefore, "protector, defender."[64] He translated עֹנֶה "call, react, appeal."[65] Together the two words enunciated the wish that the offender might be socially and cultically cut off from the community.[66]

According to Torrey, "there can be no doubt as to what sort of an expression would best suit the context here."[67] Expecting the equivalence of "all his house, remembrance, posterity," he suggested, on the basis of 3:19 where a similar threat is uttered, that originally the text read שֹׁרֶשׁ וְעָנָף—"root and branch."[68] Such an expression "would complete the prophet's threat in as forcible a manner as could be expected: "Yahwè destroy, for the man who does this, root and branch from the tents of Jacob!"[69] He maintained that an accident to one of the earliest MSS rendered these words only partially legible.[70]

A translation option that has never been examined, is that both words, עֵר and עֹנֶה, bear a sexual connotation. Indeed, for the verb [עָנָה] III in the piel, the meaning "to force a woman to have sexual intercourse," "to rape," is attested in both legal contexts (Deut 21:14;[71] 22:24, 29) and in narrative passages (Gen 32:2; Judg 19:24; 20:5; 2 Sam 13:12, 14, 22, 32; Ezek 22:11;

---

[61] S. R. Driver, *The Minor Prophets* (New York: Oxford University, American Branch, Henry Frowde, 1906) 314 and cf. R. C. Dentan, "Malachi," *IB* 6.1135.

[62] C. von Orelli, *The Twelve Minor Prophets* (Edinburgh: T. & T. Clark, 1893) 394.

[63] Ibid., 394–95.

[64] W. Rudolph, *Haggai-Sacharja-Maleachi* (KAT 13/4; Gütersloh: Gütersloher Verlagshaus Gerd Mohn, 1976) 269.

[65] Ibid., 269.

[66] Ibid., 272.

[67] Torrey, 5, n. 12.

[68] Ibid.

[69] Ibid., 5, n. 12.

[70] Ibid., and cf. Sellin, 603; G. Johannes Botterweck, "Schelt-und Mahnrede gegen Mischehen und Ehescheidung," *Bibel und Leben* 1 (1960) 182.

[71] Moshe Weinfeld notes that עֲנָה, even in the piel, does not necessarily involve rape. He points out that Targum Jonathan and Rashbam render ענתה in

Lam 5:11).[72] According to Gesenius, the fundamental idea of the piel is "to busy oneself eagerly with the action indicated by the stem . . . and an eager pursuit of an action may also consist in urging and causing others to do the same."[73] If rape is expressed by the piel, the qal of [עָנָה] III may express sexual intercourse by mutual consent. In Hos 2:16–17, the prophet develops the motif of love between God and his people. He says: "Therefore, I will allure her and bring her into the wilderness and speak tenderly to her . . . and there she will respond (ענתה), as in the days of her youth."[74] This is clearly a case of seducing a woman and, in accordance with the scene and the context of the passage, the clause should be translated, "Then she will love (me) as in the days of her youth." This scene of love is followed by another passage (2:23–25) that is inlaid with imagery of fertility and abundance. It is charged with sexual overtones and ענה in the qal is used repeatedly to describe the terrestrial fecundity and the era of love and bliss that will follow the marriage of Yahweh to Israel:

והיה ביום ההוא אענה נאם־יהוה אענה את־השמים
והם יענו את־הארץ והארץ תענה את־הדגן
ואת־התירוש ואת־היצהר
והם יענו את־יזרעאל
וזרעתיה לי בארץ
ורחמתי את־לא רחמה

The root ʿwr always refers to excitement. In the qal and passive stems it is used of being aroused or excited to some activity,[75] and in the factitive and causitive stems of arousing or stirring someone to actions (Ct 2:8; 3:5; 8:4, 5). Marvin Pope avers that "the state of activity from which one is aroused need not be

---

Deut 21:14 as "because he had intercourse with her," *Deuteronomy and the Deuteronomic School* (Oxford: Clarendon, 1972) 286, n. 5.

[72] Cf. [ענה] III, BDB, 776, "be low(ly)"; Piel, "afflict, humble, mishandle, rape." Note that scholars derive עָנָה in Mal 2:12 from ענה I, "to answer," cf. above, p. 94–95.

[73] GKC, #52f, g, 141.

[74] The RSV and NEB render ענתה as "answer." The NAB and JPS render it "respond."

[75] Cf. BDB, 734 and *Gesenius' Hebrew and Chaldee Lexicon*, 615.

sleep. The activities to which one is aroused are usually those
that require extra effort, especially strenuous endeavors like war,
work, love."[76] He remarks that the possibilities of the stem for
"suggestion of sexual excitement are patent and most obvious in
the noun ᶜayr, or ᶜîr, as a designation of the stud ass whose
sexual propensities are prodigious and scandalous."[77] Both the
hiphil and poᶜl of עוּר I (to rouse oneself, awake) are used in the
Song of Songs to mean "rouse, excite love," cf. Ct 2:7; 3:5; 8:4.
עוּר II (akin to ערה, ערר),[78] used only in the niphal (Hab 3:9),
means "to be naked, exposed,"[79] cf. Arab. عار, عُورَة —"nudity." As
with ענה in the qal, so the sexual nuances of עוּר in the qal have
not been exploited. In Ct 4:16a, b we read: עוּרִי צָפוֹן וּבוֹאִי תֵימָן.
Pope translates: "Stir, O North-wind, Come, O South-wind!"[80]
"This verse is clearly an invitation by the lady to her lover to
enjoy to the utmost all her charms which are his preserve."[81]
The call to the winds in 4:16a, b is intended to stir up the
fragrance of the garden and so waft the scent of the woman to
him. The sexual connotation of בּוֹא is well attested (cf. Gen 6:4;
16:2, 4; 38:16; Deut 22:13; Ct 5:1). The qal impv. f.s. עוּרִי, parallel
to בּוֹאִי (qal impv.) may, therefore, also have a sexual connotation.
Pope translates it "stir" in the sense of being sexually aroused.[82]

In Ct 5:2, the qal pt. of עוּר is found: אֲנִי יְשֵׁנָה וְלִבִּי עֵר,
cf. Mal 2:12. Pope remarks that the verbal forms here עֵר, יְשֵׁנָה are
stative participles "designating action begun in the past and
lasting to the present."[83] He translates, "I slept, but my mind
was alert."[84] Nevertheless, the sexual imagery that pervades
Ct 5:1-6 (cf. פָּתַח, open, i.e., receptive to sexual overtures;[85] רֶגֶל,
foot; used as a euphemism for genitals;[86] יָד, hand; used as a

---

[76] Marvin H. Pope, *Song of Songs* (AB; Garden City, New York: Doubleday & Co., 1977) 386.

[77] Ibid., 498.

[78] Cf. GKC, #77, 219.

[79] *Gesenius' Hebrew and Chaldee Lexicon*, 615.

[80] Pope, 453.

[81] Ibid., 499.

[82] Ibid., 498.

[83] Ibid., 510.

[84] Ibid., 501.

[85] Ibid., 515.

[86] Ibid.

euphemism for phallus[87]) makes it likely that עֵר, too has sexual overtones. The line might well be translated: "Although I am in a restful state (יְשֵׁנָה), my passions (heart) are aroused." In Mesopotamian usage "heart" has a sexual sense. The Sumerian ŠÀ.ZI.GA is equivalent to Akkadian *nīš libbi* and means "the rising of the heart," male sexual passion, potency.[88]

In view of the sexual connotations of both עור and ענה, it is conceivable that the qal participles used in Mal 2:12 have such overtones and may be translated, "the one who is aroused (from sexual inactivity, i.e., the aroused one) and the lover." Such a translation suits the context of the oracle unit. Indeed, both עֵר and עֹנֶה may here be veiled synonyms of זָנָה, "to play the harlot, commit fornication."[89] In the covenant concluded with the fathers (Mal 2:10, cf. Exod 34 and Deut 7), the Israelites agreed not to intermarry because foreign women go astray after their own gods (זנו בנתיו אחרי אלהיהן, Exod 34:16) and cause Israelite men to do the same (והזנו את־בניך אחרי אלהיהן, Exod 34:16). In Num 25:1 (covenant with Phinhas, cf. Mal 2:5), Yahweh's anger was kindled against the Israelites because they went awhoring (זנה) after Moabite women and joined themselves to Baal-Peor. זָנָה clearly suggests sexual activity.[90] According to H. Wolff, the use of זָנָה in Hosea suggests the "inroads of a Canaanite sexual rite into Israel in which young virgins offered themselves to the divinity and expected fertility in return."[91] He maintains that Israel's guilt is exposed as unfaithful apostasy (זָנָה) from Yahweh by participation in the Canaanite cult and way of life.[92] Indeed, the verb זָנָה occurs frequently in the immediate context of descriptions of the Baal cult (cf. Hos. 1:2; 2:7; 3:3; 4:10f; 5:3; 9:1). Further, the aspect of fertility that is associated with זָנָה (cf. also עֵר and עֹנֶה) is suggestive. בעל, a cognate to the word Baal, the god of rain and fertility, is used as a verb in biblical Hebrew to express marital relations (cf. Gen 20:3; Mal 2.11). G. W. Ahlström suggests that the weeping in Mal 2:13 may have been part of a

---

[87] Ibid., 517.

[88] Ibid., 479; Robert D. Biggs, *ŠÀ.ZI.GA. Ancient Mesopotamian Potency Incantations* (Locust Valley, New York, J. J. Augustin, 1967) 2–10.

[89] *Gensenius' Hebrew and Chaldee Lexicon*, 249.

[90] Wolff, *Hosea*, 14.

[91] Ibid., 14f.

[92] Ibid., 16.

fertility rite that was still performed in the post-exilic period.[93] The inference to be drawn is that when a Judean marries (בָּעַל) a foreign woman, he also is wedded to her cult. In that sense, according to Hvidberg, he marries a בַּת־אֵל נֵכָר, daughter of a foreign god, i.e., goddess, and must weep when her lover (בַּעַל) dies.[94] What Malachi is opposing are the syncretistic phenomena that have entered the Yahweh cult via intermarriage. The sexual connotations of עֵר and עֹנֶה support the suggestion that these rites have to do with fertility. The man (אִישׁ) who performs them is a fornicator, a prostitute (עֹנֶה, עֵר, זֹנֶה). The overwhelming fertility, sexual imagery finds its antithesis in Mal 2:15. The fornicator will be barren (i.e., without spirit); his seed will not germinate.[95]

מַגִּישׁ מִנְחָה: מַגִּישׁ is a hiphil active participle from [נגש], "to bring, offer." This suggests that the man who intermarries and accepts his wife's cult nevertheless continues to serve Yahweh. According to the prophet, such action will be of no avail. He will still be cut off from the cult community.

[2:13]—Van Hoonacker contends that the phrase "and this is a second thing that you do," serves as the heading of the divorce passage.[96] Chary maintains that this verse is parallel to v. 11: a cult profaned by intermarriage // a cult profaned by divorce.[97] Sellin avers that because no second sin is stated here, שֵׁנִית is a later insertion.[98] It must be stressed that the subject of divorce begins not here, but in v. 14. The issue in this verse is still intermarriage and its consequences. Moreover, there is indeed a second sin. Not only does a man intermarry, but he brings his wife's cultic rites to Yahweh's altar, covering it with

---

[93] Ahlström, *Joel*, 49. For other OT passages which suggest lamentation and cultic weeping for the deity, see Joel 1:9 (אבל); 2:12, 17; Hos 10:5 and cf. Wolff, *Hosea*, 228.

[94] Hvidberg, 122.

[95] See the discussion on 2:15, 103-9.

[96] van Hoonacker, 725; cf. also Rudolph, 271 and G. A. Smith, *The Book of the Twelve Prophets* (2 vols.; New York: A. C. Armstrong and Son, 1899) 2.340.

[97] Chary, 164.

[98] Sellin, 603. It should be noted that שֵׁנִית does not solely mean "second." It is a f. adj. num. ord. that may also mean "again, of a similar but not identical act, or another part in a series," cf. Ezek 4:6; 2 Sam 16:19. Thus, this sentence may be translated: "This is another thing that you do."

tears (דִּמְעָה), weeping (בְּכִי), and groaning (אֲנָקָה). As mentioned above (p. 98–99), this may refer to fertility rites. Such cultic behavior results in a negative response from Yahweh. The people's sacrifices will no longer be accepted (2:13d, e).

מֵאֵין is a compound negative (i.e., two morphemes coalesced into one word, cf. מִן + אֵין) and does double duty here negating both פְּנוֹת ("to turn," qal inf. cs.—פָּנָה) and לָקַחַת ("to take," qal inf. cs.—לָקַח). Thus, Mal 2:13c, d should be translated: "There will no longer be a turning to the offering, nor a taking of a favorable thing from your hand."

רָצוֹן: n.m., "a pleasing, agreeable thing."[99] As mentioned previously, one of the objects of offering sacrifice was to find favor with the deity, to command his good will. Malachi asserts that no matter how agreeable the offering, Yahweh will still turn away from it.

[2:14]—This verse opens with a question. The people ask עַל־מָה, "on what grounds, why does Yahweh refuse our sacrifices?" Although the question has already been answered— "because you served him with the wrong cult" (2:13)—, a second reason is tendered here: עַל כִּי, "because Yahweh bears witness between you and the wife of your youth with whom you have dealt deceitfully, although she was your companion and the wife of your covenant" (2:14). It is this verse that begins the diatribe against divorce. It is the treacherous behavior, the faithless acts (בגד) against the wives of their youth (אֵשֶׁת נְעוּרֶיךָ) on the part of those who decide to intermarry that culminate in divorce.

הֵעִיד: hiphil perfect of עוּד, "to bear witness, testify."[100] Although the combination הֵעִיד בֵּן . . . וּבֵין appears only here, it corresponds to the use of עֵד (n. witness) + בֵּן וּבֵן in Gen 31:44.[101]

The woman is first designated as אֵשֶׁת נְעוּרֶיךָ, "the wife of your youth," cf. נְעוּרִים, n.m. pl., "youth, early life," Prov 5:18; Isa 54:6.[102] She is the one he married when he was young and filled with youthful vigor. She is also called a חֲבֶרֶת (n.f., חָבֵר = κοινωνος, LXX), a companion, intimate, wife. And, she is

[99] KB, 907–8.
[100] BDB, 730.
[101] Note Gen 31:49: יצף יהוה ביני ובינך.
[102] BDB, 655. Note the parallel אַלּוּף נְעוּרִים "friend, intimate, husband of youth," Prov 2:17; Jer 3:4.

called "the wife of your covenant," אֵשֶׁת בְּרִיתֶךָ. As Torrey and Isaksson correctly point out, the בְּרִית refers not to a marriage contract, but to the covenant mentioned in 2:10, בְּרִית אֲבֹתֵינוּ, in which the fathers and, through them, the succeeding generations agreed not to intermarry.[103] The woman wedded in accordance with that stipulation is thus contrasted with the בַּת־אֵל נֵכָר in 2:11. The three-fold description of the wife as חֲבֶרְתְּךָ, אֵשֶׁת נְעוּרֶיךָ and אֵשֶׁת בְּרִיתֶךָ serves to emphasize the closeness, the intimateness of the relationship between the marriage partners and to make the treacherous behavior of the spouse even more odious.

It must be stressed that marriage is not merely an incidental transaction between two families; it cements a relationship or alliance between them. M. Burrows states that

> ... one family gives a very precious possession, a daughter; the other, to put things on an equal footing, gives a valuable present. The mohar thus establishes the prestige of the husband and his family, gives him authority over his wife, makes the contract binding on both parties and creates an alliance between two families.[104]

Similarly, J. Pedersen avers that the "mohar is not merely material compensation, but is a mental balancing of what is given by the family of the bride, for in the eyes of the Israelite, property is a living thing and is part of his soul."[105] Indeed, because the basis of Israelite marriage was the continuance of the husband's family, this required securing a wife from another family which had to be induced to give her up. "This was done by a gift, creating an obligation, sealing a contract and establishing a family alliance."[106]

Simply because the בְּרִית mentioned in this verse does not refer to a marriage covenant, but to the covenant of v. 10, does

---

[103] Torrey, 9; Isaksson, 31. According to van Hoonacker, Yahweh did not bear witness to the contract by which the marriage received its consecration, but to the cause of the divorce, i.e., to the spouse's treacherous behavior, 725.

[104] Millar Burrows, *The Basis of Israelite Marriage* (AOS XV; New Haven: American Oriental Society, 1938) 13.

[105] Johannes Pedersen, *Israel Its Life and Culture* (4 vols.; London: Oxford University) 1.68.

[106] Burrows, 15.

not mean that such contracts did not exist. However, A. Isaksson seems to suggest that any reference to a marriage contract in Malachi would be out of place because "the OT concept of berit is incompatible with what marriage meant in that period. Marriage was not a compact entered into by man, wife and Yahweh as witness but a matter of commercial negotiation between two men."[107] Such a statement does not take into account all the evidence. According to M. Weinfeld, a בְּרִית entails "first and foremost the notion of 'imposition,' 'liability' or 'obligation'; it expresses pledge and commitment."[108] A covenant can be established between individuals (Gen 21:22f; 26:23f; 31:44f), between states (1 Kgs 5:26; 15:19), between kings and subjects (2 Sam 5:3; 2 Kgs 11:17) and between man and wife (Ezek 16:8; Prov 2:17). Significantly, in Gen 31:43f, in language very similar to that of Mal 2:13, Jacob and Laban cut a covenant (כָּרַת בְּרִית) with God (אֱלֹהִים) as their witness (עֵד) that Jacob would not afflict Laban's daughters nor take other wives. Although Jacob is already married to Leah and Rachel, the stipulation that a man take no other wives is found in a marriage contract discovered at Elephantine and dated to the mid-fifth century.[109] It is thus very close in time to Malachi, cf. ch. II. S. Greengus maintains that the style of the Elephantine marriage contracts should be linked to the Aramaic scribal tradition circulating in Egypt, Babylonia and Palestine.[110] "Near Eastern influence is present, but it affected Elephantine no more than it affected Jewish law in general and not to a degree that would set Elephantine apart from Jewish legal tradition."[111] Although a written marriage contract is not attested in the OT, both Greengus and de Vaux maintain that since bills of sale and divorce (Deut 24:1f; Jer 3:8; Isa 50:1) were written up, it would be surprising if contracts of marriage did not exist at the same

---

[107] Isaksson, 31.

[108] Moshe Weinfeld, "בְּרִית berîth," *TDOT* 2.255–256.

[109] A. Cowley, ed., *Aramaic Papyri of the Fifth Century B.C.* (Oxford: Clarendon, 1923) 44, 47–50.

[110] Samuel Greengus, "The Aramaic Marriage Contracts in the Light of the Ancient Near East and the Later Jewish Materials," (Master's Thesis, The University of Chicago, 1959) 116.

[111] Ibid.

time.[112] Further, it may not have been necessary to write down the marriage agreement since some contracts acquired their binding force from recognized solemnities observed by the parties involved, i.e., a public transaction at the market-place, witnessed by the whole community (Gen 23:11f); a solemn declaration or understanding to do or not to do a particular thing (Num 30:13; Deut 23:33; Jer 17:16); by "striking the hand" (Ezek 17:18; Prov 6:1-5; 17:18); by oral vows (Deut 12:6, 11, 17, 18, 26) or by declaration on oath (Exod 20:7; Lev 19:12; Jer 12:16-17; Amos 8:14).

[2:15]—This verse, like the phrase עֵר וְעֹנֶה in 2:12, has been a riddle. Subjected to widely differing interpretations, many of them have drastically affected the MT. For example, Wellhausen translated: "Has not (הֲלֹא for וְלֹא) One (God = v. 10) made and left over (וישאר for שאר), i.e., preserved (1 Sam. 14:13; 25:22) (לנו for לו), the spirit (of life, cf. Gen. 6:17; Isa. 42:5)? And what does that one seek? A seed of God (i.e., children, cf. Ps. 127:3)."[113] Van Hoonacker, however, doubted whether השאר רוח can mean "conserver l'esprit."[114] Sellin concurred with van Hoonacker and suggested a less radical treatment of the MT that, at the same time, "continued the line of thought begun in 2:14." He translated: "Hat er (הֲלֹא für וְלֹא, nämlich Jahwe, vgl. 14a) nicht zu Einem Fleisch (שְׁאָר) und Leben (וְרוּחַ) dir (לְךָ für לוֹ, nämlich dem in v. 14 Angeredeten mit seinem Weibe) gemacht?"[115] "Offenbar hat Maleachi Gen 2:24 im Sinne, nur dass er das בָּשָׂר dort in שְׁאָר und רוּחַ = Lebensrauch, Leben zerlegt."[116] Further, he considered v. 15b to be a counter-question on the part of the hearers: "aber ihr sprecht: was anders als Nachkommenschaft fordert Jahwe?"[117] This is a reference to Gen 1:28 where "Gott verlange nichts anderes von dem neugeschaffenen Menschenpaare als Nachkommenschaft."[118]

[112] Ibid., 116; Roland de Vaux, *Ancient Israel* (2 vols; New York: McGraw-Hill, 1965) 1.33.

[113] Wellhausen, 240.

[114] van Hoonacker, 727.

[115] Sellin, 605.

[116] Ibid., 604.

[117] Ibid., 605.

[118] Ibid.

According to W. Rudolph, 2:15a alludes to the close of creation history in Gen 2 and should be translated: "Not one alone (Adam) did he create."[119] Interpretation difficulties with the rest of the line induced him to change שְׁאָר to שְׁאֵר and restore מִשְׁאֵרוֹ (easily omitted) as a reference to Eve. To make the line even clearer, he inserted כִּי אִם אִשָּׁה after עָשָׂה.[120] Thus, he translates: "Nicht einem Einzelnen hat er geschaffen, sondern auch die Frau also Ergänzung für ihn."[121] He remarks that just as 15aα reflects Gen 2:23, so αβ recalls 2:24: "Darum wird der Mann seiner Frau anhangen, und sie werden zu einem Fleisch werden."[122] In Malachi, the idea of "einem Fleisch" translates into Adam's desire to have children—זֶרַע אֱלֹהִים.[123] Rudolph adds כְּרַע (Ps 139:2, 7): זֶרַע כְּרַע אֱלֹהִים: "nach dem Willen (Gottes), to indicate that Adam's wish for descendants is according to God's will.[124]

J. Halévy believes the entire verse to be an allusion to Abraham. He translates:

> Le (père) unique (= Abraham qui est resté très longtemps un, sans avoir un enfant légitime) n'a pas fait [ainsi], (il n'a pas répudié sa femme Sara, qui demeura stérile jusqu'à sa grande vieillesse [Gen. 16:1; 18:11]) et pourtant un descendant direct (וּשְׁאָר; cf. שֵׁם וּשְׁאָר וְנִין וָנֶכֶד, Isa. 14:22), était sa volonté (רוּחַ לוֹ), רוּחַ au sens de volonté Ezek. 1:21, il désirait ardemment avoir un héritier (Gen. 15:2-3), ce père un' (= Abraham) demandait une progéniture d'Elohim (זֶרַע אֱלֹהִים).[125]

He concludes: "L'exhortation de Malachie est lumineuse: Vous chassez vos épouses juives qui vous ont donné ou vous donneront des enfants juifs pour épouser des éstrangeres: votre père Abraham n'a pas agi comme vous."[126] The interesting point that Halévy

---

[119] Rudolph, 270.

[120] Ibid. He contends that this was easily omitted because of the identity of שה and שׁה before the addition of Masoretic diacritics.

[121] Ibid., 270.

[122] Ibid.

[123] Ibid.

[124] Ibid.

[125] J. Halévy, "Le prophète Malachie," *RS* 17 (1909) 30-31.

[126] Ibid., 31.

makes when commenting on this verse, is that the אֶחָד here is
the same as the אָב אֶחָד of 2:10. Both refer to Abraham.[127]
Although his interpretation cannot be maintained if only because
the אָב אֶחָד in v. 10 refers to the paternity of Yahweh,[128] his
recognition of the structural and vocabulary similarities between
these two verses should not be ignored.

The sexual (and fertility) themes and images that have per-
vaded the rest of this oracle unit (cf. בָּעַל—2:11; עֵר וְעֹנֶה 2:12; אַנָקָה,
בְּכִי, דִּמְעָה—2:13) provide an avenue for the interpretation of
this verse that has hitherto been unexplored. The first words
spoken to Adam and Eve were, "Be fruitful and multiply,"
פְּרוּ וּרְבוּ, Gen 1:28. These words, although clearly commands, are
characterized in the biblical text as a blessing, and are sub-
sequently repeated by God whenever the promise of supreme
bliss and boon is imparted to an individual, cf. Noah (Gen 8:17;
9:1, 7), Abraham (Gen 12:2), Isaac (Gen 26:4, 24), Jacob (Gen
28:14; 32:13). Coupled with this is the well-attested belief that it
is Yahweh who 'opens' or 'closes' the womb of a woman,
cf. Sarah (Gen 16:2), Hannah (1 Sam 1:5-6). Indeed, it is Yahweh
who gives children (cf. Hos 9:14; Isa 66:9; Ps 127:3; 1 Chr 28:5).
This idea is linked with a paean to the fruitful wife and the
value of sons in Pss 127:3-5; 128. By the same token, it is
Yahweh who denies conception. In the Book of Job, Bildad the
Shuhite describes in considerable detail, the terrible consequences
of sinning. He says that the sinner, whom he calls the "wicked"
(רָשָׁע), loses his sexual power (אוֹנוֹ), is ensnared by his own
misdeeds and shall have neither son nor grandson among his
people (18:5-21). Significantly, both adultery (Lev 20:21) and
idolatry (Exod 23:24-26; Deut 11:17) result in sterility. This is
graphically described in Hos 4:10:

ואכלו ולא ישבעו

הזנו ולא יפרצו

כי־את־יהוה עזבו לשמר

H. Wolff remarks: "Whoever dedicates himself to the cult of
Baal, expecting fertility and population increase . . . will become

---

[127] Ibid., 30.
[128] Cf. p. 83.

a dying generation.''[129] Indeed, for Hosea, the practice of fertility rites is one of the distinguishing marks of the Baal cult.[130] Similarly, in Hos 9:11, Israel's fluttering away from Yahweh toward the cult of Baal results in the punishment of barrenness: מִלֵּדָה וּמִבֶּטֶן וּמֵהֵרָיוֹן.

The idea that cultic and marital deception are punished by sterility well suits the context of Mal 2:15. Far from alluding to creation history or to Abraham's patience with Sarah in the face of her inability to conceive, the prophet is directly confronting his contemporaries with the evidence of their reprehensible behavior. To those who intermarry and thus turn away from Yahweh and their Jewish wives, the germination of further life will be denied. The prophet's indictment of such behavior is ruthless and tinged with irony. That the prime object of marriage was to ensure the survival of the family by providing male successors (cf. זֶרַע אֱלֹהִים), is indisputable.[131] The prophet, however, intimates that the seeking of progeny (בקשׁ) through intermarriage will always be a fruitless enterprise.

הָאֶחָד . . . אֶחָד: This construction harks back to 2:10. "The article is, generally speaking, employed to determine a substantive when the person or thing already spoken of is mentioned again, and is consequently more definite to the mind of the hearer or reader, cf. Gen 1:3; 1 Kings 3:24.''[132] Contrasted to the one father (אָב אֶחָד), the one God (אֵל אֶחָד) who created (בָּרָא) Israel as his children, is the one (אֶחָד, i.e., one of his creations, children) who, similarly, tries to create (עָשָׂה), but who is unable to do so (וְלֹא אֶחָד עָשָׂה = and not one [i.e., one of God's children] did [it]). The use of עָשָׂה to refer to Yahweh's creative ability is well attested (cf. Gen 1:7, 16, 25; 3:1; Neh 9:6; Job 9:9; Prov 8:26). He created (עָשָׂה) man (cf. Job 31:15; 35:10; Isa 17:7; 27:11; Hos 8:14; Pss 100:3; 119:73). Although עָשָׂה is not otherwise used of man's reproductive capability, i.e., his ability to "create" children, its appearance here is suggestive. It implies that the man who commits (עָשָׂה) the sin of intermarriage will be unable to create (עָשָׂה), i.e., to have children. Further, the juxtaposition

[129] Wolff, *Hosea*, 81.
[130] Ibid., 165.
[131] Cf. Burrows, 9 and Isaksson, 35.
[132] GKC, #126d, 404.

of בָּרָא (2:10) and עָשָׂה is a telling one. Yahweh is the creator
(ברא) par excellence; he is bound by no restrictions. Man's creative
potential, however, is limited; it is subject to God's will. This is
made explicit in 15αβ וּשְׁאָר רוּחַ לוֹ. Gen 2:7 calls the divine vital
principle that makes a man a "soul" נְשָׁמָה, "breath." Elsewhere,
it is usually called רוּחַ, "spirit" (cf. Eccl 12:7: "The dust returns
to the earth as it was, and the spirit (רוּחַ) returns to God who
gave it;" Ps 104:29-30: "when you take away their breath, they
die . . . when you send forth your spirit (רוּחַ), they are created.")
According to J. Pedersen, spirit (רוּחַ) "is the motive power of the
soul. It does not mean the center of the soul, but the strength
emanating from it and, in its turn reacting upon it."[133] As a
result, the "spirit" is very often connected with feelings and
emotions. "But it is the spirit in a man, the breath of the
Almighty, that makes him understand" (Job 32:8). In other
words, without spirit there can be no life; without spirit the
emotions cannot function.[134] However, "spirit" (רוּחַ) is not
primarily an organ of cognition or desire; "it is a vital power
and will towards action," cf. Job 15:19; Gen 45:20.[135] As such it
is not at man's disposal; it is given freely by God for special
mighty deeds (Judg 6:43; 14:16), for historical tasks (Jer 51:11;
Ezra 1:1; Hag 1:14) and to sustain life (Isa 42:5; Ps 104:29-30;
Ezek 37:14). "Spirit" as vital power is, in principle, the opposite
of the feebleness of "flesh" (בָּשָׂר, Isa 31:3). Indeed, it is the spirit
(רוּחַ) of God that gives life, cf. Gen 2:7; Job 27:3; 33:4. One of the
firmest, clearest statements of the divine origin of life is Job
12:10: אֲשֶׁר בְּיָדוֹ נֶפֶשׁ כָּל־חָי וְרוּחַ כָּל־בְּשַׂר־אִישׁ. It is precisely this to
which רוּחַ refers in Mal 2:15. Indeed, because, in the final analysis,
it is Yahweh's רוּחַ, spirit, that gives life, man's reproductive
potential is directly dependent upon it. Thus, when Malachi
states וְלֹא אֶחָד עָשָׂה וּשְׁאָר רוּחַ לוֹ = "And not one does it and has a
remnant (שְׁאָר, cf. Isa 10:19-20; 14:22; Zeph 1:4)[136] of spirit"
(15a), the inference to be drawn is that the man who intermarries

[133] Pedersen, 1.104.

[134] P. van Imschoot, "Sagesse et esprit dans l'Ancien Testament," *RB* 47
(1938) 28.

[135] Georges Pidoux, *L'homme dans l'Ancien Testament* (CTH 32; Neuchâtal
and Paris: Delachaux & Niestlé, 1953) 22.

[136] *Gesenius' Hebrew and Chaldee Lexicon*, 799.

is denied the ability to procreate; he has not even a remnant of
the spirit that comes from Yahweh. In essence רוּחַ is creative
actuality on the part of Yahweh and creative potential on man's
part since man's ability to produce new life is dependent on
Yahweh, just as the ability of the seed (זֶרַע, 2:15b) to germinate is
dependent on soil condition, rainfall and the like. The juxtaposition of שְׁאָר רוּחַ (2:15a) and זֶרַע אֱלֹהִים (2:15b) is insightful,
Indeed, זֶרַע אֱלֹהִים, seed of God, can replace שְׁאָר רוּחַ with no
change in meaning: "And not one does it and has a seed of
(given by)[137] God," i.e., descendants, children. The conditions
requisite for the germination of the seed are denied by God to
the one who intermarries. The connection between רוּחַ, spirit,
and זֶרַע, seed, fertility, is made explicit in Isa 44:2f. Yahweh's
pouring out of his spirit (רוּחַ) is considered a blessing (בְּרָכָה), on
account of which the people's seed (זֶרַע), i.e., offspring, "will
spring up among the grass as willows by the watercourses," 44:5,
cf. Joel 2:18–3:5.

2:15b is ironic. Although the desire for sons (זֶרַע) was
paramount in marriage, without רוּחַ, spirit, creative potential,
that desire can never be fulfilled. The use of בְּקֵשׁ is image-
evoking. Its literal meaning is "to seek, search."[138] "This activity
has in view the finding of an object which really exists or which
is thought to exist, which is not close at hand to the subject at
the time of the seeking, but is desired most earnestly and initiates
the seeking. Biqqesh has to do with satisfying this desire."[139]
The meaning of בְּקֵשׁ varies according to the degree of intensity
and the difference in the mode of seeking. It may be translated,
"to seek out," "search," "search for," "seek," "wish," "desire,"
"long for." Its use in Mal 2:15 should be compared with its use
in Jer 2:33, where the prophet condemns Israel's efforts to rebel
against Yahweh and to run to foreign gods under the figure of
seeking lovers. Here בְּקֵשׁ does not simply mean "seeking" but
implies fulfillment of "love" (אַהֲבָה) after the lovers are together.
This is what lies behind בְּקֵשׁ in Mal 2:15. The one who intermarries is seeking the visible fulfillment of his marriage in the

---

[137] A. Cohen, *The Twelve Prophets* (The Soncino Books of the Bible;
London: Soncino, 1948) 347.

[138] *Gesenius' Hebrew and Chaldee Lexicon*, 137.

[139] Siegfried Wagner, "בְּקֵשׁ bikkesh," *TDOT* 2.279.

birth of children, זֶרַע. In virtue of his offense, however, such fulfillment is denied.

The final two lines of 2:15 proffer advice and sound a warning. They may be translated: "If you value your creative ability, be on your guard (וְנִשְׁמַרְתֶּם בְּרוּחֲכֶם). Take heed for your [own] spirit[s]), i.e., do not intermarry. Moreover, do not deal deceitfully with the wife of your youth."[140]

> The translation: "And not one does it (intermarries) and has a remnant of spirit (reproductive potential). And what is the one seeking? A seed of (given by) God? So, if you value your creative ability, be on your guard and do not deal deceitfully with the wife of your youth,"

requires no textual emendation. Further, such a translation suits the context of the oracle unit and complements the pervasive sexual imagery. Intermarriage not only implies abhorrent behavior toward a previous spouse, but also implies deceitfulness toward Yahweh as father and creator. It ruptures the covenant he concluded with the fathers long ago. Moreover, intermarriage is seductive. Men are lured not only to foreign women, but to their cults. Thus the religious practices of the new spouse contaminate the rites directed to Yahweh. The punishment for such adulterous, idolatrous behavior is enunciated here. Those who intermarry are denied the very expression of their union—children.

[2:16]—This verse has also proved textually difficult for translators. According to van Hoonacker "שָׂנֵא a été compris l° comme participe pour le verbe à la seconde personne (LXX); כִּי שָׂנֵא serait l'énoncé d'une condition, auquel שַׁלַּח ferait suite comme impératif: Si tu hais (la femme), renvoiela!" ... ἀλλὰ ἐαν μισήσας ἐξαποστείλῃς.[141] Such a command would be totally out of place here, coming as it does directly after an exhortation not to deal deceitfully with the wife of one's youth (2:15). Moreover, it is difficult to reconcile such a translation with the third person וְכִסָּה.[142]

---

[140] Some Hebrew MSS read תִּבְגֹד for יִבְגֹד, which agrees better with נִשְׁמַרְתֶּם and נְעוּרֶיךָ, cf. Cohen, 347.

[141] van Hoonacker, 728.

[142] Ibid.

Sellin, Rudolph and Botterweck believe Yahweh to be the speaker in this verse.[143] According to Rudolph, שָׂנֵא is a verbal adjective used as a participle and therefore, the pronomial subject need not be present when it can be inferred from the context.[144] He suggests the possibility that the אֲנִי, I, fell out because of its similarity to the preceding נא of שָׂנֵא.[145] To coordinate the 3m.s. כִּסָּה to the utterance, it is repointed as an infinitive absolute and prefaced with a כ = כְּכַסֵּה.[146] Thus the verse is translated: "Denn ich hasse Scheidung hat Jahwe, der Gott Israels, gesprochen, wie wenn jemand sein Gewant mit Gewalttat bedeckt, hat Jahwe der Heerscharen gesprochen."[147] Such an interpretation may be objected on the grounds that making Yahweh the subject is wholly arbitrary and requires too many inferences.

Van Hoonacker views כִּי־שָׂנֵא שַׁלַּח and וְכִסָּה חָמָס עַל־לְבוּשׁוֹ as "deux éléments d'une meme phrase," that are separated by the formula, "says Yahweh the God of Israel," cf. 2:2; 3:17.[148] He translates: "Quand quelqu'un répudie par aversion, dit Jahvé le Dieu d'Isräel, il se couvre d'injustice par-dessus son vêtement, dit Jahvé des Armées."[149] This translation preserves the consonantal text and requires only the repointing of שנא and שלח.[150] Thus, שָׂנֵא, qal pf., "to hate," is changed to שֹׂנֵא, the qal active participle, and becomes the "sujet indéterminé de שלח et כסה."[151] שַׁלַּח (piel inf. cs.) is construed as the piel perfect, שִׁלַּח,[152] "to send away, divorce," cf. Deut 22:19, 29; 24:1, 3; Jer 3:1; Isa 50:1;

[143] Cf. Sellin, 601, 605–6; Rudolph, 270; Botterweck, 155.
[144] Rudolph, 270.
[145] Ibid.
[146] Ibid., and cf. Sellin, 606.
[147] Rudolph, 270.
[148] van Hoonacker, 728.
[149] Ibid., 728.
[150] S. R. Driver remarks that the work of the Massoretes was essentially conservative. "Their aim was not to form a text, but by fixing the pronunciation and other means, to preserve a text which, in all essentials, they had received already formed from others," *Notes on the Hebrew Text and the Topography of the Book of Samuel* (2nd ed.; Oxford: Clarendon, 1966), XXXVI. He says, however, that in the period prior to the rise of the Massoretic school (7–8th c. A.D.) "there was no small laxity in the course of which corruptions of different kinds found their way into the text of the OT," XXXV.
[151] van Hoonacker, 729.
[152] Ibid.

Ezra 10:44. This construction, in which a participle stands at the beginning of the sentence as a *casus pendens*, is used to indicate "a condition, the contingent occurrence of which involves a further consequence" (cf. Gen 9:6; Ex 21:12; Ps 75:4).[153] "Almost as a rule, the participial construction beginning a sentence is continued by means of a finite verb with or without וְ," in this case, with וְכִסָּה (cf. Isa 14:7; 43:7; Ezek 22:3; Ps 136:13f).[154]

Van Hoonacker's translation should be considered superior for two reasons. First, it suits the context of the oracle unit and continues the tense pattern (perfect). The errant spouse marries (בָּעַל) a foreign woman and so profanes (חִלֵּל) Yahweh's temple; he commits (עָשָׂה) the offense of intermarriage (2:15) and divorces (שִׁלַּח) the wife he married in his youth (2:16). Second, the precise meanings given to שנא and שלח here are found in Deut 24:3: ושנאה האיש האחרון וכתב לה ספר כריתת ונתן בידה ושלחה מביתו.

כִּסָּה is piel perfect (כָּסָה) meaning "to cover." עַל + כִּסָּה is "to cover over":[155] "to cover (over) one's garment (לְבוּשׁ) with violence" (חָמָס, n.m. violence, wrong, wrongdoing).[156] The meaning of this phrase is disputed. Gesenius suggests that לְבוּשׁ, a garment, describes the wife, a metaphor in common use in Arabic (cf. Koran, Sur 2:183, "Wives are your attire and you are theirs.")[157] Van Hoonacker, however, states that "d'un pareil usage il n'y a aucune trace en hébreu."[158] Further, he questions the sense of "to cover one's wife with violence."[159] However, it may simply mean "to treat a spouse unjustly."

"Covering a garment" has also been understood through the ancient custom whereby the casting of one's garment over a woman was tantamount to claiming her as a wife.[160] In Ruth 3:9, "Ruth asks Boaz to take her into his immediate family: וּפָרַשְׂתָּ כְנָפֶךָ עַל־אֲמָתְךָ, Spread your robe over your handmaid."[161]

---

[153] GKC, #116u, 361.

[154] Ibid., #116x, 361-62.

[155] Ibid., #119bb, 383.

[156] *Gesenius' Hebrew and Chaldee Lexicon*, 288.

[157] Ibid., 428.

[158] van Hoonacker, 729.

[159] Ibid.

[160] J. M. P. Smith, 56.

[161] Jack M. Sasson, *Ruth* (Baltimore: The Johns Hopkins University, 1979) 81.

J. Sasson states that "Biblical texts containing similarly couched phrases are found in contexts in which marriage is definitely at stake."[162] He notes Ezek 16:8: וָאֶפְרֹשׂ כְּנָפִי עָלַיִךְ "I will spread my robe over you," cf. also Deut 23:1.[163] Although the syntax of Mal 2:16b, Ezek 16:8 and Ruth 3:9 seems to be identical: verb + object + עַל (obj.), in the latter two examples, the robe (כָּנָף) is the first object (coming immediately after the verb) and is spread over someone. In Mal 2:16b, however, the garment (לְבוּשׁ) is in the second object position and is itself covered over (with violence). This shift is suggestive; the images are the same but the meaning is changed. In Ezekiel and Ruth the person who is covered over is offered the protection of marriage and the expression has a positive connotation. In Malachi, that the garment itself is covered over suggests that the protection is taken away in view of the marital problems faced (חָמָס, violence, wrongdoing).

Van Hoonacker offers a third interpretation.[164] He states: "L'aversion ou la haine du mari envers la femme est déjà par ellemême une injustice: celui qui donne publiquemment suite à ce sentiment en répudiant sa femme, ne fait autre chose qu'étaler son injustice au dehors, aux yeux de tout le monde."[165] Expressed colloquially, the one who divorces his wife airs his dirty linen in full public view. The use of לְבוּשׁ is appropriate. As the outermost garment (cf. 2 Sam 20:8; Job 41:5), its defects (stains, frays) are particularly visible.

The verb בָּגַד is used three times in the last three verses (2:14–16). As mentioned previously, בָּגַד means "to act faithlessly" and can be used in connection with faithlessness in marriage (cf. p. 85f.). This contention is further strengthened by the meaning of the refrains found in 2:15, 16. As 2:15 avers, no intermarriage will result in offspring. Therefore, in order to ensure fertility, man is adjured not to deal faithlessly, i.e., divorce the wife whom he married in accordance with the stipulations of the covenant concluded with the fathers, 2:10. In 2:14, Yahweh witnessed the treacherous act, the divorce of the wife, the cause of which was the desire to marry a foreigner. Indeed, it may be

[162] Ibid.
[163] Ibid.
[164] van Hoonacker, 729 and cf. also Halévy, 31.
[165] van Hoonacker, 729.

posited that the sense of "to divorce, estrange oneself from, move away from," lies behind every occurrence of בָּגַד in this oracle unit. In 2:11, it is said, בָּגְדָה יְהוּדָה, "Judah acted faithlessly." As the rest of the verse demonstrates, the faithless act clearly implies a divorcing oneself from Yahweh by marrying a foreigner and worshiping her gods. Similarly, 2:10, acting faithlessly toward one another and profaning (חִלֵּל) the covenant of the fathers, implies not only the dissolution of the covenant bond but the dissolution of the group that contracted it. It suggests estrangement among people who were formerly close knit (cf. אָח, 2:10).

Discussion

In general this oracle unit, which has caused so many difficulties, is considered to be an attack on dissolved marriage alliances. It is assumed to refer to marriages with non-Jewish women (בַּת־אֵל נֵכָר), and divorce of the spouse married in the heyday of youth, vv. 13-16.[166] According to Driver, Malachi declares these practices "to be an offense against the love and faithfulness which as children of one Father they all owe to one another, an unnatural cruelty towards those who have been long bound to them by ties of affection and a challenge to the Divine judgment."[167]

Those who believe that these verses deal with intermarriage and divorce are very literal in their approach. The בַּת־אֵל נֵכָר the daughter of a foreign god, is a foreign woman. Because of her the Judean man divorces his first wife, and it is she who, in her sorrow and despair, covers Yahweh's altar with tears (2:13). Accordingly, Mal 2:13f is considered to contain a diatribe against divorce. Because marriage is described as a covenant (בְּרִית, v. 14) between man and woman entered into before God, it follows that the husband cannot arbitrarily dissolve it. Further, the fact that the first wife has already borne her husband children makes divorce all the more unsavory, especially since the foreign woman could not give him "godly offspring," v. 15. Finally, v. 16 has been taken proof that Yahweh himself hates divorce.[168]

---

[166] Cf. Rudolph, 271; van Hoonacker, 721f; J. M. P. Smith, 52f; Driver, *The Minor Prophets*, 312; Sellin, 601f; Halévy, 25f.

[167] Driver, *The Minor Prophets*, 312.

[168] Cf. Driver, *The Minor Prophets*, 312 and J. M. P. Smith, 52.

That intermarriage and divorce increased in this period is often attributed to the depressed condition of the Jews returning from exile. Desirous of up-grading their economic and social status, many men chose to marry women from wealthy foreign families. However, the relatives of these women demanded, as a condition of the proposed marriage, that the men first divorce their Jewish wives so that the new spouse would not be neglected.[169] Although such a scenario is plausible, to impute all intermarriage and divorce to this is extremely risky. The openness of the Persian administration fostered a more intimate acquaintance with and acceptance of the peoples round about, and this, too may have contributed to the increase in intermarriage.[170] Although divorce need not necessarily follow on the heels of intermarriage, economic considerations would make it difficult for the majority of men to have more than one wife. Indeed, polygyny seems to have been restricted to men who occupied leading positions, who were rich or who had some other claim to distinction, i.e., David (1 Sam 25:39f), Solomon (1 Kgs 9:16).[171] To maintain as do Torrey and Isaksson, that another marriage or intermarriage was no cause for divorce is to miss the point.[172] As mentioned, polygyny was a mark of high status, prestige and wealth, conditions which were not widespread among the Judeans at this time (cf. ch. II). Further, the general practice of monogamy cannot be denied. The creation account in Genesis describes the first marriage in clearly monogamous terms (2.24). Many of the laws strongly imply this type of marriage (Exod 20:7; 21:5; Lev 18:8, 16; 20:10; 21:13; Num 5:12; Deut 5:21; 22:22). The book of Proverbs is silent on polygamous life (12:4; 18:22; 19:13, cf. also Qoh 9:9; Sir 26:1-4). De Vaux remarks that "it is noteworthy that the books of Samuel and Kings, which cover the entire period of the monarchy do not record a single case of bigamy among commoners (except that of Samuel's father, 1 Sam. 1.2, at the very beginning of the period)."[173]

---

[169] J. M. P. Smith, 52.

[170] Torrey, 11.

[171] Cf. Raphael Patai, *Sex and Family in the Bible and the Middle East* (Garden City, New York: Doubleday and Co., 1959) 39-41.

[172] Torrey, 9; Isaksson, 30.

[173] de Vaux, 1.25.

G. A. Smith questioned the integrity of 2:11-12.[174] He contended that originally there was only an attack on divorce, vv. 10, 13-16. Verses 11-12, which deal with mixed marriage, were considered a later interpolation reflecting the campaign carried on by Ezra and Nehemiah.[175] Indeed, as Morgenstern states: "Opposition to intermarriage came only with Ezra and Nehemiah in the spirit of Jewish particularism and isolationism."[176] To support the charge that vv. 11-12 are secondary, Smith pointed to the change from first to third person and the break in thought between the charge of mutual faithlessness in v. 10 and the application of that charge in vv. 13-16 which speak of the harsh treatment accorded to Jewish wives. To this the charge of intermarriage is unrelated. As Smith maintained: "Marriage with heathen women . . . is not proof of faithlessness between Israelites."[177] Further, the finality of the curse in v. 12 was used to support the assumption that these verses are an addition.[178] Such an hypothesis severely damages the text and is unnecessary. To assume that Ezra and Nehemiah were the first to combat intermarriage is contrary to the textual information we possess. The book of Judges implies that such marriages became common after the Israelites settled in Canaan (Judg 3:6) and were condemned as evil in Yahweh's sight; they endangered Israel's religious faith (Judg 3:7; 1 Kgs 11:4). The covenants found in Exod 34 and Deut 7 (cf. Mal 2:10) forbade intermarriage for the same reason. It lured Israelite men and their children away from Yahweh. Further, the statements in Nehemiah and Ezra attest to the fact that it was a prevalent and long standing abuse (Neh 6:17-19; Ezra 9-10). It is therefore, unrealistic to assume that the problem was non-existent in Malachi's time. Indeed, that the prophet inveighs against it should not be surprising. Concerned as he was about the purity of the cult (cf. 1:6-2:9), any practice that violated that purity, violated Yahweh and was a target for Malachi's invectives. Further, to

---

[174] G. A. Smith, 340.
[175] Ibid., cf. also Otto Eissfeldt, *The Old Testament: An Introduction* (New York; Harper & Row, 1965) 442.
[176] J. Morgenstern, "Jerusalem—485 B.C.," *HUCA* 28 (1957) 21.
[177] G. A. Smith, 340.
[178] Ibid.

state as does G. A. Smith, that intermarriage is not an instance of faithless behavior among Israelites, is to misconstrue the scope of 2:10.[179] The covenant concluded with the fathers expressly forbids intermarriage (cf. Exod 34; Deut 7). Thus, any Israelite who intermarries violates the covenant obligations and severs his ties with his fellows and with God. Finally, questions of mixed marriage and divorce were so inextricably intermingled in actual practice that in discussing one, the other was involved, especially since, given the economic circumstances of the period (cf. pp. 12, 17), monogamy was more the rule than the exception. Thus, intermarriage and divorce are not two separate and distinct subjects, but two phases of one subject, viz. the obligations of the Judean to be faithful to his people and his God.[180]

C. C. Torrey suggested that the prophet's attack was not upon mixed marriages and divorce at all, but upon apostasy to a foreign cult practiced in Jerusalem itself.[181] On this basis, the "daughter of a foreign god" becomes the "cult of a foreign god" and the "wife of your youth" (2:14) becomes the religion of Yahweh to which Israel had formerly been true.[182] The language is thus figurative. Agreeing with Torrey, both Hvidberg and Isaksson affirm that it is apostasy to a foreign cult to which the prophet alludes.[183] Indeed, the expression בַּת־אֵל נֵכָר must mean "a goddess"[184] and "the statement that Judah married (baʾal) her is immediately intelligible to the person who, e.g., knows the mention by a prophet like Hosea of Yahweh as the husband of Israel," v. 11.[185] This marriage is equal to a תוֹעֵבָה, an abomination, an illegitimate practice and constitutes a profanation of Yahweh's temple. Those who take part in the worship of the goddess cover Yahweh's altar with tears, weeping and groaning. Hvidberg considers this to be an allusion to ritual mourning,[186] and remarks that,

[179] Ibid., 340.
[180] Rudolph, 271.
[181] Torrey, 9f.
[182] Ibid.
[183] Hvidberg, 120; Isaksson, 30f and cf. Ahlström, *Joel*, 49f.
[184] Cf. Ahlström, *Joel*, 49; Hvidberg, 121.
[185] Hvidberg, 122.
[186] Hvidberg, 120 and cf. Isaksson, 31; Helmer Ringgren, *Israelite Religion* (Philadelphia: Fortress, 1966) 127.

it is a drastic thought that it is Yahweh's altar that is
affected by cultic weeping. But, their 'marriage' to the
goddess is altogether a profanation of the altar . . . since
those who have married (ba°al) her must weep when her
lover (ba°al) dies.[187]

Further, Hvidberg contends that "it cannot be doubted that this
deity is of the Anat-Astarte type and that her lover, for whom the
weeping is done is an 'Adonis' deity."[188] The Malachi passage
suggests to Hvidberg that "even at that late period the dying
deity had so great a power over Jewish minds that the temptation
to apostasy seemed probable."[189] G. W. Ahlström remarks that
the cultic weeping may have been "part of a fertility rite still
being performed in the second temple," and thus we can "assume
that reminiscences and survivals of the pre-exilic rituals associated with a goddess (Asherah) had played a certain role, even
after the Exile."[190]

The result of this ritual mourning (v. 13b) is that Yahweh
turns away from the sacrifices of Judah (v. 13c, d). By marriage
to a foreign deity and participation in her cult, they betrayed the
"wife of your youth," who was "your companion" and the "wife

---

[187] Hvidberg, 122. Cf. Also J. G. Matthews, "Tammuz Worship in the Book
of Malachi," *JPOS* 11 (1931) 42-50. Matthews interprets these verses as "an
appeal against an insidious, false ritual like Tammuz worship," 45. He remarks
that as a fertility cult, centered around the idea of the changing seasons, Tammuz
worship "so appealed to the masses that it was a menace to the higher morality
and the purer worship of Israel," 45-46. He believes that the phrase עֵר וְעֹנֶה,
"inciter and respondent" is an "admirable characterization of those who take
part in the dance or in the antiphonal responses in Tammuz worship," and that
"covering Yahweh's altar with tears," is most naturally interpreted as part of the
ritual of the dying god, 46-47. Finally, Matthews goes so far as to identify the
goddess described in the phrase בת־אל נכר, v. 11, as אשרה נתעבה, "abominable
Asherah," 47. This identification was reached by slightly changing the consonants
of אשת נעוריך, v. 14, a phrase he considered to be the *bête noir* of the oracle unit
since it had no connection with the ritual considerations of the work, 47.

[188] Hvidberg, 123 and cf. Isaksson, 31.

[189] Hvidberg, 120.

[190] G. W. Ahlström, *Joel*, 49. Ahlström remarks that "the tears covering the
altar cannot be anything other than an allusion to a rite of which the prophet
disapproves. Since women are not allowed to approach Yahweh's altar, it cannot
be the divorced wives who are weeping in sorrow and grief at the altar of
Yahweh. Therefore, by using the word תּוֹעֵבָה, in v. 11, the prophet is registering
his disapproval of a non-Yahwistic ritual," 49.

of your covenant.''[191] According to Hvidberg and Isaksson, these terms are nothing other than similies denoting the cult of Yahweh, who was the wife of youthful Israel.[192] That Yahweh, who is otherwise represented as the husband in the marriage between Yahweh and Israel (cf. Hos 3; Ezek 16:8; Jer 3:4), is here designated the wife results from the imagery begun in v. 11.

> There Judah is mentioned as the man who married the daughter of a foreign god. This marriage means treachery towards Yahweh, the wife of his youth and the wife of his covenant. In order to enable the author to carry on using the image from v. 11, Yahweh must be represented as a wife.[193]

Both Isaksson and Hvidberg aver that to interpret these verses as an attack on apostasy to a foreign cult is in agreement with the thematic starting point in v. 10.[194]

> Such participation in an alien cult implies treachery towards their brothers in the covenant and causes division in the people, so that one side opposes the other, although all who are included in the covenant have the same creator and father.[195]

Further, Isaksson maintains that such an interpretation is in agreement with the context of the rest of the prophecy since "the prophet's attention is concentrated . . . on the true religion. He is a priestly reformer and not a prophetic renovator of the ethics of marriage.''[196] Similarly, G. W. Ahlström concludes that Malachi was interested "in what he himself considers to be a pure and right Yahweh cult, and the social and moral problems are not his main concern here.''[197]

Those who interpret literally and view this oracle unit as a diatribe against intermarriage and divorce, and those who con-

[191] Hvidberg, 123.
[192] Cf. Hvidberg, 123; Isaksson, 33.
[193] Isaksson, 33.
[194] Hvidberg, 122; Isaksson, 32.
[195] Isaksson, 32.
[196] Ibid.
[197] Ahlström, *Joel*, 50.

tend that these verses contain an attack on syncretistic practices in Jerusalem, straddle opposite sides of a fence; they consider their views to be mutually exclusive and self-contained. Nevertheless, it must be asked whether either of these views presents a full picture or does full justice to Malachi's words. Those who interpret literally fail to recognize that the covenant concluded with the fathers (2:10; cf. Exod 34; Deut 7) banned intermarriage precisely because the seduction practiced on the Israelite spouse lured him away from Yahweh to the worship of other gods. And those who take the syncretistic approach view Malachi solely as a cultic reformer and downplay his social consciousness (3:5). Further, although they base their entire interpretation on the existence of syncretistic practices in the post-exilic cult, they rarely discuss how such illegitimate rites entered the Yahwism of that period. Is it not possible to state that intermarriages, which were prevalent at that time (cf. p. 114f.), led to an increase in syncretism?[198] Finally, those who consider this a diatribe against foreign cultic influence have difficulty fitting vv. 15-16 on divorce into their schema. Indeed, Torrey and Hvidberg go so far as to say that the text is completely unintelligible.[199]

Malachi was not dealing with a purely social offense, nor was he dealing with a purely religious one. The prophet was confronting a problem, prevalent in his period, that had both religious and social consequences. That problem was intermarriage. Its social consequences were two: it broke the bond that united all Israel as brothers (2:10) and it resulted in the divorce of the Jewish wife. Religiously, intermarriage resulted in the incorporation into Yahwism of syncretistic phenomena, a fact assiduously pointed out by both Nehemiah (13:2f) and Ezra

---

[198] G. W. Ahlström suggests the survival of pre-exilic cult phenomena that were perhaps rooted in Canaanite festivals, *Joel*, 49, 128. This is certainly correct. Indeed, there is ample evidence that idolatrous practices continued after the exile, cf. Ahlström, *Joel*, 111f; P. R. Ackroyd, *Exile and Restoration* (London: S. C. M., 1968) 205, n. 116. At the same time, however, the prevalence of syncretistic practices to which Malachi alludes in this oracle unit, seems to be the result of an increase in intermarriage. Ezra (Ch. 9) passes the same negative judgment on intermarriage as does Malachi. It is to be banned because it leads the people into idolatry. Although G. W. Ahlström, *Joel*, 127-28, seems to recognize the connection between intermarriage and apostasy in Ezra 9, he does not bring the observation to bear on Mal 2:10-16.

[199] Torrey, 10; Hvidberg, 123.

(9-10). The בַּת־אֵל נֵכָר was neither foreign woman nor goddess; she was both at once. Those married to her were lured to her cult and her gods. These apostates, however, did not give up the cult of Yahweh any more than did the Elephantine Jews who also worshiped Anat.[200] They continued to bring him sacrifices (2:12-13) while using his altar to carry out the mourning rites associated with the gods of their spouses (2:13). Because of the abomination (2:11) they committed, they are cut off from Yahweh and their sacrifices rejected (2:13).

The last three verses deal with divorce (2:14-16). As a consequence of the desire to intermarry, it also has religious and social overtones. Just as the בַּת־אֵל נֵכָר (2:11) is woman and goddess, so the terms חֲבֶרְתְּךָ, אֵשֶׁת נְעוּרֶיךָ and אֵשֶׁת בְּרִיתֶךָ (2:14) refer both to the first spouse and to Yahweh, the spouse of Israel.[201] The religious consequence of divorce is alienation from Yahweh and his cult as the Judean man follows the gods of his new wife. The social consequence is the first wife's loss of protection (לְבוּשׁ), 2:16. The punishment for this defection from Yahweh and wife is graphically described as infertility. The marriage with the foreign woman will never bear fruit (2:15) since it is Yahweh himself who blesses a couple with children; it is he who opens and closes the womb and it is he who gives man spirit (רוּחַ), or reproductive capacity.

The literal rendering that views these verses as a condemnation of intermarriage and divorce gives a not undue prominence to the social aspects of these actions. The figurative or syncretistic interpretation brings the religious consequences to the forefront and gives full rein to the sexual (fertility) imagery that saturates these verse. Taken alone, however, each of these interpretations is incomplete. Indeed, it is their interrelationship that adds pathos to the text by heightening the severity of the offense. Thus, any attempt to penetrate the *ipsissima verba* of this oracle unit must take both into account.

[200] Cf. Hvidberg, 122.
[201] Isaksson, 33.

CHAPTER VIII

MALACHI 2:17–3:5

ABC	^{17}הוגעתם יהוה בדבריכם
DA_1^2	ואמרתם במה הוגענו
D_1E^3	באמרכם כל־עשה רע
E^3	טוב בעיני יהוה
E_{11}^3	ובהם הוא חפץ
(Z) F^3	או איה אלהי המשפט
A^2B	$^{3:1}$הנני שלח מלאכי
B_1^3	ופנה־דרך לפני^1
A^2B^2	ופתאם יבוא אל־היכלו
C D^2 E	האדון אשר־אתם מבקשים
$C_1^2D^2E_1$	ומלאך הברית אשר־אתם חפצים
A_1^2	הנה־בא אמר יהוה צבאות
A B C^3	^{2}ומי מכלכל את־יום בואו
A B_1C_1	ומי העמד בהראותו
A^2 B C	כי־הוא כאש מצרף
B_1C_1	וכברית מכבסים
A B^2 C	^{3}וישב מצרף ומטהר כסף
A_1 D	וטהר את־בני־לוי
A_{11} C_1 C_1^2	וזקק אתם כזהב וככסף
A^2	והיו ליהוה
B^2 C	מגישי מנחה בצדקה
A_1^2	^{4}וערבה ליהוה
B_1^3	מנחת יהודה וירושלם
C D	כימי עולם
C_1 D_1	וכשנים קדמניות

^{1} In this schematization, the relation of B to B_1^3 is the relation of the messenger to his task. It is also possible to diagram the sentence grammatically: $A^2B \parallel A_1B^2$ = verb and object $\parallel$ verb + object.

A BC	וקרבתי אליכם למשפט⁵

$A_1{}^3$ והייתי עד ממהר
D D_1 במכשפים ובמנאפים
$D_{11}{}^2$ ובנשבעים לשקר
$D_{111}E^2$ ובעשקי שכר־שכיר
$E_1E_{11}F^2$ אלמנה ויתום ומטי־גר
$F_1{}^2$ ולא יראוני אמר יהוה צבאות

(2:17) *You have wearied Yahweh with your prattle.*
    Yet you say, "How have we wearied him?"
    By saying: "Everyone that does evil
     is good in Yahweh's eyes
     and in them he delights;"
    Or "Where is the God of justice?"
(3:1) *"I am about to send my messenger,*
     and he shall clear the way before me.
    And suddenly, the Lord whom you seek
     will come to his temple.
    And the messenger of the covenant in whom you delight,
     he will come," says Yahweh of Hosts.
(3:2) *But who can endure the day of his coming*
    or stand when he appears?
    For he is like a refiner's fire
    and like fullers' soap.
(3:3) *And he shall sit as a refiner and as a purifier of silver.*
    And he will cleanse the sons of Levi,
    And purge them as gold and as silver.
    And there will be those who offer an offering in
     righteousness to Yahweh.
(3:4) *Then shall the offering of Judah and Jerusalem be*
    pleasing to Yahweh,
    as in days of old and as in former years.
(3:5) *"And I will draw near to you for judgment*
    and I will be a swift witness
    against sorcerers, adulterers
     and false swearers;
    and those who extort the wages of the hireling,
     and oppress the widow and the orphan,
    and who thrust aside the stranger and fear me not,"
    says Yahweh of Hosts.

Content and Structure

In this the fourth oracle unit, 2:17-3:5, the prophet turns his visage toward those within the community who, because of the troubles and social anomalies which they saw around them, came to question God's justice and to doubt whether he would ever interpose to distinguish between good and evil (cf. also Mal 3:13-21; Jer 12:1f; Ps 73; Job 21). The problem, in short, is retribution, and it is obvious that it was much discussed because, as the *"hingestellte Behauptung"* avers, the people have wearied Yahweh with their constant prattle on the subject, הוֹגַעְתֶּם יהוה בְּדִבְרֵיכֶם, 2:17a. Reacting strongly, the people retort, בַּמָּה הוֹגָעְנוּ, "How have we wearied him?" (2:17b). Having lived with the almost magical assumption that good begets good and evil begets evil, they were standing on a precipice.[2] They could find no evidence for the existence of a just judge of the world when they saw the wicked prosper and God showing no sign of intervention. It was their concern with the problem of reconciling God's supposed justice with the evident inequalities of life that led them to question God, and that questions of such paramount importance to their lives were wearying to him was inconceivable to them. Significantly, it is not the act of questioning itself that Malachi decries; rather, it is what the questioning symbolizes— in this case, blasphemy and loss of faith. Indeed, the people have reversed a divine principle. In their attitude of despondence and doubt they are driven to one of two conclusions: either evil is pleasing to God, or there is no God of justice (2:17c-f). Although Malachi censures their impatience, their desire for instantaneous gratification, he does not dwell on it. Rather, he tries to restore their faith by announcing the imminence of God's intervention; the day of judgment is near at hand when He will show himself to be the judge in spite of the prevailing skepticism. The evil doers will be punished (3:5) and the priests and people will be purified, brought back to the right relationship with their God (3:2-4). Powerful as the prophet's words were, they were obviously shopworn and could no longer placate the people. Indeed, in the sixth oracle unit, 3:13-21, the impatient people are once again heard murmuring at the ways of God.

[2] Cf. Deut 28.

One of the characteristics of the previous three oracle units was the repetition of key terms, a device that strengthened the force of the utterances and underscored the people's guilt. Significantly, there is little vocabulary repetition in the fourth oracle unit. What is impressive is the sensation of constant activity (cf. 3:3, טהַר, מְטַהֵר, מְצָרֵף, יָשַׁב מְצָרֵף, זִקַּק ;3:5, הָיִיתִי עֵד מְמַהֵר) and constant movement; Yahweh is always moving toward Israel, the center (cf. 3:1, בָּא, הִנְנִי שֹׁלֵחַ, פִּנָּה־דֶרֶךְ ;3:5, קָרַבְתִּי). The sensation of motion is enhanced by the prophet's use of alliteration and terminal rhyme, above all in 3:1–2; it underscores the claim that the day of judgment is imminent.

Text and Commentary

[2:17]—This verse introduces not only the fourth oracle unit (2:17–3:5), but serves as the stage-setter for the rest of Malachi's prophecy (3:6–3:24). At issue throughout is God's justice or the lack of it. It is never more explicit than in Deut 30:15f that men's actions are consequential. Obedience to God's will brings blessing while suffering is the outgrowth of sin and disobedience. To the men of Malachi's day just the opposite appeared to be true. It was the evil men among them who prospered. Their evil deeds were not chance occurrences or things done under the stress of desire, but had become almost habitual, so as to cause justifiable anger, even dissipation of faith. Thus, the people requested a demonstration of Yahweh's judgeship, proof of the biblical axiom. "If" they ask, "it is not true that evil doers are Yahweh's favorites, then why doesn't he come to punish them?" (cf. 2:17f, אַיֵּה אֱלֹהֵי הַמִּשְׁפָּט). Malachi responds decisively by affirming that Yahweh will surely come and soon (3:1). He will first cleanse the priesthood that proper sacrifices might be offered (3:2–4). Then he will cleanse the immorality of the people (3:5). When all have been reconciled to him, blessing and fertility will ensue (3:6–12). Such words, however, had lost their ability to engender hope and trust; overuse and experience to the contrary had divested them of their power. Indeed, the prophetic defense of God's justice had failed to convince the people. Malachi's contemporaries were unable to accept promises of future vindication at face value; they wanted Yahweh himself—now! And they challenged him again, as if daring him to appear. "In what way does religion pay?" they asked; "What is to be gained by being so meticulous in the ritual observances?" After all, it was the wicked who prospered! (3:13–15). To these condemnations Malachi again responds by announcing the imminence of Yahweh's day of judgment, when the wicked will be annihilated and the faithful vindicated (3:16–21). This time, however, Malachi goes beyond shopworn phrases; he announces that prior to judgment Yahweh will send his messenger to prepare the way, to restore harmony and turn the hearts of all to Yahweh (3:22–24). It is not the nameless messenger of 3:1; this time he has a name—Elijah. Clearly, succinctly, Mal 2:17 outlines the dilemma that motivates the remainder of the prophecy. The people have stated their case—God is unjust; it is left to Malachi and through him, Yahweh, to prove them wrong.

It is of primary importance to know just which people are being addressed in this oracle unit. M. J. Lagrange remarks:

> Ce sont des gens qui croient remplir leur devoir envers Iahwé et qui s'etonnent de ne pas recevoir de bénédictions plus abondantes.[3]

Further, he continues:

> A ses interlocuteurs, qui seraient beaucoup plus disposés à condamner les lenteurs du jugement de Dieu qu'à s'examiner eux-mêmes, Malachie fait deux réponses. D'abord ils offensent Dieu, même lorsqu'ils ont la prétention de se conformer à la loi, dans les répudiations et les dimes. Surtout il ne fait pas douter de lá venue du jugement, terrible dans son approche, mais définitivement heureux dans ses résultats.[4]

In view of the charges that Malachi has already leveled against the people (cf. 1:14; 2:10–16), Lagrange's argument is tenable. Indeed, the charges brought against the people in the fifth oracle unit, 3:6–12, lend weight to his hypothesis. The people are

---

[3] M.-J. Lagrange, "Notes sur les prophéties messianiques des derniers prophètes," *RB* 15 (1906) 79.

[4] Ibid., 79.

condemned for robbing God, skimping in their tithes and offerings; they give only the bare minimum and believe their obligations are fulfilled. Such disrespect for the cult is not important for its own sake, but because it is a symbol of a general indifference to God, an indifference that is leading to negation (cf. 2:17f אַיֵּה אֱלֹהֵי הַמִּשְׁפָּט).

Van Hoonacker and Sellin maintain that the people addressed in this oracle unit are the pious who are contesting what they believe to be the injustice of God.[5] As van Hoonacker states: "Les gens pieux se plaignent de ce que les injustes soient heureux,"[6] contravening the biblical axiom. The unjust within the community have been described as those who have intermarried (2:10-16), allied themselves with powerful families, acquired wealth and so turned away from their poorer kinsmen.[7] In more general terms, the unjust ones could refer to rich Judeans. As Nehemiah 5 emphasizes, the poor within the community were reduced to slaves and were forced to sell their children and pawn their fields in order to feed themselves, pay their taxes, and permit their wealthy brethren to live in luxury (5:1-5). The hypothesis that it is the pious who are speaking here, bitterly lamenting their fate, should be considered superior. In the sixth oracle unit, 3:13-21, which is most certainly parallel to the fourth, the speakers are called the יִרְאֵי יהוה, and are designated his סְגֻלָּה, treasure, to be spared at the time of judgment (3:16-17).[8] The problem can be reduced to one of perception— man's understanding of justice versus God's, man's timetable versus God's. It is man's inability to trust in the unseen and the unproven that leads him to desire tangible proof that his faith is not in vain. The longer that proof is withheld, the more skeptical man becomes of its reality. This is the point reached in this oracle unit. The people have questioned God's justice and surely, the next step is to question whether there is indeed a god of

[5] A. van Hoonacker, *Les douze petits prophètes* (Paris: Gabalda, 1908) 729; Ernst Sellin, *Das Zwölfprophenbuch übersetzt und erklärt* (KAT 12/2; Leipzig: A. Deichertsche, 1930) 606.

[6] Ibid., 729.

[7] Ibid.

[8] Cf. the discussion of these verses, 217f.

justice. It is this that the prophet tries to combat when he proclaims that Yahweh will come (3:1f; 19f).

הוֹגַעְתֶּם—hiphil perfect of יגע, "make to toil, weary."[9] Its appearance here is reminiscent of Isa 43:24: אַךְ הֶעֱבַדְתַּנִי בְּחַטֹּאותֶיךָ הוֹגַעְתַּנִי בַּעֲוֹנֹתֶיךָ, where Yahweh is irritated by constant provocation. In Mal 2:17b, בַּמָּה הוֹגָעְנוּ "In what way have we wearied," the expected direct object, "him," is missing. Both the LXX, ἐν τίνι παρωξύναμεν αὐτόν and the Peshitta, ܒܡܢܐ ܐܠܐܝܢܝܗܝ supply it. To accord with the Versions, von Bulmerincq and M. P. Smith read הוֹגַעְנוּהוּ.[10] Such an addition is not strictly necessary since the correct object, Yahweh, can readily be inferred from the context.

דָּבָר can mean either a single word (2 Kgs 18:36) or words, speech (2 Sam 23:1), conversation (Jer 38:24).[11] The translation "prattle" aptly communicates a sense of tension and irony. Questions that are of paramount importance to the people are classified by Malachi as foolish, idle talk, childish babble by men who should know better.

The expression כָּל־עֹשֵׂה רָע טוֹב בְּעֵינֵי יהוה can be broken down into its components: עָשָׂה (אֶת־) הָרַע בְּעֵינֵי יהוה (cf. Deut 4:25; 9:18; 17:2; Judg 2:11; 3:7; 4:1; 6:1; 10:6; 1 Kgs 11:6; 14:22) and עָשָׂה הַטּוֹב (וְהַיָּשָׁר) בְּעֵינֵי יהוה (cf. Deut 12:28); עָשָׂה (הַיָּשָׁר וְהַטּוֹב) בְּעֵינֵי יהוה (cf. Deut 6:18). Malachi combined these two formulas to produce the ultimate irony and a sharp antithesis: men consider the upheaval in their lives to be the result of a reversal in the divine sphere. Yahweh, who had previously reacted favorably to the good, now has cast his lot with the wicked. Those who do evil, כָּל־עֹשֵׂה רָע are further described as the זֵדִים, the proud, 3:15, 19; עֹשֵׂה רִשְׁעָה, 3:15, 19: and רְשָׁעִים, 3:21, in the parallel sixth oracle unit.

חָפֵץ, 2:17d, is a verbal adjective meaning "delighting in."[12] The clause וּבָהֶם הוּא חָפֵץ continues the irony begun in 2:17c-d.

---

[9] BDB, 388.
[10] A. von Bulmerincq, *Der Prophet Maleachi* (2 vols.; Tartu: J. G. Krüger, 1926-1932), 2.322; J. M. P. Smith, *Malachi* (ICC: Edinburgh: T. & T. Clark, 1912) 61, 67.
[11] BDB, 338.
[12] Ibid., 342.

In 1:10c, Yahweh tells the priests that he "has no delight," חָפֵץ (n.m.), in them because the sacrifices they offer are inferior. The people are implicated by association. They are the ones who bring the blemished offerings that the priests then put on the altar, 1:14. Because blemished offerings reveal a blemished, interior disposition, Yahweh punishes the sacrificer by refusing to accept his offering. In this oracle unit, the people maintain that it is precisely the ones who offer blemished fare in whom Yahweh delights (חָפֵץ). Their prosperous state is evidence of Yahweh's favor.

אוֹ—van Hoonacker translates אוֹ as a disjunctive "ou bien."[13] "S'il n'est pas vrai que les méchante soient les favoris de Jahvé, alores où est le Dieu—pourquoi ne punit-il pas les méchants ?"[14]

אֱלֹהֵי הַמִּשְׁפָּט, "the god of justice" is also found in Isa 30:18, אֱלֹהֵי מִשְׁפָּט. J. Halévy remarked that אַיֵּה אֱלֹהִים "est une interrogation qui suppose la non-existence ou l'impuissance du dieu afférent" (Mic 7:10; Joel 2:17; Jer 2:25).[15] The phrase אַיֵּה אֱלֹהֶיךָ is often put in the mouths of the enemies of the psalmist, who ask triumphantly: "Where is the god with whom you have had a relationship and from whom you expect help?" (cf. Pss 42:4, 11; 79:10; 115:2). This question hints scornfully that Yahweh is not fulfilling his function as god of the person addressed, i.e., "What a useless god you have!" The impotence of the deity is made startingly clear in the speech of the Rabshakeh in 2 Kgs 18:34f: "Where are the gods of Hamath and Arpad? . . . Which of the gods for all these lands ever rescued his land from my hand?" In this oracle unit the people's question implies that Yahweh is not fulfilling his function as judge with respect to them. Hitherto they had recognized justice, מִשְׁפָּט, as an attribute of god (cf. Isa 30:18; Gen 18:25; Job 40:8; Deut 32:4, Ps 111:7; he loves it, Pss 33:5; 37:28; 99:4; he will not pervert it, Job 8:3; 34:12). In the face of their experience, they question the validity of what was once a firmly held belief. In what follows (3:1-5), Malachi intones that Yahweh will surely come.

[3:1]—This verse is an interpretive crux. Just who is being spoken of here and how many are involved? Is the מַלְאָךְ of 3:1a to

---

[13] von Hoonacker, 730 and cf. GKC, #150g, 475.

[14] van Hoonacker, 730.

[15] J. Halévy, "Le prophète Malachi," *RS* 17 (1909) 32.

be identified with the מַלְאַךְ הַבְּרִית of 3:1e or are they distinct? Do הָאָדוֹן of 3:1d and מַלְאַךְ הַבְּרִית of 3:1e have the same referent? How much of the verse is original to the prophecy?[16] To answer these questions intelligently is to provide a key to the entire prophecy, for this verse is pivotal; it looks back to the past of the prophecy itself (1:11), answers questions posed by the present (2:17) and points toward the future (3:22f).

D. L. Petersen contends that

> to be dogmatic about Mal 3:1 would be unwise. In this Yahweh speech, we are told that a messenger, the prophetic 'author' of the book, is to be sent before Yahweh arrives. Verses 1–5, with the exception of "and the Lord whom you seek will come suddenly into his temple," apparently all refer to the action of this malʾākî. He is the judging figure whose work of purification will allow the requisite purity of cult for Yahweh to appear. The action of this messenger is defined by his cleansing of the Levites. Only when the Levites have been cleansed, and the offerings of Israel are thus acceptable, will Yahweh himself draw near in judgment.[17]

Petersen makes two salient points. First, the messenger, מַלְאָךְ, is a prophetic figure who is part of a scenario *praeparatio;* his task is preparatory to the coming of the day of Yahweh. Second, the

[16] Rex Mason, *The Books of Haggai, Zechariah and Malachi* (Cambridge: Cambridge University, 1977) 152. Mason removes all the difficulties of this oracle unit by contending that vv. 1b–4 are secondary. He remarks that these verses are in the third person while 1a and 5 are in the first. Thus they are "an elaboration of the original oracle," 152. Sequentially, v. 5 "concerns itself with wrong-doers in general and continues the answers to the questions of 2:17," 152. His analysis is extremely short-sighted. Such abrupt changes of person in poetic (or prophetic) language are not unusual, cf. Isa 42:20; 54:14; 61:7; Deut 32:15; Job 16:7; Lam 3:1.

W. Rudolph, *Haggai-Sacharja-Maleachi* (KAT 13/4; Gütersloh: Gütersloher Verlagshaus Gerd Mohn, 1976) 278. Rudolph contends that Yahweh's speaking of himself in the third person "elevates not only the solemnity but underlines the majesty of his appearance," 278. Finally, these verses are integral to the sense of the oracle unit and are paralleled in 3:13–21.

[17] David L. Petersen, *Late Israelite Prophecy: Studies in Deutero-Prophetic Literature and in Chronicles* (SBL Monograph Series, 23; Missoula: Scholars, 1977) 42.

terms מַלְאָךְ and מַלְאַךְ הַבְּרִית both refer to the prophetic forerunner. Thus, in this verse we are dealing with two figures—the מַלְאָךְ = מַלְאָךְ הַבְּרִית and the אָדוֹן, lord = Yahweh.

It is this second part of Petersen's thesis which, although intriguing, is unlikely because of the context of the prophecy. To understand the significance of this passage, it is necessary to look at Exod 23:20f. In the Book of the Covenant too, the messenger of Yahweh appears. The relationship between Mal 3:1 and Exod 23:20 is too striking to be accidental. In fact, the passage in Malachi appears to be a reworking of the מַלְאָךְ text in the Book of the Covenant:

Mal 3:1   הנני שלח מלאכי
                               ופנה־דרך לפני

Exod 23:20   הנה אנכי שלח מלאך לפניך
                                  לשמרך בדרך

The messenger of the Exodus passage is to bring the Israelites to the place Yahweh has prepared for them. Yahweh says: "Be attentive to him and heed his voice. Do not rebel against him, for he will not forgive your sin for my name is in him. But if you heed his voice and carry out all I tell you, I will be an enemy to your enemies and a foe to your foes" (23:20-22). Petersen contends that the coming help of Yahweh by means of the messenger (מַלְאָךְ) is dependent upon Israel's obedience to the laws of the Book of the Covenant. He says that "in Malachi, the coming of Yahweh depends upon the arrival of the messenger (מַלְאָךְ) who will function as a covenant enforcer"—מַלְאַךְ הַבְּרִית.[18] Several objections to this hypothesis can be raised. First, the verse itself seems to make a sharp distinction between the מַלְאָךְ on the one hand and the אָדוֹן and the מַלְאַךְ הַבְּרִית on the other. Yahweh sends his messenger preparatory to his own coming, to announce his imminent arrival. To effect a transition, the adverb פִּתְאֹם is used. Then, suddenly (פִּתְאֹם) Yahweh himself arrives in his temple, the messenger of the covenant comes. The verse itself equates not the מַלְאָךְ and the מַלְאַךְ הַבְּרִית, but the אָדוֹן and the

---

18 Ibid., 43.

מַלְאַךְ הַבְּרִית. This corresponds well with the Exodus passage where the roles of Yahweh and his messenger seem to merge (22:21f). There are many other instances in the Old Testament of such coalescence—the messenger blends into and is swallowed up by Yahweh (cf. Gen 16:7, 13; Exod 13:19, 24f; Num 22:22-35). In Exod 3, the call of Moses, a מַלְאַךְ יהוה appeared to him in fire flaming out of a bush (3:2). When the curious Moses approached the sight, it was Yahweh himself who spoke to him from the bush (3:4f). A similar situation is found in Judg 6:11f. A מַלְאַךְ יהוה appeared to Gideon and said that Yahweh was with him. When Gideon expressed skepticism, Yahweh turned to him (וַיִּפֶן אֵלָיו יהוה) and spoke. In all these instances, the messenger (מַלְאַךְ) is Yahweh's mode of self revelation.[19]

Petersen's equation of the forerunner מַלְאַךְ and the מַלְאַךְ הַבְּרִית is problematic in another sense. As covenant enforcer, Petersen says, it is the task of the מַלְאַךְ הַבְּרִית to bring Israel back into line. Obedience to the law becomes the prerequisite for Yahweh's coming. The curse in 3:24b, however, recognizes the distinct possibility that the מַלְאַךְ will be unable to create the requisite ritual and ethical purity necessary for Yahweh's coming. If this is the case, it must be inferred from Petersen's argument that Yahweh will not come. This is plainly contrary to the tenor of this verse, the prophecy as a whole (cf. 3:12-21; 22-24) and Israelite prophecy in general (cf. Joel 1:15; Zeph 1:4f; 2:1-11; Hag 2:22; Obad 1b f; Zech 14:6f).

If the אָדוֹן is identified with the מַלְאַךְ הַבְּרִית, the covenant enforcer, the verse assumes an unprecedented power. This oracle unit is replete with Yôm Yahweh imagery. The יוֹם יהוה is cultic in origin. "This day is one in which the deity shows himself as he really is—a 'showing' which takes place in the temple where he lives," (cf. Mal 3:1-2).[20] The Yôm Yahweh is the "day of his enthronement as king," (cf. Mal 1:11, 14; Pss 47:1, 8f; 96:1, 3f; 98:3f).[21] It is the day when he "comes" (Mal 3:2a; cf. Pss 96:13; 98:9) and "makes himself known," i.e., reveals himself and his

[19] Robert North, S. J., "Angel-Prophet or Satan-Prophet?" ZAW 82 (1970) 33-34.

[20] G. W. Ahlström, Joel and the Temple Cult of Jerusalem (SVT 21; Leiden: Brill, 1971) 66.

[21] Sigmund Mowinckel, The Psalms in Israel's Worship (2. vols.; New York: Abingdon, 1962), 1.107.

will (Mal 3:2b; cf. Pss 98:2; 93:5; 99:7); it is the day when he repeats the theophany of Mt. Sinai (Pss 97:3f; 99:7). Specifically, it is the day when he renews the election of Israel (Ps 47:5) and the covenant with his people (Pss 95:6f; 99:6f). As G. W. Ahlström maintains: "The cultic day of Yahweh is a day of his coming, his theophany, his war against his enemies, and his reestablishment of the covenant, complete with its accompanying ṣĕdāqāh, for his people."[22] Therefore it can be none other than Yahweh who is the מַלְאַךְ הַבְּרִית, the covenant enforcer of Mal 3:1e. On his day, he will reestablish his covenant and enforce its justice thereby satisfying those who questioned him in 2:17. This description of Yahweh accords well with Malachi 3:13-21, an oracle unit parallel in thought to 2:17-3:5. On Yahweh's day, he will spare all those who serve him (3:17, 20) and totally annihilate all the wicked among them (3:19).[23]

Finally, ascribing all the action in verses 1-5, with the exception of 3:1a, b, to Yahweh creates a dramatic flow, a crescendo that is denied by Petersen's analysis. By contending that these verses describe the function of the מַלְאָךְ, he is ascribing to the messenger traits generally associated with Yahweh alone. It is not the messenger who appears (3:2) in order to purify (3:2-4) and judge (3:5), as Petersen would have it; it is Yahweh. As the text states: "And suddenly the Lord whom you seek will enter his temple" (3:1c, d), and when he comes, "who will be able to stand when he appears?" (3:2a, b). Indeed, the day of Yahweh is the festival of his epiphany, the day of his cultic coming;[24] it is the day when he purifies (Mal 3:2f and cf. Isa 1:25; 4:4-5; Ezek 36:25) and the day when he judges (Mal 3:5 and cf. Jer 21:13; 49:4; 25:31; Isa 59:19f; 65:15f; Zech 14:5; Joel 4:12f).

The central characters of this verse are two: the forerunner messenger whose task it is to smooth the way and Yahweh, the אָדוֹן, the מַלְאַךְ הַבְּרִית, who is coming for judgment and restoration.

[22] Ahlström, *Joel,* 69.
[23] Mason maintains that the covenant referred to in מַלְאַךְ הַבְּרִית is the covenant with Levi mentioned in 2:4-7 because the attention of vv. 3:2-4 centers on the Levites and their purification, 153. Because this hypothesis does not take into account either the dependence of 3:1 on Exod 23:20f or the pervasive Yôm Yahweh imagery, it should be rejected.
[24] Mowinckel, 1.119; Ahlström, *Joel,* 69.

The analyses of van Hoonacker[25] and Chary,[26] among others[27] support the hypothesis espoused here. As van Hoonacker insists:

> Dans Malachie l'ange de l'alliance indique personelle-ment Jahvé, comme ayant donné la loi en apparition d'ange. On concevait l'alliance actuellement existante comme ayant été contractée entre le peuple hébreu et Jahvé se manifestant par le Mal'akh; c'est en vertu de cette conception que Jahvé porte le titre d'ange de l'alliance.[28]

Malachi employed that title in order to evoke themes through contextuality: the somber aspect of the day of Yahweh could not be missed, for the allusion to the messenger of the covenant was inevitably related to the contextual sequence of the Exodus passage. It was to insinuate that Yahweh was coming to contract "une alliance nouvelle que Malachie rappelle que le Seigneur qui va paraître est l'ange de l'alliance d'autrefois."[29]

The messenger, מַלְאָךְ, of 3:1a is a forerunner whose task it is to prepare the people for Yahweh's coming. Petersen affirms that this messenger (מַלְאָךְ) is a prophet.[30] A prophetic connotation for messenger is not novel in post-exilic literature. Deutero-Isaiah defines the activity of the "servant" with the appellation "messenger," (42:19; 44:26). In Haggai 1:13 we find the phrase: "Haggai the messenger of the Lord," חַגַּי מַלְאַךְ יהוה, in place of the more typical, "Haggai the prophet," cf. 1:1, 3-2:1, 10. Similarly, in the Chronicler's history, prophets are designated as messengers: "Persistently did Yahweh, the God of their fathers, send his messengers to them, for he had compassion on his people and his dwelling place. But they mocked the messengers of God, despising his warnings and scoffing at his prophets until the anger of Yahweh against his people was so inflamed that

---

[25] van Hoonacker, 730-31.

[26] Th. Chary, *Les prophètes et le culte à partir de l'exil* (Tournai: Desclée, 1954) 176-79.

[27] Rudolph, 278; Lagrange, 82.

[28] van Hoonacker, 731.

[29] Ibid.

[30] Petersen, 42.

there was no remedy" (2 Chr 36:15-16). Petersen lists several reasons why a prophet was deemed necessary to appear before Yahweh came in judgment. He suggests that "it was part of a more general expectation consistent with the Joel text," 3:1.[31] More important is the fact that Israel had already experienced the appearance of prophets prior to Yahweh's judgment in the debacle of 587 B.C.

> Such is the sum and substance of the Chronicler's observation on the place of Israel's earlier prophets. They had come to warn the nation. Yahweh then appeared in judgment; and since Israel had not repented, his judgment fell on them. The Chronicler observed that the prophets preceded Yahweh's coming, that they attempted to prepare the people for it. Now this memory was turned into an expectation for prophecy to precede Yahweh's appearance on his day.[32]

Petersen contends not only that the messenger (מַלְאָכִי) is a prophet, but more specifically, that he is "the prophetic 'author' of the book" (מַלְאָכִי).[33] The implications of this are fascinating, especially since it is expressly stated in Mal 3:23-24 that Elijah is the precursant messenger. For those, Petersen included, who maintain that Mal 3:23-24 are a later addition, this dichotomy presents no problems. As Eissfeldt states: "Mal. 3:23-24, however, are intended to make precise the proclamation of 3:1, of a heavenly messenger who is to precede Yahweh when he appears for judgment, and to correct this by indicating that Elijah is this messenger."[34] According to this view then, verses 23-24 provide a clarification and a specification of the earlier expectation. However, if these verses are original to the prophecy[35] an attempt to resolve the tension between מַלְאָכִי, the messenger, the prophetic 'author' in 3:1, and Elijah in 3:23 must be undertaken. The simplest solution is to suggest that מַלְאָכִי (3:1) refers purely and

[31] Ibid., 44.
[32] Ibid.
[33] Ibid., 42.
[34] Otto Eissfeldt, *The Old Testament: An Introduction* (New York: Harper and Row, 1965) 442.
[35] Cf. the discussion on 3:23-24, 252f.

simply to an unspecified messenger or prophet whose name was revealed only at the prophecy's close. There was a prophet who, because he did not die, was available for such a reappearance as was deemed necessary to precede Yahweh's coming. This was Elijah (cf. 2 Kgs 2:11; Enoch 89:52). Nevertheless, Petersen's suggestion that the מַלְאָכִי of 3:1 is our prophetic author, is too titillating to be disregarded out of hand. Perhaps a *double entendre* was intended here. The people were clamoring for Yahweh to exercise his judgeship thereby eradicating the wicked (2:17). Despite his impatience at their unbelief, Malachi assured his contemporaries that Yahweh will surely come and they will know the time has arrived because a messenger (מַלְאָכִי) will precede him with the news. The people, however, were beyond promises, no matter how near to fulfillment; they wanted immediate action. That the name Malachi—מַלְאָכִי means "messenger" may have offered them some concrete hope. The messenger who was to clear a path for Yahweh was none other than the man speaking to them! It may have suited Malachi to continue this deception in the hope that the people would return to Yahweh strengthened in their belief. It was only at the close of his words, when he was reiterating his thesis of the imminence of Yahweh's day, that Malachi enlightened his hearers as to the true identity of the מַלְאָך—Elijah (3:23-24).

הִנְנִי שֹׁלֵחַ: The participial form (שֹׁלֵחַ) is used to announce a future action or event, cf. also 1 Kgs 2:2; 2 Kgs 4:16. "If it is intended to announce the event as imminent, or at least near at hand (and sure to happen)"—the *futurum instans*, the participle is often introduced by הִנֵּה or a suffixed form as here (cf. also Gen 6:17; Exod 3:13; Isa 3:1; 7:14; 17:1; Jer 30:10; Zech 2:13).[36] Thus the clause should be translated, "I am about to send my messenger."

שֹׁלֵחַ is the verb ordinarily used to describe the sending of a messenger and is common both in accounts of the prophets' inaugural visions and in the introduction, to subsequent oracles (cf. Gen 24:7, 40; Exod 23:20; Num 20:16; Hag 1:12; Zech 2:12, 13, 15; Jer 1:7; 7:25). There is a close relationship between the messenger and the one who sent him because the messenger's

---

[36] GKC, #116p, 359-60.

authority is that of the master. "Thus a messenger is to be treated as if he were his master."[37]

פְּנָה־דֶרֶךְ: to clear a road, path. פִנָּה is a piel pf., "to turn away, put out of the way, free from obstacles."[38] דֶּרֶךְ is used in the literal sense of road, movement (Gen 38:16; Num 22:23), and for the direction of life which an individual takes for himself or which is set for him by others (1 Sam 23:20).[39] דֶּרֶךְ as road implies movement, in this case, movement towards Israel.

There is a striking parallel to פְּנָה־דֶרֶךְ לְפָנָי found in Isa 40:3:

במדבר פנו דרך יהוה
ישרו בערבה מסלה לאלהינו

The theme of דֶּרֶךְ plays an important role in 2 Isaiah. Yahweh's power is apparent when he opens a "road" for historical movements, as in the exodus of Israel from Egypt (43:16, 19; 51:10) and the sending of Cyrus (45:14; 48:15). In particular, as Isa 40:3 demonstrates, Yahweh will soon prepare a marvelous highway through the wilderness. Deutero-Isaiah's proclamation gives signs of encounter with the world in which he lived, the sphere of influence of the Babylonian empire. "The highway" has its own peculiar place in the Babylonian hymns, the layout of the city of Babylon is itself proof of the importance of the great processional way.[40] The highways of the gods and the highways of kings meet.

> From hostile Elam he entered upon a road of jubilation,
> a path of rejoicing . . . of success to Su-an-na. The people
> of the land saw his towering figure, the ruler in (his)
> splendor. Hasten to go out (Nabu), Son of Bel, you who

---

[37] James F. Ross, "The Prophet as Yahweh's Messenger," *Israel's Prophetic Heritage: Essays in Honor of James Muilenberg* (eds. Bernhard W. Anderson and Walter Harrelson; New York: Harper and Brothers, 1962) 101.

[38] BDB, 815. The use of פנה is interesting. It implies that there are obstacles in the way (דרך), perhaps physical (i.e., stones, unevenness of terrain), but more likely mental (i.e., the people's unbelief, skepticism). It was the messenger's task to prepare the people for Yahweh's coming, to turn them to him, cf. 3:22f. In view of their present disposition, such a task would be quite difficult.

[39] BDB, 202-4.

[40] Cf. Fr. Stummer, "Einige keilschriftliche Parallelen zu Jes 40-66," *JBL* 45 (1926) 171-89.

know the ways and the customs. Make his way good,
renew his road, make his path straight, hew him out a
trail.[41]

In Babylon, the processional road, prepared and made level
for the entry of the god or the king, was called Airburshabu and
"it was decorated with lions and inscriptions in blue and white
faience."[42] For exiled Israelites in Babylon, such imposing roads
were symbols of the might that brought about Israel's own downfall. Although this is not said until the motif is further developed,
the highway about which the prophet writes is the one that will
enable Israel to return home (cf. 42:16; 49:9–11). Here however, it
is designated a highway "for Yahweh our God" just as the roads
of Babylon were processionals for divinity. Its designation as the
highway for Yahweh is more precisely explained in verse 5,
"And the glory of Yahweh shall be revealed." This, too, can be
read against the Babylonian backdrop: there, the primary function of the highways was to allow the great processions to
display the power and majesty of the gods in visible form.[43] But
this backdrop highlights the difference in the essence of Yahweh:
his "glory," כָּבוֹד, cannot be manifested in the same way as that
of the gods of Babylon; because what created the impression of
majesty in the Babylonian processions—the images of the gods—
is absent here. What reveals Yahweh's glory is his action in
history. Therefore, the highway which is to be made through the
desert, is the way on which Yahweh now gives proof of himself,
in a new historical act—the way for leading his people home.
    The idea of a "processional road" was not unique to the
Babylonians; it "always belonged to the cultic processions at the
great temples of the orient, a *via sacra*, as it was called by the
Romans."[44] Jerusalem had a *via sacra* as well (cf. Ps 84:6).[45]
Among the rites belonging to the festival of the enthronement of
Yahweh,

---

[41] Quoted in Paul Volz, *Jesaja* II (KAT; Leipzig: Deichert, 1932) 4; cf.
Stummer, 172 for the original text.
[42] Mowinckel, 1.170.
[43] Ibid., 170.
[44] Ibid.
[45] Ibid., 170–72.

> a main event was evidently the great festal procession,
> the victorious coronation entry of the Lord, to which
> reference is made in Ps 47:6. . . . The personal presence
> of Yahweh in the festive procession was most probably
> symbolized by his holy shrine (the ark).[46]

It is this appearance and enthronement day of Yahweh which
was originally called 'the day of the Lord,' 'the day of the feast
of Yahweh' (cf. Hos 7:5; 2:15; 9:5). The "day of Yahweh" was
the day when he was to appear, become enthroned as king,
"establish his kingdom and thus secure justice and a future for
his people." [47]

To a large extent, the message of Deutero-Isaiah has been
couched in the language of the enthronement festival. Yahweh is
about to appear in triumph, like a king, his 'glory' revealed,
40:3, 5. He is coming to Jerusalem, his temple, 40:9. In Isa 52:7
messengers announce his coming saying, "Your God reigns."

> Here we find almost word for word the acclamation of
> the enthronement psalms: 'Yahweh is king.' From the
> fact that Yahweh is the creator of the world—a motif
> that also plays an important role in the enthronement
> psalms—the prophet draws the conclusion that Yahweh
> is unique and incomparable, the lord of all the world
> and its history. (Cf 40:22f.)[48]

Yahweh will triumph over his enemies (51:9-11) and renew the
covenant with his people (54:9f). Finally, all nations will assemble
in Jerusalem to worship the one true god (Isa 45:15; 49:14-23).

The scenario envisioned by Deutero-Isaiah and the enthronement psalms is complemented strikingly by Mal 3:1 and other
verses within the prophecy. As Sellin commented, "Yahweh's
coming is like that of a king entering his palace" (הֵיכָל), that is,
his temple in Jerusalem (Mal 3:1; Isa 40:3).[49] His arrival is
presaged by a messenger (3:1a; Isa 52:7). Malachi too emphasizes
Yahweh's kingship (cf. 1:14, כִּי מֶלֶךְ גָּדוֹל אָנִי, cf. Isa 52:7) and his

[46] Ibid., 115.
[47] Ibid., 189.
[48] Helmer Ringgren, *Israelite Religion* (Philadelphia: Fortress, 1966) 289.
[49] Sellin, 607.

creatorhood (2:10, אֵל אֶחָד בְּרָאָנוּ) with the implicit assumption
that he alone should be worshiped (cf. 2:10f). On his day,
Yahweh will triumph over his enemies (cf. 3:13-21) and renew
the covenant with his people (cf. 3:1, Yahweh as מַלְאַךְ הַבְּרִית).
Finally, he will be worshiped by all people (cf. 1:11).

The imagery contained in this verse is powerful, designed as
a response to the people's skepticism (2:17). Yahweh's day is the
day of his epiphany (3:2), the day when he will refute the empty
claim that there is no god of justice (cf. 2:17).

פִּתְאֹם is an adverb that functions here as a transitional
device separating the action of the מַלְאָךְ from that of Yahweh.
The messenger is sent to prepare a highway and suddenly, in a
twinkling (פֶּתַא) Yahweh appears on it; he comes to his temple
(הֵיכָל) where he lives (1 Kgs 8:10f; 2 Chr 4:13f; Ezek 43:4f) and
where man and deity confront one another (cf. Ps 65).

בּוֹא is one of the most frequently used verbs in the OT and
heads the list of verbs expressing motion, i.e., to come in, enter.[50]
It is used as a technical term of the cult describing man's
approach to a sanctuary (i.e., entering the sacral sphere) either
Yahwistic, Ps 65:3; Deut 31:11; 2 Sam 7:18; Isa 30:29; Isa 66:23; or
non-Yahwistic, cf. Hos 9:10; 2 Kgs 10:21; Ezek 20:29.

Yahweh is a judge (cf. Pss 50:6; 67:5; 75:8; 94:2) and his
coming in judgment is often designated by the use of בּוֹא. Amos
says בָּא הַקֵּץ אֶל־עַמִּי יִשְׂרָאֵל (cf. also Hos 9:7). בּוֹא appears in the
announcement of judgment on Eli's house (1 Sam 2:31) and in
Isaiah's announcement of judgment on Hezekiah (2 Kgs 20:17).
Isaiah proclaims that Yahweh comes (יבוא) in a judgment assem-
bly in order to judge the elders of his people (3:14) and cries
"woe" to those who do not believe that the judgment which has
been announced will come to pass (תְּבוֹאָה, תִּקְרַב, 5:19). This use
of בּוֹא to delineate Yahweh's coming in judgment accords well
with the thematic concerns of Malachi's fourth oracle unit. The
people are waiting for the god of judgment (2:17). His arrival as
such is imminent (3:1); he will draw near to his people in
judgment (3:5, וְקָרַבְתִּי אֲלֵיכֶם לַמִּשְׁפָּט).

Integrally related to Yahweh's coming (בּוֹא) in judgment is
the coming of the day of Yahweh (יוֹם יהוה), also spoken of in
connection with בּוֹא. Ezekiel proclaims that the day draws near,

---

[50] BDB, 97.

בָּא הָעֵת הִגִּיעַ הַיּוֹם (7:12). Zephaniah exhorts the shameless nation to gather together בְּטֶרֶם לֹא־יָבוֹא עֲלֵיכֶם חֲרוֹן אַף־יהוה (2:2). According to Malachi 3:19, Yahweh's day comes burning like a furnace, devouring the wicked. According to Joel 1:15, the day of Yahweh comes (יָבוֹא) as a destruction from שַׁדַּי. At that time the nations are to come (בּוֹא), to gather (קָבַץ), to go up (עָלָה) for judgment (4:11-12). The day of Yahweh is coming and is near: כִּי־בָא יוֹם־יהוה כִּי קָרוֹב , Joel 2:1. Significantly, Yahweh is said to dwell on Mt. Zion, his holy mountain—שֹׁכֵן בְּצִיּוֹן הַר־קָדְשִׁי, 4:17, the mountain of his sanctuary.[51] Both Mal 3:1f and Joel offer the same basic promise—that Yahweh will come, tabernacle on Mt. Zion, his temple, and act specifically in judgment. That Yahweh's coming and his judgment are so inextricably linked should not be surprising. On Yahweh's day, the day of his enthronement, he was acclaimed as king (cf. יהוה מָלָךְ, Pss 93:1; 97:1; 47:8; 96:10), and it was one of his tasks as king to set conditions on earth in the right order. As Mowinckel observes, judgment (מִשְׁפָּט) does not merely indicate judicial activity,

> but all activity on the part of kings and leaders for the purpose of maintaining the balance and 'harmony' and 'peace' of society, and to secure to everybody what according to the covenant is his 'right,' i.e., what we would call to 'rule' or to 'govern.' Thus when the king displays his 'judgment' and 'righteousness,'—ṣedheq, ṣĕdhaqâ—it means his power to do the 'right' thing in all senses of the word, and create 'right order,' i.e., blessing, peace, good morals and victory for his people— 'justifying them' (hiṣdîq), i.e., creating for them the right social, moral and religious conditions. In this way Yahweh also is going to 'rule' or 'judge' his people.[52]

The forensic aspect, the fundamental 'act of judgment' at the coming of Yahweh is also prominent. Yahweh summons his antagonists to him and judges them. In Ps 75:8 he speaks severe words of reproof to all the inhabitants of the earth; he is the judge who lowers one and lifts another (cf. also Ps 149;

---

[51] Hans Walter Wolff, *Hosea* (Philadelphia: Fortress, 1974) 81.

[52] Mowinckel, 1.149; Johannes Pedersen, *Israel Its Life and Culture* (4 vols.; London: Oxford University), 2.336f.

Isa 59:18f; 66:15f). In Mal 3:1f, Yahweh's coming incorporates both the forensic action of judging (3:5) and the more general aspect of restoration of the 'right order.' No more will the people say that Yahweh favors the wicked (2:17).

One other aspect of בּוֹא remains to be discussed. The connection between Mal 3:1 and Ps 24 is too close to be ignored. In both, the processional way, the דֶּרֶךְ, is featured. In Malachi, the way is being prepared for Yahweh's entrance; in Ps 24 the procession on the "way" has reached the gates of the temple (v. 7).

> The psalm falls into three parts: the introductory hymn to the creator and ruler of the world (vv. 1-2), the dialogue between the leader of the procession and the gatekeepers as to who is allowed to enter the sanctuary (the 'conditions of entry'), with the assurance from the side of the pageant (the congregation) that they fulfill the demands (vv. 3-6) and finally the request for the gates to open to the one who is coming, 'the King of glory, Yahweh Zeboath' (vv. 7-10), יהוה . . . הַכָּבוֹד מֶלֶךְ וְיָבוֹא צְבָאוֹת.[53]

The use of בּוֹא in Ps 24 to indicate the cultic entrance of Yahweh to his temple parallels Mal 3:1c perfectly: וּפִתְאֹם יָבוֹא אֶל־הֵיכָלוֹ. In this verse therefore, בּוֹא delineates Yahweh's cultic coming, that is, his entrance into the temple to inaugurate his day and its attendant judgment.

הָאָדוֹן אֲשֶׁר־אַתֶּם מְבַקְשִׁים: Significantly, Ps 24 describes those desirous of a confrontation with Yahweh as מְבַקְשֵׁי פָנֶיךָ—seekers of your face, v. 6. It should be noted that they fulfill the conditions for entry into Yahweh's presence, v. 4. "Seeking" (מְבַקֵּשׁ—piel active participle) the deity ostensibly refers to a comprehensible cultic rite at a holy place where it would have been possible to seek God directly or immediately. Hosea 5:6 speaks of "going with flocks and herds to seek Yahweh" and thus refers to a cultic act connected with sacrifice (cf. also 2 Chr 11:16; 15:15). Zech 8:21f has in mind seeking Yahweh at his temple (cf. also Ps 27:8). Those who praise God are called

---

[53] Mowinckel, 1.177.

"the seekers of God" in 1 Chr 16:10-11.[54] According to Mal 3:1, when Yahweh enters his temple, it will then be possible to seek him, i.e., have a cultic meeting with him. The idea that one must be pure, in the right condition before such a meeting can take place, is attested to in Ps 24 and is implied in Hos 5:6. Those who go to seek Yahweh are defiled (5:3), without knowledge of God (5:4), iniquitous (5:5). Therefore, they will not find him (5:6). Mal 3:2-5 suggests that purificatory rites will be performed before God and man meet—the priests will be cleansed so that proper sacrifices can be offered, and those who do not fear the Lord will be purged from the community (3:5 and cf. 3:19).

The use of בּוֹא and בָּקַשׁ in this verse emphasizes the pervasive sense of movement. God comes (יָבוֹא) to man, man seeks (בָּקֵשׁ) God; they move toward one another and the meeting ground is Yahweh's temple.

אָדוֹן is a masculine noun meaning "lord" and is often applied to Yahweh, cf. Exod 23:17; 34:23.[55] L. Köhler emphasizes that אָדוֹן refers to Yahweh in his capacity as ruler while בַּעַל means Yahweh as possessor and owner.[56] Similarly, O. Eissfeldt maintains that אָדוֹן "is used to emphasize Yahweh's rule over all the world" (cf. Josh 3:13; Isa 1:24; 3:1; 10:16, 33; Mic 4:13; Zech 6:5; Pss 97:5; 135:5).[57] The use of אָדוֹן in Mal 3:1 aptly continues the יוֹם יהוה imagery. On his day Yahweh becomes king, "the world-ruler who uses all nations and kingdoms as his instruments" (cf. Mic 4:13; Zech 4:14).[58] Indeed, there can be no doubt that Malachi is providing a description of the coming day of Yahweh and this description is enhanced by the verses that follow.

[3:2]—This verse introduces the effects of Yahweh's coming. His day will be a day of distinctions, of separating the good from the evil, the pure from the impure. Yahweh is pictured as a metal refiner, an especially apt simile because it is through the

---

[54] Other instances of "seeking" God in a cultic sense can be found in Deut 4:29; Hos 3:5; 5:1; Jer 50:4; 2 Chr 7:14; 15:4 and cf. C. Westermann, "Die Begriffe für Fragen und Suchen im AT," *KuD* 6 (1960) 2-30.

[55] BDB, 11.

[56] L. Köhler, *Old Testament Theology* (Philadelphia: Westminster, 1957) 31.

[57] Eissfeldt, "אָדוֹן ᵓadhôn; אֲדֹנָי ᵓᵃdhōnāi, *TDOT* 1.62.

[58] Mowinckel, 1.114.

process of the liquifaction of the ore that the useless elements are isolated; the dross rises and is easily skimmed off the top.

וּמִי: This separation process is indicated by the first word of the verse, 3:2a and cf. 3:2b—וּמִי "but who?"[59] As van Hoonacker maintains: "וּמִי serves to eliminate all the impure elements from the bosom of the nation."[60] Indeed, Malachi is proffering a warning to those so eager for the arrival of Yahweh's day (3:1).[61] His coming will not be a boon to everyone but will presage destruction for the wicked, cf. Amos 5:18, Zeph 1:17. Only those who are already pure, those who fear Yahweh (3:5), will endure it; only they will be exempt from Yahweh's refining action.[62]

מְכַלְכֵּל (3:2a)—עֹמֵד (3:2b): מְכַלְכֵּל is a pilpel participle of כּוּל ("to contain, measure, of liquid or dry measure")[63] meaning "to contain, support, endure."[64] The obvious answer to the question וּמִי מְכַלְכֵּל אֶת־יוֹם בּוֹאוֹ "But who can endure the day of his coming?" is—those who fear Yahweh. Certainly they will tremble at the awesomeness of his epiphany but only they will be able to present themselves before Yahweh with equanimity because his day is the day of their vindication (3:20f). However that may be, the question can be answered in a totally different way that more sharply defines the images of the oracle unit. To the question "But who can endure the day of his coming?" the answer may be given—"Certainly not the wicked!" For them Yahweh's arrival signals their fiery destruction (3:19). In view of their ignominious, in fact, terrifying end, their pride is shattered, their bones refuse to support them; the day of Yahweh is unendurable.[65]

---

[59] For the adversative use of וֹ = but, see *Gesenius' Hebrew and Chaldee Lexicon* (Grand Rapids, Michigan: William B. Eerdmans, 1949) 235 and cf. Hos 1:7; Gen 2:17.

[60] van Hoonacker, 731.

[61] Cf. 3:1d, e—אתם חפצים; אתם מבקשים.

[62] Cf. also Rudolph, 279.

[63] BDB, 465.

[64] *Gesenius' Hebrew and Chaldee Lexicon*, 386.

[65] In Joel 2:11, in a context similar to Mal 3:2, the hiphil of כול is found: כי־גדול יום־יהוה ונורא מאד ומי יכילנו, "The day of Yahweh is great a very terrible and who can endure it?" The answer is—no one; the people are all wicked. However, as vv. 12f enunciate, those who turn to Yahweh will find in him a compassionate God (2:13) who will willingly avert his anger and its consequences. Malachi's prophecy provides the same escape hatch. Yahweh will again look with favor on those who return to him, 3:7.

The theme of both this oracle unit and 3:13-21 is the sureness of Yahweh's coming with its attendant separation of the good from the evil within the community. Malachi describes the cleansing or separating process using the image of the refiner's fire (3:2c; 3:3). Under extreme heat, the smelter liquifies his ore causing impurities to rise to the surface where they are quickly skimmed off.[66] Only when that step is completed does he turn his attention to the resultant pure metal, giving it the time and consideration it deserves, molding it into objects of beauty. So too, Yahweh's purificatory work deals first with the evil-doers so that he can then concentrate his extended care on those who have served him well.[67] This sequence of events is suggested most forcefully when the question, "Who can endure the day of his coming," is answered with "Certainly not the wicked." The implication is that they are rooted out at the very beginning of the process leaving only the God-fearers standing firmly before him.

The parallel question וּמִי הָעֹמֵד בְּהֵרָאוֹתוֹ "But who can stand when he appears?" (3:2b), can be answered the same way. The verb עָמַד means not only "to stand," but "to remain standing" (2 Kgs 13:6), "to make a stand, hold one's ground" (Amos 2:15; 2 Kgs 10:4) and "to present oneself" (i.e., before Yahweh, Deut 19:17; Jer 7:10; 18:20).[68] As the entrance liturgies of Pss 15 and 24 (cf. also Mic 6:6-8; Isa 33:14-16) demonstrate, standing in Yahweh's presence is not the prerogative of all.[69] Only those who have fulfilled certain requirements, i.e., having clean hands, pure hearts and guileless tongues (cf. Ps 24:4) are permitted to go up to him. Certainly, therefore, the question וּמִי הָעֹמֵד בְּהֵרָאוֹתוֹ may be answered, "the God-fearers, the righteous." Because they have served Yahweh well they may hold

---

[66] Alan Robinson, "God, the Refiner of Silver," *CBQ* 11 (1949) 189.

[67] This does not mean that Yahweh spares no thought for them until the wicked are destroyed. As Malachi avers, those who fear Yahweh will be able to participate actively in the destruction of the evildoers, 3:21. Moreover, Yahweh's purificatory work is not totally destructive. While this seems to be the case for evildoers who refuse to return to Yahweh (cf. 3:19), the priests will be purified in the literal sense of the word—cleansed both outwardly and inwardly so that they will again offer Yahweh proper sacrifices, 3:3-4.

[68] BDB, 763-64.

[69] Mowinckel, 1.177f.

their ground before him without faltering. However, just as surely, the question may be answered, "Certainly not the wicked!" Their slovenly behavior in cultic matters (3:6f) and in their relationships with their fellow Judeans (3:5) makes them unworthy to present themselves, to stand (עמד) before Yahweh. Again, the inference is that a sharp distinction is made between the righteous and the evildoers at the moment of Yahweh's epiphany. The wicked are immediately weeded out; the righteous are left standing.

הֵרָאוֹתוֹ (3:2b)—בּוֹאוֹ (3:2a): Both words indicate clearly the יוֹם יהוה setting of this oracle unit. It is the day when Yahweh comes (בּוֹא qal inf., cf. Pss 96:13; 98:9); it is the day of his epiphany (רָאָה niphal inf. cs.—to appear, cf. Ps 102:17).

בְּרִית מְכַבְּסִים (3:2d)—אֵשׁ מְצָרֵף (3:2c): refiner's fire—fullers' soap. On the day of his coming Yahweh is likened to both. The images are clear and devastating. The prophet symbolizes Yahweh's cleansing action by two common trades, the gold— and silver refiner and the clothes-cleaner. As the refiner removes the dross from the precious metal and the cleaner washes away the stains from clothes, so will Yahweh test all and remove the vile from the precious.

אֵשׁ fire (n.m. and f.) is not limited to any form; it blazes up to an intensity pure and inaccessible, it disseminates light and heat and can be beneficial or destructive. All this gave it the nimbus of the mysterious, the terrifying. Fire plays an important role in statements concerning Yahweh, his appearances and his actions.[70] Indeed, one of the ways Yahweh reveals himself is through fire, the best example of which is the Sinai theophany (cf. Exod 19:18; 24:16f; Deut 4:11, 12, 14, 33, 36).[71] Jeremias emphasizes that at Sinai "fire is the phenomenon that accompanies or mediates the manifestation of Yahweh."[72]

Fire (אֵשׁ) is also an actualization of Yahweh's burning anger (cf. Isa 29:6; 30:27, 30; Nah 1:6, Jer 15:14; Ezek 36:5). Zephaniah

---

[70] P. O. Miller, "Fire in the Mythology of Canaan and Israel," *CBQ* 27 (1965) 256-61.

[71] Cf. Gen 15:17; Exod 3:2; 13:21; Num 9:15; Ps 78:14 for other examples of the fire through which Yahweh's presence is made known.

[72] J. Jeremias, *Theophanie* (WMANT 10; Neukirchen-Vulyn: Neukirchener Verlag, 1958) 108.

describes the imminent day of Yahweh as a day of wrath, a day
when God's anger will be displayed with terrifying effects (1:14–
17), and he concludes:

גם־כספם גם־זהבם
לא־יוכל להצילם
ביום עברת יהוה
ובאש קנאתו תאכל כל־הארץ
כי כלה אך־נבהלה יעשה
את כל־ישבי הארץ

"Neither their silver nor their gold will be able to deliver them
in the day of the Yahweh's wrath; but the fire of his zeal will
devour the whole earth; for he will make an end, indeed, a
terrifying end of all them who dwell on earth" (1:18 cf. also Isa
66:15–17; Joel 1:19–20; 2:3).

Ezekiel sees in the hot smelting furnaces, the kind of treatment that Yahweh will accord wicked Israel (22:20–21); to
Zechariah, the heat of the fire is purificatory (13:9):[73]

והבאתי את־השלשית באש
וצרפתים כצרף את־הכסף
ובחנתים כבחן את־הזהב
הוא יקרא בשמי ואני אענה אתו
אמרתי עמי הוא
והוא יאמר יהוה אלהי

In Malachi, the symbolism of fire possesses this versatility of
content. The prophet says that when Yahweh appears he will be
like a refiner's fire, אֵשׁ מְצָרֵף (מְצָרֵף, piel active participle of צָרָף,
"to smelt, refine"). Thus, fire represents Yahweh's energetic self
revelation. It suggests the anger long held in check that he will
unleash on his errant people on his day. Finally, the phrase
'refiner's fire' points to Yahweh's cleansing work. Just as the
smelter retrieves pure metal from ore so Yahweh will refine his
people. That Yahweh was likened not just to fire but to a
refiner's fire is significant. Because smelting was a common craft,[74]
the people were cognizant of the intense, burning heat that the
smelter needed to generate in order to liquify the ore and thus

---

[73] Cf. also Isa 22:25; Jer 6:27–30; Dan 11:35; Ps 66:10.
[74] F. V. Winnett, "Metallurgy," *IDB* 3.336–38.

Yahweh's actions attained experienced meaning. In other words, by equating Yahweh with a refiner's fire, Malachi likened the quality of Yahweh's heat to something directly out of the people's own experience thereby strengthening the image.

בֹּרִית is a feminine noun meaning "lye," a cleansing agent that can be made out of the ashes of the soap plant.[75] It is derived from the root בָּרַר meaning "to purify, purge, separate out" (cf. Ezek 20:38; Isa 52:11).[76] The adjective בַּר means "pure" (cf. Pss 24:4; 73:1). The abstract noun בֹּר means "purity" (cf. Job 22:30; Ps 18:21, 25).[77] As a noun בֹּר (n.m.) also means "lye, potash, alkali" (cf. Job 9:30; Isa 1:25). More generally, בֹּר means something which cleanses, purifies (the root meaning of בָּרַר), something which has a cleansing property—an alkali, soap.[78] בֹּרִית (from בֹּר with the adj. fem. termination ־ית) has essentially the same meaning (cf. Jer 2:22). Malachi describes Yahweh as בֹּרִית מְכַבְּסִים, washers' soap.[79] Just as the refiner's fire purifies ore and the fuller's soap cleans clothes,[80] so Yahweh will cleanse his people. At issue here is the separation of the impure from the pure.

Both von Bulmerincq and van Hoonacker suggest that in view of Mal 3:3, where Yahweh is described as a refiner of silver, and Isa 1:25, where Yahweh states that he will refine dross as with lye, the phrase בֹּרִית מְכַבְּסִים in Mal 3:2 should be understood against the background of metal refining.[81] Indeed, בֹּרִית (an alkali) was used in smelting metals to make them melt more quickly.[82] Specifically, an alkali such as potash or lye could be used as the reducing agent in the refining of silver. Since silver is mined in an impure form, an agent is required to help reduce the ore to metallic purity, to help separate the dross from the

[75] BDB, 141.

[76] Ibid., 140.

[77] Ibid., 141.

[78] *Gesenius' Hebrew and Chaldee Lexicon*, 142.

[79] Note Jer 2:22 where both כבס and ברית appear. Soap is usually produced by the action of an alkali such as lye or potash on a fat or oil.

[80] מכבסים is a piel m. pl. ptc. from כבס, "to wash garments by treading on them under water," cf. BDB 460; *Gesenius' Hebrew and Chaldee Lexicon*, 382. כבס refers especially to the cleaning of clothes, cf. Gen 49:11; Exod 19:10; Lev 13:6, 34; Num 19:7, 19.

[81] von Bulmerincq, 2.358; van Hoonacker, 731 and cf. also Sellin, 609.

[82] *Gesenius' Hebrew and Chaldee Lexicon*, 138.

metal. A caustic substance such as lye or potash was a good reagent.[83]

Further, potash and lye are by-products of the smelting process itself. Charcoal was used to heat the furnaces.[84] The resultant ashes were leached to get a strongly alkaline solution, lye. Similarly, potash could be derived from the flue dusts of the furnace or from ashes.[85] This understanding of בֹּרִית, as an agent in the refining process, continues the language of 3:2c and strengthens the overall image of Yahweh's purificatory work.[86]

Malachi's creative ability should not be underestimated. He has provided his hearers with an interesting play on words. A simple repointing of בֹּרִית (3:2d), alkali, gives בְּרִית, covenant, the מַלְאַךְ הַבְּרִית of 3:1.[87] Yahweh's work as covenant enforcer includes cleansing the community of those elements who refuse to abide by its precepts.[88]

---

[83] This information was gathered in discussions with J. Hoke, Associate Professor of Metallurgy at The Pennsylvania State University. He also suggested that the dross removed in the purification process may have had some silver in it that could be retrieved by mixing it with an alkali, cf. Isa 1:25.

[84] Winnett, 3.366.

[85] This according to J. Hoke, see above n. 83.

[86] von Bulmerincq remarks: "Doch ist das noch kein zureichender Grund, in v. 2 für מכבסים eine sonst im A. T. nicht zu belegende Bedeutung anzunehmen und damit auch das in Gl. b vorliegende Doppelbild auf ein einziges zu reduzieren. . . . Die beiden Bilder veranschaulichen die Idee der Läuterung und der Reinigung," 2.358. Since ברית was probably best known as a substance used in the cleaning (כבס) of clothes, Malachi may have used the phrase ברית מכבסים to ensure that his hearers understood the full implication of Yahweh's cleansing action.

[87] It is likely that this play on words was intended for a reader (for whom the forms would have been identical) rather than for a listener since בְּרִית, 3:1, is not in the immediate vicinity of בְּרִית, 3:2 (though the preceding verse might be considered close enough for an oral/aural play on words).

[88] Malachi's creativity, the fluidity of his poetry is evidenced in addition by his use of alliteration and terminal and internal rhyme both in 3:2 and in 3:1. Note in 3:1:

הנני־מלאכי ;האדון אשר אתם ;מבקשים־חפצים ;פתאם־יבוא־היכלו־
האדון־יום־בואו־עמד־הראתו ;מי־מכלכל־יום־העמד ;כי־כאש־כברית

It is precisely these conventions that create the very perceptible sense of motion which characterizes this oracle unit.

[3:3-4]—According to Rudolph, these two verses disturb the unity of the oracle unit.[89] Whereas in 3:2 Yahweh simply eliminates evildoers from the heart of the community, in 3:3-4 the implication is that the Levites as a group, despite their irresponsible attitude toward Yahweh and his cult, will be cleansed. Rudolph suggests that these verses owe their present place to what he calls "the catchword principle of the redactor:" מְצָרֵף (3:2c)—מְצָרֵף (3:3a),[90] and he concludes that they belong with 1:6-2:9 where the prophet discusses the need for a Levitical renovation.[91] In point of fact, these verses do not disturb the unity of the unit but are integral to it. There is a very perceptible progression and specification within this section. Yahweh's coming will bring with it a purification of his people (3:2). That this does not necessarily involve an irrevocable elimination of the wicked can be inferred from Mal 3:7, שׁוּבוּ אֵלַי וְאָשׁוּבָה אֲלֵיכֶם. The cleansing work will first be done to Levi (3:3) who was also the principle object of the reproaches formulated in 1:6-2:9. Then the immorality of the people will be purged (3:5). The cult will be purified through the purification of the Levites. The post-exilic community will regroup around the temple, their sacrifices once again pleasing to Yahweh (3:3d-3:4). The new era envisioned by Malachi appears to be the epoch of the heroic fidelity of Levi (cf. Mal 2:6-7; Exod 32:26f; Num 25:11f).

יָשַׁב: qal pf., "to sit." Again the Yôm Yahweh imagery prevails. It is the day when Yahweh becomes king and sits (יָשַׁב) himself on the throne, cf. Ps 99:2.[92] Yahweh's day is a day of judgment and the idea of Yahweh sitting as a judge is also expressed by the verb יָשַׁב (cf. Ps 9:8f).[93]

מְטַהֵר: piel participle of טָהַר "to purify, cleanse."[94] The use of the verb to indicate the cleansing of metal is found only here but the adj. טָהוֹר "clean, pure" is often employed to describe

---

[89] Rudolph, 279-80.

[90] Ibid., 280.

[91] Ibid.

[92] Mowinckel, 1.102; E. Lipínski, *La royauté de Yahwé dans la poésie et le culte de l'ancien Israël* (Brussels: Paleis der Academiën, 1965) 394. Other passages that describe Yahweh as sitting enthroned include Pss 2:4; 9:8; 22:4; 29:10; 1 Sam 4:4; 2 Kgs 19:15.

[93] Cf. Mowinckel, 1.149 f.

[94] *Gesenius' Hebrew and Chaldee Lexicon*, 318; cf. Lev 14:11.

זָהָב טָהוֹר .[, Exod 25:11, 17, 24, 29, 31, 36, 38, 39; Exod 28:14, 30:3; 37:2, 6, 11, 16, 17, 22, 23, 24, 26;[95] 1 Chr 28:17; 2 Chr 3:4; 9:17.)[96]

כֶּסֶף n.m. "silver." Sellin, J. M. P. Smith and G. A. Smith excise כֶּסֶף as a dittography from 3:3c; it destroys the meter of the line and is believed to be unsuitable to the comparison.[97] However, the images used in his oracle unit flow from one verse to the next. In 3:2 Malachi described Yahweh as a metal refiner whose cleansing would be as caustic as בֹּרִית. Since it appears from both Isa 1:25 and Mal 3:2 that בֹּרִית was used for the smelting and purification of silver, the use of כֶּסֶף in 3:3a is not superfluous but is part and parcel of the prophets' continuum of imagery.[98]

וְטִהַר אֶת־בְּנֵי־לֵוִי—As mentioned previously in connection with מְטַהֵר (3:3a), the only use of the verb to indicate the cleansing of metal is found in Malachi. Its employment was deliberate—to extend the imagery begun in 3:2 and to provide a point of comparison that is fully explained in 3:3b. As the smelter refines metal, so Yahweh will refine, purify (טִהַר, piel pf.) the Levites. And just as the refined silver is more precious than the ore, so a cleansed priesthood will be more worthy of serving Yahweh. Indeed, purification implies the removal of the obstacles[99] which hindered them from coming near to God. Because everything which was related to God was holy, "nothing could penetrate within the realm of the divine unless it had first been 'sanctified,' i.e., unless it had been withdrawn from the realm of things profane.[100] The verb טָהַר specifically indicates the idea of suppression or removal of the profane to induce closeness with Yahweh. This is made especially clear in the accounts of the reforming efforts of Kings Hezekiah and Josiah. The desire to

[95] These are all P.

[96] For further discussion of מטהר, see below under טהר, pp. 151f.

[97] Sellin, 609; J. M. P. Smith, 68; G. A. Smith, *The Book of the Twelve Prophets* (2 vols.; New York: A. C. Armstrong and Son, 1899), 2.344.

[98] Cf. van Hoonacker, 731. A. Robinson believes that emphasis is placed on silver because the process of refining it is a very delicate and anxious operation, 189. As the silversmith lavishes care on his metal, so Yahweh will be extremely careful with the Levites.

[99] Cf. 2:1–9.

[100] Roland de Vaux, *Ancient Israel* (2 vols.; New York: McGraw-Hill, 1965) 2.464.

reestablish the correct relationship with Yahweh was evidenced by the commands to cleanse (טהר) the temple from unclean things (2 Chr 29:15, 16, 18) and Judah and Jerusalem from the במות with their images, i.e., Asherim (2 Chr 34:3, 5, 8). Similarly, Nehemiah cleansed (טהר) the temple chambers from household gods (13:9) and the priests from foreign contamination (13:30).

The verb טָהַר also expresses the idea of a ceremonial cleansing or purification, especially in preparation for sacred duties. In Num 8 Moses is told to separate the Levites from the rest of the Israelites, purify (טהר) them (v. 6) and so dedicate them to Yahweh's service (v. 16). It is made abundantly clear that only after the Levites were cleansed of sin and dressed in clean garments could they enter Yahweh's service in the tent of meeting, vv. 15, 22. The parallels between Num 8:5–22 and Mal 3:3–4 are too significant to be ignored. In both cases, purification is the means by which the Levites are separated out and dedicated to the proper performance of their work. As Malachi attests, only when the Levites have been cleansed will they perform their tasks correctly and in a manner pleasing to Yahweh (3:3d–3:4a). In essence, it is the act of purification that binds the Levites closely to Yahweh, cf. Num 8:14: והיו לי הלוים; Mal 3:3d והיו ליהוה מגישי מנחה בצדקה. It is reckoned by Malachi as one of the traits marking the coming day of Yahweh.

The very words the prophet employs to describe Yahweh's method of cleansing the priesthood are used by the psalmist to describe Yahweh himself. It is said:

אמרות יהוה
אמרות טהרות
כסף צרוף בעליל לארץ מזקק שבעתים

"Yahweh's words are words that are pure,
silver refined in a furnace on the ground
and purified seven times" (12:7).[101]

The emphasis here is on Yahweh's trustworthiness and his otherness. In fundamental contrast to the hypocritical and impure men of the psalmist's generation, Yahweh keeps his word and

---

[101] Ringgren, 216.

remains faithful to it. The promised deliverance will come to those devoted to his service.

Malachi's announcement of Yahweh's purification of the priesthood does not imply that the Levites will thereby become godlike, i.e., pure (טָהוֹר) like Yahweh. Rather, when Malachi says that they will be refined (צָרף) and cleansed (טָהַר) like silver (כֶּסֶף), purified (זָקַק, piel pf.) like gold and silver (3:3), he is simply asserting that the conditions necessary for a proper relationship with Yahweh will be reestablished; through purification, the obstacles which hindered their coming near to God will be removed (cf. 1:6–2:9).

Malachi's use of the term בְּנֵי־לֵוִי, sons of Levi, i.e., Levites, is another example of the continuity of his prophecy. In the second oracle unit (1:6–2:9), Malachi constructed a "levite-*cohen*" model in which the term *"cohen"* was used to represent the current degenerate priesthood and "levite" the priestly ideal.[102] It is through Yahweh's cleansing work (3:3–4) that the levitical ideal will be attained once again.[103]

. . . וְהָיוּ לַיהוה: "und sie werden Jahve Opfergaben darbringen in Gerechtigkeit bzw. dass sie dem Jahve werden Darbringer von Opfergaben in Gerechtigkeit."[104] "Bei dieser Übersetzung sind Subjekt die Levisöhne, Prädikat ist מַגִּישֵׁי מִנְחָה wahrend לַיהוה dätivisches Objekt bzw. Dativus commodi ist."[105] This translation is accepted by the majority of scholars, including von Orelli, van Hoonacker, Sellin and J. M. P. Smith.[106] As van Hoonacker asserted:

> . . . la tournure est choisie à l'effet de signifier que non seulement les actions rituelles des Lévites seront accomplies conformément aux exigences divines; mais que les Lévites euxmêmes, purifiés, comme il vient d'être dit,

[102] Cf. pp. 72–80.

[103] His use of "levite" here may also have been conditioned by his reliance on Num 8.

[104] von Bulmerincq, 2.366. For the use of the participle + הִנֵּה see GKC #119s, 381.

[105] von Bulmerincq, 2.366 and cf. GKC #116r, 360.

[106] C. von Orelli, *The Twelve Minor Prophets* (Edinburgh: T. & T. Clark, 1893) 392.

exerceront leur ministère avec les dispositions subjectives
voulues.[107]

There is, however, another option that should be explored.
Numbers 8 describes the selection of the Levites for service at the
tent of meeting. They are first separated from the Israelites at
large and then they are cleansed. The consequence of these
actions is their dedication to Yahweh: והבדלת את־הלוים מתוך בני
ישראל והיו לי הלוים (8:14). This same sequence of events is
perceived in Malachi. The Levites are singled out for Yahweh's
attention; they are purified, they become Yahweh's own. The
clause וְהָיוּ לִי הַלְוִים, "and the Levites will be mine," in Num 8:14,
is paralleled in Mal 3:3 by וְהָיוּ לַיהוה "And those (i.e., the
Levites) who bring[108] an offering with the proper intent will be
Yahweh's." Further, this translation option clearly points out
the syntactic similarity between Mal 3:3d and 3:4a: וְעָרְבָה לַיהוה
מִנְחַת יְהוּדָה וִירוּשָׁלָם, "Thus the offering of Judah and Jerusalem will be pleasing (ערב, qal pf. 3 f.s., 'to be sweet, pleasing,' cf. Jer 6:20)[109] to Yahweh." In both cases the predicate
(vb + ל + obj.) is placed before the subject in order to lay special
emphasis on it.[110] Malachi's intent is obvious. He is signaling
the contrast between the priests as they have been and the priests
as they will be. In Mal 1:6-2:9 the priests are anything but
dedicated to Yahweh. They regard it as of no consequence
whether the sacrificial ritual is properly conducted or not; they
find their service a contemptible burden (1:7f). Significantly, the
priests have become estranged from Yahweh; they have abandoned his צְדָקָה, norm. Moreover, as 1:14 elucidates, they permit
the people to bring blemished unworthy offerings for sacrifice
on Yahweh's altar. His displeasure with prevailing attitudes and
conditions is signaled by his refusal to accept anymore offerings
from the priests hands (1:10)—

---

[107] van Hoonacker, 731-32.
[108] הגיש, hiphil of [נגש] is the verb used by Malachi to designate the bringing
near of offerings, cf. 1:7.
[109] BDB, 787.
[110] GKC #141L, 454.

אֵין־לִי חֵפֶץ בָּכֶם ...
וּמִנְחָה לֹא־אֶרְצֶה מִיֶּדְכֶם

This state of affairs will be righted when Yahweh comes (3:1f).
No longer will the priests despise Yahweh (1:6) but through
purification they will be rededicated to him (וְהָיוּ לַיהוה) 3:3, and
the cult will be reoriented—the priests will offer sacrifices with
the proper intent, according to the divine norms (בִּצְדָקָה). As
Ringgren maintains, the word צְדָקָה, generally translated "righteousness," does not mean what we usually understand by that
word. "It is neither exclusively nor even primarily a juristic or
moral concept. On the basis of Arabic, the original meaning of
the root is something like "be right, stable substantial," ... "conformity to a norm."[111]

צֶדֶק and צְדָקָה, " ... refer to the divine order that regulates
the world and universe, expressed in the regular cycle of the
seasons, in the alternation of day and night, heat and cold
and infertility of the earth. In other words, it is the order of
creation ..." that was instituted by God.[112] Significantly, in
human terms, righteousness designates behavior which is in
keeping with that order. G. W. Ahlström remarks that צְדָקָה,
right order, can only be maintained,

> ... through a right covenant relationship with Yahweh.
> This means that all Yahweh's commands and statutes
> given in the covenant must be kept.... Only through
> a rightly established and a rightly kept covenant can
> life in all aspects be guaranteed; for Joel, as for all
> other prophets, this can be established only by a correct
> Yahweh cult.[113]

Malachi's use of the word צְדָקָה is pivotal here. Indeed, it gives
perspective to the oracle unit as a whole. The right order (צְדָקָה)
can be established only by a proper covenant relationship with
Yahweh since, after all, that order was instituted by him.[114] It is

[111] Ringgren, 83.
[112] Ibid., 131.
[113] Ahlström, *Joel*, 97.
[114] Ibid., 97; Ringgren, 134.

especially significant that Malachi describes Yahweh as the covenant enforcer, reestablishing the correct relationship with his people on the day when he comes (3:1). The maintenance of the covenant relationship, however, is contingent upon a correct Yahweh cult.[115] Therefore, it should not be at all surprising that Yahweh's first order of concentration is the priests (3:3). Their cleansing results in an interior rededication to God's service that manifests itself in the offering of sacrifices according to covenant stipulations, in accordance with the divine norms (בִּצְדָקָה). Moreover, it follows that a reverent conscientious priesthood will not permit improper, blemished offerings that the people were previously wont to bring (1:14). Thus, the sacrifices of Judah and Jerusalem, the cult congregation,[116] will once again be pleasing to Yahweh (3:4); they will be ritually correct and properly offered.

. . . כִּימֵי עוֹלָם: The particular period to which reference is made cannot be known. It may be that Malachi is simply reflecting a common view that "the good old times" were all that could be desired, whereas the present age leaves everything to be desired. It is more probable, however, that by "the good old days" Malachi is referring to the time when the covenant with Levi bore its richest fruits, cf. 2:5f. This phrase, while exhibiting no parallelism with either 3:3d or 3:4a, is, nevertheless, internally parallel (עוֹלָם // קַדְמֹנִיּוֹת[117] // שָׁנִים // יְמֵי). The repetitiveness serves to emphasize the abrupt change in conditions that Yahweh's coming will bring.

[3:5]—Malachi now moves to the second stage of Yahweh's work of purification: the cleansing of the people at large. Here it becomes evident that Malachi is no mere ritualist, in the sense of being preoccupied with cultic sins to the exclusion of sins against humanity. The fulfillment of man's obligations to God does not release him from certain obligations to his fellow man, but involves the full discharge of the former as well as the latter.

The parallelism between these lines and the beginning of the oracle unit (2:17; 3:1) is striking and evidences once again the prophetic emphasis on continuity. קָרַב אֶל (qal pf.) means "to

---

[115] Ahlström, *Joel*, 97.
[116] Cf. pp. 89f.
[117] קַדְמֹנִיּוֹת, f. pl. adj., "front, east, aforetime," BDB, 869; cf. also Isa 43:18.

come, draw near, approach"[118] and corresponds to יָבוֹא in 3:1.[119]
The image is identical; Yahweh's day is the day when he comes,
draws near to his people.[120] That he draws near for the purpose
of judging (לַמִּשְׁפָּט) is an integral part of his work on that day
and, in fact, answers the question posed by his people at the
beginning of this oracle unit—אַיֵּה אֱלֹהֵי הַמִּשְׁפָּט, 2:17.[121] Although
קָרַב and בּוֹא are indeed synonymous, Malachi's use of קָרַב here
adds another dimension to the oracle, heightening the Yôm
Yahweh imagery. The noun קְרָב means "struggle, battle, war,
hostile approach,"[122] and drawing near to the other party was
primarily for the purpose of overcoming him by force.[123] The
Day of Yahweh signified essentially the moment of his epiphany
as king, which was the highlight of the autumn festival. Significantly, Yahweh became king, not just of Israel but of the
world, because he created it, because he established himself as
effective in cosmic conflict (cf. Pss 89:10-13; 93:1-4; 104:5-9).[124]
The result of his battle against the forces of chaos (unruly water,
monsters)[125] is מִשְׁפָּט, "right order," imposition of the effective
rule of Yahweh as King.[126] On his cultic day, the day of his
enthronement as King, Yahweh re-creates, that is, he battles
chaos once again, establishes an ordered cosmos, "an earth where
men can live (Isa. 45:18). He (again) establishes the 'right order,'
without which heaven and earth cannot exist. It is this establishment of the right order which the Hebrews express by the verb
šāphaṭ and the noun mišpāṭ."[127]

---

[118] BDB, 897; cf. also Gen 31:18; Num 18:42; [Exod 14:20; Judg 20:24—in an
angry sense].

[119] Note Isa 5:19 for the synonymity of בּוֹא // קרב.

[120] Mowinckel, 1.107, 118.

[121] Cf. pp. 139f. for a discussion of the judgment aspect of Yahweh's day.

[122] BDB, 898.

[123] Z. W. Falk remarks that 'it is only in a civilized state of society that the
conflict must be referred to the judgment of an arbitrator or to the divine
decision by ordeal. Language, however, has preserved the memory of the old
custom," "Hebrew Legal Terms," *JSS* 5 (1960) 354.

[124] Mowinckel, 1.143.

[125] Cf. Pss 46:13f; 89:10f; 74:12-14; Isa 51:9.

[126] Mowinckel, 1.146.

[127] Ibid., 146. Note also the specific association of the Day of Yahweh with
מִשְׁפָּט, Jer 25:30f; Joel 4:1-3; 9-12; Isa 2:5f; Zeph 1.

This theme of God's demonstration of effective kingship in the cosmic conflict with chaos was eventually historified in Israel to reflect God's day of reckoning with his enemies, his victory and the imposition of his government.[128] Mowinckel remarks that

> Yahweh's claim to the complete surrender of the people to him as their one and only God, and the inherent ethical approach of the Yahweh religion, resulted in picturing the just judgment of his coming as a judgment not only of their demonic and historical enemies and of the sinners within Israel, but as judgment of his own people as well.[129]

The yardstick against which his people are judged is their obedience to the covenant (cf. Ps 50), a yardstick implied by Malachi when he speaks of Yahweh's return as covenant enforcer (3:1).[130] The idea that Yahweh on his day will approach (קָרַב) to do battle is not unknown in the OT. Joel chapter 2 opens with the command to "Blow the horn" (תקעו שופר), "sound an alarm" (הריעו), a signal for men to be on their guard against an invading army. H. W. Wolff maintains that the "alert is motivated not by the approach of just any powerful enemy (v. 2b); rather 'the day of Yahweh' itself is 'coming'."[131] Zeph 1:14–16a also associates Yahweh's final day of judgment with the sounding of an alarm, calling the day of Yahweh explicitly a יום שופר ותרועה. Wolff continues:

> Joel presents the call to sound the horn-blast in the same form in which warning is given of an unnamed enemy in Hos. 5:8, and of the enemy from the north

---

[128] John Gray, "The Day of Yahweh in Cultic Experience and Eschatological Prospect," *SEÅ* 39 (1974) 14. Elsewhere Gray remarks "that Amos as well as his contemporaries related the cultic experience of Yahweh's effective power to prevail over chaos to the historical situation," 27.

[129] Mowinckel, 1.161.

[130] For a more detailed analysis of the relationship between the Yôm Yahweh and the covenant, see Gray, 1–37 and Mowinckel, 1.154f.

[131] H. W. Wolff, *Joel and Amos* (Philadelphia: Fortress, 1977), 43.

(cf. Joel 2:20), whom Yahweh will bring near, in Jer.
4:5-6 (cf. Jer. 6:1). Thus the association of the ancient
warning cry with the threat of a punitive campaign of
Yahweh himself already has its prehistory in Hosea
and Jeremiah. . . . In Zeph. 1:14-16 this topic was linked
closely with the theophany account in the Sinai tradition
and for the first time was combined with the catchword "Day of Yahweh" as the day of wrath against
Jerusalem.[132]

In Joel, the approaching army shows itself to be a disciplined,
irresistible conqueror of cities (2:7-9); its commander in chief is
none other than Yahweh himself (2:11). Jerusalem is in danger.[133]
In Zech 14, Yahweh's day, the day when he will reign as king
(14:9), has a double emphasis: He will lead the nations in battle
against Jerusalem, i.e., against his people (1-3), and in a turn
about, he will himself go forth and fight against those very
nations (14:3). Yahweh's day is a day of battle, יוֹם קְרָב (14:3).[134]

Malachi's use of קָרַב אֶל in this inimical sense, "to approach
with the purpose of overcoming by force," adds both scope and
power to the Yôm Yahweh imagery and intensifies the sense of
motion the prophet has created. Yahweh does not merely come
quietly to pass judgment (מִשְׁפָּט) on his people; he approaches
rapidly (מַהֵר), in full battle array. The implication is that just as
Yahweh first established 'right order,' מִשְׁפָּט through his pri-
mordial battle with the chaos monsters, cf. Ps 74:12-17, so he
will re-create that order by vanquishing the evildoers, the covenant offenders (Mal 3:5c-g) within his own community.[135]
Malachi used language to the greatest effect. By employing the
familiar image of Yahweh terrible in combat, he emphasized the
severity of the people's guilt. Their offenses were so manifold

---

[132] Ibid., 44.

[133] Ibid., 46.

[134] Cf. also Joel 4 where Yahweh appears both to lead an army against his
enemies and to judge them (vv. 9f). For a more detailed description of the
connection between the Day of Yahweh and his coming in battle, see G. von
Rad, *Old Testament Theology* (2 vols.; New York: Harper and Row, 1962-1975),
2.119f where he lists appropriate passages. See Gray, 12f for a critique of von
Rad's argument.

[135] For a discussion of משפט, see Ringgren, 132 and L. Köhler, Old Testament Theology (London: Lutterworth, 1957), 204f.

(cf. 3:5; 3:6-12) that mere threats on Yahweh's part no longer served to keep them in line. Malachi implies that it is time for decisive action.

עֵד מְמַהֵר בְּ :עֵד is a n.m. meaning 'witness.'[136] The combination of עֵד + בְּ means "to witness against" (cf. Num 5:13; Deut 19:15f; 31:26; Josh 24:22; 1 Sam 12:5; Mic 1:2; Prov 24:28). That Yahweh comes to witness or give testimony against the evildoers (cf. 3:5c–g) suits the thematic concerns of this oracle unit for, indeed, the Day of Yahweh is a day of judgment. However, the implications are far greater than this. As creator, as king of the world, Yahweh is also the supreme judge (Isa 33:22; Pss 50:6; 75:8; 94:2; 96:13). Therefore Yahweh not only testifies against his people, but also as judge, passes sentence on them. He is, in effect, witness, judge and jury.[137] Further, he describes himself as a 'swift witness,' עֵד מְמַהֵר (מהר, piel act. ptc., m.s.).[138] This suggests that the people's guilt is so patently visible that both testifying to their offenses and passing judgment on them can be done with all haste. Significantly, מְמַהֵר provides a fitting parallel to פִּתְאֹם in 3:1. As von Bulmerincq remarks: "Doch der Parallelismus mit פִּתְאֹם in v. 1 . . . legt es näher . . . an das Plötzliche, Unverhoffte des göttlichen Auftretens zu denken."[139]

מְכַשְּׁפִים is a piel m. pl. ptcpl. from כָּשַׁף, "to practice sorcery," hence "sorcerers," cf. Exod 7:11.[140] מְכַשְּׁפִים heads the list of those within the community against whom Yahweh testifies. In Exod 22:17 it is said—מכשפה לא תחיה, "You shall not allow a sorceress to live." The feminine form 'sorceress' may indicate the frequency with which the practice was identified with women, although the masculine form does occur, cf. Exod 7:11; Dan 2:2. Sorcery was a form of mantic practice identified with foreign cults (cf. Deut 18:12f; 2 Kgs 9:22), and was obviously a threat to

---

[136] BDB, 729. עֵד is derived from a middle weak verb עוּד meaning "to return, turn back, repeat, do again," cf. Arab. عاد, "return, do again." עֵד, as a the probable qal participle of עוּד, therefore means "reiterating," hence "emphatically affirming."

[137] Note Ps 50:6-7 where Yahweh as judge (שפט) testifies against (הֵעִיד בְּ) his people.

[138] Cf. also Gen 41:32; Prov 6:18.

[139] von Bulmerincq, 2.377.

[140] BDB, 506.

Israel's worship of Yahweh. It was labelled an 'abomination' (תּוֹעֵבָה) to Yahweh (Deut 18:12). According to Isa 47:9f, sorcerers laid claim to a power both of interpreting and controlling the future which opposed the authority of God. As a supposed source of divine help, sorcery was ridiculed by the prophets (Isa 5:11; 8:18f). Significantly, in Deut 18:15f, the office of the prophet is set over against diviner and sorcerer. The Israelites are enjoined to listen only to the prophet. When Isaiah (3:2-3) placed the "diviner" (קֹסֵם), the "skillful magician" (חֲכַם חֲרָשִׁים) and the "expert" in charms (נְבוֹן לָחַשׁ) on the same plane as mighty men, soldiers, judges and prophets, he merely stated a known fact— namely, the importance attached to these practitioners in the life of the people and the state. And in keeping with this high regard for magicians King Manasseh made public use of their services (2 Chr 33:6). The people, of course, did likewise. Jeremiah (27:9) appeals directly to the people not to put trust in "your diviners (קֹסְמֵיכֶם), your soothsayers (עֹנְנֵיכֶם), or your sorcerers (כַּשָּׁפֵיכֶם)." It is obvious that belief in the efficacy of the magic arts was deeply rooted.[141] Von Rad remarks that Yahwism's "unyielding inflexibility against magic" begins "from the moment magic reveals itself as a well-tried technique for influencing the deity, or when man, with its aid, takes into his own control, to further his own needs, events or powers that belong to the deity."[142] He continues:

> Jahweh's invasive power . . . was absolutely incompatible with the impersonal, automatic action of the operation of the forces of magic. Neither was this Jahweh made available by being influenced by magic; nor could people ward him off by means of magical invocations; nor was it possible, by, as it were, a highhanded drawing upon his powers, to achieve effects which did not proceed in the most direct and personal fashion from himself.[143]

That sorcerers are included in Malachi's list of those who will be punished on Yahweh's day should not be surprising. First, they presumed to appropriate for themselves powers that, by rights, belong to Yahweh alone as king (1:14), lord (3:1) and creator (2:10). Second, they lied to the people, estranging

[141] Pedersen, 1.125.
[142] von Rad, 1.34-35.
[143] Ibid., 35.

them from Yahweh by telling them what they wanted to hear rather than what Yahweh willed (cf. Jer 23:9f; 27:9f). Third, sorcerers obviously tried to influence gods other than Yahweh (cf. Deut 18:9f; 2 Kgs 9:22), creating divided loyalties that he will no longer tolerate.

מְנָאֲפִים: piel m. pl. ptc. of נאף, "to commit adultery."[144] In the OT adultery is viewed as a "violation de la fidélité conjugal, à laquelle homme et femme etaient également tenus"[145] (cf. Exod 20:14; Deut 5:18; Lev 18:20; 20:10; Deut 22:22f). It has been observed that according to the Hebrew idiom "the man can only commit adultery against a marriage other than his own, the woman only against her own."[146] The punishment for adultery is death (Deut 22:22), while seduction or violation of a virgin requires that the man either marry her or offer monetary compensation (Exod 22:15; Deut 22:28f). The evidence within the OT clearly suggests that adultery was placed in a different category from fornication; the commandments refer specifically to the former.

Perhaps the best commentary on the seriousness with which Israel viewed adultery is reflected in the narratives dealing with the subject. "It is the 'great sin' mentioned in certain Egyptian . . . texts, the 'great sin' which the king of Gerar almost committed with Sarah" (Gen 20:9).[147] Joseph rebuffs Potiphar's wife lest he "do this great wickedness and sin against God" (Gen 39:9). In Job, adulterers are linked with murderers (24:14f) and in Jer 9:2, with treacherous men. As a social offense, adultery not only destroyed the intimacy of the family unit but caused a breach of community solidarity as well.[148]

---

[144] BDB, 610.

[145] Walter Kornfeld, "L'adultère dans l'Orient antique," *RB* 57 (1950) 93.

[146] J. J. Stamm and M. E. Andrew, *The Ten Commandments in Recent Research* (SBT 2.5; London: SCM, 1967), 100; cf. also de Vaux: "The husband is exhorted to be faithful to his wife in Prov. 5:15-19, but this infidelity is punished only if he violates the rights of another man by taking a married woman as his accomplice," 1.37.

[147] de Vaux, 1.37. Cf. also, W. L. Moran, "The Scandal of the 'Great Sin' at Ugarit," *JNES* 18 (1959) 280-88; J. J. Rabinowitz, "The 'Great Sin' in Ancient Egyptian Marriage Contracts," *JNES* 18 (1959) 73.

[148] Kornfeld remarks: "Pour Israël, l'adultère est considéré comme un obstacle à la volonté de Yahvé, ce crime retombant sur le peuple tout entier. En raison de cette solidarité morale le peuple est chargé de la vengeance ou du maintien de la justice originaire. A la base de cette jurisdiction, il y avait non un désir

Adultery is not just a social offense against one's neighbors
and community; it also refers metaphorically to idolatrous
worship and thus becomes a sin against Yahweh. Hos. 2:4 reads:

ריבו באמכם ריבו
כי־היא לא אשתי
ואנכי לא אישה
ותסר זנוניה מפניה
ונאפופיה מבין שדיה[149]

> Accuse your mother! Accuse!
> For she is not my wife
>   and I am not her husband.
> Let her remove her harlotries from her face,
>   her adulteries from between her breasts.

In this verse Yahweh appears as the plaintiff against his unfaithful spouse. Her lovers are the *ba'alīm* and to them she offers
sacrifice (2:15), thanking them for gifts which had, in reality,
been bestowed by Yahweh (2:10). When the people turned for
support to lovers, i.e., other gods (2:7), they severed their intimate
relationship with Yahweh just as adultery destroyed the marriage
bond. Isa 57:3f is a scathing denunciation of those who indulged
in idolatrous rites. They are called בְּנֵי עֹנְנָה, children of the
sorceress,[150] and זֶרַע מְנָאֵף, seed of the adulterer, and they indulge
their lust among the oaks and under every green tree, slaying
their children in the valleys and under the clefts of rocks.[151]
    In Malachi, the adulterers, מְנָאֲפִים, have committed not just
a social offense against their wives and community, but have
committed a religious breach as well. It is very probable that
Malachi is referring to those who intermarry, cf. 2:10-16. Not
only do they leave their Judean spouses, their legitimate wives,
but they are also lured by their new wives to the worship of
foreign gods (2:11f), leaving Yahweh as well.
    נִשְׁבָּעִים לַשֶּׁקֶר: נִשְׁבָּעִים is a niphal m. pl. ptc. from שבע, "to
swear;"[152] שֶׁקֶר is a n.m. meaning "deception, disappointment,

---

d'intimidation mais un sentiment typique de solidarité et de responsabilité
collective," 95.
[149] נאוף, n. [m.], "adultery," BDB, 610.
[150] Note that both here and in Mal 3:5 sorcerers and adulterers are allied.
[151] Cf. also Jer 3:8; 13:27; Ezek 23:37.
[152] BDB, 989.

falsehood,"[153] hence, "those who swear falsely." It is significant that just as there are religious and social implications involved in the actions of the מְנָאֲפִים, the adulterers, so too do "false swearers" commit offenses against both Yahweh and the community. It is evident from a study of the OT that the use of the name of God played an important part in Israel's faith. One 'called' on the name (קרא, cf. Gen 4:26), 'blessed' the name (ברך, Ps 72:19), 'praised' the name (הלל, Ps 69:31), 'trusted' (בטח, Isa 50:10) and 'sought refuge in' the name (חסה, Zeph 3:12).[154] Similarly, in swearing an oath the name of Yahweh was called upon (Lev 19:12; Deut 6:13; 10:20; 1 Sam 20:42). However, the misuse of the name was obviously a continuing threat. Therefore, it was forbidden to 'profane' his name (חלל, Lev 20:3), to 'curse' his name (קלל, 2 Kgs 2:24), to 'defile' his name (טמא, Ezek 43:8), to 'swear falsely' by his name (שבע לשקר, Lev 19:12). The prohibitions against the misuse of Yahweh's name were attempts to protect the divine name, identified with God's being itself, from abuse within the cultic sphere and without. This is reflected most clearly in the command in Lev 19:12: ולא־תשבעו בשמי לשקר וחללת את־שם אלהיך אני יהוה, which focuses on the one concrete abuse of using the name to support a false oath which was intended to inflict evil on another (cf. 19:11).[155] Indeed, because "every genuine oath was accompanied by invocation of the deity," a false oath in testimony profaned Yahweh and had the potential to injure one's fellow man.[156] This connection is made clear in Zech 8:16-17:[157]

(16)   אלה הדברים אשר תעשו
דברו אמת איש את־רעהו
אמת ומשפט שלום שפטו בשעריכם

(17)   ואיש את־רעת רעהו אל־תחשבו בלבבכם
ושבעת שקר אל־תאהבו
כי את־כל־אלה אשר שנאתי נאם יהוה

---

[153] Ibid., 1055.
[154] von Rad, 1.184f.
[155] Note Exod 22:10 where a man takes an oath in the name of Yahweh that he has not stolen.
[156] von Rad, 1.184.
[157] Cf. also Lev 5:20f.

Jeremiah gives two startling examples of the relationship between false swearing and serving other gods. Although the people say, "As Yahweh lives," they swear falsely (5:2, לשקר ישבעו). They commit adultery (ינאפו) by swearing by gods that are not (5:7). Because they have abandoned Yahweh to serve other gods, so he will abandon them to the mercy of strangers (5:19, זָרִים). In Jer 7, Yahweh lists the offenses committed by his people. They oppress (עשק) the widow, orphan and resident alien;[158] they steal, murder, commit adultery (נאף) and swear falsely (הִשָּׁבֵעַ לַשֶּׁקֶר) 7:6-9. Although they burn incense to Baal and go after other gods, they still come to stand before Yahweh in his house and, believing that they are forgiven, they go out and commit these abominations (תוֹעֵבוֹת) all over again (7:9-12). Only when the people return to Yahweh alone may they again swear by his name, 4:1-2.

The false swearers condemned in Mal 3:5 have committed this double abuse. They have allied themselves with other gods (2:11) and yet come to Yahweh's altar swearing their devotion (2:13-14).[159] They have invoked his name in testimony and yet lie and so defraud their neighbors.[160]

עשְׁקֵי :וּבְעשְׁקֵי שְׂכַר־שָׂכִיר אַלְמָנָה וְיָתוֹם is a qal. m. pl. ptc. from עָשַׁק, "to oppress, to treat violently, to defraud, extort."[161] שְׂכַר is a n.m. cs. (שָׂכָר) meaning "wages" (of a hireling);[162] שָׂכִיר is a n.m. meaning "hireling,"[163] cf. שָׂכַר (Arab. شكر, "to hire.")[164] Van Hoonacker suggests changing שְׂכַר־שָׂכִיר to שכר שכר or just שכיר since "it is evidently the mercenary and not the wages that is the object of עשק."[165] Moreover, the combination עשק שכיר

---

[158] Cf. Mal 3:5.

[159] That the people believe they are wholehearted in the fulfillment of Yahweh's demands is revealed in their questioned disbelief of his refusal to accept future sacrifices from them (2:14).

[160] Admittedly this is a subjective interpretation. Nevertheless, since the people are accused of defrauding the hireling of his wages and oppressing the widow and orphan, such conduct in court does not seem unlikely, cf. also Zech 8:16-17. Note that von Bulmerincq contends that נשבעים לשקר should be enlarged to נשבעים בשמי לשקר, 2.380-381. Such a clarification is unnecessary since Yahweh's name can easily be inferred from the context.

[161] *Gesenius' Hebrew and Chaldee Lexicon*, 660.

[162] Ibid., 790.

[163] Ibid., 789.

[164] Ibid., 790.

[165] van Hoonacker, 732.

coordinates better with אלמנה and יתום.[166] Von Bulmerincq emends to ובעשקי שכיר וּשְׂכָרוֹ on the basis of Deut 24:14-15.[167] The Deuteronomy passage commands the people not to oppress (עשק) the hireling (שכיר) whether Israelite or sojourner. He is to receive his wages (שָׂכָרוֹ) on the day he earns them; they are necessary because of his poverty. Should he not be recompensed, his cry to Yahweh will indicate that an offense has been committed (והיה בך חטא), Deut 24:15.[168] Similarly, Lev 19:13 states that the laborer's wages (פְּעֻלַּת שָׂכִיר) should not be withheld overnight. Obviously, according to both Deut 24:14-15 and Lev 19:13, the hireling is oppressed or treated unjustly when his wages remain unpaid. Viewed in this manner, the emendations proposed by both van Hoonacker (עשק שכיר) and von Bulmerincq (עשק שכיר ושכרו) have merit. However, the need to emend the text is obviated when it is recalled that עָשַׁק also means "to defraud," "rob." Thus, the phrase may be translated, [I will be a swift witness] "against those who rob the wages of the hireling." Significantly, the idea of oppressing or treating the laborer unjustly is implicit in this rendering—he is oppressed when his wages are withheld, cf. Deut 24:14-15. Moreover, the precise meaning "to oppress" comes to the fore in coordination with אלמנה and יתום: [והייתי עד ממהר] בעשקי אלמנה ויתום, [and I will be a swift witness] against those who oppress the widow and the orphan. This same use of עשק to mean both "rob" and "treat unjustly" within the same sentence can be found in Mic 2:2. Those devising iniquity (2:1), עשקו גבר וביתו ואיש ונחלתו, "oppress a man and wrest away his house, [oppress] a man and rob him of his heritage."

The protection of the widow (אלמנה) and the orphan (יתום) was a common policy of the ancient Near East. They were individuals who had lost their natural protectors and were thus in need of special consideration (cf. Zech 7:10; Isa 1:17; 10:2; Jer 7:6; Exod 22:21-24; Deut 24:17f; 26:12; Prov 13:31; 19:17; 22:9). From the earliest times on, a strong king promulgated stipulations in connection with the protection of this group. Indeed, such protection was viewed as a virtue of gods, kings and

---

[166] Ibid., 732. Cf. also, Sellin, 609; J. M. P. Smith, 65, 68.

[167] von Bulmerincq, 2.383.

[168] Note that Deut 24:17 also cautions the people with regard to their behavior with the sojourner (גר), orphan (יתום) and widow (אלמנה), cf. Mal 3:5.

judges.[169] It is also obvious that this policy was closely connected with social reform or a new legal promulgation. In bad times, in times of decay, the protection of the widow and orphan was neglected.[170] In the OT the protection of the weak is regarded vertically and horizontally. The vertical protection comes from God while the horizontal protection comes from the people. This is made clear in the Covenant Code, Exod 22:21-24, where the oppression of widows and orphans was forbidden and a severe punishment pronounced for offenders (וחרה אפי והרגתי אתכם בחרב). As a direct command from God to his people (כל-אלמנה ויתום לא תענון, Exod 22:21), the vertical line is drawn and closely linked with the horizontal responsibility. The divine concern for the widow and orphan is also revealed in Deut 10:18. Yahweh, "the great god, mighty and awesome," is also the god who עשה משפט יתום ואלמנה. Further, according to Deut 27:19, anyone who abuses the rights of the widow and orphan comes under Yahweh's curse.

The prophetic protestations against injustices toward widows and orphans[171] reveal that they were not merely sporadic evidences of man's inhumanity to man. As people without relatives, money or influence, the widow and orphan were easy targets for abuse by the unscrupulous. Their position was tenuous at best and that it deteriorated during Malachi's time should not be surprising. The general poverty induced by the Persian economic policy (cf. Neh 5) coupled with poor harvests (Mal 3:11) were probably directly responsible for the lack of concern for orphans and widows and for the apparent inability to pay laborers promptly. Despite this, however, Mal 3:5 views the situation from the divine perspective. Man's inhumanity to man reveals a contempt for Yahweh. The weak within the community were objects of Yahweh's special care and protection (Deut 10:18) and he commanded his people to extend a like consideration. Failure to do so creates a breach between Yahweh and the community and results in severe punishment (cf. Exod 22:21-24; Deut 27:19).

---

[169] F. Charles Fensham, "Widow, Orphan and the Poor in Ancient Near Eastern Legal and Wisdom Literature," *JNES* 21 (1962) 129.

[170] Ibid.

[171] Cf. Zech 7:10; Isa 1:17; 10:2; Mic 2:9; Jer 5:28; 7:6.

מַטֵּי־גֵּר מַטֵּי: is a hiphil m. pl. (cs.) ptcpl. from נטה "to extend, incline, turn, turn away" (qal); "to incline, turn away; decline" (hiphil). [172] הַטָּה usually has as its direct object "justice" (מִשְׁפָּט) (cf. Prov 17:23; Exod 23:6; Deut 16:19; 1 Sam 8:3). Von Bulmerincq remarks that "הַטָּה ist hier wie Jes. 29, 21. Amos 5, 12 mit dem Akkus. der Person Konstruiert, doch mit Recht erklären schon Kimḥi and I.-Ezra מַטֵּי־גֵּר als elliptische Ausdrucksweise für מַטֵּי מִשְׁפָּט גֵּר." [173] According to H. W. Wolff, the clause ואביונים בשער הטו, Amos 5:12, is an abbreviated form of הטה משפט. [174] "The expression 'in the gate' (בשער) shows that it is the whole of the local judiciary proceeding which is in view." [175] Similarly, in Amos 2:7, נטה דרך is an abbreviated equivalent of "to pervert the courses of justice" (הטו ארחות משפט) (cf. Prov 17:23; 18:5). [176] The tenor of Malachi suggests that he too is using this abbreviated form הטה גר for הטה משפט גר.

> The term gēr describes a person who lives in a community which is not his own. [177] He may be an Israelite, a stranger, or a traveler. [178] But the word has its own special sphere as a designation of a great class of fellow citizens who are not born Israelites, but attach themselves to the Israelitic community. That their importance was considerable may be inferred from the fact that the laws very often mention them together with the native Israelite (ʿezrāh). [179]

Generally speaking they were poor. When the towns in which they lived were taken over by the Israelites, the latter appropriated their land and the "gērīm were reduced to penury." [180] They supported themselves as paid workmen (Exod 20:10; Lev 22:10;

---

[172] *Gesenius' Hebrew and Chaldee Lexicon*, 546.
[173] von Bulmerincq, 2.386 and cf. the LXX—ἐκκλίνοντας κρίσιν προσηλύτου.
[174] Wolff, *Joel and Amos*, 249.
[175] Ibid., 248.
[176] Ibid., 166.
[177] Cf. T. M. Horner, "Changing Concepts of the 'Stranger' in the OT," *ATR* 42 (1960) 49-53; H. Wildberger, "Israel und sein Land," *EvTh* 16 (1956) 402-22, esp. 417-20.
[178] Pedersen, 1.40.
[179] Ibid., 40.
[180] Ibid., 41.

25:6). Like the poor they were to be permitted to gather what was left behind in fields and vineyards (Lev 19:10; 23:22; Deut 24:16) and like the widow and orphan, the *gēr* was to be allotted a share of the tithe (Deut 14:28-29). No special laws were created for them. On the contrary, they were to be judged according to the same principles as the Israelites; they were to be treated righteously in judgment (Deut 1:16; 24:17; 27:19). Deut 10:18 says that Yahweh loves the *gēr* and thus gives him food and clothing. Out of this it is concluded that the Israelites are to love the *gēr* (10:19) because they themselves were *gērīm* in Egypt.

> The constantly repeated admonitions, which even recur in writings full of hatred against the foreign, especially the Canaanite spirit, can only mean that these *gērīm* have gradually become so closely allied with the Israelites that the original difference has vanished.[181]

Just as with widows and orphans, the protection of the *gēr* is regarded vertically and horizontally. Yahweh's love for the *gēr* and his responsibility for feeding and clothing him becomes the people's responsibility (Deut 10:18-19). Significantly, in Deut 27:16, the widow, orphan and *gēr* are linked together. Those who violate their rights (מַטֶּה מִשְׁפָּט) come under Yahweh's curse.

יְרֵאוּנִי וְלֹא יְרֵאוּנִי: is a qal pt. m. pl. + suffix from ירא, "to fear, stand in awe of, have reverence for."[182] The phrase יראת יהוה, "fear of Yahweh," contains within it the notion of obedience to his commands and statutes, Deut 6:2, 24; 8:6; 13:4; 28:58; 31:13. "Dans tous ces passages *jir°at Jhwh* indique l'obéissance de l'homme à Dieu. Il s'est soumis à Dieu et s'est placé envers Lui dans un rapport de servitude. Craindre Jhwh veut dire servir Jhwh,"[183] Deut 6:13; 10:20; Josh 24:14; 1 Sam 12:14, 24. Man is not, however, a mere slave since "fear of Yahweh" is synonymous with loving him (אהב), Deut 10:12, clinging to him (דבק), Deut 10:20, and following him (הלך אחרי יהוה), Deut 13:5. It expresses

---

[181] Ibid., 41.

[182] BDB, 431.

[183] H. A. Brongers, "La Crainte du Seigneur (Jir°at Jhwh, Jir°at °Elohim)," *OTS* 5 (1948) 161.

la base des normes de la vie qui doivent être respectées dans le monde. La crainte de Dieu impose à l'homme certaines obligations vis-à-vis du prochain. C'est une attitude pieuse qui prouve son authenticité et sa vérité justement dans les rapports avec lui. Aussi l'humanité, chez les Israelites, n'a-t-elle pas une base rationaliste et utilitaire, mais, au contraire, elle a ses racines dans la crainte de Dieu. En d'autres termes, l'éthique n'y est pas autonome, mais elle est liée étroitement avec la religion.[184]

Sellin correctly observes that "Das לֹא יְרָאוּנִי fasst alle vorher aufgezählten Sünden zusammen und nennt ihr Wurzel: die mangelnde Gottesfurcht. Die ganze Klasse der Gottlosen wird also verurteilt, das ist die tröstende Verheissung für die Gottes-fürchtigen."[185] Although Malachi does indeed take issue in this verse with man's inhumanity to man, the thrust is far deeper. Yahweh's demands upon men should be fulfilled; the vertical line is inseparable from the horizontal responsibility. In the final analysis therefore, man's inhumanity to man is sympto-matic of a profound contempt for Yahweh himself.

Discussion

Malachi's eschatology finds expression in this oracle unit and in 1:11. The problem has been to reconcile these passages. Van Hoonacker remarks that the messianic renovation announced in v. 11 was envisaged as a "répudiation du sacerdoce et des sacrifices lévitiques. Au chap. 3 la note dominante est tout autre."[186] According to M. Rehm, Mal 1:11 looks forward to a messianic age in which the prescriptions of the law of the single sanctuary and the Levitical priesthood will be impossible, when the plan of salvation must revert to former institutions, as when sacrifice was the prerogative of every family head.[187] His analysis, however, seems to leave out of perspective the prophecy of 3:1-5 on the Levitical priesthood. When Malachi's obvious devotion to cult and priestly purity is taken into account, it is hardly realistic to

---

[184] Ibid., 164.
[185] Sellin, 610.
[186] van Hoonacker, 729.
[187] Martin Rehm, "Das Opfer der Völker nach Mal. 1.11," *Lex Tua Veritas: Festschrift für Hubert Junker* (Trier: Paulinus-Verlag, 1961) 201.

interpret his messianic teaching apart from these. Therefore, if 1:11 is to be taken as a reference to the messianic age, it must be reconciled with 3:1-5; the solution cannot be found in denying the manifestly messianic character of 3:1-5.

It is extremely important to recognize that Malachi is a unity. The individual oracle units do not stand alone but are, in fact, interrelated and thus, the thematic dependence of one on the other requires that the whole be viewed before judgments can be passed on individual parts. Significantly, both the oracle unit in which 1:11 appears (1:6-2:9) and 3:1-5 deal with priest and cult and both advance the thesis that prevailing conditions will be transformed; the future will be the inverse of the present. Taken as complementary parts of a single vision, it becomes evident that there is movement from a general formulation (1:11) to one that is more specific (3:1-5). According to 1:11, sacrifices will not cease but the manner in which they are offered and those who offer them will be changed. A pure sacrifice, a sacrifice made with the proper intent, will replace the impure (מֻקְטָר מֻגָּשׁ לִשְׁמִי וּמִנְחָה טְהוֹרָה). These thoughts are particularized in 3:1-5. Those who offer the sacrifice, the Levites, will be cleansed (3:3) and it is their purification and reorientation that will result in offerings proffered בִּצְדָקָה (3:3), in offerings that are pleasing to Yahweh (3:4). Significantly, M.-J. Lagrange contends that in 1:11 Malachi "songe encore aux Lévites mais aux Lévites purifiés (3:3), à un sacrifice offert au nom de Iahvé connu comme tel,"[188] Recognizing the interrelatedness of 1:11 and 3:1-5, Chary remarks that "les deux pointes messianiques du livre relèvent du domaine cultuel: au jour de Yahweh, il purifiera les lévites pour les rendre aptes au culte parfait: Mal. 3:3-4, et de même, a l'époque messianique, l'offrande sacrificielle sera parfaite: 1:11."[189]

The movement from general (1:11) to particular (3:3-4) is complemented by parallel movement from the nations (1:11) to Israel (3:3-4), a movement from universalism to particularism. In 1:11 it is stated that proper sacrifice will be offered everywhere (בכל־מקום) and that Yahweh's name will be great among the nations. In 2:17f "l'horizon est limité à Israel et même plus

---

[188] Lagrange, 81.
[189] Chary, 178.

strictement à Juda et Jerusalem, c'est-à-dire la communauté postexilienne regroupée autour du temple."[190]

The description of movement that begins on the outer reaches and culminates in the center is not uncommon in the OT. In Joel 2:21f,

> the admonition to rejoice and be glad is given first to the country, then to the beasts of the field, and finally in v. 23 to the בני ציון, the population and cult congregation of Jerusalem. The composition starts with the outer circle and proceeds to the inner circle, the center, so that the בני ציון get an assurance that what is necessary for life will be restored, namely the life-giving rain which gives an abundant harvest.[191]

Similarly, Ps 89:6f begins with the cosmic aspects of Yahweh's actions and moves to the center (vv. 15ff), that is, the cult congregation of Jerusalem, the cultic procession and the people rejoicing over Yahweh's deeds[192] (cf. also Amos 1–2; Isa 66:18–24; Gen 1:1f; Pss 24; 29; 95:3–8; 97).

What characterizes this oracle unit above all else is the constant sensation of movement toward Israel;[193] Yahweh is coming (בָּא, יָבוֹא, 3:1), drawing even nearer (קָרַב אֶל, 3:5). Only by viewing this oracle unit within the wider context of the prophecy as a whole does this sense of movement find its highest expression. The renewal that begins with the nations (1:11) culminates in the transformation of Yahweh's own people (3:1-5).

---

[190] Ibid., 179.

[191] Ahlström, *Joel*, 6–7.

[192] G. W. Ahlström, *Psalm 89: Eine Liturgie aus dem Ritual des leidenden Königs* (Lund: G. W. K. Gleerups, 1959) 91.

[193] Cf. p. 124.

CHAPTER IX

MALACHI 3:6-12

$Z\ A^2B^2$	6כי אני יהוה לא שניתי
$A_1{}^3B_1{}^2$	ואתם בני־יעקב לא כליתם
A^2BC	7למימי אבתיכם סרתם מחקי
$B_1{}^2$	ולא שמרתם
DED_1E_1	שובו אלי ואשובה אליכם
F^3	אמר יהוה צבאות
$F_1D_1{}^2$	ואמרתם במה נשוב
$A\ B\ C$	8היקבע אדם אלהים
$(Z)\ B\ A_1\ C$	כי אתם קבעים אתי
$D\ A_{11}{}^2\ (C)$	ואמרתם במה קבענוך1
E^2	המעשר והתרומה
$A\ B\ C$	9במארה אתם נארים
$A_1B\ C_1$	ואתי אתם קבעים
$B_1{}^\varrho$	הגוי כלו2
$A\ B^3\ C^3$	10הביאו את־כל־המעשר אל־בית־האוצר
$D\ B_1\ C_1$	ויהי טרף בביתי
$A_1{}^3$	ובחנוני נא בזאת אמר יהוה צבאות
$A^3\ B$	אם־לא אפתח לכם
C^3	את ארבות השמים
$A_1\ B$	והריקתי לכם
$C_1{}^4$	ברכה עד־בלי־די
$A_{11}\ B\ C_{11}$	11וגערתי לכם באכל
$A^2\ B\ C^3$	ולא־ישחת לכם את־פרי האדמה
$A_1{}^2\ B\ C_1{}^2$	ולא תשכל לכם הגפן בשדה

---

[1] Note that the suffix ך (c) on קבענו refers to אלהים, אתי identified by ''C'' in 3:8a, b.

[2] Both במארה (3:9a) and אתי (3:9b) are objects of the ensuing participial clauses and as such are designated by the same letter (A). Note also the parallelism between 3:9b and 3:8b.

אמר יהוה צבאות
non-parallel unit}   ¹²ואשרו אתכם כל־הגוים
כי־תהיו אתם ארץ חפץ
אמר יהוה צבאות

(3:6)   "For I, Yahweh, do not go back on my word.
        But as for you, O sons of Jacob, you are not destroyed.
(3:7)   From the days of your fathers you turned aside
            from my statutes, and did not keep them.
        Return to me and I will return to you," says Yahweh of
            Hosts.
        But you say: "In respect of what shall we return?"
(3:8)   "Will a man rob God?
        Yet you are robbing me.
        But you say: 'Wherein have we robbed you?'
        In the tithe and in the levy.
(3:9)   You are cursed with the curse,
        Yet you continue to rob me—the entire nation.
(3:10) Bring the entire tithe to the store-house
            that there may be food in my house.
        And test me through this," says Yahweh of Hosts.
        "I will indeed open the sluices of heaven for you,
            and pour out a blessing for you until there is no more
                need.
(3:11) And I will restrain the devourer for you,
        And he shall not destroy the produce of your land;
        Neither shall the vine in the field fail to bear for you,"
            says Yahweh of Hosts.
(3:12) "And all the nations shall consider you fortunate;
        For you will be inhabitants of a desirable land," says
            Yahweh of Hosts.

Content and Structure

This the fifth oracle unit flows directly out of the closing
verse (3:5) of the fourth.[3] In 3:5, the evildoers within the community are sentenced for their crimes. It should be recalled that

[3] Ernst Sellin, *Das Zwölfprophetenbuch übersetzt und erklärt* (KAT 12/2;
Leipzig: A Deichertsche, 1930) 611, maintains that this oracle unit is not linked
to the preceding section. Instead of the desired announcement of Yahweh's

their offenses are not merely sins against their fellowmen, but
sins against Yahweh himself, i.e., cultic sins.[4] The exact nature
of their cultic failings is enunciated in 3:6-12. It is significant
that the evildoers here and the priests in the second oracle unit,
1:6-2:9, are adjudged guilty of the same sorts of crimes. Both are
condemned for dishonesty and fraudulent practices in the offering of sacrifices (cf. 1:7-9; 12-13; 3:8). Both have turned aside
from Yahweh's laws (cf. 2:8; 3:7) and, as a result, both are cursed
(cf. 2:2; 3:9). The similarity of the abuses should not be surprising. In 1:14 it is implied that the priests' contemptuous
attitude toward their cultic responsibilities has spilled over onto
the people. They too bring blemished offerings and think nothing of their deceit. Conversely, 3:3-4 explicitly aver that when
the priests are cleansed, when they again honor their duties and
stand in the proper relationship to Yahweh, their realignment
will result in the realignment of the people; the sacrifices of
Judah and Jerusalem will again be pleasing to Yahweh.[5]

Structurally, this oracle unit employs the same question-
and-answer schema found in the previous four. It opens in 3:6a,
b with a double-barreled 'hingestellte Behauptung.'[6] Yahweh
has not gone back on his word (3:6a) to judge the sins of the
evildoers and execute the sentence (3:5). However, they are not

---

coming we hear about cheating Yahweh, p. 610. He avers that 3:6-12 belong
with 2:2-5. Not only is Jacob the subject of both, but 3:12 provides a striking
antithetical parallel to 1:4, 5, p. 611. Sellin's argument is tenuous at best. In
1:2-5, Jacob is the beloved object of Yahweh's words; in 3:6ff, he is the object of
Yahweh's reproach. In 1:4, which Sellin views as the opposite of 3:12, the subject
is not Jacob's land (as it is in 3:12) but Esau's. Finally, the content of this oracle
unit springs directly out of Yahweh's judgmental activity enunciated in 3:5,
cf. 235f. Although Wilhelm Rudolph, *Haggai-Sacharja-Maleachi* (KAT 13/4; Gütersloh: Gütersloher Verlagshaus Gerd Mohn, 1976) agrees that 3:6-12 are not out
of place, he contends that the oracle unit is a non-eschatological piece sandwiched
between two future-directed oracles (2:17-3:5; 3:13-21), 282. His assessment is
shortsighted. As a corollary of 2:17-3:5 which are eschatological, 3:6-12 share
their future orientation cf. אָשׁוּבָה, 3:7 אֶפְתַּח; וַהֲרִיקֹתִי, 3:10; וְגָעַרְתִּי, 3:11. More
significant, both 2:17-3:5 and 3:13-21 describe the coming Yôm Yahweh which
presupposes a cultic *Sitz im Leben*, cf. above, 131f. The cultic setting of 3:6-12 is
obvious in Malachi's use of the words אני יהוה (3:6) and שוב (3:7), cf. 177f.

[4] Cf. 159f.

[5] Cf. 149f.

[6] Cf. Egon Pfeiffer, "Die Disputationsworte im Buche Maleachi," *EvTh* 19
(1959) 561.

yet destroyed (3:6b). Although they have continually been derelict in their obligations (3:7a), if they return whole-heartedly to Yahweh, he will return to them, i.e., forgive them (3:7b). The evildoers object: "In respect of what sins shall we return?" thus pretending not to know of any shortcomings in their conduct that call for amendment (3:7c). Yahweh's indicting reply is incisive. They have robbed him, scanting in their payment of the tithe and the levy (3:8). Thus, they are cursed (3:9). Finally, Yahweh substantiates his assertion that if the evildoers turn once again to him, he will return to them (3:7b). If they bring the required tithe and so fill Yahweh's house (בַּיִת), he will pour out upon them an abundant blessing (בְּרָכָה עַד־בְּלִי־דָי), and the resultant prosperity will be so conspicuous that they will become the envy of all nations, 3:10-12.

The fourth oracle unit (2:17-3:5) is characterized by action and a sense of constant movement—Yahweh is drawing ever nearer to his people.[7] These are carried over to the fifth (3:6-12) thereby creating a continuum of thought and deed. Yahweh will return (שׁוּב) to those who return to him (3:7). He will open for them (אֶפְתַּח לָכֶם) the windows of heaven; he will pour out for them (וַהֲרִיקֹתִי לָכֶם) an abundance of blessing (3:10); he will restrain for their benefit (וְגָעַרְתִּי לָכֶם) the devourer (3:11).[8]

Text and Commentary

[3:6]—Scholars have isolated two main problems in this verse. The first has to do with the meaning of the verse and revolves around how the verbs שׁנה and כלה should be translated. The second concerns the relation of the verse to the preceding oracle unit, 2:17-3:5. Van Hoonacker contends that because Yahweh is described as unchangeable or constant in 3:6a (לֹא שָׁנִיתִי), 3:6b must include an affirmation of the behavior of the sons of Jacob.[9] Therefore, he repoints כְּלִיתֶם (qal pf., כָּלָה "to be complete, spent, used up, destroyed")[10] to כִּלֵּיתֶם (piel pf., כלה, "to

---

[7] Cf. 124, 171.

[8] The use of poetic conventions in this oracle unit is minimal. There is some key word repetition, cf. שׁוב (3:7, 2x); קבע (3:8-9). What is most eye-catching is the abundant use of the ʾaleph both alliteratively and as the dominant sound within words, cf. 3:6a, b; 3:7b; 3:8a, b; 3:9a, b; 3:10d; 3:11a, b.

[9] A. van Hoonacker, *Les douze petits prophetès* (Paris ; Gabalda, 1908) 733.

[10] BDB, 477.

end, make an end")[11] and translates, "I, Yahweh, do not change; and you, Sons of Jacob, do not put an end (to your abuses)."[12] In this way Yahweh is pictured as the constant avenger of evil and the Sons of Jacob as the constant committers of it. Such an understanding provides a clear link with 3:7a where the people are upbraided for failing to keep Yahweh's statutes.[13] Moreover, van Hoonacker asserts that his translation is more in harmony with the context of the prophecy because it allows for a liaison with 3:5 by the transitional particle כִּי—Yahweh is coming to judge his errant people (3:5) for, כִּי, he is constant in the exercise of justice (3:6).[14] Significantly, van Hoonacker also affirms that his translation links 3:6 to 2:17.[15] Seeing the evildoers prosper, the people came to question whether there was a god of justice, אַיֵּה אֱלֹהֵי הַמִּשְׁפָּט, 2:17. According to van Hoonacker, 3:6 strongly affirms that a god of justice does indeed exist. Yahweh has not abandoned them; he is always the avenger of evil. This interpretation is questionable. If Yahweh had indeed been the constant avenger of evil as van Hoonacker would have it (3:6a), the people would have had no need to question his existence as a just judge (אַיֵּה אֱלֹהֵי הַמִּשְׁפָּט, 2:17). Moreover, it appears that 3:6a flows directly out of 3:5. There Yahweh avers that he will be a swift witness (עֵד מְמַהֵר) against the evildoers. 3:6a affirms that he has not changed (לֹא שָׁנִיתִי) with regard to that assertion. This interpretation, which will be discussed more fully below,[16] creates a dramatic flow between the oracle units and suits the context far better than does van Hoonacker's. Indeed, those addressed in this oracle unit are the evildoers (cf. also 3:5) and not the pious. Finally van Hoonacker's translation calls for too much from the imagination of the reader specifically with regard to 3:6b. By repointing כְּלִיתֶם to piel כִּלִּיתֶם, one is forced to supply an object in order to complete the sentence. Although it is true that van Hoonacker's insertion [you do not put an end] "to your

---

[11] BDB, 478.

[12] van Hoonacker, 733 and cf. also Rudolph, 281.

[13] Ibid. Note that the LXX also appears to link 3:6b with 3:7a: 3:6b καὶ ὑμεῖς υἱοὶ Ιακωβ, οὐκ ἀπέχεσθε (from כלא), 3:7a, ἀπο τῶν ἀδικιῶν (perhaps understanding לְמִימֵי as לְמוּם, moral blemish, cf. Deut 32:5) τῶν πατέοων.

[14] van Hoonacker, 733.

[15] Ibid.

[16] Cf. 179f.

abuses,"[17] coordinates well with 3:7, it must be questioned whether any repointing of כלה is necessary.[18]

J. M. P. Smith remarks that

> ... if any of the guilty have thought that Yahweh has lost all his interest in righteousness and goodness ... they are now to be completely disabused of that error. The moral character of Yahweh remains unchanged; hence sinners must undergo the punishment they so richly deserve. This, it is clear, is not an abstract proposition that Yahweh cannot change in any respect, but simply a positive affirmation that he has not changed in this specific particular.[19]

Smith's interpretation recognizes the continuity between 3:5 where Yahweh avows that he will judge the evildoers, and 3:6a where that promise is reiterated. However, Smith maintains that the לֹא כְלִיתֶם "not consumed"[20] in 3:6b "hardly satisfies the demands of the context."[21] "It is not the kind of thought to be expected at the close of such an arraignment of Israel's sins."[22] Therefore, he regards the לֹא as the emphatic $l\bar{a}^{\flat}$ and translates, "You will surely be destroyed."[23] At first glance, in view of 3:7a which sums up the evildoers offenses, Smith's translation "you will surely be destroyed" seems perfectly suitable. Nevertheless, 3:7b explicitly states that if the people return to Yahweh, he will return to them. Although they are now under a curse (3:9a), if they give the requisite tithe, they will receive an abundant blessing (3:10). Such thoughts suggest that although the evildoers will be judged for their crimes (3:5; 3:6a), they "will not be destroyed" yet (3:6b). They will be given one final chance to make reparations.

A full interpretation of this verse rests on an understanding of its relationship to what precedes and follows and on an understanding of its vocabulary. There can be no doubt of the

[17] van Hoonacker, 733.
[18] Cf. below, 179f.
[19] J. M. P. Smith, *Malachi* (ICC; Edinburgh: T. & T. Clark, 1912) 66.
[20] Ibid.
[21] Ibid.
[22] Ibid., 67.
[23] Ibid., 58.

cultic setting of the fourth oracle unit. Verses 2:17–3:5 are per-
vaded by Yôm Yahweh imagery; the Day of Yahweh is the day of
his cultic coming, the day when he reveals himself to his people
(3:2).[24] The continuation of this imagery can be seen in the first
words of 3:6—אני יהוה. In his basic study, W. Zimmerli designated
it as a 'self-introductory' formula, which demonstrates at the
outset its origin in the cult.[25] "In this form, which is widespread
throughout the Old Testament, the divine 'I' enters into the
presence of the cultic community and addresses it as his own
possession."[26] The revelation of Yahweh's name serves as a
prologue to the Decalogue "to make clear that they are understood as the will of Yahweh who has delivered his people from
bondage. Yahweh has identified himself as the redeemer of God.
The formula identifies the authority and right of God to make
known his will because he has already graciously acted on Israel's
behalf."[27] Leviticus 19 is addressed to "the congregation of the
people of Israel," כל־עדת בני־ישראל, and deals with the correct
behavior of individuals (i.e., according to God's will), in the
circumstances of daily life, within the framework of the community to which they belong. Each of the commands beginning
with 19:2 and ending with 19:18, concludes with the obviously
substantiating clause אני יהוה or אני יהוה אלהיכם, which von Rad
contends "was quite certainly a liturgical usage."[28]

The connection of Yahweh's day with his self-revelation is
made explicit in Ezek 7. Yahweh says that the end has come (בא
הקץ בא, 7:6), the day has drawn near (קרוב היום, 7:7).
Iniquity piled on iniquity calls forth judgment. Yahweh will
have no mercy on his people but will judge them according to
their conduct (7:9, 27) and thus they shall know that he is
Yahweh—וידעו כי אני יהוה (7:9, 27). Significantly, in Ezekiel

[24] Cf. above, 131f.

[25] W. Zimmerli, *Gottes Offenbarung: Gesammelte Aufsätze* (Münich: Kaiser,
1963) 11f.

[26] Gerhard von Rad, *Deuteronomy* (OTS; Philadelphia: Westminster, 1966)
56.

[27] Brevard Childs, *The Book of Exodus* (OTS; Philadelphia: Westminster,
1974) 401.

[28] Gerhard von Rad, *Old Testament Theology* (2 vols.; New York: Harper
and Row, 1962–1975) 1.197, and cf. B. Gemser, "The Importance of the Motive
Clause in Old Testament Law," VTSup 1 (Leiden: Brill, 1965) 50f.

chapters 7, 20:42 and 37:15f, the words כי אני יהוה occur in connection with utterances against idolatry. Israel's history, characterized as it was by constant apostasy, evokes not only the outpouring of Yahweh's wrath and his judgment (Ezek 20:33f), but his manifestation as the holy one (20:41), an act which causes his people to remember their pollutions with self-loathing (20:43). Indeed, Yahweh says that when he so deals with his people, they will know that he is Yahweh: וידעתם כי־אני יהוה בעשותי אתכם למען שמי, 20:44. In Mal 3:6-7, Yahweh's self-proclamation (אני יהוה, 3:6a) is linked with a demand that the evildoers return (שוב) to him (3:7b), a demand that clearly implies the worship of other gods (cf. Joel 2:12; Hos 2:21f).[29]

לֹא שָׁנִיתִי: שָׁנִיתִי is a qal perfect (1 sg.) from שנה meaning "to change."[30] As J. M. P. Smith remarked, the words לא שנה do not hint of the abstract proposition that Yahweh cannot change in any respect, but contain the positive affirmation that he has not changed in his intent to punish the evildoers, 3:5.[31] The expression "not changing" has a connotation which is brought out by an Akkadian parallel. The Akkadian enû, "change," which is semantically parallel to שנה, is used both transitively and intransitively in the G form.[32] N. Waldman lists several examples of "the intransitive use of enû in the sense "go back on one's word, change, renege": ša inūma 20 MA.NA. KÙ. BABBAR Ì-LÁ-E, "whoever goes back on the agreement will pay 20 minas of silver;" eme u ḫatānu aḫameš ul innû, "the father-in-law and the son-in-law shall not mutually revoke their agreement;" ana a[q]bima eni, "I promise but I reversed myself."[33] The context of Malachi 3:5-6 is quite consistent with an interpretation in terms of keeping one's word. The assertion that Yahweh will come to judge the evildoers (3:5) is solidly substantiated in 3:6a by the categorical assertion, "For (כִּי) I am Yahweh, I do not go back on my word." Indeed, the link between this oracle unit (3:6-12) and 2:17-3:5 is

---

[29] G. W. Ahlström. *Joel and the Temple Cult of Jerusalem* (SVT 21; Leiden: Brill, 1971) 26 and cf. 182f. Note that in 3:5, the evildoers were charged with adultery, an abuse with both social and cultic implications.

[30] BDB, 1039.

[31] J. M. P. Smith, 66.

[32] Nahum Waldman, "Some Notes on Malachi 3:6; 3:13 and Psalm 42:11," *JBL* 93 (1974) 543.

[33] Ibid.

assured not only by the continuation of the revelatory aspect of Yahweh's day (cf. 3:2b, וּמִי הָעֹמֵד בְּהֵרָאוֹתוֹ 3:6a, אֲנִי יהוה)[34] but also by the particle כִּי, "for, because," which introduces causal clauses assigning reasons for or legitimizing previously made statements, demands or threats.[35] Malachi 3:6a, כִּי אֲנִי יהוה לֹא שָׁנִיתִי is syntactically similar to Exod 20:3-5 where the commands prohibiting the serving of other gods and the making of images are theologically substantiated by the clause, כִּי אָנֹכִי יהוה אֱלֹהֶיךָ אֵל קַנָּא, "For I, Yahweh your God, am a jealous God," 20:5b.

כְּלִיתֶם :לֹא כְלִיתֶם is a qal perfect, 2 m.pl. from כלה, "to be complete, at an end," "come to an end, vanish = perish, be destroyed"[36] (cf. Isa 1:28; 16:4; 29:20; Jer 16:4; Ezek 5:12; 13:14; Job 4:9). The perceived problem with this line stems from the fact that punishment of the wicked is upheld in 3:5, 3:6a and then seemingly withdrawn here, "But as for you, O sons of Jacob, you are not destroyed," 3:6b.[37] The arraignment of the sins of the evildoers in 3:5 and 3:7a leaves no doubt that they are deserving of Yahweh's punishment. Nevertheless, they are still the same בְּנֵי-יַעֲקֹב, the sons of Jacob, so lovingly addressed in the first oracle unit, 1:2-5. And it is as such that they are given one final chance to allay their punishment. If they return to Yahweh, he will return to them (3:7b). Thus, understood, Yahweh is not reneging on his promise to chastise the wicked (3:5, 6a) in 3:6b; he is simply delaying it: "But as for you, O sons of Jacob, you are not destroyed . . . yet."[38]

[3:7]—In the most straightforward terms, this verse enunciates the cause of the people's estrangement from God (סרתם מחקי ולא שמרתם) and the avenue of their reconciliation (שובו אלי ואשובה אליכם). It is made patent that wrongdoing is not a present aberration but has been, in fact, part and parcel of the community's life since its inception. Indeed, Yahweh says that

---

[34] The Yôm Yahweh imagery which figures so prominently in 2:17-3:5 and is continued in 3:6-12, is also an integral part of the sixth oracle unit, 3:13-21, especially 3:17f. It is precisely this imagery continuum that links these three units together.

[35] GKC, #158b, 492.

[36] BDB, 477.

[37] J. M. P. Smith, 66-67.

[38] The thought here is akin to Jer 30:11: "I will correct you in measure and will not utterly destroy (כלה) you."

the people have turned away from him since the days of their fathers (3:7a).

לְמִימֵי אֲבֹתֵיכֶם: The word לְמִמֵי is a combination of לְ (to) + מִן (from) + יְמֵי (days, cs.pl. יוֹם). The function of the לְ is "to indicate expressly the starting point, as an exact *terminus a quo* (of place or time)"[39] (cf. Judg 19:30; 2 Sam 7:19; Jer 7:7; 42:8; Mic 7:12). Thus it is avowed that the misdeeds "go back to" (i.e., begin with) and have "continued from" the days of the fathers (cf. also Jer 7:25f; Ezek 2:3; 20:5-26; Isa 43:27; Zech 1:2-4). J. M. P. Smith contends that "the period covered by this indictment includes at least the lifetime of the prophet's hearers up to the time of this address. It probably reaches back also into the previous generation and, possibly, even further."[40] A clue to the precise *terminus a quo* can be found in the third oracle unit, 2:10-16. The major theme of these verses is intermarriage, the prime pitfall of which is the resultant incorporation into the Yahweh cult of the cultic rites of other gods (cf. 2:13). In 2:10d, those who intermarry are accused of profaning the covenant of their fathers (לחלל ברית אבתינו). Such a covenant was made at Mt. Sinai with the Exodus fathers and is detailed in both Exod 34:10f and Deut 7:1f. Not only does it make explicit the connection between intermarriage and apostasy,[41] but it avows that turning away from Yahweh can be the result of any close contact between the Israelites and their neighbors (cf. Exod 34:15; Deut 7:16). Yahweh alone is to be Israel's God, Exod 34:14; Deut 7:9. Although the Exodus fathers agreed to abide by the covenant stipulations enjoined at Sinai, their promise was forgotten almost immediately, cf. Num 25. Moreover, the prophetic indictments of both Jeremiah (7:25f) and Ezekiel (20:5-26) which highlight Israel's recalcitrance, her refusal to obey Yahweh's injunctions assert that the rebellion which began with the Exodus fathers has continued to the present time (cf. Jer 7:30f; Ezek 20:27f). This appears to be the thrust of Malachi's argument also. Although he condemns in detail the covenant faithlessness of his own generation—they intermarry (2:10-16), they commit adultery (3:5)[42]—it is not viewed as a

[39] GKC, #119c, note 2, 378.
[40] J. M. P. Smith, 69.
[41] For a fuller discussion, 87f.
[42] Cf. 161f.

contemporary aberration. In 3:7a Malachi is at great pains to point out that apostasy had its roots in the wilderness with the very generation that contracted the covenant. It is significant that Malachi defines the people's sin as "turning away from and not observing Yahweh's statutes" (סַרְתֶּם מֵחֻקַּי וְלֹא שְׁמַרְתֶּם).[43] In the Deuteronomic exposition of the covenant with the Exodus fathers Yahweh states: "Therefore you shall observe the commandment, the statutes and the decrees which I enjoin upon you today,"—ושמרת את־המצוה ואת־החקים ואת־המשפטים אשר אנכי מצוך היום לצשותם. The use of the word חֹק (cf. חקק, "to cut, inscribe, engrave")[44] strongly implies the immutability of the covenant stipulations. Therefore, Malachi's avowal that unfaithfulness began in the wilderness days is not intended to reduce the guilt of his contemporaries, but to increase it. The covenant has not been abrogated; its conditions have not been changed. The people should have known better; they should have learned from the lessons of the past.

The prophetic emphasis on continuity is visible not only in the strong link between 3:7 and 2:10-16 but in the link between these verses and the second oracle unit (1:6-2:9). The priests have defiled the covenant made with Levi by turning aside from (סַרְתֶּם מִן) the correct path (2:8a). The people have profaned the covenant made with the fathers (2:10) in their refusal to abide by its strictures; they have turned away from (סַרְתֶּם מִן) and not observed (וְלֹא שְׁמַרְתֶּם) Yahweh's statutes (3:7a). Malachi begins in the center with the priests (1:6-2:9) and then moves outward to encompass the population at large in his indictment (3:7).[45] Not only does he stress the inclusiveness of guilt but the inclusiveness of punishment—both groups are under the power of a divine curse (2:2e; 3:9). Nevertheless, reconciliation is still possible. The priests need only give honor to Yahweh (2:2); the people need only return to him (3:7).

---

[43] J. M. P. Smith, 74 and A. von Bulmerincq, *Der Prophet Maleachi* (2 vols.; Tartu: J. G. Kruger, 1926-1932) 2.409, repoint שְׁמַרְתֶּם לֹא to לֹא שְׁמַרְתֶּם, "you did not observe them," i.e., the statutes. However, because it is quite obvious that חֻקַּי is the object of שָׁמַר, such repointing is not strictly necessary.

[44] BDB, 349.

[45] Note that in 3:3-4, the cleansing process begins with the priests and from there it extends to the people.

שׁוּבוּ אֵלַי וְאָשׁוּבָה אֲלֵיכֶם: "Turning" (שׁוּב) is the essence of the prophetic concept of repentance[46] and the culmination of the message of the Deuteronomistic history.[47] It represents the divine demand for human decision, a demand for total reorientation to Yahweh, a return to him alone.[48] For the Deuteronomistic historians especially, the notion of "turning" (שׁוּב) to Yahweh was integrally related to the theology of covenant. Indeed, covenant as a category for describing the past history of the people of Israel in relation to Yahweh is most clearly expressed in Deuteronomy and it was the Deuteronomists who used covenant as a regulative principle.[49] In their ideology, two interrelated points stand out prominently. The first of these is that Israel's existence and continuance as a nation is made dependent upon its obedience to the covenant (cf. esp. Deut 4:13-14; 2 Kgs 17:15). Second, disobedience to covenant stipulations ruptures the relationship between Yahweh and Israel and entails summary punishment of a catastrophic nature (cf. Jer 11:10f; Deut 27: 28:15f). Within the Deuteronomistic account of history which was written during the exile,[50] these points served to explain why it was possible for Yahweh to reject his people. Deuteronomy 4 clearly enunciates that Israel was condemned to be scattered because of its worship of idols (25f), because it forgot the covenant made with Yahweh.[51] Nevertheless, the saying that

> ... at every time of judgment the way stands open
> for Israel to return to Yahweh appears ... in each climax
> of the Deuteronomistic history. This work is concerned
> to introduce variations on this theme with such great
> urgency because just at this time, i.e., in the situation

[46] Cf. Joel 2:12-14; Zeph 2:3; Jer 3:22; 4:1; 5:3; 8:4-5; 18:7-10; Ezek 3:17-21; 14:7; 17:21-32.

[47] Cf. Deut 4; 29-31.

[48] Hans Walter Wolff, *Joel and Amos* (Philadelphia: Fortress, 1977) 49.

[49] See L. Perlitt, *Bundestheologie im Alten Testament* (WMANT 36; Neukirchen-Vulyn: Neukirchener Verlag, 1969) and E. Kutsch, *Verheissung und Gesetz. Untersuchungen zum sogenannten 'Bund' im Alten Testament* (BZAW 131; Berlin: Alfred Töpelmann, 1973).

[50] von Rad, *Deuteronomy*, 342.

[51] Note that von Rad, *Deuteronomy*, 183 and H. W. Wolff, "Das Kerygma des deuteronomistischen Geschichtswerk," *ZAW* 73 (1961) 180f, consider Deut 4:29-31 and 30:1-10 to be part of the "Great Deuteronomistic historical work."

after God's judgment in 587, it is endeavoring to show
its contemporaries this one and only way to salvation.[52]

Both Deut 4 and 30 make it clear that if Israel takes Yahweh's
punishment to heart and if she turns (שׁוּב) to Yahweh, so he will
have compassion on his people; he will gather them from all the
nations in which they have been scattered, return them to their
own land and bestow even greater blessing on them (cf. esp.
Deut 30:1–10). In the Deuteronomistic schema, therefore, the
concept of "turning" (שׁוּב) serves as a corrective to the traditional
dogmatic covenant theology in which obedience to covenant
stipulations issues in blessing and life (cf. Deut 28:1f) while
disobedience results in curse and death (cf. Deut 27:14f).
    Israel's prophets too, placed great emphasis on "turning"
(שׁוּב) to Yahweh. The absence of covenant terminology in the
eighth-century prophets especially is due to their not having had
access to the deuteronomistic categories that came to be utilized
only in the following century. The field of metaphor used by the
prophets to describe the relationship between Yahweh and Israel
is that of familial and personal association (e.g., Isa 30:1, 9;
Amos 3:2; Hos 1:3; 11:1–4; 13:13; Jer 2:2–3; 31:20). Isaiah says:
בנים גדלתי ורוממתי והם פשעו בי "Sons I have reared and brought
up, but they have rebelled against me," (1:2). The dissolution of
the relationship between father and son leads to punishment
(1:7–8, 11–15). Only the son's return to obedience can repair the
broken relationship and ensure blessing (1:19). In Isa 30, Yahweh
punishes his "rebellious children" (בָּנִים סוֹרְרִים) 30:1f, and avows
that only "in turning (בְּשׁוּבָה) and rest shall you be saved," 30:15.
    It is significant that the close familial relationship between
Yahweh and Israel was established at the time of the Exodus
(cf. Exod 4:22–23). G. Fohrer remarks that "the Sinai event
intended to establish a permanent relationship between Yahweh
and the Moses host in the sense of an ongoing community. The
community constituted at the mountain of Yahweh was thought
of as a blood relationship, in which the Moses host represent the
ʿam of Yahweh, that is his clan or family."[53] Therefore, although

---

[52] Cf. von Rad, *Deuteronomy*, 50 and Wolff, "Das Kerygma," 177f.
[53] Cf. Georg Fohrer, *History of Israelite Religion* (New York: Abingdon,
1972) 81. Note that the husband-wife metaphor employed by Hosea and Jeremiah
may have been a prophetic development of that basic relationship.

covenant terminology is lacking in the deuteronomistic sense, the prophets nevertheless interpreted Israel's actions on the basis of a relationship established at Sinai. Indeed, the aggressive critique of society propounded by the prophets was essentially a spelling out of the broken condition of that relationship and the call to turn from rebellion and to return to Yahweh (Jer 3:22; 4:1; cf. 15:19) was the prophetic attempt to repair it. The covenant concept is implicit in prophecy.[54] Therefore, it must be asked whether the absence of covenant terminology in the early prophets can be attributed solely to the fact that the deuteronomistic categories had not yet been formulated. The prophets' indictments of corrupt practices and their announcement of Yahweh's coming judgment were designed to shock the people into an awareness of their plight and to drive them to repentance (cf. Amos 5:4, 6; Isa 1:10f; 10:1-4). Strictly speaking, the notion of repentance does not belong to a covenant paradigm. According to the political-juridical treaties of the Ancient Near East with which the prophets may have been acquainted, "When a people fails to fulfill the obligations of the covenant, the covenant actually ceases to be in force."[55] This notion is not foreign to OT covenant formulary. Continuance of the relationship between Yahweh and Israel depends on obedience to the stipulations of that relationship (cf. Exod 34:10f). It may be, therefore, that the known covenant paradigm was too rigid for the prophets and we should see in their proclamations a change of direction. By drawing on the analogy of human and social relationships rather than political-juridical treaties, they added a certain flexibility and naturalness to the bond linking Yahweh and Israel since broken relationships are entities that can be repaired and made whole again.

Although the prophets employed the verb שׁוּב to describe a turning away from evil behavior in a general sense (cf. Ezek 3:16-21; 18:21-32), it was most regularly used to call for a return to the exclusive worship of Yahweh (cf. Hos 2:9[7]; 3:5; 4:1f; Amos 4:6-11; Ezek 14:16)—a demand that correlates well with the first covenant obligation (cf. Exod 20:3; 34:14; Deut 5:7f). In Joel 2:12f, the phrase "turn to me" indicates that Joel is addressing "a people which has not only worshipped Yahweh but other

[54] Helmer Ringgren, *Israelite Religion* (Philadelphia: Fortress, 1966) 255.
[55] Ibid., 118.

gods. He stresses that the people must return to no other god than Yahweh because they are Yahweh's own covenant people."[56] The terrible visions, denunciations and prophetic threats of destruction should be seen as a summons to the decision to return (cf. Isa 1:10-15, 21-23; 2:6-8; 3:13-15; 5:8-25; 10:1-14; Amos 5:4, 6; Jer 26:17-19). Indeed, Joel 2 and Zeph 2:3 (cf. Mal 3) associate the theme of return with the threat of the day of Yahweh. "The announcement of catastrophe is designed to awaken repentance in the hearer"[57] and cause him to turn to (שׁוּב אֶל) a way of life appropriate to the familial relationship between Yahweh and Israel.

Of central importance to Malachi is the relationship between Yahweh and Israel, a relationship initiated at Mt. Sinai and based on the exclusive worship of Yahweh (cf. Exod 20:3-6; 34:14; Deut 5:7-10). His prophecy revolves around the covenant concept (cf. 2:5, 8; 2:10; 3:1, 7) and like both his prophetic predecessors and the deuteronomists, Malachi created a covenant paradigm as an overview of Israel's history. Faithfulness to Yahweh insures blessing (3:10f; 3:16-17, 20-22); unfaithfulness brings disaster (3:9). Malachi's contemporaries profaned the covenant concluded with the Exodus fathers (2:10; 3:7). Chief among their sins is apostasy. They are adulterers (3:5), worshipers of foreign gods (2:10-16). Therefore, they stand under a present curse (3:9) and under the threat of future judgment (3:1-5). Malachi's description of the the Yôm Yahweh (3:1-5) issues as a challenge, a summons to decision (cf. 3:0-7). If his people remain on their present course, they will feel the devastating strength of Yahweh's anger (3:2). If, however, they heed his warnings and return to Yahweh alone, curse will turn into blessing, judgment will be averted (3:10-11).[58] Indeed, the phrase וְאָשׁוּבָה אֲלֵיכֶם indicates that human repentance will lead to a responsive turning on Yahweh's part. The possibility of the restoration of the covenant relationship is implicit in the very nature of that association. Using the prophetic metaphor, Malachi describes Yahweh as Israel's father and Israel as Yahweh's son (2:10). It is

---

[56] Ahlström, *Joel,* 26.
[57] Wolff, *Joel and Amos,* 49.
[58] Cf. also Joel 2:3, 19; Deut 7:13; 16:10, 15, 17.

because he loves his children, the בְּנֵי יַעֲקֹב (1:2), that he has not yet destroyed them (3:6), but has provided instead one final opportunity for them to repair the relationship they shattered.

It must be recognized however, that the possibility of repentance after the announcement of the Day of Yahweh cannot be expected as a matter of course. The prophets were generally skeptical that the people would change (i.e., "turn" to Yahweh) because corruption, injustice and apostasy had become such a way of life with them (cf. Amos 4:4, 5, 6-12; 5:10-13; Isa 3:9; 30:8-14; Jer 3:22; 4:1; 5:3; 8:4, 5; Joel 2:12; Zeph 2:3). Malachi shares this awareness of his people's incapacity to reorient their lives. In 3:7c he records their query in which they seem to be quite unaware of any shortcomings in their conduct that call for amendment (cf. בַּמֶּה נָשׁוּב, "In respect of what sin shall we return?").[59]

[3:8]—To the people's question in 3:7c, במה נשוב Yahweh responds with one of his own, הֲיִקְבַּע אָדָם אֱלֹהִים "Will man rob God?" To ask the question is to answer it; a reply in the negative is the only possible one. Nevertheless, Yahweh accuses his people of doing the inconceivable, כִּי אַתֶּם קֹבְעִים אֹתִי, 3:8b, "Yet you are robbing me." The foregoing question (3:8a) is couched in the most general of terms, viz. "man" and "God"; Yahweh's accusation (3:8b) is direct and highly personal, viz. "you" and "me," the intent being to arouse the guilt of those addressed, to impress strongly upon them that it is God whom they are scanting. Their counter-query evidences their surprise, their total ignorance of any wrongdoing. In the same personal tones they demand to know, בַּמֶּה קְבַעֲנוּךָ, "Wherein have we robbed you?" (3:8c). Yahweh does not content himself with hazy and indefinite generalizations. Their question demands and receives a specific answer—הַמַּעֲשֵׂר וְהַתְּרוּמָה, "In the tithe and the levy" (3:8d).[60] The precise statutes from which the people have turned aside (3:7a) are now made explicit.

קָבַע: The Hebrew קָבַע is found only in Mal 2:8, 9 and Prov 22:23. As a verb it is used extensively in Talmudic literature

[59] Cf. also 3:24 in which Malachi recognizes the possibility that even Elijah will be unable to reorient the people and thus avert judgment.

[60] Grammatically, הַמַּעֲשֵׂר וְהַתְּרוּמָה is best treated as depending upon the בְּ carried over from the question in 3:8c.

with the meaning "to rob," "to take forcibly."[61] In Prov 22:23 קָבַע is a parallelism with גָזַל (22:22) "to rob, seize, tear away."[62] This suggests that the use of קָבַע in the sense of "to rob" was operative in the Biblical period also. The Peshitta employs the verb ܓܠܙ, "to wrong, defraud" and especially, "to withhold that which is due,"[63] to translate קָבַע and thus has captured the nuance of the verse. Yahweh avers that the people have robbed or scanted him, that is, they have withheld from him that which is his due in the way of tithes and levies.

Several scholars have suggested that קבע is simply a mis-writing of עקב, "to deceive."[64] Further, they contend that the original text which is reflected in the LXX's translation, cf. πτερνίζειν, thus includes a play on words with the בְּנֵי יַעֲקֹב of 3:6.[65] The narrative of the birth of the twins Jacob and Esau (Gen 25:26) derives the name יַעֲקֹב from עָקֵב, since he grasps Esau's "heel." יַעֲקֹב is first connected with "to deceive" (עָקַב) in Esau's description of the underhanded way in which Jacob obtained Isaac's blessing, Gen 27:36, cf. Jer 9:3; Hos 13:3. In the immediately preceding verse (27:35), Jacob's deed is characterized as מִרְמָה, "deception." It should be noted however, that Jacob is never represented as "deceiving" Yahweh. As J. M. P. Smith remarked, " . . . one may in a certain sense 'rob' God, as it is there stated Israel has done; but it is not possible to 'deceive' or 'cheat' him."[66] Although the root קבע is not well attested in the OT, the mere fact that the precise meaning of a word is unknown is, in itself, insufficient reason for emending the text in a literature so limited as the Hebrew. Moreover, not much stress may be laid on the fact that עָקַב would furnish a pun on בְּנֵי יַעֲקֹב of v. 6. Close connection between the two verses is broken by 3:7, and furthermore, Malachi is not characterized by the use of paronomasia. Finally, Yahweh's demand that the people bring

[61] J. M. P. Smith, 74 and A. Cohen, *The Twelve Prophets* (London: Soncino, 1948) 351.

[62] BDB, 159.

[63] R. Payne Smith, *A Compendious Syriac Dictionary* (Oxford: Clarendon, 1903) 175.

[64] Cf. Sellin, 612; von Bulmerincq, 2.415 and Rex Mason, *The Books of Haggai, Zechariah and Malachi* (Cambridge: Cambridge University, 1977) 155.

[65] Cf. above, 180.

[66] J. M. P. Smith, 70.

the whole tithe (כָּל־הַמַּעֲשֵׂר) to the temple (v. 10) implies that the people have been remiss in that area and thus supports the charge that they have robbed or scanted him (cf. קבע, 3:8).

מַעֲשֵׂר וְהַתְּרוּמָה:הַמַּעֲשֵׂר is a n.m. meaning "tenth part, tithe," cf. עֶשֶׂר, "ten." [67] תְּרוּמָה is a n.f. from רוּם, "to be high, exalted, rise," cf. הֵרִים, "to raise, lift, take off." [68] It denotes properly what is 'taken off' from a larger mass and so separated from it for sacred use; a contribution, offering. According to G. R. Driver, תְּרוּמָה is based on the Assyrian *tarāmu*, "to levy, remove" (cf. Talmud תְּרַם "removed"), found in a small group of Assyrian texts.[69]

> These [texts] say that the tenant of a fief liable to requisitions for food or other charges, kaspa ina eli (še'i) tarāme išakkan eqilšu ušêṣa, "shall put (down a sum of) silver against the levy (of corn and then) shall take over his field or lease." In other words, the tenant may not occupy the field until he has given a guarantee that he will meet the customary requisitions when they fall due, i.e., after the harvest. Here the √TRM applied generally to the levying of an impost or payment due as a charge on land; cp. Heb. אִישׁ תְּרוּמוֹת "a man of levies," i.e., one who is extortionate in levying charges or exacting payment (Prov. 29:4), which is in form analogous to אִישׁ תככים "a man of oppressions," i.e., exacting in demanding repayment of debts (Prov. 29:13).[70]

In Deuteronomy, the tithing laws (מַעֲשֵׂר) provided for an annual tithe of דגנך תירשך ויצהרך ובכרת בקר וצאנך, Deut 14:23. It was to be brought to Jerusalem and eaten there by the offerer לפני יהוה, Deut 14:23. The people were enjoined not to neglect the Levite within their gates כי אין לו חלק ונחלה עמך, Deut 14:27. Every third year the tithe was to be given to the Levite, the stranger, the widow and the orphan for their sustenance, Deut 14:28f; 26:12f. These requirements do not accord fully with Malachi's charge and demand. Deut 26:12f contemplates no

[67] BDB, 796-98.
[68] Ibid., 926-27.
[69] G. R. Driver, "Three Technical Terms in the Pentateuch," *JSS* 1 (1956) 102.
[70] Ibid., 102.

storage of the מַעֲשֵׂר as is implied in Mal 3:10; Deut 14:28f calls for storage in the various cities while Mal 3:10 evidently conceives of it as stored in Jerusalem only. Malachi's presuppositions are best met by the provisions found in the priestly code, cf. Lev 27:30f and Num 18:21-31.[71] Lev 27:30f states unequivocally that the entire tithe belongs to Yahweh—ליהוה הוא קדש ליהוה, v. 30. Only after the tithes are given to Yahweh are they then reapportioned to the Levites as recompense for their service at the tent of meeting, Num 18:21f. In their turn the Levites give back to Yahweh a tenth of what they have received as their tithe, v. 26.

In Num 26:26f the תְּרוּמָה, "levy, contribution" is considered part of the מַעֲשֵׂר, "tithe." This should not be surprising since תְּרוּמָה "denotes, literally, 'that which is raised up' (*scil.* from a larger portion).'"[72] The levitical tithe of the tithe is thus their תְּרוּמָה.

תְּרוּמָה appears to have a wider frame of reference than does מַעֲשֵׂר. It refers not only to animal and vegetable offerings (cf. Deut 12:6, 11, 17; Num 15:19-21; 18:11, 24; Ezek 44:30; Neh 10:37, 39; 12:44), but to "contributions of money, spoil etc., offered for sacred purposes as Exod 25:2, 3; 20:13-15; Num 31:29, 41; Ezra 8:25; Ezek 45:1, 6, 7."[73] Like the tithe, a תְּרוּמָה is an offering "made to God, but received for the use of the officiating priest."[74]

The community of which Malachi was a part was economically depressed as a result of Persian taxation and perhaps drought and plague,[75] cf. 3:10f. J. M. P. Smith has remarked that

> ... when receipts decrease, or expenses increase with
> no accompanying increase of income, the first thing
> to suffer is the cause of religion. It needs seem more
> remote and less pressing than the necessities of food,
> raiment, housing, education, and the like, which are ever
> with us. This cause, together with a general decline of
> religious fervour that was directly due to the fact that the

[71] Cf. also Rudolph, 284; van Hoonacker, 734; Mason, 155.

[72] J. M. P. Smith, 74.

[73] S. R. Driver, *The Minor Prophets* (New York: Oxford University, American Branch, Henry Frowde, 1906) 322.

[74] G. R. Driver, 104-5.

[75] Cf. above, 11f.

community as a whole was unable to see wherein zeal for
Yahweh was yielding any returns in terms of prosperity
and influence, had brought about a serious diminution
in tithes and offerings, which the prophet does not
hesitate to brand as robbery.[76]

In the days of Nehemiah, the people entered into a covenant and
pledged themselves to pay the entire tithe, 10:38f, cf. Mal 3:10.
Unfortunately however, during Nehemiah's absence that pledge
was quickly forgotten and the tithe allowed to go by the default
as here, cf. Neh 13:10f.

[3:9]—Although the people have been threatened with severe
punishment when Yahweh appears, cf. 2:17-3:5, there is a far
more immediate emergency. As a consequence of their intolerable
actions, cf. 3:8, they are already under a curse, בַּמְּאֵרָה אַתֶּם נֵאָרִים.[77]
Specifically, the conditions requisite for fertility have been withheld by a divinely imposed ban, 3:10-11. There is an undeniable
parallelism between this verse and 2:2. In answer to the unworthy
actions of the priests, Yahweh is sending a curse (מְאֵרָה, 2:2c)
upon them, a curse that will block off fertility (בְּרְכוֹת)[78] so that
the fields will not yield produce from which they might benefit,
2:2d. Indeed, because the priests have not taken Yahweh's warnings to heart (2:2f), the curse is already effective, וְגַם אָרוֹתִיהָ, 2:2e.

וְאֹתִי אַתֶּם קֹבְעִים, "But you continue to rob me." The emphasis
is on the אֹתִי, me, the intent being to impress strongly on those
addressed that they are not robbing just anyone; they are robbing
Yahweh himself. This line suggests that despite the curse effected
by God (3:9a), the people continue their dishonest and fraudulent
ways undeterred.

הַגּוֹי כֻּלּוֹ: The sins denounced are confined to no one class,
but are characteristic of the community as a whole. In the OT,
Yahweh's "people" are most frequently called an ʿam; the quasi-
synonym gôy is ordinarily reserved for the foreign nations.[79]

[76] J. M. P. Smith, 70.

[77] For ʾarr see above, 64f. J. Scharbert, "'Fluchen' und 'Segnen' im A.T.,"
Bibl 39 (1959) 2-5. The LXX translation—καὶ ἀποβλέποντες ὑμεῖς ἀποβλέπετε
appears to derive מְאֵרָה (n.f. curse, spell), נֵאָרִים (niphal pt., ארר) from רָאָה rather
than אָרַר. This difficulty may have stemmed from the fact that the niphal of אָרַר
appears only once in the OT.

[78] Cf. above, 65.

[79] Cf. E. A. Speiser, "'People' and 'Nation' of Israel," JBL 70 (1970) 157-63.

Although the immediate impression is that the OT writers do not like to call their people a *gôy*, there are texts, in fact, in which this is the case. *Gôy* is used of Israel growing into the status of a nation (גּוֹי) like all the other nations, cf. Gen 12:12; 18:18; 35:11; 46:3, as well as in a context of taking possession of a geographical territory or land (cf. Josh 3:17; 4:1; 5:6, 8; 10:13; Isa 26:2, 15). *Gôy* is also used to express horizontal socio-political relations, that is, Israel as a political entity capable as such of entering into relations with other *gôyîm*, Mic 4:7; Ezek 37:22; Exod 19:6.[80] In contrast, *ʾam* describes all the internal relations of the people with one another as well as vertical theological relations, the relations of Israel to her God; she is Yahweh's *ʾam*, people.[81] Theologically however, Israel can become a *gôy* when she is unfaithful and unworthy to be distinguished from other *gôyîm*, (cf. Deut 32:28; Judg 2:20; Isa 1:44; 10:6; Jer 5:9, 20; 7:28; 9:8; 12:12; 33:34; Ezek 2:3). Although, according to Deuteronomy, Israel was to have its own place among the *gôyîm* (7:7; 9:14), there is an implied hostility toward these other nations on the grounds that their religion is not pleasing to Yahweh and represents a temptation to Israel. This adverse estimate of the *gôyîm* is even more strongly expressed in 2 Kings, which explains the downfall of the northern kingdom as a consequence of its imitating ways of the *gôyîm* (cf. 17:8, 11, 15 and Ezek 20:32; 2 Chr 28:3). Malachi's use of *gôy* to describe his people has this theologically pejorative nuance. It signals Yahweh's rejection of Israel in view of her cultic misdeeds.

[3:10]—Malachi does not urge obedience in religious matters as an end in itself. Obedience is seen as a pre-condition for experiencing God's blessing, which is expressed in terms of the fertility of the soil. Here Yahweh gives the assurance that at the very moment when the people give him that which is his due, i.e., return to him (3:7), he will send the fructifying rains (3:10a, b, d, e); he will turn to them (3:7).

H. C. Brichto suggests that the first two clauses of this verse "be attached to the preceding verse, that hābīʾū be read as hābīʾ

---

[80] Here *Gôy* is frequently in parallelism with מַמְלָכָה kingdom, cf. also, Isa 15:6, 18; 41:2; Jer 25:14.

[81] Cf. L. Rost, "Die Bezeichnungen für Land und Volk im AT." *Festschrift Otto Procksch zum sechzigsten Geburtstag am 9 August 1934* (ed. Albrecht Alt et al; Leipzig: A Deichert, 1934) 125–48.

(inf.), and *terep* be understood as analogous to *mošḥat* in 1:14."[82]
Thus he translates: v. 9 "You are in the grip of a curse/spell, for
it is me whom you are scanting—the whole lot of you—(v. 10)
bringing the full tithes into (your own) storehouses, while in my
temple there is but carrion."[83] In support of his interpretation
Brichto contends that בֵּית הָאוֹצָר, "storehouse, treasury,"[84] is never
used elsewhere for the temple (or its granaries)."[85] Moreover, the
support for the rendering of טֶרֶף as 'food' is weak (cf. only
Ps 111:5 and Prov 31:15).[86] The more common meaning is
'prey' (cf. Gen 49:9; Num 23:24; Amos 3:4). Both Lev 22:8 and
Ezek 44:31 indicate that the priests may not eat טְרֵפָה, an animal
torn (by wild beasts), because it will render them unclean and
thus unfit for cultic service.[87] Therefore, a מַעֲשֵׂר, tithe, which
consists of טְרֵפָה would be a totally inappropriate offering since,
in the final analysis, it is received for the use of the officiating
priests (cf. Lev 27:30f, Num 18:21-31). Finally, Brichto contends
that Malachi's complaint throughout is not in regard to the
quantity but to the quality of the offerings.[88] The use of טֶרֶף
implies inferiority since "it is well established that *terep* or
terepa does not constitute first-class food."[89] Brichto's analysis
suggests that the people are keeping the best for themselves (the
מַעֲשֵׂר, 3:10a) and giving to Yahweh what they will not deign to
eat and what the priests by law cannot eat (טֶרֶף, 3:10c).

בֵּית הָאוֹצָר means "storehouse," cf. אָצַר "to lay up, store
up."[90] Brichto's remark that "bēt haʾ ôṣar is never used elsewhere for the temple (or its granaries)"[91] is shortsighted. According
to 1 Chr 9:26, the levites had charge of the chambers (לשכות)
and the treasure-chambers (אצרות) of the temple (בֵּית־הָאֱלֹהִים),
cf. also 1 Chr 26:20, 22, 24, 26. When David gave Solomon the

---

[82] Herbert Chanan Brichto, *The Problem of "Curse" in the Hebrew Bible*
(Philadelphia: Society of Biblical Literature and Exegesis, 1963) 105.

[83] Ibid.

[84] BDB, 69.

[85] Brichto, 105.

[86] Ibid., 105.

[87] The common Israelite may eat טְרֵפָה, cf. Brichto, 105.

[88] Brichto, 104-5.

[89] Ibid., 105.

[90] BDB, 69.

[91] Brichto, 104.

temple plans (1 Chr 28:11f), these included plans for storerooms (אצרות) to house קדשים, that is, consecrated things, i.e., tithes, cf. Lev 27:30. Nehemiah reports that the people agreed to bring the first fruits "to the chambers (לשכות) of the house of our God," 10:38. The tithes were to be brought to the Levites who, in turn, would bring a tenth of it to the treasure-house (בית האוצר) of the temple, 10:39. In a passage similar to Mal 3:10, Nehemiah asks, מדוע נעזב בית־האלהים, "Why is the house of God forsaken?" To remedy the situation he had all Judah bring the tithe (מַעֲשֵׂר) to the treasuries (אוצרות), 13:11–12.

"Every large temple had its treasure (ʾoṣār), thus the temple at Shechem (Judg 9, 4); and at Jerusalem Solomon's temple was filled with treasures presented by the kings but removed again when they had to pay tribute to an enemy."[92] cf. 1 Kgs 7:51; 2 Chr 5:1; 2 Kgs 12:18. Obviously the treasures needed to be stored and the biblical texts refer to such storage places as אצרות, cf. בית־האוצר (1 Kgs 7:51; 1 Chr 28:11f; Neh 10:38f; 13:11–12). They were probably found in the side buildings along the temple and along the outer walls of the temple court.[93] Such buildings housed not only gold, silver and precious cult objects but any gift consecrated to God, i.e., the tithe (cf. Neh 13:11–12).[94] Thus Malachi's use of the term בֵּית הָאוֹצָר to refer to the temple storehouse is in line with other OT references.

טֶרֶף: Normally טֶרֶף is the word used for an animal's prey (cf. Amos 3:4; Job 4:11; 38:39; Gen 49:9; Num 23:24); but poetically it is used of food for human consumption (cf. Prov 31:15; Ps 111:5). There is no implication in these verses that such food is second-class.[95] Indeed, Yahweh gives טֶרֶף, food, to those who fear him, Ps 111:5. Brichto's assessment of טֶרֶף as inferior food rests on the assumption that טֶרֶף is totally synonymous with טְרֵפָה, an animal torn (by wild beasts) and as such forbidden to the priests (cf. Lev 22:8; Ezek 44:31).[96] If this in the case, then טֶרֶף

---

[92] Johannes Pedersen, *Israel Its Life and Culture* (4 vols.; London: Oxford University, 1973) 4.332.

[93] Ibid., 3.253; cf. T. A. Busink, *Der Tempel von Jerusalem, von Salomo bis Herodes; ein archäologisch-historische Studie unter Berücksichtigung des westsemitischen Tempelbaus* (Leiden: E. J. Brill, 1970).

[94] Pedersen, 4.332.

[95] Cf. Brichto, 103.

[96] Ibid., 105.

in Yahweh's storehouse would be totally inappropriate.[97] However, the complete congruity of טֶרֶף and טְרֵפָה must be questioned. טֶרֶף is never categorized as forbidden food. The root meaning of טרף is "to tear, rend, pluck," cf. טָרָף.[98] In Gen 8:11 the adj. טָרָף describes a fresh, newly plucked leaf, cf. Ezek 17:9. טֶרֶף then is a portion, something plucked off or separated from the rest. According to Prov 31:14–15, the ideal wife is one who procures the choicest of food (לחם) for her table, v. 14. After rising early to prepare it, she allocates it in this way: her household receives a טֶרֶף, her maidservants, a חֹק. The parallelism of חֹק, "portion" (31:15c) and טֶרֶף (31:15b) suggests that טֶרֶף is that part of the food which has been set aside for the family. Malachi's use of the word טֶרֶף in 3:10b corresponds well with this. It is parallel to מַעֲשֵׂר, tithe (3:10a), and indicates that portion of the people's produce that is reserved for Yahweh.

בַּיִת: M. Haran emphasizes that every sanctuary and every temple is a house of God, a בית.[99] Although בית, "house," occurs in the pre-exilic texts as a synonym for היכל, "temple," cf. 2 Sam 5:8; 7:8f, 13; 1 Kgs 6:25, 37f; Isa 2:2; Hos 9:15, in the later writings it appears to be the more common designation. In Joel the usual term for temple is בית,[100] cf. 1:9, 13f, 16; 4:18, and the word appears fifty times in Ezekiel's temple reorganization program, cf. 40–48. In Mal 3:10a, b, the parallelism between בֵּית הָאוֹצָר (3:10a) and בַּיִת (3:10b) implies that within the temple compound there was storage space to accommodate the gifts brought there.

וּבְחָנוּנִי נָא בָּזֹאת: The intent of Yahweh's command that he be put to the test is to reveal to his people the boons reserved for those who serve him well. They have already experienced Yahweh's reaction to abhorrent behavior; they have been cursed because of their cultic misdeeds, i.e., refusing to follow Yahweh's laws, 3:7; robbing Yahweh, 3:8. The people will find, however, that if they test him with proper cultic conduct, i.e., bringing the entire tithe to the temple, 3:10a,[101] they will evoke from him

---

[97] Cf. above, pp. 192–94.

[98] BDB, 382.

[99] M. Haran, "Biblical Studies: The Idea of the Divine Presence in the Israelite Cult," *TARBIZ* 38 (1968) 105–19.

[100] Ahlström, *Joel*, 18.

[101] בָּזֹאת, "Through this, in this manner," refers to the command issued in 3:10a—הָבִיאוּ.

the opposite response—blessing, 3:10d, e. The thought that Yahweh may be subjected to specific tests in order to verify the truth of his promises is not uncommon in the biblical texts (cf. Exod 4:1-9; Jud 6:36-40; 1 Kgs 18:22f; Isa 7:10f; Jer 28:16f).[102]

According to J. M. P. Smith, that Malachi "should condition the bestowal of Yahweh's favour upon the payment of the tithe alone" provides telling evidence that his conception of the nature of religion is much "less ethical and spiritual than that of his great predecessors, viz. Amos, Hosea, Isaiah and Jeremiah. It is inconceivable that they could have represented Yahweh as contented with the performance of any single act, least of all one in the sphere of ritual."[103] Such an assessment *must* be questioned. The theme of this oracle unit is encompassed in the demand to return, שׁוּב, 3:7b, to Yahweh wholeheartedly, to totally reorient oneself toward him, to return to his cult according to his ṣĕdāqāh.[104] It is not simply the payment of the full tithe that ensures Yahweh's favor since dues may be paid carelessly, without the requisite interior dedication. Blessing is wholly contingent upon the return to Yahweh; payment of the tithe is the exterior manifestation of that return.

אִם־לֹא אֶפְתַּח: This is the apodosis to the protasis implied in the preceding imperatives, cf. בְּחָנוּנִי, הָבִיאוּ. If the people bring[105] the full tithe to the storehouse (3:10a) then Yahweh will surely open the windows of heaven for them; he will surely pour out a blessing for them (3:10d, e).[106]

In the creation account, Yahweh separated the upper water (rain) from the lower water (sea) by means of a solid expanse called the רקיע, "firmament" or the שׁמים, "heavens" (cf. Gen 1:6-8). To enable the upper water to descend, the windows or

---

[102] It is worth noting that Brichto's analysis admits of no such test. He has linked 3:10a, b with 3:9 and translated: (v. 9) "You are in the grip of a curse/spell, for it is me whom you are scanting—the whole lot of you—(v. 10) bringing the full tithe into (your own) storehouses, while in my temple there is but carrion," 105. In so doing, 3:10c . . . וּבְחָנוּנִי stands without a referent.

[103] J. M. P. Smith, 72.

[104] Ahlström, *Joel*, 26.

[105] The apodosis might also be rendered—"If you test me in this way by bringing the full tithe to my storehouse . . . then I will open . . ."

[106] אִם־לֹא, "certainly, surely," governs both 3:10d, e. For the force of אִם־לֹא see, GKC, #149b, 472.

sluices of heaven אֲרֻבּוֹת הַשָּׁמַיִם, must be opened (cf. Gen 7:11-12:
וארבת השמים נפתחו ויהי הגשם על־הארץ); to confine the rains, the
sluices are close (cf. Gen 8:2: ויסכרו מעינת תהום וארבת השמים). It
is significant that the opening and closing of heaven's sluices is
dependent upon man's response to Yahweh.[107] Deut 11:16f makes
it abundantly clear that if the people turn away from Yahweh to
serve other gods, he will close up the heavens (עצר את־השמים) so
that no rain will fall and the soil will not yield its crops. This
idea is also found in Malachi. Evidently the land was suffering
from drought, ravishment by locusts and crop failure, v. 11,
which the prophet interprets as due to the curse, מארה, of
Yahweh, v. 9. Because proper respect has not been paid to him
or his cult, the conditions requisite for fertility, i.e., rain, have
been barred to man.[108] Mal 3:10, however, indicates that human
repentance, man's return to God (3:10a-c), will lead to a responsive turning on Yahweh's part (3:10d, e). The curse will be lifted
and blessing (בְּרָכָה) will take its place in the form of the rains
needed to fructify the soil (cf. 3:11). Similarly, according to Joel,
blessing (בְּרָכָה) ensues from the return to Yahweh. Instead of
scorched earth and barren desert (1:10f; 2:3) God will leave behind
a blessing (2:14), that is, the rain that creates fertility so that
threshing floors will be full of grain and vats will overflow with
new wine and olive oil (2:23f).

בְּרָכָה: As the antithesis of the מְאֵרָה "curse" of sterility (cf. 3:9,
11), the בְּרָכָה, "blessing" of 3:10e, must be equated with fertility
and more specifically, with the rain upon which growth depends.
The identification of בְּרָכָה with rain is confirmed by the parallel
expression אֲרֻבּוֹת הַשָּׁמַיִם in 3:10d. The result of opening heavens'
sluices is the emptying out[109] of the rains stored above the
firmament. Moreover, since the blessing of rain makes the ground
fruitful, it is in no way surprising that the conception of blessing
also indicates the yield of the fields, cf. 3:11 and Joel 2:14, 23f.
These ideas are similarly connected in Ezek 34:26f.[110] ונתתי
אותם וסביבות גבעתי ברכה והורדתי הגשם בעתו גשמי ברכה יהיו : ונתן
עץ השדה את פריו והארץ תתן יבולה.

---

[107] Cf. Deut 28:9f; 15:22.

[108] Cf. also 2:2-3 where the priests' abhorrent cultic behavior has resulted in
a ban on fertility.

[109] Cf. הֲרִיקֹתִי, hiphil pf. of ריק, "to empty out, pour out," cf. BDB, 937-38.

[110] von Bulmerincq, remarks that on analogy with Ezek 34:26, the בְּרָכָה of
Mal 3:10e may be a shortened form of גשמי ברכה, 2.439.

עַד־בְּלִי־דָי: This last clause has been translated and interpreted in a variety of ways. Gesenius translates: "I will pour you out a blessing עַד־בְּלִי־דָי until (there is) not sufficiency, until all my abundance be exhausted, and as this can never be, it means, for ever."[111] C. Rabin suggests that *"dai* itself is an old dual of *d* 'hand,' and means 'power ability,' just as do *yādh* and *yādhayîm,"*[112] thus, "I will pour you out a blessing until my power be exhausted," i.e., forever. Van Hoonacker[113] and J. M. P. Smith[114] translate, "And I will pour you out a blessing until there is no more need." Although all the translations stress the abundance of blessing, in view of the identification of בְּרָכָה with rain, the latter interpretation best suits the context. The people need only as much as is necessary to saturate the soil and so initiate fertility. An unlimited supply, i.e., rain 'forever' would produce flooding and would be just as much a curse as is the present drought. Literally, עַד־בְּלִי־דָי should be translated, "until there is no sufficiency."[115] However, as J. M. P. Smith remarks, "'sufficiency' and 'need' are closely related ideas" and translating דָי "need" makes "no such demands upon the imagination as does any rendering based upon the meaning 'sufficiency.'"[116]

[3:11]—Continuing the theme of 3:10, this verse also enunciates the effects of a wholehearted return to Yahweh. The locusts, (cf. אכל), voracious eaters who have devastated the earth's produce, will be rendered incapable of continuing their destruction (3:11a). It is probable that 3:11a וְגָעַרְתִּי לָכֶם בָּאֹכֵל, "And I will restrain the devourer for you," is governed by the אִם־לֹא of 3:10d. The resultant tri-colon (3:10d, e; 3:11a), each line of which contains identical syntactic elements, cf. v. + i.o. + d.o., states in the strongest possible way, the benefits of properly directed cultic service.

---

[111] *Gesenius' Hebrew and Chaldee Lexicon* (Grand Rapids, Michigan: Wm. B. Eerdmans, 1949) 195; cf. BDB, 191.

[112] C. Rabin, "Hebrew D = Hand," *JSS* 6 (1955) 114.

[113] van Hoonacker, 736.

[114] J. M. P. Smith, 73 and cf. Sellin, 612.

[115] דָי, subst., "sufficiency, a large enough quantity," cf. *Gesenius' Hebrew and Chaldee Lexicon*, 195.

[116] J. M. P. Smith, 73. It should be noted that Cyrus Gordon (Review of Johannes Friedrich *Phönizisch-punische Grammatik, OR* 21 [1952] 119–123) translates דָי, "enough" (["my] two hands [full]"), 121, i.e., that which is needed to fill both hands.

בְּ + גָּעַר: In the previous discussion of גער (2:3),[117] it was suggested that "in origin g‹r denoted an aspect of the physical expression of anger; it is used to denote angry protest. When Yahweh is the subject, its connotation is both his anger and the effective working out of such."[118] Significantly, the anger of Yahweh "may be seen to effect the paralysis of the curse in its object"[119] (cf. Zech 3:2; Nah 1:4). This understanding accords well with Mal 3:11a. Yahweh is not "rebuking"[120] the devourer; he is restraining or paralyzing him thus ending his destructive activities.[121] Yahweh's anger, which effected the curse enunciated in 3:9, was directed against the people because of their cultic misdeeds. Rain was restrained (3:10e) and fertility decreased. Locusts were unleashed resulting in the devastation of whatever did germinate (3:11). That the locust here becomes the recipient of Yahweh's invective[122] is a consequence of the people's return to proper cultic service.

אֹכֵל is a qal active participle of אָכַל, "to eat." אכל is commonly used to express destructive or other hostile activities.[123] Israel is said to "devour her enemies" (cf. Deut 7:16; Ezek 19:3, 6; 36:13; Zech 12:6); other nations "devour" or "consume" Israel and its land (cf. Isa 1:7; Jer 8:16; 10:25; Ps 79:7). The fire of God "devours" the sons of Aaron (Lev 10:2), the rebels associated with Korah (Num 16:35; 26:10) and part of Job's possessions (1:16). Scholars agree that in Mal 3:11a the participle אֹכֵל describes the locust.[124] There is no better epithet of its genre since locusts are prodigious eaters who "devour" everything in their path. The most common designation for locusts is ארבה (cf. Exod 10:4, 12, 13f; Deut 28:38; Judg 6:5; Jer 46:23; Nah 3:15;

---

[117] Cf. above, 66–68.

[118] A. A. Macintosh, "A Consideration of Hebrew גער," *VT* 21 (1971) 479.

[119] Ibid., 474.

[120] Cf. BDB, 172.

[121] Similarly in 2:3, Yahweh is not "rebuking" the seed; he is paralyzing its ability to germinate.

[122] The preposition בְּ is used to denote the recipient of the invective, cf. also Isa 13:17; Nah 1:4.

[123] Cf. also Akk. "Akalu" in *CAD* I/1, 245–58.

[124] Cf. Sellin, 612; van Hoonacker, 737; J. Halévy, "Le prophète Malachie," *RS* 17 (1909) 38.

Joel 1:4), which refers specifically to the fully developed ones.[125] It is significant that even the larvae (= יֶלֶק, "hopper") like the fully grown insects are able to consume grass, seed crops, tree fruits and to strip branches, cf. Joel 1:6f. In his description of the infestation of Palestine by locusts in 1915–1916, G. Dalman reports:

> In Jerusalem the locusts appeared at that time in flights lasting for hours. . . . At the end of May and the beginning of June the first hatching of eggs . . . appeared as wingless larvae . . . , which wander about and eat up everything green that they encounter. Wild growth, grain, the leaves of fig trees, vines, even olive trees, everything disappears where they move along.[126]

The scope of the economic crisis caused by the locusts is illustrated in Joel (cf. 1:4f; 2:25) by the fact that they have carried out their destructive work so effectively that it will be felt for years to come.

Locust infestations are one of the ways in which Yahweh punishes his errant people (cf. Joel 1:4; 1 Kgs 8:37; Amos 4:9; Deut 28:42). In Joel (ch. 1), Amos (4:4f) and Malachi they are Yahweh's angry response to improper cultic activities and his call for repentance (cf. Amos 4:9; Job 2:12f; Isa 33:4; Deut 28:38). Only in return will the people find respite from the locusts' voracious appetites (cf. Joel 2:21–25; Mal 3:10–12).[127]

וְלֹא־יְשַׁחֵת . . . וְלֹא־תְשַׁכֵּל: These two lines detail further restorative effects of a return to Yahweh. The paralysis of the locust will end crop destruction (3:11b); the blessing of rain (3:10e) will ensure the ripening of the vines (3:11c).[128]

Both אדמה (n.f. ground, land) and שדה (n.m. field, land) designate arable land that is to be cultivated (cf. Gen 47:20–24; Deut 21:1; Joel 1:10; 2:21). It is significant that the ground's

---

[125] Cf. Gustaf Dalman, *Arbeit und Sitte in Palästina*, 1/2 (Gütersloher Verlagshaus Gerd Mohn, 1928; reprint ed., Hildesheim: George Olms, 1964) 394.

[126] Ibid., 393.

[127] Note that in Joel, the locusts are harbingers of the Day of Yahweh, cf. 1:15.

[128] Cf. 201–2.

productivity depends on man's response to Yahweh. His food
is God's gift; he eats according to the blessing of Yahweh
(cf. Deut 12:15f; 32:13; Hos 11:4). As long as Israel is faithful to
the covenant, the land gives sufficient harvest and the people
have enough to eat (cf. Lev 25:19; 26:35; Joel 2:23f). Refusal to
abide by the covenant stipulations results in judgment manifested
by a lack of nutriment (cf. Deut 28:17f, 23, 31, 33; Lev 26:26;
Isa 9:19; Amos 4:9; Mic 6:14). A return to the right relationship
with Yahweh restores the fertility of the land; the people will eat
and be satisfied (cf. Joel 2:12-26). So too in Malachi, the paralysis
of the locusts, the result of a return to Yahweh, enables the
people and not the voracious insects to harvest the produce (פְּרִי,
n.m. "fruit, produce") of their land; the return to Yahweh causes
the sluices of heaven to be opened (3:10d) and so provides the
rain necessary for the maturation of grape-bearing vines (גֶּפֶן, n.f.
"vine").[129]

All of the lines from 3:10d through 3:11c are similarly constructed: vb. + לָכֶם (Dativus commodi)[130] + n. Such syntactic
parallelism not only emphasizes the message contained in these
lines but highlights the continuity of that message. This constant
combination of vb. + לָכֶם + n. does not lead to an absence of
movement since progression of thought is achieved by changing
the verbal subject. In 3:10d, e; 11a, Yahweh is the speaker and
the verbs are in the first person (cf. אֶפְתַּח, הֲרִיקֹתִי, גָּעַרְתִּי). The
emphasis is on Yahweh's actions in response to his people's
return to proper service: he will open (vb.) for them (cf. לכם) the
sluices of heaven (n. = d.o.); he will pour out (vb.) for them
(cf. לכם) a blessing (n. = d.o.); he will restrain (vb.) for them
(cf. לכם) the devourer (n. = d.o.). 3:11b (vb. + לכם + n. = d.o.)
flows directly out of 3:11a but the subject is no longer Yahweh; it
is the devourer (אֹכֵל) which occupied the n. = d.o. slot in the
preceding line. As the result of Yahweh's paralyzing action the
locust will be unable to destroy (vb. = 3 m.s.—יַשְׁחִת, hiphil of
שחת, "to ruin, spoil") the people's (cf. לכם) produce (n. = d.o.).
In 3:11c, there is another subject change (vb. = 3 f.sg.) and the
noun (גפן) is no longer the direct object as in the preceding lines,
but is the subject. Continuing the thought initiated in 3:11b,

this line details a further positive result of Yahweh's response to his people's return. Although 3:11c may imply that prior to Yahweh's paralyzing action, the locusts either ate the immature grapes before they were ripe enough to be harvested or ate the vines, it is more likely that a drought accompanied and intensified the locust plague which resulted in a poor harvest (cf. Joel 1:10, 12, 18). This interpretation is suggested by 3:10d, e which imply the need for rain. Indeed, the shift from the preceding vb. + לכם + n. = d.o. to vb. + לכם + n. = subj. may be the prophet's way of alerting his hearers to the change of direction and bringing his message full circle so that it begins (3:10d) and ends (3:11c) with the blessing of rain. Finally, the vb. שכל in the piel means "to make childless, cause barrenness, abort,"[131] i.e., fail to grow to full-term (cf. 2 Kgs 2:19). This line does not imply that the vines were devastated as by locusts, but that they were unable to fully ripen. This inability is due to the lack of nourishing rain.

[3:12]—The fifth oracle unit closes with a non-parallel line[132] that succinctly restates the benefits of a return to Yahweh. The people's prosperity, the result of the outpouring of Yahweh's favor, will be so conspicuous that they will be the envy of all other nations (3:12a). With the return of the conditions requisite for fertility, the present lamentable state of the soil will give place to a fruitful and well nourished land.

אִשְּׁרוּ is a piel pf. of אשר, "to go straight, advance,"[133] and means "to pronounce blessed, happy, fortunate."[134] Waldemar Janzen remarks that in the OT, "the ᵓašrê-formula is a statement made to or about someone which somehow magnifies or extols the person's condition as a desirable one."[135] It is expressive of envious desire and it is spoken "upward"—i.e., "by one who is in a less desirable situation than the one he addresses."[136] Significantly, there exists a relationship between ᵓašrê and the forms of blessing (ברכה). According to J. Pedersen, the content

---

[131] BDB, 1013.
[132] Note the ᵓaleph alliteration.
[133] BDB, 80.
[134] Ibid.
[135] Waldemar Janzen, "Ašrê in the Old Testament," *HTR* 58 (1965) 215.
[136] Ibid., 225.

of blessing may be summarized as (I) children, descendants, (II) fertility of flocks, herds, fields, (III) defeat of enemies.[137] "The basis of the ᵓašrê-ascription consists of precisely the same content . . . descendants, fertility, security, cf. Ps 144:12-15, 127-128."[138] As can be clearly seen from Job 29:11 where the people consider Job fortunate (ᵓašr) after they have observed his state of blessing, "receipt of that which blessing has to bestow qualifies a person or group to be called ᵓašrê."[139] Similarly, in Mal 3:10-12, the people are blessed by Yahweh while the nations acknowledge it by calling them happy (ᵓašr).

כָּל־הַגּוֹיִם: In 3:9b, Israel was designated a gôy because her reprehensible cultic conduct rendered her unworthy to be distinguished from other gôyîm.[140] The result of her return to Yahweh, however, is that she is once more set apart from the nations as the beneficiary of his blessings.

אֶרֶץ חֵפֶץ: The land (אֶרֶץ) belongs to Yahweh (Lev 25:23). Disobedience to his commands violates its sacral character (cf. Isa 24:5f; Jer 2:7; 16:18) and turns a once fruitful land (ארץ פרי, Ps 107:34) into a desolate waste (cf. Lev 26:19f; 23:23f; Deut 28:23; 29:21f; Jer 12:11; Ezek 12:19; Zech 7:14). To the contrary, obedience carries with it the blessing of fertility (cf. Deut 11:10f; 28:9f) and makes the land a pleasant, desirable place in which to live (cf. ארץ חפץ, Mal 3:12b; ארץ חמדה, Jer 3:19; Ps 106:24). Indeed, it is the renewed fertility that induces the envy of the nations for (כִּי) Israel dwells in a fruitful and well nourished land, that is, a desirable one.[141]

This oracle unit begins with a threat of annihilation (3:7) and ends with a promise of blessing and life (3:10-12). It moves from a people in whom Yahweh finds no delight because of their cultic misdeeds (3:7-9) to a people in whom Yahweh will find

---

[137] Pedersen, 2.206-213.

[138] Janzen, 222.

[139] Ibid., 223.

[140] For a fuller discussion of the theologically pejorative use of גוי, see 191-92.

[141] In a general sense, men are called יֹשְׁבֵי־הָאָרֶץ, "inhabitants of the earth, land," cf. Isa 24:5, 17; Jer 25:29; Zeph 1:18. It is possible that the word יֹשֵׁב is implied in Mal 3:13b, cf. Ps 33:8: ייראו מיהוה כל־הארץ ממנו יגורו כל־ישבי תבל. Thus the line would read: "For you will be [inhabitants] of a desirable land."

the greatest pleasure because of their wholehearted return to his commands (3:10-12). Because a return to Yahweh would restore the sacral character of the land, it is possible that Malachi is affirming in this final line that the people will live in a land in which Yahweh can once again take delight.[142]

---

[142] Note the same scenario in Joel chapter 2 where turning to Yahweh (2:12-13) evokes a positive response from him. A land devastated by locusts (cf. ch. 1) will be made into a land of plenty, 2:18f.

CHAPTER X

MALACHI 3:13-21

A^3 B^2	¹³חזקו עלי דבריכם אמר יהוה
B_1 A_1^3	ואמרתם מה־נדברנו עליך
A B C D	¹⁴אמרתם שוא עבד אלהים
B_1^2 C_1^2 D_1	ומה־בצע כי שמרנו משמרתו
C_{11}^2	וכי הלכנו קדרנית
D_{11}^3	מפני יהוה צבאות
(Z) A^2 B	¹⁵ועתה אנחנו מאשרים זדים
C^2 B_1^2	גם־נבנו עשי רשעה
C_1^3 C_{11}	גם בחנו אלהים וימלטו
(Z) A B^2	¹⁶אז נדברו יראי יהוה
B_1^3	איש את־רעהו
C^2 C_1	ויקשב יהוה וישמע
D E^2 F	ויכתב ספר זכרון לפניו
B_{11}^2 B_{111}^2	ליראי יהוה ולחשבי שמו
A^2 B^3	¹⁷והיו לי אמר יהוה צבאות
C^4 D	ליום אשר אני עשה סגלה
A B	וחמלתי עליכם
A_1^3	כאשר יחמל איש
B_1^4	על־בנו העבד אתו
A^2 B^2 C	¹⁸ושבתם וראיתם בין צדיק לרשע
B_1^3	בין עבד אלהים
C_1^3	לאשר לא עבדו
(Z) A B C	¹⁹כי־הנה היום בא
C_1 D	בער כתנור
E F^2 F_1^3 G	והיו כל־זדים וכל־עשה רשעה קש
C_{11} F_{11} B_1^2	ולהט אתם היום הבא אמר יהוה צבאות
C_{111}^3 F_{111} G_1^2	אשר לא־יעזב להם שרש וענף
A B B_1^2 C^2	²⁰וזרחה לכם יראי שמי שמש צדקה
D_1^2	ומרפא בכנפיה

A A₁ B²   ויצאתם ופשתם כעגלי מרבק

A₁₁ C   ²¹ועסותם רשעים

C₁³ D³   כי־יהיו אפר תחת כפות רגליכם

E⁴   ביום אשר אני עשה

                      אמר יהוה צבאות

(3:13) *Your words have become too much for me," says Yahweh.*
Yet you say: "What have we spoken against you?"

(3:14) *You have said: "It is worthless to serve God;*
And what profit is it that we have kept his charge,
And that we have walked earnestly before Yahweh Sebaot?

(3:15) *So now we deem the arrogant happy;*
Indeed, the committers of wickedness are built up;
They even test God and escape."

(3:16) *Then the Yahweh fearers spoke together, each with*
his fellow;
And Yahweh paid attention and heard,
And a book of remembrance was written before him
regarding those who fear Yahweh and esteem his name.

(3:17) *"And they will become," says Yahweh Sebaot,*
"on the day when I act, a special possession of mine.
And I will have compassion on them just as a
man has compassion on his son who serves him."

(3:18) *"And you shall again distinguish between the*
righteous and the wicked,
between him who serves God and him who does not."

(3:19) *"For the day is indeed coming,*
burning like an oven;
And all the arrogant and all those who commit
wickedness will be stubble;
And the coming day will set them ablaze," says
Yahweh Sebaot;
"it will leave them neither root nor branch."

(3:20) *"But as for you who fear my name the sun of righteousness*
will arise with healing in its wings;
And you shall go out and gambol like well-fed cattle.

(3:21) *And you shall tread down the wicked*
for they will be as ashes under the soles of your feet
on the day when I act,"
says Yahweh Sebaot.

3:13-21: Content and Structure

The sixth and final oracle unit is addressed to the pious[1] within the community who have come to question the value of their piety in Yahweh's eyes. The facts of experience seem to militate against the profitableness of godliness. Indeed, the contrast with what ought to have been is striking. The people who have scorned the requirements of God have prospered while those who have feared him look upon them, the evildoers, with envious eyes (3:13-15). The thematic parallelism between this oracle unit and the fourth (2:17-3:5), the repetitiveness of the claims, amply demonstrates the acuteness of the problem—the desire to reconcile Yahweh's supposed justice with the evident inequalities of life. The fifth oracle unit (3:6-12) unequivocally proclaimed that "return" (שׁוּב) to Yahweh would be rewarded by an abundance of blessing. To the pious who had never left and who were suffering privation as a result of heavy taxation and locust infestation,[2] this must have seemed the greatest of injustices. Their disgruntled murmurings, however, disturbed Yahweh as is clear from the *hingestellte Behauptung*, חָזְקוּ עָלַי דִּבְרֵיכֶם "your words are too much for me" (3:13a). When the people query: מַה־נִּדְבַּרְנוּ עָלֶיךָ, "What have we spoken against you?" (3:13b), Yahweh responds by listing their grievances against him (3:14-15). Although their impatience is rebuked and the tone of their murmurings is censured, the pious are not condemned. After all, they are the יִרְאֵי יהוה, "the fearers of Yahweh" (3:16a); the great day of judgment will signal their vindication (3:17-21). The evildoers will be totally consumed and the righteous will actively participate in their destruction (3:19). On the day of Yahweh all will see that virtue is rewarded and vice is punished (3:18). There will no longer be any excuse for the pious to question the existence of a just judge (cf. 2:17); Yahweh too, will be vindicated.

Text and Commentary

[3:13]— . . . חָזְקוּ עָלַי: The *hingestellte Behauptung* of this final oracle unit, חָזְקוּ עָלַי דִּבְרֵיכֶם "Your words have grown strong

---

[1] Cf. J. M. P. Smith, *Malachi* (ICC; Edinburgh: T. & T. Clark, 1912) 76; A. von Hoonacker, *Les douze petits prophètes* (Paris: Gabalda, 1908) 737.

[2] Cf. Mal 3:10-11.

against me,''[3] admits the seriousness of the problem faced by the pious. Their continued failure to receive the blessings promised for faithfulness and meticulous ritual observance (cf. 3:6–12) has induced them to speak out harshly against Yahweh's brand of justice.

The verb חָזַק in the qal means "to be or grow strong, firm, strengthen, to grow stout, rigid, hard, with the idea of perversity''[4] (cf. Exod 7:13; 8:15; 9:35). According to N. Waldman, the Hebrew has a semantic range "partially paralleled by Akkadian *danānu* "be strong" and the derived words, *dannu*, "strong, severe" and *dannatu*, "strength, severity, difficulty.''[5] The Hebrew חָזַק עַל—finds its Akkadian parallel:

> in a construction limited to Neo-Assyrian and Neo-Babylonian, dān eli, dān eli muhhi, and dān ana, "be too much for, be too strong for." LÚ. GAL. MEŠ-*ia qitrub tāḫazi* LÚ. KUR *elišun idninma ul ili'u maḫaršu,* "as for my officers, the onslaught of the enemy became too strong for them;" *dulla ina muḫḫini idnini,* "the work has become too much for us.''[6]

Waldman remarks that "there are a number of instances of *ḥzq* *ᶜl* in the OT which do not have the sense we are considering, but the obviously related one of "prevail over, overpower, urge" (cf. Exod 12:33; Dan 11:5). However, in the light of the parallel material, Mal 3:13 might be rendered: "Your words have been too much for me,''[7] or perhaps, "your words have become too much for me." This translation provides a striking contrast to the parallel *hingestellte Behauptung* of 2:17a. Words that Yahweh once found merely tiresome (הוֹגַעְתֶּם יהוה בְּדִבְרֵיכֶם, 2:17a), he now finds intolerable.

נִדְבַּרְנוּ :מַה־נִּדְבַּרְנוּ עָלֶיךָ is a niphal pf. 1 c. pl. of דָּבֶר "to speak";[8] "the niphal expresses reciprocal or mutual action,"[9]

---

[3] Notice the LXX ἐβαρυνατε has דִּבְרֵיכֶם as its object.

[4] BDB, 304.

[5] N. Waldman, "Some Notes on Malachi 3:6; 3:13 and Psalm 42:11," *JBL* 93 (1974) 545.

[6] Ibid., 545–46.

[7] Ibid., 546.

[8] BDB, 180–81.

[9] *GKC* #51d, 137.

e.g., "to speak to one another," "to talk together." The people's
retort, מַה־נִּדְבַּרְנוּ עָלֶיךָ "What have we spoken against you?",[10]
does not deny that Yahweh's ways have been the object of
criticism in conversational circles. Rather, Yahweh's avowal that
their words are intolerable (too strong, 3:13a), leads the people to
wonder just what they have said that is untrue. Their question
challenges Yahweh to prove the error of their logic and he
accepts the challenge. In the verses that follow Yahweh first
enumerates their grievances against him (3:14-15) and then
assures the pious that the blessing they so ardently seek will be
fully realized on the great day of judgment that is coming
(3:16-21).

[3:14-15]—In the Israelite view there was a definite and
clearly recognizable connection between a man's actions and the
state of his life, "a connection frequently interpreted as a consequence of divine retribution."[11] Observance of God's commandments guaranteed the preservation of life and blessing; violation
resulted in punishment, suffering and death (cf. Deut 28; 30:15f).
In Exod 20:5f Yahweh is characterized as a jealous god who
visits "the iniquity of the fathers upon the children to the third
and fourth generation" of those who hate him, yet shows
"steadfast love to the thousandth generation" of those who love
him. These verses illustrate the general principle of collective
responsibility (cf. also Deut 28:1, 15).

> The family or clan constitutes a single unit within which
> each individual is responsible for the actions of the other
> members. Not only does this mean that children must
> answer for the sins of their fathers, but also that all
> members of a clan, or even all the inhabitants of a city or
> of the whole land, share this responsibility. If a murder
> is committed in a city and the murderer remains uniden-
> tified, guilt rests on the entire region and expiation must
> be made (Deut 21:1-9). The king's sin brings misfortune
> upon the entire land (2 Sam 24). On the other hand, how-
> ever, the presence of a small number of righteous men can

---

[10] For דִּבֶּר + עַל, "to speak against," see Amos 3:1; Hos 7:13; Ezek 36:5;
Dan 9:12.

[11] Helmer Ringgren, *Israelite Religion* (Philadelphia: Fortress, 1966) 137.

> save an entire city, as the story of Abraham's intercession
> on behalf of Sodom presupposes (Gen 18:23-33).[12]

This idea of collective responsibility must not be oversimplified as meaning that the individual was robbed of his individuality. A man's actions directly affected both the integrity of the group to which he belonged and his own life (cf. Prov 12:4; Job 34:11).[13] That there was a real expectation of individual reward and punishment is evident from the frequently asked question, "Why do the wicked prosper?" The psalmist is enraged when he sees how the godless live without pain and suffering (cf. 73:5f). Persecuted by enemies, Jeremiah asks why all the treacherous thrive (12:1-2). However, so long as appeal could be made to the family or the clan, the unjust suffering of one individual posed no real problem for faith. After all, one's merits might fall to a succeeding generation. But a painful questioning of God's justice did arise in "the final years of the monarchical period with their political catastrophe,"[14] and especially in the exilic period and beyond with the disappearance of a free society based on collective guilt and punishment. As von Rad remarked, the new generation

> ... knew itself to be cut off from that of the fathers and
> made responsible for itself alone: it can no longer con-
> ceive of the possibility that the sowing of the fate
> bringing action might in certain circumstances only
> ripen in later generations. Because of this it looked upon
> its relationship with God as threatened.[15]

Indeed, with the loss of the nation and the resultant loss of the solidarity with past and future generations, a single example of innocent suffering called into question Yahweh's justice and power. It is this sort of situation that confronts Malachi in 3:14-15. The harsh words of the people that are recounted here should not be viewed as the symptom of an exhausted piety, but

---

[12] Ibid., 137-38.

[13] G. von Rad, *Old Testament Theology* (2 vols.; New York: Harper and Row, 1962-65) 1.387.

[14] Ibid., 391.

[15] Ibid., 392.

as the symptom of an anguished faith as the pious question how it could be consonant with God's righteousness to compel the devout to endure sufferings they have not merited.

[3:14]—שָׁוְא . . . וּמַה־בֶּצַע: The root meaning of שָׁוְא (n.m.) is "to be empty," "groundless."[16] "Because something without substance was considered worthless, the term almost always carries pejorative overtones."[17] Isaiah 1:13 speaks of מִנְחַת־שָׁוְא worthless offerings. Idols are called הַבְלֵי־שָׁוְא because they are without substance (Ps 31:7). To flatter a person is to speak שָׁוְא, words devoid of truth, unable to be substantiated, Ps 12:3. The people's complaint in Mal 3:14a is that it is worthless (שָׁוְא) to serve (עֲבֹד, qal, inf, cs.)[18] God. Piety yields no tangible benefits. There is no profit (בֶּצַע, n.m.) to keeping Yahweh's commands. The verb בָּצַע originally meant "to cut off," "and presumably it was used at an early period as a technical term in the manufacture of carpets with reference to the weaver 'cutting off' a ready-woven piece of material from the thrum."[19] This gave rise "to the figurative meaning . . . 'to cut off a piece, i.e., to take one's cut, profit'. . . . The meaning of the noun is limited almost entirely to this . . . idea. In almost all the passages in the OT where it occurs, beṣaᶜ means 'a piece that is cut off, (illegal) profit or gain.' "[20] In and of itself, profitmaking was not illegal according to OT thought (cf. Gen 30:25-43; Job 22:3; Sir 42:5). However, greed, profits gained by unjust dealings were condemned (cf. 1 Sam 8:3; Isa 59:9-12; Jer 6:13, 22:13-19; Ezek 21:12f; Prov 1:19, 15:27; 28:16). In Mal 3:14b, the noun בֶּצַע does not convey the negative idea of "unjust gain;" it carries the neutral connotation of "profit."[21]

According to J. M. P. Smith, the people's remarks in 3:14a-b reveal that they view piety in the same light as a commercial venture. "If Yahweh received the gifts, obedience and worship of

---

[16] BDB, 996.

[17] Brevard Childs, *The Book of Exodus* (OTL; Philadelphia: Westminster, 1974) 410.

[18] עֲבַד, "to serve" describes man's proper conduct toward God, i.e., "to worship," cf. C. Lindhagen, *The Servant Motif in the Old Testament* (Uppsala: Lundeqvist, 1950) 152f.

[19] Kellerman, "בצע bṣᶜ; בֶּצַע betsaᶜ," *TDOT* 2.206.

[20] Ibid., 206-7.

[21] For the combination בֶּצַע + מַה see Gen 37:26; Ps 30:10.

his people, it is incumbent upon him to make liberal returns in the form of material prosperity, political influence and supremacy, and the like. If such things are not forthcoming, why worship him?"[22] Although the juxtaposed use of שָׁוְא (worthless) and בֶּצַע (profit) does indeed suggest that if piety is to continue it must be, to some extent, self-serving, it would be misguided to argue that the people's standard of value for religion was crass and commercial. Throughout Malachi's prophecy there is great stress placed on the connection between one's relation to Yahweh and the state of one's life. When the Levites abided by God's strictures, they lived in peace; when they turned away from him, Yahweh brought them low (2:5-9). In Mal 3:5 the evildoers were warned of the precariousness of their situation before Yahweh; in 3:7; 11-12, they were told that if they reoriented their lives they would experience an abundance of blessing. It is in view of this situation that the pious seek to ascertain their position before God (3:14). With the growth of the consciousness of individualism,[23] it became necessary for each man to explore the nature of his relationship to Yahweh, to ask what part he had in God's salvation and when he could expect to receive his due (cf. Isa 33:15b). The desire to "profit" now from piety, to experience present tangible benefits (3:14a-b) may be the reaction of the pious to the boons promised to the evildoers in return for their reorientation.

מִשְׁמַרְתּוֹ is a n.f. from שָׁמַר meaning "to guard, watch,"[24] also "charge, function."[25] According to J. M. P. Smith שָׁמַר מִשְׁמַרְתּוֹ, "to guard his charge," Mal 3:14b, "is practically equivalent to 'his commands' or 'statutes'; it refers to religious duties in general and is not to be identified with any particular ritualistic obligations."[26] In Gen 26:4-5, Isaac is told that his descendants will be as numerous as the stars in the sky עֵקֶב אֲשֶׁר שָׁמַע אַבְרָהָם בְּקֹלִי וַיִּשְׁמֹר מִשְׁמַרְתִּי מִצְוֹתַי חֻקּוֹתַי וְתוֹרֹתָי, "because Abraham obeyed my voice and guarded my charge, my commandments, my statutes and my instruction." Deuteronomy 11:1 urges the Israelites to love Yahweh by guarding his charge (שמר

---

[22] J. M. P. Smith 76-77.

[23] Cf. above, 210-11.

[24] Cf. 2 Kgs 11:5-7; 1 Chr 12:30— שמר משמרת "keep the watch."

[25] BDB, 1038.

[26] J. M. P. Smith, 77.

משמרת), his statutes (חק), his ordinances (משפט) and his commandments (מצות). Such conduct which is synonymous with "walking
in the way," הלך בדרך, laid down by Yahweh at Horeb, ensures
life and prosperity (cf. Deut 11:22-24). On his deathbed, David
advises his son, Solomon, to guard Yahweh's charge (ושמרת את־
משמרת יהוה), and to walk in his ways (ללכת בדרכיו) for such
conduct will guarantee success in all his undertakings (1 Kgs
2:1-3, cf. also Zech 3:7; Josh 22:3f). It is this clearly stated
connection between following Yahweh, guarding his charge
(שמר משמרת) and success and prosperity that the pious are
refuting in 3:14b. Despite their faithfulness, they have profited
(בָּצַע) not at all.

הלכנו קדרנית: קדרנית is an adverb[27] from קָדַר, "to be dark."[28]
Deriving it from the Arabic قَدِر, "to be dirty, filthy," most scholars translate קדר, "to mourn, be in mourning," "be unkempt,
sloppily dressed," "to go in filthy garments as mourners."[29]
According to J. M. P. Smith, הָלַךְ קֹדְרַנִּית, to go "in mourning"
"probably refers primarily to the outer garb."[30] Sellin remarks:
"Das קֹדְרַנִּית, eigentlich schmutzig, dann im Trauerhabitus . . .
ist bezeichnend für die damalige Frömmigkeit, dieselbe mani-
festiert sich in Fasten, Sichkasteien, Büssen und Klagen."[31]
These translations must be challenged. The Hebrew stem קדר
does not mean "dirty." The sky, the day, the stars darken or
become obscured (cf. Jer 4:28; Mich 3:6; Joel 2:10; Ezek 32:7f;
1 Kgs 18:45); they do not become dirty or squalid. In Pss 35:14,
38:7; 42:10; 43:2 the LXX translates קדר with σκυθρωπάζειν "to
be vexed, of a sad countenance."[32] The translator obviously
recognized that קדר, "to be dark" = "to mourn" refers to the
countenance and not to the clothes, cf. also Syriac ܟܡܪ "to be
gloomy, sad,"[33] Jer 8:21; Pss 38:7; 42:10; 43:2; Job 30:28. In Job

---

[27] Cf. אחרנית, GKC #100g, 295.

[28] BDB, 871.

[29] Cf. BDB, 871; J. M. P. Smith, 83; Gesenius' Hebrew and Chaldee Lexicon,
(Grand Rapids, Michigan: Wm. B. Eerdmans, 1949) 729. A. Cohen, The Twelve
Prophets (London: Soncino, 1948) 353.

[30] J. M. P. Smith, 77.

[31] Ernst Sellin, Das Zwölfprophetenbuch übersetzt und erklärt (KAT 12/2;
Leipzig: A Deichertsche, 1930) 614.

[32] LSJ, 1616.

[33] R. Payne Smith, A Compendious Syriac Dictionary (Oxford: Clarendon,
1903) 217.

5:11, שפלים and קדרים are parallel. The lowly, humiliated ones (שפלים) will be put on high; the wretched (קדרים) will be exalted. Jeremiah is wretched (קָדַרְתִּי) over the collapse of the בַּת־עַמִּי, "the daughter of my people," 8:21. The translation "blue, wretched," "to have a serious, troubled or worried face" suits the tenor of Mal 3:14c. The pious are the God-fearers, the יִרְאֵי יהוה (3;16), those who obey Yahweh, who keep his charge (שמר מִשְׁמֶרֶת) (3:14b). Here they question the profitability of their earnestness, the seriousness with which they have taken their obligations to Yahweh. The phrase הָלַךְ קְדֹרַנִּית מִפְּנֵי may be rendered "[and what profit is it] that we have walked earnestly,[34] i.e., with an earnest, serious face, before (מִפְּנֵי, in the presence of 'um seinetwillen'[35]) Yahweh." There is, however, another possibility. The pious may have "walked mournfully" (הָלַךְ קְדֹרַנִּית), i.e., with woebegone, wretched faces, when in Yahweh's presence in an attempt to draw his attention to their precarious state. Nevertheless, that ploy yielded no profit either.

[3:15]—זֵדִים אַשְּׁרִים זֵדִים: זֵדִים is a m. pl. verbal adj. from זוּד, זִיד, meaning "proud (properly swelling up, inflated), with the connected idea of insolence and impiety."[36] It is used substantively as a *terminus technicus* for godless, rebellious men (cf. Prov 21:24; Isa 13:11; Jer 43:2; Pss 19:14; 86:14; 119:21, 51, 69, 78, 85, 122. In Mal 3:15a זֵדִים, "the proud, presumptuous ones," is parallel to עֹשֵׂי רִשְׁעָה, "the committers of wickedness," those who turn away from Yahweh's statutes, (cf. Ezek 18:27; 33:19).[37] To the righteous they are objects of envious desire (cf. מְאַשְּׁרִים)[38] because, in spite of their impiety, their evilness, they prosper (3:15b); they try Yahweh repeatedly and escape unpunished (3:15c).

גם: The particle גם introduces intensive clauses[39] often serving to make a sentence emphatic (cf. Job 18:5; 1 Sam 24:12;

---

[34] For the combination הלך + קדר cf. also Pss 38:7; 42:10; 43:2; Job 30:28.

[35] A. von Bulmerincq, *Der Prophet Maleachi* (2 vols.; Tartu: J. G. Kruger, 1926–1932) 2.478.

[36] *Gesenius' Hebrew and Chaldee Lexicon*, 238.

[37] Note Ps 119:21 where זֵדִים is in parallelism with השגים ממצותיך, "those who stray from your commandments."

[38] מְאַשְּׁרִים is a piel m. pl. ptcpl. of אָשַׁר, "to go straight, advance." For a discussion of אשר, cf. Mal 3:12, 202f.

[39] *GKC* #153, 483.

Hos 9:12). In Mal 3:15b, c גם should be translated, "indeed, even, = moreover." The intent of these lines is not simply to list the reasons why the godless are envied. Above all, they express the incredulity of the righteous that such conduct is sanctioned by Yahweh (cf. 3:15c, "They even test God and escape").

נִבְנוּ is a niphal pf. 3 m. pl. of בָּנָה "build" and means "to be built, established,"[40] "built up."[41] According to Israel's strongly deterministic theological world view, nothing can be built "unless Yahweh builds it; the builders labor in vain without Yahweh (Ps 127:1)."[42] If God tears down, no one can rebuild without his help (cf. Job 12:14). In Jer 31:4 Yahweh avows: עוד אבנך ונבנית בתולת ישראל, "Again I will build you and you will be built, O virgin Israel." Yahweh is regarded as the master builder of Jerusalem and its sanctuary (Pss 78:69; 147:2; he will rebuild the ruined Zion, Ps 102:15-17). He is also regarded as the architect of men's lives. Indeed, "a man's good fortune is understood as "being built up" by God,"[43] cf. Job 22:23, אם־תשוב עד־שדי תִּבָּנֶה "If you return to Shaddai, you will be built up," i.e., you will prosper. In Ps 28:5, the righteous pray that Yahweh will destroy the prosperity of the evildoers, ואל־מעשה ידיו יהרסם ולא יבנם. To Malachi's contemporaries the contrast with what ought to have been is striking. The wicked who have scorned the requirements of Yahweh have not received the punishment they so well merit. Rather, they escape all trouble and are built up (נִבְנוּ) by God; they prosper on every hand.

בָּחֲנוּ . . . וַיִּמָּלֵטוּ: In Mal 3:15c the righteous level their final accusations at both the evildoers and at Yahweh. The wicked are accused of trying or testing[44] (בָּחֲנוּ qal pf. 3 m. pl., בָּחַן) God. God is accused of permitting their conduct to go unpunished (cf. וַיִּמָּלֵטוּ). According to J. M. P. Smith, "the 'test' is probably an allusion to the 'test' proposed in 3:10,"[45] וּבְחָנוּנִי נָא בָּזֹאת. As an enticement to the evildoers, Yahweh suggests that they "try" something out on him, that they "test" his reaction to the

[40] BDB, 125.
[41] S. Wagner, "בָּנָה bānāh," TDOT 2.173.
[42] Ibid., 173.
[43] Ibid.
[44] M. Tsevat, "בָּחַן bḥn," TDOT 2.71
[45] Ibid., 77.

receipt of the full tithe (3:10a–c) to see if he does indeed reward proper service with an abundance of blessing (3:10d–12). What is significant here is that the evildoers are asked to test God and that their testing will induce a positive response from him; it is seen as the first step in a return (שׁוּב) to Yahweh, the major theme of the fifth oracle unit (3:6–12). That the testing referred to in Mal 3:15c alludes to this scenario is questionable.[46]

There is no implication in 3:15 that the evildoers have been asked to test Yahweh. Rather, the tenor of the sixth oracle unit (cf. esp. 3:14–15) suggests that they are provoking him, "trying" him beyond endurance and in spite of that, they do not receive the punishment they merit; they escape, וַיִּמָּלֵטוּ (niphal impf., 3 m. pl., מָלַט, "to slip away, escape"[47])

Psalm 95:9f recounts Israel's wilderness experience. At Massah and Meribah Yahweh provided water for a contentious people who challenged (נסה, "test, try,"[48] בָּחַן) his presence among them, a people who had seen repeatedly Yahweh's great works, גם־ראו פעלי 95:9. Indeed, Yahweh's signs should have led Israel to an unconditional trust in her God. That she must continually "try, test" (בחן, נסה) Yahweh reveals her lack of faith, a shortcoming which is punished by God's refusal to let that generation enter the promised land, 95:11. These sentiments are echoed in Num 14:11f. The discovery that Canaan was strongly fortified led the people to doubt their ability to conquer the land and to grumble against their leaders (14:29). Angered, Yahweh wonders how long (עד־אנה) they will continue to spurn him (ינאצני), to refuse to believe in him (לא־יאמינו בי), 14:11. Because they tested (נסה) Yahweh ten times, because they failed to listen to him (לא שמעו בקולי) despite all the signs he performed in their midst, 14:22, they are refused entry into the promised land (14:23).

From these passages it is evident that to "test" God (בחן, נסה) may be indicative of a lack of faith in him and a defiant self will. This is precisely the sense of בָּחַן in Mal 3:15c. The evildoers, called the זֵדִים, the proud, arrogant, 3:15a, are those who have faith solely in their own ability and consequently defy or challenge Yahweh's authority at every turn. That Yahweh has not

---

[46] Cf. also von Bulmerincq, 2.486.

[47] BDB, 572.

[48] Tsevat, 69.

punished the testers (cf. וַיִּמָּלֵטוּ) as he did in the past the righteous find objectionable.

[3:16-21]—The final section of the sixth oracle unit revolves around the imminent "Day of Yahweh" (cf. also 3:1-5), a day which will vindicate Yahweh in the eyes of the righteous and the righteous in the eyes of the wicked. What is significant in these verses is the concept of a division within the community between evildoers on the one side and the faithful on the other. The final day of Yahweh is seen as the occasion for revealing what is "good" and what is "bad."

[3:16]—אָז: Based on the LXX reading ταῦτα, most commentators change the particle אָז, "then," to זֶה,[49] זֹה[50] or זֹאת,[51] "this, these things." According to both J. M. P. Smith and E. Sellin, "this rendering . . . shows unmistakably that the words of vv. 14-15 are spoken by those who worship Yahweh,"[52] i.e., "These things have those who feared Yahweh spoken together." The MT אָז, "then," "involves assigning the foregoing doubts to the godless in Israel, interpreting 'the arrogant' as characterizing the heathen, and leaving the words of the pious unrecorded. Furthermore, no definite point of attachment in time can be found for 'then'."[53] However, the emendation of the MT אָז, "then," to זֶה or זֹאת, "this, these things," is thematically unsuitable. In both 3:13 and 3:16 the righteous speak among themselves. According to 3:13, Yahweh refuses to listen to their words; he finds them intolerable (חָזְקוּ עָלַי דִּבְרֵיכֶם). It is inconceivable, therefore, that "these" same words (cf. the emendation, זֹאת, זֶה נדברו) should now elicit a favorable response from him (cf. 3:16b, וַיַּקְשֵׁב וַיִּשְׁמָע). Yahweh's contrasting reactions suggest that the tone of the God fearers words changed, a change presaged by the particle אָז, "then." It may be that after they listened to Yahweh's enumeration of their grievances, אָז, "then, at that time, after that,"[54] they spoke with one another in a more conciliatory vein,

---

[49] Cf. J. M. P. Smith, 81; van Hoonacker, 738.
[50] Cf. von Bulmerincq, 2.490; Sellin, 614.
[51] Cf. also Sellin, 614.
[52] J. M. P. Smith, 78; Sellin, 614.
[53] J. M. P. Smith, 78.
[54] "The perfect is used after אָז when stress is to be laid on the fact that the action has really taken place," GKC #107c, 314.

perhaps revising their assessment, and as a result, Yahweh was able to listen to them (cf. 3:16b).

יְרָאֵי יהוה: The יְרָאֵי יהוה are the fearers of Yahweh, those who honor him and serve him well. As a group, they stand in contrast to the זֵדִים, the "arrogant" ones (3:15a, 19a), the עֹשֵׂי רִשְׁעָה, those who commit wickedness (3:15b, cf. 3:19b) and the רְשָׁעִים, the wicked (3:21a), that is, all those who disregard Yahweh's authority, who refuse to obey his commands, who would be masters of their own fate.[55]

Man's proper attitude toward God is described by the word יָרֵא, "fear," "reverence," "a word frequently used to designate the religious attitude in general,"[56] (cf. Deut 6:13; Ps 2:11). However, religion was never confined to fear. No matter in what small measure, there was always a feeling of longing for the presence of God, trust in God's benevolence and helpfulness, and even love. Deut 10:12 clearly exhibits the characteristic ambivalence of the religious experience. Because God is both *tremendum* and *fascinosum,* man must fear him and love him. These are the "two poles between which man's appropriate reaction moves."[57]

Although the fear of Yahweh may express itself as real fear and trembling, cf. Exod 15; 20:18-19; Pss 33:8, 76:8f, "usually the fear of God means reverence before God,"[58] the awe inspired by his presence. As H. A. Brongers remarks,

> La révélation de la redoutable majesté divine effraye l'homme et le met fuite. Mais l'homme ne peut pas continuer à fuir Dieu; cetter attitude étant tout à fair stérile d'un point de vue spirituel. L'homme revient à son Dieu, parcequ'il reconnaît en ce Dieu son supérieur et qu'il est prêt a se soumettre à Son autorité. Il veut être lié avec son Dieu malgré tout, et il veut faire tout ce que ce Dieu exige de lui. Aussi nous ne sommes point étonnés de voir prendre la notion de jirᵓat Jhwh le sens de: obeissance à Ses commandments(מצותיו) et à Ses statuts (חקתיו) Deut. v 28, vi 2, 24, viii 6, xiii 4.[59]

---

[55] Cf. above, 214-15.
[56] Ringgren, 126.
[57] Ibid.
[58] Ibid., 127.
[59] H. A. Brongers, "La Crainte Du Seigneur," *OTS* 5 (1948) 161.

In other words, the fear of Yahweh refers not only to the experience of awe, but to its consequence, that is, obedience. Fear of Yahweh means to serve Yahweh (Deut 6:13; 10:20; Josh 24:14; 1 Sam 12:14, 24). It is synonymous with loving God (אהב), Deut 10:12; being devoted to him, Deut 10:20; and following him (הלך אחרי יהוה), Deut 13:15. Indeed, in itself, the expression fear of God combines *tremendum* and *fascinosum*, fear and love.

The God fearers are the faithful, the cult congregation, "les hommes pieux, qui ont la bonne attitude vis-à-vis de Dieu, qui d'un côté savent ce qu'ils peuvent attrendre de Jhwh, et qui, d'un autre côté, savent très clairement ce qu'ils Lui doivent."[60] Those who fear Yahweh are those who heed his words (Exod 9:20), who receive his correction, Zeph 3:7, who are trustworthy and hate dishonest gain (Exod 18:21). They observe the Sabbath (Lev 19:3), swear only by Yahweh's name (Deut 6:13; 10:30), and exhibit social justice (Lev 19:14; 25:36, 43). According to Brongers, "dans tous ces passages la *jir²at Jhwh* exprime la base de normes de la vie qui doivent être respectées dans le monde."[61]

To the man who fears Yahweh, who stands in the proper relationship to him, the benefits are considerable. He is the recipient of Yahweh's blessing (Ps 115:13) and his eternal kindness (Pss 103:11, 17). He prospers (Deut 5:29) and receives the homage of his contemporaries (Prov 22:4); his name is inscribed in Yahweh's book of remembrance (Mal 3:16). Superficially it appears as though fearing God is grounded in utilitarianism, that is, it is good to fear Yahweh because one is suitably recompensed. Brongers remarks however,

> Mais à regarder de plus près on s'aperçoit que la vie et ses biens ne doit pas être considérée dans le sens d'un matérialisme vulgaire. Cette vie est unie à Dieu et ne cesse pas de l'être. On ne se le représente pas sans Dieu. C'est pourquoi cette vie est dans le sens le plus absolu du terme une vie dans la crainte de l'Eternel.[62]

---

[60] Ibid., 162.
[61] Ibid., 164.
[62] Ibid., 166-67.

וַיִּכָּתֵב סֵפֶר זִכָּרוֹן: The root כָּתַב, "to write, inscribe," is used "as a *terminus technicus* for determining the fate of man,"[63] (cf. Pss 69:29; 139:16). That Yahweh himself does not write (cf. וַיִּכָּתֵב, niphal, "it was written") the book described by Malachi accords with "the well documented motif of the divine book-keeper"[64] (cf. Pss 32:2; 51:3; 69:28–29; 78:8; 87:6; 130:3; 139:16).

The combination סֵפֶר זִכָּרוֹן, "book of remembrance," appears only in Mal 3:16 and in Est 6:1 (סֵפֶר הַזִּכְרֹנוֹת).[65] Nehemiah, however, asks God to remember (זכר) him and not wipe out his good deeds, presumably from the book in which such deeds were recorded, 13:14, cf. 5:3. In Exod 17:14 Yahweh commands Moses to record (כתב) as a memorial (זכרון) in a book (בספר) his intention to wipe out the name of Amalek.

The concept of books preserved in heaven is well known. In the apocryphal literature reference is made to 'heavenly tablets' which record "all the deeds of mankind . . . to the remotest generation," 1 Enoch 81:2; they foretell the whole history of the world (1 Enoch 93:2, cf. Jub. 5:13; 23:30f; 30:21–22; 32:21–22; T. Asher 7:5; 2:10; T. Levi 5:4). These heavenly tablets "appear in the Babylonian sources as 'tablets of destiny' and play a significant part in the New Year ritual in the ceremony of fixing the destinies. Thus, when Marduk defeats the dragon Tiamat the tablets are placed in his hands, signifying that now the power and the victory belong to him."[66] The belief that world events and men's lives were predetermined by God is also found in the OT. The psalmist writes:

גלמי ראו עיניך
ועל־ספרך כלם יכתבו
ימים יצרו ולא אחד בהם   139:16.

---

[63] Mitchell Dahood, *Psalms III* (AB; Garden City, N.Y.: Doubleday, 1970) 295.

[64] Mitchell Dahood, *Psalms II* (AB; Garden City, N.Y.: Doubleday, 1968) 163.

[65] In Esther 6:1 the reference is not to a heavenly book but to a daily chronicle. Such a memorandum book, in which the reports of messengers coming in from the empire were recorded, was common throughout the ANE, cf. Otto Kaiser, *Isaiah 1-12* (OTL: Philadelphia: Westminster, 1972) 55.

[66] D. S. Russel, *The Method and Message of Jewish Apocalyptic* (OTL; Philadelphia: Westminster, 1976) 125.

In Dan 10:21, the "writing of truth," כתב אמת "is represented as containing an account of events to come."[67]

The heavenly books in which events are predetermined by God and in which the names of the righteous or the evil, as predetermined by God, are inscribed are obviously somewhat different from the heavenly books in which the deeds of men are recorded after they occur (cf. Ps 58:8-9). It is probable that the latter were ledger-like, listing men's deeds, good and evil. These could be tallied and used for judgment purposes.[68] In Isa 65:6 Yahweh says that the tale of his people's vile practices has been duly recorded; their iniquities will be requited. According to Dan 7:10, the judgment commences with the opening of the books (וספרין פתיחו), presumably those containing the evil deeds of the beast destined to be destroyed by fire (cf. 7:11). Corresponding to the book of evil deeds is the book of life, ספר חיים, (Ps 69:29), in which are recorded men's good deeds, cf. also Isa 4:3. It is to this book that the סֵפֶר זִכָּרוֹן of Mal 3:16, the memorial record, book of remembrance is analogous.[69] According to Nötscher, to be listed in the ספר חיים means in the first instance that one's earthly life is maintained for as long a time as possible.[70] Similarly, entry into the ספר זכרון of Mal 3:16 guarantees the preservation of life.[71] The godfearers whose names are recorded therein, cf. Mal 3:16d, will be spared on the day Yahweh comes to execute judgment (cf. Mal 3:17f).[72]

---

[67] Norman W. Porteous, *Daniel* (OTL; Philadelphia: Westminster, 1965) 155.

[68] The conception of a heavenly book in which the deeds of men are listed for judgment is also found in the religion of Zoroaster, cf. *Yasna* 31:14: "I ask you, O Ahura, for what is true and what will come. What demands will be made of the righteous on the basis of what has been written down, and what, O Master, to the liars—what will they be like, when the end comes?" From F. König, "Die Religion Zarathustras," *CRE* 2 (Wien: Herder, 1951) 649.

[69] In a general sense, a סֵפֶר זִכָּרוֹן may refer to a book in which good deeds (cf. Neh 13:14) or bad (cf. Exod 17:14) are recorded. J. M. P. Smith, p. 78, remarks that "this conception of the deity as provided with books or tablets to aid his memory in preserving the records of human deeds is not uncommon," cf. Dan 7:10; Ps 69:28; Isa 4:3; 65:6; Exod 32:32.

[70] Cf. F. Nötscher, *Altorientalischer und Alttestamentlicher Auferstehungsglauben* (Würzburg: C. J. Becker, 1926) 163f.

[71] Cf. Rudolph, p. 28.

[72] According to Dahood, in Ps 69:29 חיים refers to "everlasting afterlife." Thus the ספר זכרון "records the names of those who share in everlasting afterlife,"

חֹשְׁבֵי שְׁמוֹ: On the basis of the LXX's καὶ εὐλαβουμενοις, J. M. P. Smith emends the text to read ולחסי בשמו, "those who take refuge in his name."[73] He remarks that חֹשְׁבֵי שְׁמוֹ, "those who think of his name,"[74]

> ... creates a difficult and isolated Hebrew idiom and yields a rather weak sense. The emended text describes the pious as solicitous to obey Yahweh perfectly and as placing their whole confidence in him under even the most trying circumstances. To 'take refuge in Yahweh's name' is to take refuge in Yahweh himself, for in the Hebrew mind the name and personality were inextricably intermingled and practically identified.[75]

This emendation (לחסי בשמו < לחשבי שמו) based on the LXX, was justified on the grounds that since חשבי שמו is in parallelism with יְרָאֵי יהוה, "those who fear, revere Yahweh," its meaning must be analogous. Because, according to J. M. P. Smith, חָשַׁב "does not ordinarily mean 'hold dear' or 'esteem,'" which would correlate well, but "think" or "plan," textual alteration is necessary.[76] However, the justification for the emendation and thus the emendation itself, must be questioned. As R. Gordis points out, "In Rabbinic Hebrew חָשַׁב means 'to regard highly, esteem' as e.g., Ber. 14a: במה חשבתו לזה ולא לאלוה 'Why did you esteem this man above God,' and the common adjective חָשׁוּב 'important, esteemed.'"[77] This precise meaning occurs in Isa 13:17, אשר־כסף לא יחשבו וזהב לא יחפצו־בו, and Isa 33:8, חפר ברית מאס ערים לא חשב אנוש. It is this meaning of חָשַׁב, "to regard highly, esteem," which should be applied to

---

cf. 2 Aqht: 6:26–29, a Ugaritic text describing immortality, *Psalms II, 164.* However that may be, there is no implication in Mal 3:16f that the Yahweh fearers will share in everlasting afterlife, only that they will live through the destruction of the wicked.

[73] J. M. P. Smith, 78. Note that Halévy emends to חשקי, "to be attached to, love," "Le prophète Malachie," *RS* 17 (1909) 41.

[74] חֹשְׁבֵי is a qal act. ptcpl. (m.pl.cs.) from חָשַׁב, "to think, plan," cf. BDB, 362.

[75] J. M. P. Smith, 78.

[76] Ibid., 84.

[77] R. Gordis, *The Word and the Book: Studies in Biblical Language and Literature* (New York: Ktav, 1976) 163.

Mal 3:16d. The חֹשְׁבֵי שְׁמוֹ, "those who esteem his name," are thus parallel to the יִרְאֵי יהוה, "those who revere Yahweh," and both describe the righteous within the community who will be spared punishment on Yahweh's day (cf. 3:17f). Significantly, that חֹשְׁבֵי שְׁמוֹ means "those who esteem, highly regard his name" is confirmed by the contrasting expression בּוֹזֵי שְׁמִי, "those who despise my name," Yahweh's designation for the unscrupulous, contemptuous priests (cf. 1:6d).[78] Like the זֵדִים (3:15a, 19a) and the רְשָׁעִים (3:21, cf. עֹשֵׂי רִשְׁעָה, 3:15b, 19b) of this oracle unit, they too will experience the heat of Yahweh's anger when he comes to judge (cf. 3:2-3; 3:19).[79]

[3:17]—The day of Yahweh which figures so prominently in the fourth oracle unit (cf. 3:1-5) is the theme of 3:17f. It is the day when Yahweh comes to his temple (3:12), manifests himself before his people (3:2) and initiates judgment (3:5). It is the day (הַיּוֹם, 3:17b; 19a, c; 21c) of discrimination between the good and wicked when all men will see clearly that virtue is rewarded and vice punished (cf. 3:17-18).

הָיוּ לִי ... סְגֻלָּה: היה in combination with לְ is used as a periphrastic idiom for "belong to," "have," for which Hebrew does not have a corresponding verb.[80] The phrase וְהָיוּ לִי, "And they will be mine," connotes a most intimate relationship between Yahweh and those who are inscribed in his book of remembrance (סֵפֶר זִכָּרוֹן) (cf. 3:16).

The noun סְגֻלָּה appears eight times in the OT. It is applied to Israel six times (cf. Exod 19:5; Deut 7:6; 14:2; 26:18; Ps 135:4; Mal 3:17) and to gold and silver twice (cf. Eccl 2:8; 1 Chr 29:3). On analogy with its Akkadian cognate *sikiltum*, "private hoard, accumulation, fund,"[81] it is clear that סְגֻלָּה was originally an economic term. Indeed, the literal usage is found in 1 Chr 29:3 and Eccl 2:3. According to M. Greenberg, later "a more spiritual connotation became attached to the word. The material aspect of 'private savings' gave way to the spiritual attachment to objects

[78] Cf. Isa 53:6: נבזה ולא חשבנוהו, "He was despised and we esteemed him not."

[79] The expression חשבי שמי is exactly in line with the thought with which the prophet's mind is filled, cf. 2:2—לתת כבוד לשמי.

[80] GKC #119r, 381.

[81] Moshe Greenberg, "Hebrew Segullā: Akkadian Sikiltu," *JAOS* 71 (1951) 173. Cf. also his remarks on סְגֻלָּה in Rabbinic Hebrew, 172.

diligently and patiently acquired. Thus *sᵉgūllâ* comes to mean a dear personal possession, a treasure,"[82] In a text from Ugarit, a vassal is called the *sglt* of his sovereign.[83] M. Weinfeld concludes that *sglt* and סְגֻלָּה "belong to the treaty and covenant terminology and that they are employed to distinguish a special relationship of the sovereign to one of his vassals."[84] Significantly, at Mt. Sinai where Yahweh and Israel entered into a covenant relationship, Yahweh announces: והייתם לי סגלה מכל־העמים כי־לי כל־הארץ Exod 19:5. Just as an individual's private accumulation of wealth (סְגֻלָּה) is precious to him, so Israel is the precious treasure (סְגֻלָּה) of Yahweh. This analogy, however, should not be over emphasized. The explicit statement, כי־לי כל־הארץ, "for the whole earth is mine," stresses that "Israel is God's segulla only insofar as its dearness to God may be compared to the dearness of a segulla to its human owner; it must not be supposed, however, that God, like man, had to scrape his segulla together from the property of others, for, indeed, there are no proprietors on earth other than him."[85]

In Exod 19:5 as in Deut 7:6; 14:2; 26:8; Ps 135:4, סְגֻלָּה, "special possession, treasure," is descriptive of all Israel. Indeed, the term is applied to Israel as the object of Yahweh's election and it is often parallel to the word בחר, "choose," (cf. Deut 7:6): כי עם קדוש אתה ליהוה אלהיך בך בחר יהוה אלהיך להיות לו לעם סגלה מכל העמים אשר על־פני האדמה (cf. also Deut 14:2; 26:18; Ps 135:4). In Mal 3:17, סְגֻלָּה does not have as its referent all Israel; it is applied narrowly to the faithful minority within the community (cf. 3:16d). As Yahweh's סְגֻלָּה, "special possession," they alone will be spared (חָמַל, 3:17) the judgment and destruction that will accompany Yahweh's appearance on his day, cf. 3:19f. Malachi's use of סְגֻלָּה to describe the faithful within the community and not the entire community should not be regarded as novel. It is clear from both Exod 19:5 and Deut 26:18 that to be Yahweh's סְגֻלָּה, special possession, required faithfulness to covenant obligations. By implication, refusal to accept such responsibilities will result in the forfeiture of that status with its attendant blessings

---

[82] Ibid., 174.

[83] Cf. PRU V no. 60: 7, 12. Cites in M. Weinfeld, *Deuteronomy and the Deuteronomic School* (Oxford: Clarendon, 1972) 226, n. 2.

[84] Ibid.

[85] Greenberg, 174.

(cf. Deut 7:12f; 26:19). What is new is Malachi's connection of
the concept of סְגֻלָּה, "special possession," with the יוֹם יהוה. To
the prophet, covenant faithlessness (cf. 2:4-9; 2:10f; 3:7) is the
cause of his contemporaries' disabilities. Thus he urges them to
return to Yahweh and their covenant responsibilities and so
ensure blessing (cf. 3:7b, 10f). Should they fail to heed his plea,
Yahweh's day will signal destruction for some (cf. 3:19f). For
others, that day with its purificatory aspect, will serve to renew
the neglected covenant relationship. Indeed, Yahweh avows that
when the priests are cleansed, the offerings they will oversee will
once again be pleasing to him as they had been in bygone days,
presumably when the covenant with Levi (cf. 2:4-5) was effected
(cf. 3:4).[86] For the faithful, elevation to the status of סְגֻלָּה is a
guarantee of life when Yahweh's day arrives. Those so designated
will experience neither purificatory rites nor destruction. Instead,
their loyalty and integrity will be vindicated; they will actively
participate in the extirpation of wickedness (cf. 3:20-21). According to von Bulmerincq: "Offenbar denkt sich . . . Maleachi die
Endzeit . . . vor allem als Wiederkehr der mosaischen Gründungs
periode."[87] In Exod 19:5f, three terms spell out the uniqueness
of the pristine covenant community: סגלה מכל־העמים (a special
possession in distinction from all other peoples), ממלכת כהנים (a
kingdom of priests) and גוי קדוש (a holy nation). Malachi may be
affirming that Yahweh's סְגֻלָּה, those who survive the devastation
of his day, will form the nucleus of a renewed community which
will once again aspire to those ideals. Covenant responsibility
will once again encompass Israel's whole life, "defining her
relationship to God and to her neighbors and the quality of her
existence."[88]

     J. M. P. Smith contends that because the distance of סְגֻלָּה
from "הָיוּ לִי, with which it must be taken, is abnormal," סְגֻלָּה is
"best treated as a gloss on הָיוּ לִי."[89] Halévy circumvents the
distance problem by connecting סְגֻלָּה with עָשָׂה and translating
"le jour où je constituerai un trésor de choix."[90] However, as

[86] Cf. above, 74f.
[87] von Bulmerincq, 2.505.
[88] Childs, 367.
[89] J. M. P. Smith, 84.
[90] J. Halévy, "Le prophete Malachie," RS 17 (1909) 42. Halévy also remarks
that סְגֻלָּה "peut encore être pris adverbialement: »au jour où j'agirai partic-
ulièrement,«" 42.

J. M. P. Smith notes, עָשָׂה סְגֻלָּה "would naturally mean 'acquire property': cf. Gen. 12:15; 31:1; Deut. 18:17f; Isa. 19:19."[91] סְגֻלָּה should not be treated as a gloss. Von Bulmerincq states that "mit der Mehrzahl der Augsleger סְגֻלָּה trotz der weiten Entfernung als Prädikat zu סְגֻלָּה zu ziehen."[92] Significantly, Torrey notes that its position gives it added emphasis.[93] The sentence should thus be translated, "And they will be to me on the day when I act, a special possession."

לַיּוֹם אֲשֶׁר אֲנִי עֹשֶׂה[94]: The coming day of Yahweh is, of course, before the prophet's mind (cf. היום בא, 3:19a; היום הבא 3:19d). It is the day when Yahweh comes (יוֹם בּוֹאוֹ, 3:2a), the day "on which the deity shows himself as he really is" (3:2b)—"a 'showing' which takes place in the temple where he lives," cf. 3:1b.[95] It is the day of his judgment (3:5), the day of his wrath (3:19a–b, d); it is the day when he reestablishes his covenant and צְדָקָה for his own people.[96] Malachi's use of יוֹם אֲשֶׁר אֲנִי עֹשֶׂה incorporates all the foregoing concepts. Yahweh's day is the day when he acts, takes action (עשה, cf. Ps 118:24: זֶה־הַיּוֹם עָשָׂה יהוה).

J. M. P. Smith, von Bulmerincq and von Orelli treat אֲשֶׁר as "a relative particle representing the object of עֹשֶׂה," and translate, "the day which I am about to make."[97] Such an understanding of אֲשֶׁר is problematic because it requires that עֹשֶׂה (qal act. ptc.) be translated "make." In his remarks on Ps 118:24, זֶה־הַיּוֹם עָשָׂה יהוה, G. W. Ahlström states: "This verse does not refer to 'the day which the Lord has made' (RSV) He has made all the days. In this particular verse, עשה must be translated 'act,' 'work,' because the psalm is talking of Yahweh's acts of deliverance. Because of these acts the people rejoice, v. 24."[98] The same reasoning holds for Mal 3:17b. The oracle units in which יום יהוה imagery figures prominently are action filled (cf. 2:17–3:5; 3:13–

---

[91] J. M. P. Smith, 84.

[92] von Bulmerincq, 2.504; Cf. also van Hoonacker, 738; Sellin, 614.

[93] C. C. Torrey, "The Prophet Malachi," *JBL* 17 (1898) 12.

[94] For לְ of time when, cf. Gen 8:11; 17:21; Isa 10:3 and *GKC* #119r, 381.

[95] G. W. Ahlström, *Joel and the Temple Cult of Jerusalem* (SVT 21; Leiden: Brill, 1971) 66.

[96] Ibid.

[97] J. M. P. Smith, 84; von Bulmerincq, 2.507; C. von Orelli, *The Twelve Minor Prophets* (Edinburgh: T. & T. Clark, 1893) 402.

[98] Ahlström, *Joel*, 66, n. 1.

21). The day of Yahweh is described as the day when Yahweh comes (3:2a), appears (3:2b), judges (3:5), delivers (3:17a, 20) and destroys (3:19). It is not a day which he "makes" like any other; it is the day when he takes decisive action. Therefore, it is best to treat אֲשֶׁר with von Hoonacker and Sellin as introducing a temporal clause, viz. "when I act (take action)." [99]

וְחָמַלְתִּי ... הָעֹבֵד אֹתוֹ: The compassionate love (cf. חָמַל, "to spare, have compassion") of a human father for his son is the classic symbol for the compassionate paternal love of Yahweh, cf. also Ps 103:13. Just as a father shields his son requiring others to undertake the more difficult or dangerous tasks, so Yahweh shields his סְגֻלָּה, his "special possession" from the unpleasantness of judgment and destruction (cf. 3:20).[100]

The juxtaposition of בֵּן, son, and עָבַד, "serve, work," is extremely rare, appearing elsewhere in the OT only in Exod 4:23. There Yahweh calls Israel "my son" (בְּנִי) and, through Moses, urges the pharaoh to let him go וְיַעַבְדֵנִי, "that he may serve me." In the cultic sphere the verb עבד, "serve" describes man's proper conduct towards God, conduct that arises from the attitude of fear or reverence, יִרְאָה.[101] In Mal 3:17d, the participle עֹבֵד means "to be dutiful toward." It describes the proper conduct of a son to his father, conduct that should originate from the command to honor him (cf. כַּבֵּד Exod 20:12; Deut 5:16). Such a "dutiful" son is patently distinct from the stubborn and rebellious son of Deut 21:18f who, by the mutual agreement of his parents, may be brought before the elders of the city to be punished by death.

Malachi's use of עֹבֵד in 3:17d is related to its use in 3:14a. Dismayed by the evident inequalities of life, by their depressed circumstances in contrast to those of the evildoers (cf. 3:15), the fearers of Yahweh announced that displaying the proper conduct towards God yields no tangible benefits (שָׁוְא עֲבֹד אֱלֹהִים). Refuting their claim, Yahweh avows that proper service is not worthless for it is precisely that which evokes a compassionate response from him (3:17d and cf. 3:18).

[99] van Hoonacker, 738; Sellin, 613.

[100] Cf. J. M. P. Smith, 79.

[101] C. Lindhagen, *The Servant Motif in the Old Testament* (Uppsala: Lundeqvist, 1950) 152f.

[3:18]—It is clear from Malachi's prophecy that real, not imaginary, lines of division have been consciously drawn in the community (cf. also Isa 26:7f). On the one side are the good men who fear Yahweh and who should be the beneficiaries of blessing; on the other are the arrogant who scorn Yahweh's requirements and who should, consequently, be punished. According to the pious, however, Yahweh's failure to act as the God of justice (cf. 2:17) has caused the dividing lines to be obliterated and the positions of the two groups to be reversed. The reward of the faithful is humiliation and privation: the punishment of the wicked is elevated status and prosperity (cf. 3:13-15). In Mal 3:18, Yahweh avows that the situation will change. The day of Yahweh is here described as a day when distinctions blurred by time and circumstance will once again become crystal clear. On that day Yahweh will act to restore "the cosmos and the right conditions for his people according to his covenant with them and, in so doing ṣĕdāqāh," right order, will be established.[102] The righteous who have suffered will receive their just reward (3:20; the now triumphant godless will be destroyed (3:19, 21).

שַׁבְתֶּם is a qal pf. (2 m. pl.) of שׁוּב, "turn back, return." Van Hoonacker renders וְשַׁבְתֶּם וּרְאִיתֶם, "you will return (i.e., from your present state of mind) and see."[103] But, the adverbial use of שׁוּב to denote repetition, i.e., "again" is very common[104] and its adoption here avoids the necessity of leaving so much to the imagination. With the restoration of the "right order" the people will "again" be able to distinguish[105] between the righteous and the wicked.

צַדִּיק—רָשָׁע // עֹבֵד אֱלֹהִים—לֹא עֲבָדוֹ: A dividing line rigidly enforced will separate the righteous from the wicked, those who

---

[102] Ahlström, *Joel,* 60.

[103] van Hoonacker, 738.

[104] Cf. *GKC* #102d, 386.

[105] According to von Bulmerincq, ראה "bedeutet hier wie Deut. 11, 2. Hi. 11, 11. Koh. 8, 16 (// ידע). Jer. 5, 12, Pss. 34, 13; 89, 49. u.ö. erfahren, Einsicht gewinnen, aus eigener Anschauung kennenlernen, erleben . . . Man übersetze . . . ראה בן ל . . . den Unterschied kennen lernen, erkennen, erfahren bzw. aus eigener Anschauung erfahren, es erleben, was es um den Unterschied bzw. das Verhältnis ist, 2.514-515. For בן ל cf. *GKC* #119s, 381.

serve God from those who do not.[106] The word צְדָקָה means "right order," "conformity to a norm."[107] A צַדִּיק therefore, is one who embodies this order, who "lives according to the prevailing norms of society."[108] Since this order is ultimately divine, instituted by God, a צַדִּיק is an עֹבֵד אֱלֹהִים, a server of God, obedient to him, one whose life is consistent with the maintenance of God's order. As mentioned above, man's proper attitude toward God is one of fear or reverence (יִרְאָה).[109] To be a צַדִּיק, a righteous one, an עֹבֵד אֱלֹהִים, a server of God, requires the possession of this primary quality because it is precisely the fear or reverence of Yahweh that evokes the desire to serve (עָבַד) him and sustain his order (cf. צְדָקָה).

Von Bulmerincq notes that "Malachi steht auch hier ganz auf den Schultern Ezechiels, für den das kennzeichen des צַדִּיק in der Erfüllung einer Summe kultischer und ethischer Verordnungen besteht,"[110] (cf. 18:5-9). Significantly, Ezekiel claims that the man who is צַדִּיק, who observes God's ordinances, shall live, חיה יחיה (18:9). In Mal 3:18, the terms צַדִּיק and עֹבֵד אֱלֹהִים[111] circumscribe Yahweh's cult community, the יִרְאֵי יהוה, the fearers, reverers of Yahweh (3:16a, d; 3:20a; cf חֹשְׁבֵי שְׁמוֹ, 3:16d).[112] As individuals whose lives are consonant with the divine norms, they are designated Yahweh's סְגֻלָּה (3:17a, b) and it is as such that they will be spared the destruction that awaits the wicked on his day (3:17c, d; cf. 3:19).

Those who do not fear Yahweh are, by contrast, the wicked, רְשָׁעִים.[113] They refuse to recognize their dependence on Yahweh

[106] Note that each word pair contains antithetical elements: צדיק—רשע; לא עבדו—עבד אלהים.

[107] Cf. Ringgren, 83; Ahlstrom, *Joel*, 77.

[108] Ringgren, 132.

[109] Cf. above, 218f.

[110] von Bulmerincq, 2.516.

[111] These terms are employed in a collective sense as are רשע, לא עבדו, cf. *GKC* #126 1, m, p, 406.

[112] Cf. also Isa 26:7; 57:1; Pss 33:1; 75:11; 97:11f; 118:15; 125:3 (צדיק); Isa 68:5f, 13f (עבד).

[113] רשע is an adj., "wicked, criminal"; "usu. as subst., one guilty of crime, deserving of punishment"; opp. צדיק, BDB, 957. J. Pedersen remarks: "One of the strong appellations of a sinner, rāshāᶜ, is often used . . . about him who is wrong in a special case, quite corresponding to ṣaddîk, which denotes him who is right," *Israel Its Life and Culture* (4 vols.; London: Oxford University, 1973) 2.418.

but would be masters of their own fate (cf. Ps 10:4, 6, 11; Deut 8:11–18; Isa 14:13–14). They are proud and defiant, infected with hybris (cf. זֵדִים, Mal 3:15a, 19c). "To trust in one's own strength means to make oneself equal to God; such pride is a sign of rebellion against God" (cf. Ps 52:7, 9).[114] Indeed, the wicked, רְשָׁעִים (cf. also עֹשֵׂה רִשְׁעָה, 3:15b, 19c) challenge (cf. בָּחַן, 3:15c) and defy him. Unlike the צַדִּיקִים who obey Yahweh and do his will, the רְשָׁעִים disregard his precepts. Self-serving, they do not serve God, cf. לֹא עֲבָדוֹ. Committers of wickedness (cf. עֹשֵׂה רִשְׁעָה, 3:15b, 19c), they overturn his order (cf. Isa 26:10). According to the prophets the worst of all is that in their self-conceit, the wicked say that God cannot be angry (cf. Amos 9:10; Isa 5:18f; Mic 2:7; Zeph 1:2). "This is a denial of the majesty of God, as is also the derision of those who think that there is an escape from God's punishment" (cf. Isa 28:14f).[115] There is no escape, as Malachi makes clear. The wicked will be judged (3:5) and destroyed (3:19, 21, cf. also Prov 10:21; 11:9; Ps 78:13f; Job 20:6f).

[3:19][116]—It is the imminence of Yahweh's day (הַיּוֹם) that is stressed here. According to Gesenius, the participle is frequently used to announce future actions or events. If it is "intended to announce the event as imminent, or at least near at hand (and sure to happen)"—the *futurum instans*—the subject is generally introduced by הִנֵּה[117] (cf. הִנֵּה הַיּוֹם בָּא, "the day is indeed coming").[118]

בֹּעֵר is a qal act. ptc. (m.s.) from בָּעַר meaning "to burn."[119] The root appears in descriptions of theophanies. When Yahweh revealed himself at Horeb, the mountain burned with fire (בער באש, cf. Deut 4:11; 5:23; 9:15).[120] It frequently appears in connection with the wrath of God (cf. Isa 30:27; הנה שם־יהוה בא ממרחק בער אפו;[121] Isa 30:33; 42:25; Jer 4:4; 7:20; Pss 2:12; 89:47). Further,

---

[114] Ringgren, 129.

[115] Th. C. Vriezen, *An Outline of Old Testament Theology* (2nd ed.; Newton, Mass.: Charles T. Branford Co., 1970) 306.

[116] Note that the RV, following the LXX and Vulgate begins a new chapter with this verse.

[117] *GKC* #116p, 360–61.

[118] For a discussion of the significance of בא in relation to the day of Yahweh, cf. above on 3:1, 139–41.

[119] BDB, 128.

[120] Cf. also Exod 3:2f; Ps 18:9.

[121] Note that the description is like theophany.

the representation of Yahweh's judgment upon the wicked as a consuming fire is a common one. In Num 11:1, Yahweh's anger flared upon hearing his people's complaints, ותבער־בם אש יהוה ותאכל בקצה המחנה. According to Isa 10:17, the Holy One of Israel will become a flame ובערה ואכלה שיתו ושמירו ביום אחד (cf. also Isa 9:17; Zeph 1:18; 3:8; Amos 1:3f; Jer 21:14; Ps 106:8).

In Mal 3:18b, the participle בֹּעֵר not only emphasizes the burning power of the divine wrath, but hints at the means of God's judgment as well. Yahweh's day burns like an oven (cf. תַּנּוּר n.m. "oven, furnace, fire-pot" [122] generally used for baking bread, cf. Lev 2:4; 7:9; 26:26; Hos 7:4, 6) constantly stoked. Its heat is such that it immediately ignites and consumes anything which comes into contact with it (cf. 3:18d, e). Significantly, this is the second time in Malachi's prophecy that the day of Yahweh has been characterized as a day of intense heat (cf. 3:2-3). When Yahweh deals with the priests his action is compared to a purifying fire (3:2-3). With regard to the evildoers, however, this action becomes an all-consuming fire of destruction (cf. 3:19; Obad 18). It may be that the priests' deficiencies (cf. 1:6-2:9), were regarded as correctable (through purification) while those of the wicked were not. Consideration should also be given to the possibility that the priests were purified and not destroyed [123] because of their function within the community. Unlike the evildoers, the priests were necessary to its ongoing cultic life. As Malachi makes clear, they served as mediators between Yahweh and his people. The proper priestly performance of the sacrificial ritual ensured the acceptance of the people's offerings (cf. 3:3-4).

וְהָיוּ כָל־זֵדִים ... קַשׁ: The victims of Yahweh's avenging justice are designated in the same manner as in 3:15 (cf. זֵדִים, "proud, arrogant"; עֹשֵׂה רִשְׁעָה,[124] "committers of wickedness, evildoers"). They are likened to קַשׁ, "stubble," the refuse from the threshing process. Dry grain stalks, the קַשׁ was collected and used to activate fires where it was quickly consumed. As a figure

---

[122] *Gesenius' Hebrew and Chaldee Lexicon,* 869.

[123] It is likely that some priests were to be destroyed. In the purification of gold and silver, the dross is separated from the precious metal and discarded, cf. above, 147-48. Analogously, Yahweh will separate the priests capable of correction from those who are not and will discard the latter, cf. 3:3.

[124] Note that עשה רשעה is a collective expression, cf. "All those who do evil."

of speech, קַשׁ denotes the worthless or evil that are about to be destroyed (cf. Mal 3:19-20; Isa 5:24; 47:14; Joel 2:5; Obad 18; Nah 1:10).

לִהַט is a piel pf. (3 m.s.) meaning to "set ablaze," cf. לָהַט, "blaze up, flame."[125] According to E. Lipínski, on analogy with Akkadian *laṭu*, "encircle, surround, shut in, include, contain," the verb לָהַט can evoke the image of enveloping or encircling fire (cf. Mal 3:19; Pss 83:15; 97:3; 104:4; 106:18).[126] It is a synonym of אָכַל, "eat, devour, consume," (Deut 32:23; Joel 1:19; 2:3); בָּעַר, "burn" (Isa 42:24; Ps 83:15), יקד, "be kindled, burn" (Deut 32:33) and קדח, "be kindled, kindle" (Deut 32:22). The verb is used in Mal 3:19, as elsewhere, to express the total destruction of the wicked (cf. Joel 1:19; 2:3; Isa 42:25, a favorite theme of the prophets, cf. Amos 9:10; Isa 10:1-4; Jer 7:29-34; 10:22; Ezek 13:8-16). The day of Yahweh will envelop them in a fire from which there is no escape.

. . . אֲשֶׁר לֹא-יַעֲזֹב: According to van Hoonacker, in place of יַעֲזֹב (qal, impf., 3 m.s. "to leave"), niphal יֵעָזֵב should be read with שֹׁרֶשׁ וְעָנָף, root and branch as its subjects—"so that neither root nor branch will be left (remain) of them,"[127] cf. LXX ὑπολειφθῇ = יֵעָזֵב. Von Bulmerincq contends however, that

> Doch ist das Nifᶜal von עָזַב in der Bedeutung »übriggelassen wereden, übrigbleiben« = נשאר (vgl. Gen 14, 10; Exod 10, 19; 2 Chron 10, 21) bzw. נותר (vgl. Jes. 1, 8; 1 Chron 19, 20; Exod 12, 10) sonst nicht im A.T. nachzuweisen: wo es vorkommt, bedeutet es stets "verlassen werden" (Lev 26, 43; Jes. 7, 16, 27, 10; 62, 12; Exod 36, 4; Pss 37, 25; Hi. 18, 4; Neh 13, 11) und einmal auch »überlassen werden« (Jes. 18, 6). Für das Ḳal dagegen ist die Bedeutung übriglassen . . . auch sonst belegen, vgl. Ri. 2, 21; Ru. 2, 16.[128]

According to von Bulmerincq, J. M. P. Smith, E. Sellin and J. Halévy, אֲשֶׁר should be treated as a "Konsekutivpartikel »dass«

---

[125] BDB, 529.

[126] E. Lipínski, *La Royauté de Yahwé dans la poésie et le culte d'ancien Israël* (Brussels: Palais der Academiën, 1965) 223-24.

[127] van Hoonacker, 739.

[128] von Bulmerincq, 2.525-526.

oder »so dass,«[129] and the vocalization of the M.T. should be retained. The subject of the verb עָזַב "Ist das gleiche wie von לְהַט, d.h. der kommende Tag (היום הבא)."[130] Therefore, Mal 3:19e should be translated: "so that it (היום הבא) will leave them neither root nor branch."

שֹׁרֶשׁ וְעָנָף: The juxtaposition of שֹׁרֶשׁ (n.m., root) and עָנָף (n.[m.], branch) appears elsewhere only in Ps 80:10 (שרשיה) // (ענפיה). עָנָף is more frequently linked with פְּרִי, "fruit" (cf. Lev 23:40; Ezek 17:8; 36:8); שֹׁרֶשׁ with קָצִיר, "bough, branch" (Job 18:16; 29:19), פְּרִי (Isa 37:31; Hos 9:16; Amos 2:9) or פרח "bud, sprout" (Isa 5:24). These word pairs are used figuratively to connote the firmness and permanence of Israel when she consigns herself to Yahweh's care (cf. Hos 14:6-8; Isa 37:31). By contrast, the destruction of root and branch, fruit is the punishment inflicted on those who turn away from God (cf. Isa 5:24; Hos 9:16-17; Amos 2:9). Von Bulmerincq remarks that,

> Ein Baum, dessen Wurzel vernichtet und dessen Äste abgetan sind, ist für immer tot; jede Möglichkeit der Neubelebung (vgl. Jes. 11, 1; Hi. 14:7ff) ist dann ein für allemal ausgeschlossen. Eine treffende Erläuterung des Bildes bietet Hi. 18, 16-20: einem abgestorbenen Baume gleich werden, heisst ohne Andenken und Namen (v. 17), ohne Nachkommen und Nachwuchs (v. 19) zu hinterlassen, aus dem Licht des Lebens in die Nacht des Todes hinausgestossen werden (v. 18), um lediglich ein Gegenstand schaudernden Entsetzens für alle Welt zu bleiben (v. 20).[131]

According to Mal 3:19, the fate that awaits the godless on Yahweh's day is complete extirpation. Their roots will be destroyed, their branches will wither, they will die.[132]

[3:20]—The imagery in this verse is striking. Yahweh's day is the day of his epiphany.[133] In Mal 3:20 his theophanic approach is described through the use of solar categories. He is

---

[129] Ibid., 525.
[130] von Bulmerincq, 2.526; Sellin, 612; J. M. P. Smith, 84; Halévy, 42.
[131] von Bulmerincq, 2.527.
[132] Notice the complete contrast between the wicked who will die on Yahweh's day and the righteous who will be inscribed for life, cf. 3:16-17.
[133] Ahlström, *Joel*, 66.

pictured as the rising sun (שֶׁמֶשׁ) whose rays radiate healing and life (מַרְפֵּא)[134] for the long-suffering righteous. On Yahweh's day the destruction of the wicked (3:19) will have as its corollary the triumph of the just.

וְזָרְחָה . . . שֶׁמֶשׁ צְדָקָה: The verse begins with a *Waw* adversative, but, to introduce the contrast between the fate of the evildoers and that of the Yahweh fearers. The former will be consumed, "but as for you, O fearers of my name, the sun of righteousness will arise."

זָרְחָה . . . שֶׁמֶשׁ צְדָקָה: G. W. Ahlström remarks that "Man sieht . . . deutlich, dass der israelitische Himmelsgott eng mit Lichphänomenen verknüpft ist und geradezu mit der Sonne oder ihrem Licht assoziert wird."[135] Yahweh is אוֹר, light, (cf. ps 27:1; Isa 10:17; 60:1; Mic 7:8). In Ps 84:12 he is called שֶׁמֶשׁ, "sun." According to Ezek 8:16, the priests waited at the temple between the altar and the porch "for the rising of the sun which was seen as an expression for the epiphany of Yahweh."[136] He "shines forth or out" when he comes (cf. הוֹפִיעַ, Deut 33:2; Pss 50:2; 80:2; 94:1). His radiance (נגה) rivals that of the rising sun (cf. Isa 60:3; Hab 3:4; Ezek 10:4). "Das Aufgehen Jahwes oder seines *kābōd* wird durch das Verb זָרַח ausgedruckt (Isa. 60:1f). Dieses Verb wird im Alten Testament hauptsächlich vom Aufgang der Sonne gebraucht, Gen. 32:32; Exod. 22:2; Judg. 9:33; 2 Kings 3:22; Nah. 3:17; Mal. 3:20; Ps. 104:22."[137] According to Ahlström,

> Der solare Aspekt im Charakter des Himmelgottes Jahwe ist also nicht zu leugnen. Jahwe lässt sein Angesicht leuchten über seine Kultgemeinde, Deut 6:25, er ist das Licht selbst, Ps 27:1. Weil nun Jahwe das Licht selbst ist, wird er zur Existenzbedingung des Lebens, zum Lebensprinzip, Ps 56:14, und damit derjenige, der den Kosmos am Leben erhält, Ps 36:10.[138]

F. Schnutenhaus explains this close association of Yahweh with light phenomena as a result of the transference of charac-

---

[134] Cf. 236f.

[135] G. W. Ahlström, *Psalm 89: Eine Liturgie aus dem Ritual des leidenden Königs* (Lund: C. W. K. Gleerup, 1959) 86.

[136] Ahlström, *Joel*, 53.

[137] Ahlström, *Psalm 89*, 88.

[138] Ibid.

teristics of the Babylonian sun-god to him.[139] Ahlström however, contends that

> Diese Verbindung wird besonders deutlich durch die Identifzierung Jahwes mit dem solaren El Eljon in Jerusalem, ja, sie wird so deutlich, dass es streng genommen unmöglich ist, den »vorjerusalemitischen« Charakter Jahwes klar zu beschreiben, den er ist im Textmaterial in der Regel aus den Aspekten einer jerusalemitschen Gottesauffassung heraus charakterisiert.[140]

According to Malachi, there is a twofold purpose to Yahweh's theophanic approach on his day. On the one hand it signals the destruction of the wicked (cf. 3:19, 21), and on the other, the deliverance and salvation of those who fear him (3:20). Significantly, light is a symbol of the salvation given by God (cf. Isa 9:1; 58:8; Pss 18:29; 36:10; 43:4; 97:1). Two light-related terms in Mal 3:20a indicate this motif: שֶׁמֶשׁ,[141] sun, a symbol of well-being and salvation (Judg 5:31; Jer 15:9) and זָרְחָה (qal 3 f.s.) "to arise," as the sun (cf. Isa 60:2). Numerous biblical texts affirm that Yahweh's intervention to save man comes in the morning, with the light (cf. Pss 5:4; 46:6; 88:14; 119:147; 130:6; 143:8; Isa 8:20; 58:8; Hos 6:3). According to Lam 3:22f, God's mercies are "new every morning." In Ps 46:3f, Yahweh's help which comes at the break of dawn, means the restitution of creation threatened by the powers of chaos. Similarly, it is probable that Job 38:4-15 means that morning signifies a renewal of creation and order. In the light of dawn, the earth's shape becomes visible (v. 14) and the wicked are removed from it (vv. 13, 15). This appraisal of morning may be connected with experiences Israel had in the distress of battle (cf. 2 Kgs 19:34f; Ps 46:6f). It is also likely that the custom of holding trials and vindicating the righteous in the morning contributed to this (cf. Ps 101:8; 2 Sam 15:2; Jer 21:12; Job 7:8).

---

[139] F. Schnutenhaus, "Das Kommen und Erscheinen Gottes," *ZAW* 76 (1964) 9.

[140] Ahlström, *Psalm 89*, 86.

[141] Note that שֶׁמֶשׁ, "sun," is usually masculine, but is feminine here and in Gen 15:17; Jer 15:9; Nah 3:17; Isa 45:6. J. M. P. Smith, p. 85, opines that "the choice of the feminine here may be due to the influence of the genitive צְדָקָה."

In Mal 3:20a, Yahweh arises (זָרְחָה) as the sun (שֶׁמֶשׁ). In this line light represents both the restitution of the "right order" (צְדָקָה) and the salvation of the Yahweh fearers which is attained through צְדָקָה. Indeed, Yahweh is called שֶׁמֶשׁ צְדָקָה, the sun of righteousness.[142] Both J. M. P. Smith and von Bulmerincq maintain that "righteousness is here practically equivalent to vindication and victory, as is so often the case in Isa, chs. 40-60; e.g., 41:2; 45:8; 46:13; 15:5, 6, 8; 56:1; 62:1."[143] Broadly speaking, they are correct. However, in the sixth oracle unit, the Yahweh fearers lament the dissolution of the proper order. Instead of the promised correlation between following Yahweh and success, the facts of experience suggest that prospering evildoers are the ones blessed by God (cf. 3:15). According to Mal 3:20, it is precisely the "right order," צְדָקָה which Yahweh, the שֶׁמֶשׁ צְדָקָה will restore on his day. The wicked will be judged (3:5) and destroyed (3:19). The regular cycle of the seasons which is so necessary for human life[144] will be reinstituted (cf.מַרְפֵּא).[145] The righteous will be vindicated. Thus the salvation and victory of the Yahweh fearers is the direct consequence of God's צְדָקָה restoring actions.

Von Bulmerincq, J. M. P. Smith and Mason all maintain that the picture of Yahweh rising like the sun to establish righteousness was influenced by the Babylonian conception of Shamash, the sun god, the universal judge.[146] It must be stressed, however, that when the Israelites entered Canaan, the land of the god El, "they had to follow El's *mišpāṭ*."[147] According to Ahlström, this led to the identification of El and Yahweh which made possible "an ever-increasing adoption and adaptation to

---

[142] צְדָקָה is a *genit. explicativus* or *epexegeticus*, cf. *GKC* #128k, 1, 416-17. Von Bulmerincq suggests that צדקה "als Subjekt zu זרחה und שמש im Sinne von כשמש zu stehen kame. Allerdings werden die ganz analogen Vergleiche Jes. 58, 8 (והוציר כאור צדקך). Ps. 37, 6 (אז יקבע כשחר אורך)," 2.532.

[143] J. M. P. Smith, 80; von Bulmerincq, 2.533.

[144] Cf. Ahlström, *Joel*, 97.

[145] Cf. 237f.

[146] von Bulmerincq, 2.533; J. M. P. Smith, 80; Rex Mason, *The Books of Haggai, Zechariah and Malachi* (Cambridge: Cambridge University, 1977) 158.

[147] G. W. Ahlström, "Some Remarks on Prophets and Cult," *Essays in Divinity VI; Transitions in Biblical Scholarship* (Chicago: The University of Chicago, 1968) 128.

the cult and ideology of Canaan." [148] It is significant that El was considered to be the author and preserver of order and the judge among the gods. [149] Further, as mentioned above, El Elyon, the El of Jerusalem, had solar characteristics. [150] It may be that the absolute impartiality of the sun's rays gave rise to the association of justice and righteousness with the sun. In view of the close relation between Yahweh and El, it is very likely that Canaanite conceptions influenced the description of Yahweh.

מַרְפֵּא is a n.m. meaning "healing, cure, health," [151] cf. רָפָא, heal. Marvin Pope considers the biblical Rephaim (cf. רפא) and the Ugaritic RPUM/RPIM to be "the spirits of the dead, the denizens of the netherworld, the heroes of generations past." [152] They were regarded as "the source of fertility as life eventually returns to the earth whence it came." [153] The connection of the root RPA with fertility "is confirmed by the explanation of the name Hammurapi as meaning "extensive family" (^{d}Ha-am-mu-ra-pi: ^{d}Kim-ta-ra-pa-aš-tum). The old Arab blessing for newly-weds, bi'r-rifāᶜi wa'l-banīna, "with health (?) and children," also shows the connection with fertility." [154] The verb רפא is found with precisely this significance in connection with the restoration of fertility to Abimelech and his harem in Gen 20:17. In Prov 4:22 the noun מַרְפֵּא is in parallelism with חיים, "life," with שלום, "peace, well-being" in Jer 8:15; 14:19, and with ארכה, "healing of a wound, restoration," [155] in Jer 33:6. For Malachi, מַרְפֵּא, "healing fertility" is the result of Yahweh's coming to establish the "right order," cf. שֶׁמֶשׁ צְדָקָה, 3:20a. The land which

[148] Ibid., 128-29.

[149] Othmar Keel, The Symbolism of the Biblical World (New York: Seabury, 1978) 207.

[150] Cf. 235-236.

[151] BDB, 951.

[152] Marvin Pope, "Notes on the Rephaim Texts from Ugarit," Essays on the Ancient Near East in Memory of Jacob Joel Finkelstein (Hamden Ct., CT: Anchor Books, 1977) 163 and cf. also John Gray, "The Rephaim," PEQ 81 (1959) 127-39.

[153] Pope, 167 and cf. also Ringgren, 245.

[154] Pope, 167. Note that BDB, 952 and Otto Kaiser, Isaiah 13-39 (OTL; Philadelphia: Westminster, 1974) 35, consider רפה, "to sink" to be the root of רפאים. The רפאים would thus be the sunken or powerless ones.

[155] BDB, 74.

was ravaged by drought and locust infestation (3:10–11) will once again yield an abundant harvest.[156]

In Jer 33, וּרְפָאתִים, "I will heal them," v. 6, is synonymous with וְהֲשִׁבֹתִי אֶת־שְׁבוּת יְהוּדָה וְאֵת־שְׁבוּת יִשְׂרָאֵל, "I will turn the fate of Judah and Israel," v. 7. The phrase שׁוּב שְׁבוּת should "be seen in connection with the day of Yahweh, the day upon which Yahweh acts and restores the cosmos and right conditions for his people according to the covenant with them."[157] As in Mal 3:20, so too in Jeremiah, Yahweh's healing and restorative work will transform a desolate land into a land of abundance (cf. Jer 33:12f). Apropos of שׁוּב שְׁבוּת, Ahlström remarks that "the idea of restoration, a turning of the fate, or a coming back to stability, i.e., the harmonious order, includes a restoration of the people."[158] This concept is implicit in Mal 3:20. The reinstitution of צְדָקָה, "right order," affects not only the fertility of the earth but man's relationship to his God. Not only the wounds of the ravaged earth, but the wounds of the people will be healed (cf. רפא, Jer 30:17), and thus, the anguished cry אַיֵּה אֱלֹהֵי הַמִּשְׁפָּט, "where is the god of justice?" will be silenced (cf. Mal 2:17).

בִּכְנָפֶיהָ: According to J. M. P. Smith, the phrase "in its wings," בִּכְנָפֶיהָ (n.f.pl. + 3 f.s. suffix), "at once suggests the winged solar disk of Egypt, Babylonia, Assyria and Persia."[159] E. Sellin and R. Mason maintain that the wings refer to the portrayal of the winged solar disk in Egyptian and Mesopotamian art.[160] John Gray remarks that the sun of righteousness with healing in its wings

> refers to the winged solar disc familiar in oriental iconography. This was the symbol of the sun god in Egypt and Mesopotamia, and the qualification of 'righteousness' might possibly reflect the conception in Egypt and Mesopotamia of the sun-god as the god of justice. But,

[156] Note that this boon was also promised to the evildoers who returned to Yahweh, cf. 3:12.

[157] Ahlström, *Joel*, 60. Cf. also Sigmund Mowinckel, *The Psalms in Israel's Worship* (2 vols.; New York: Abingdon, 1962) 2.250.

[158] Ahlström, *Joel*, 60–61.

[159] J. M. P. Smith, 80.

[160] Sellin, 615; Mason, 158.

Ahuramazda, whose province was also righteousness, was also so represented in the symbolism of Persian Zoroastrianism, and in virtue of the date of Malachi in the Persian period and the association with the fiery consummation, a distinctive feature of Zoroastrian eschatology, we think it likely that it is the Persian conception reflected in 3:19-21.[161]

According to O. Keel, in Egyptian iconography wings originally represented the sky. "But the sun fixed between the two wings . . . soon became the central feature, and the wings of the sky came to be understood as a winged sun. In that form the image spread from Egypt throughout the whole of Asia Minor." [162] As a rule, he continues, "wings appear in Egyptian iconography as a means of shelter rather than as instruments of flight," an image that may be traced to the idea of a heavenly bird whose giant wings spread protectively over the earth.[163] Similarly, in the Psalms, wings are linked with refuge and symbolize Yahweh as the protector of his people (cf. 17:8; 36:8; 57:2; 63:8; 91:4).[164] In Ps 61 the suppliant asks to be set high upon a rock (צור), v. 3, and to be permitted to dwell in Yahweh's tent (אהל), v. 5, that is, his temple, for there he will find shelter under the wings of God, signifying the sky, אחסה בסתר כנפיך, v. 5, (cf. also Pss 15:1; 27:4-5; 43:3). These verses merge images of temple (אהל) and heaven (כנף)[165] in a manner quite similar to Isaiah 6. It is out of place to inquire whether the suppliant in Ps 61 wishes to be taken to the temple or to heaven. The temple is on earth but, as the locus of the presence of Yahweh, it is identical to heaven (cf. Ps 11:4).

In Mal 3:20 Yahweh is depicted as "the sun of righteousness with healing in its wings." To surmise with Gray that these

[161] John Gray, "The Day of Yahweh in Cultic Experience and Eschatological Prospect," *SEÅ* 29 (1974) 6, n. 1.

[162] Keel, 27-28. Keel points out that in Assyrian examples the winged solar disc is "primarily a symbol of the heavens, less so of the sun," 29.

[163] Keel, 28; cf. also, 192.

[164] Note that Deut 32:11 compares Yahweh to an eagle that spreads out its wings.

[165] For wings as a symbol of heaven, cf. Keel, 27.

images derive from Persian conceptions of Ahuramazda is short-sighted.[166] Because the adoption of such representations in Syria-Palestine can be traced back to the close of the second millennium,[167] there is no necessity to postulate borrowing from the Persians. It is more likely that Malachi incorporated traditions which had long circulated throughout the ancient Near East.[168] It is the interrelatedness of these images which is striking in Mal 3:20. The wings symbolize Yahweh's protective presence, a presence which spreads over the earth ensuring its prosperity. The association of the wings (or rays) of the sun (= Yahweh) with healing is significant for it is precisely the sun generating light and warmth which guarantees fertility and thus, life. Further, there is a connection between the sun and world order, cf. שמש צדקה. In the ancient Near East, the sun god was considered to be the author of the world order.[169] According to Ps 85:12, righteousness, צֶדֶק (in the sense of world order) goes before Yahweh. Ps 19 suggests an association between the sun and world order (law) when it celebrates the sun (vv. 5-7) and then praises the law of Yahweh which enlightens the eyes (vv. 8-11). In Mal 3:20, the rising of the sun (= Yahweh) ensures the restoration of צדקה, right order, and thus of harmonious relations between heaven and earth, between Yahweh and man.

וִיצָאתֶם וּפִשְׁתֶּם: פְּשְׁתֶּם is a qal pf., 2 m.pl. of פוש, "to spring about,"[170] (cf. Jer 50:11). Gesenius suggests that the verb is related to "Arab فاش Med. Ye, to be proud, then used of a horseman leaping proudly and fiercely, Hab 1:8."[171] The hiriq in פְּשְׁתֶּם is probably due to attentuation from the usual pathah.[172]

---

[166] Gray, "The Day of Yahweh," 5, n. 1. Moreover, Gray's remark that Zoroastrian eschatological categories are reflected in Mal 3:19-21 must be questioned. Malachi is not speaking of an eschatological conflagration of the world. He is describing the day of Yahweh which will usher in "an ideal future for Yahweh's own people in the land that he has given them . . . a future in this world, and not at or after the end of this world," Ahlström, *Joel*, 89. Further, the eruption of Yahweh's anger into a fire of destruction appears not only in Malachi, cf. 3:19, but in Isa 5:25; 30:27f; Nah 1:6; Zeph 1:18 and cf. Ps 18:18; it is a characteristic of the day of Yahweh.

[167] Keel, 192.

[168] Cf. also J. M. P. Smith, 80; von Bulmerincq, 2.535-536.

[169] Keel, 207-8.

[170] BDB, 807.

[171] *Gesenius' Hebrew and Chaldee Lexicon*, 670.

[172] Cf. GKC #44d, 120.

מַרְבֵּק :כְּעֶגְלֵי מַרְבֵּק n.m. is always associated with עֵגֶל, n.m.,
"calf" (cf. Amos 6:4, 1 Sam 28:24; Jer 46:21). It is derived from
the Arabic رَبَق, "to tie up,"[173] and denotes the stall in which
cattle were tied for feeding purposes. עֶגְלֵי מַרְבֵּק thus are well-fed,
or fattened cattle, and are symbolic of prosperity.[174]

   In Mal 3:14 the Yahweh fearers assert that they walk mournfully, הָלַךְ קְדֹרַנִּית. Such a depressed state (cf. קָדַר, "to be dark,
blue, wretched")[175] is quite possibly the result of God's failure to
judge the evildoers and mete out the punishment they so clearly
deserve. According to Mal 3:20c, however, their dark depression
will lift and will be replaced by an exuberance of vitality and
joy. Like calves released from their dark stalls who gambol in
the freedom of open pastures, the God fearers will break into life
and energy. The catalyst is Yahweh's arrival on his day. As the
sun of righteousness, שֶׁמֶשׁ צְדָקָה 3:20a, he will restore order
צְדָקָה,—the wicked will be destroyed, 3:19, 21, the righteous
vindicated, 3:20a, b—and initiate a healing process, מַרְפֵּא, 3:20a.
Indeed the healing power of the sun is illustrated through the
imagery of Mal 3:20c. It renews vitality (וִיצָאתֶם וּפִשְׁתֶּם), it ensures
fertility and prosperity (cf. עֶגְלֵי מַרְבֵּק); it guarantees life.

   [3:21]—The triumph of the pious over the wicked is one of
the standing features of the Day of Yahweh, though it assumes
varying forms (cf. Mic 4:13; 7:17; Zeph 2:9; 3:8; Obad 17f, Isa
11:13f; 66:24; Ps 149:7-8). According to Mal 3:21, the Yahweh
fearers will actively participate in the destruction of the evildoers
on the day when Yahweh acts (cf. ביום אשר אני עשה 3:21c).

   עַסּוֹתֶם is a qal pf. 2 m.pl. from עסס, "to press, crush, by
treading, tread down,"[176] cf. Arab. عَسَّ, "go the rounds, tramp,
prowl,"[177] and the Talmudic עסיסית, "zerdrückłe, zerstampfte
Weizenkörner."[178] It is a synonym of רמס, "to trample," (Isa

---

[173] BDB, 918.
[174] von Bulmerincq remarks: "Allerdings kann durch Jes. Sir. 38, 26 . . . für
מרבק im späteren Sprachgebrauch die Bedeutung Mast bezeugt werden, jedoch
wohl nur als Metonymie für Maststall. Der ursprüngliche Sinn der Nominalform
makṭil . . . kann entsprechend dem Etymon רבק . . . nur gefasst werden als Ort,
wo man etwas anbindet, speziell der Ort, wo das Vieh angebunden wird, d.h. der
Stall, sei es der Futter—, sei es der Maststall," 2.541-542.
[175] Cf. above, 213-14.
[176] BDB, 779.
[177] Ibid.
[178] von Bulmerincq, 2.544.

41:25; 63:3; Pss 7:6; 91:13); בוס, "tread down, trample," (Isa 14:
25; 63:6; Pss 44:6; 60:14); דוש, "tread," Job 39:15 and דרך, "tread,
march," (Isa 63:6; Ps 91:13). The noun עסיס means "sweet wine,"
i.e., "pressed" from the grapes. According to Joel 4:18 and Amos
9:13, the blessing of fresh, sweet wine dripping from the mountains is consequence of the day of Yahweh and is symbolic of
abundant fertility. It is probable that the imagery in Mal 3:21a is
borrowed from treading grapes in the winepress. God's judgment
upon his own people or upon the nations "is often expressed in
terms of a cup of wine which he will force them to drink so that
they will reel and stagger, cf. Pss 60:5; 75:9; Jer 25:15; 51:7."[179]
Similarly judgment is compared to the treading out of grapes
(cf. Joel 4:13; Isa 63:2-6 and cf. Mal 3:21a). Further, just as
treading on grapes produces wine which is symbolic of blessing
and fertility, so the total destruction of the wicked (by trampling
them) will signal the return of life sustaining conditions. Finally,
the use of the verb עסס in Mal 3:21a continues the imagery
begun in 3:20c of the cattle romping through open pastures,
treading on whatever is in their path.

אֵפֶר כִּי־יִהְיוּ אֵפֶר:[180] is a n.m. meaning "ash." According to
Num 19:5f, אֵפֶר is a result of burning (cf. also Ezek 28:18;
Isa 44:19-20). Von Bulmerincq remarks that, "An unserer Stelle
ist . . . die Bedeutung Asche direkt durch den Kontext an die
Hand gegeben."[181] Because the evildoers will be set ablaze on the
day of Yahweh (cf. 3:19), "Es ist daher das denkbar Natürlichste,
ihre Überrest als Asche zu bezeichen."[182] Since it is clearly stated
in Mal 3:19 that the fire of Yahweh's day will consume the
wicked, it is unlikely that the God fearers will directly participate
in their destruction. However, they will participate indirectly by
stamping on the remains of the evildoers. Such an action would
enable the righteous to feel as though they were contributing to
the extirpation of the evil they had bemoaned for so long
(cf. 2:17; 3:13-15).

רֶגֶל :תַּחַת כַּפּוֹת רַגְלֵיכֶם: (n.f.) means "the soles of the foot"
(cf. Gen 8:9; Josh 3:13; 4:18; 2 Kgs 19:24; Ezek 43:7). The combination תחת כף רגל, "under the sole of the foot" is found
elsewhere only in 1 Kgs 5:17.

[179] J. F. Ross, "Wine," *IDB* 4.851.
[180] For the causal use of כִּי, "for," see von Bulmerincq, 2.545.
[181] Ibid., 546.
[182] Ibid.

CHAPTER XI

MALACHI 3:22-24

²²זכרו תורת משה עבדי אשר צויתי אותו בחרב
על־כל־ישראל חקים ומשפטים
²³הנה אנכי שלח לכם את אליה הנביא
לפני בוא יום יהוה הגדול והנורא
²⁴והשיב לב־אבות על־בנים
ולב בנים על־אבותם
פן־אבוא והכיתי את־הארץ חרם¹

*"Remember the law of Moses my servant, to whom I commanded
   at Horeb
   statutes and ordinances for all Israel.
I am about to send to you Elijah the prophet before the coming
   of the
   great and terrible day of Yahweh.
And he will turn the heart of the fathers together with that of
   the children.
And the heart of the children together with that of their fathers
   [to me];
So that I will not smite the land with a ban of destruction when
   I come."*

[3:22-24] Introduction

There is a general agreement on the critical assessment of
the last three verses of Malachi's prophecy as consisting of two

¹ Note that these verses exhibit neither the question and answer schema
characteristic of the six oracle units nor poetic structure. Such an abrupt change
in form throws these verses into sharp relief. It is the prophet's task to convey the

243

separate appendices. The evidence turns chiefly on the form and content of these concluding verses. Verse 22 is thought to be a summarizing admonition stemming from a 'legalistic' rather than a prophetic editor which connects "with neither the foregoing nor the following context."[2] The last two verses offer a secondary attempt to identify the figure promised in 3:1.[3] Dentan characterizes these verses as "a bit of speculative exegesis."[4] W. Rudolph has argued for seeing these verses as a final redactional conclusion to all the prophetic books.[5]

J. M. P. Smith remarks that although the linguistic usage of Mal 3:22-24 "is not conclusive in itself," it adds weight to the thesis that the verses are of late origin.[6] He stresses that "Malachi's term is not יום יהוה, nor יוֹם הַגָּדוֹל וְהַנּוֹרָא, but הַיּוֹם הַבָּא or הַיּוֹם אֲשֶׁר אֲנִי עֹשֶׂה. Malachi speaks of הַתּוֹרָה, but not of תּוֹרַת מֹשֶׁה. Malachi constantly cites אָמַר יהוה; these verses never. אָנֹכִי stands here as against אֲנִי elsewhere in Malachi."[7] Finally, Smith suggests that the נ majuscula found in the MT is the mark of an addition to the text "as the beginnings of books are so marked in certain cases, viz. Gen 1:1; Prov 1:1; Ct 1:1; Ecc 1:1; 1 Chron 1:1; Isa 40:1."[8]

Scholars generally conclude that these verses reflect the conditions of the Hellenistic period. They view the "irreconcilable conflict"[9] between fathers and their sons (3:24) as the result of

---

words of Yahweh to his people and to do so in the most effective manner possible. Mal 3:22-24 comprise the climax of the prophecy. As the last words directed to the people they not only summarize themes previously introduced but emphasize in the clearest, most straightforward way that the dire consequences of Yahweh's wrath can be averted only by a wholehearted return to him.

[2] So J. M. P. Smith, *Malachi* (ICC; Edinburgh: T. & T. Clark, 1912) 81; Ernst Sellin and George Fohrer, *Introduction to the Old Testament* (Nashville: Abingdon, 1968) 470; A. Robert and A. Feuillet, *Introduction to the Old Testament* (New York: Desclee, 1968) 355.

[3] Sellin and Fohrer, 470; J. M. P. Smith, 82; A. van Hoonacker, *Les douze petits prophètes* (Paris: Gabalda, 1908) 739f.; Rex Mason, *The Books of Haggai, Zechariah and Malachi* (Cambridge: Cambridge University, 1977) 160.

[4] R. C. Dentan, "Malachi," *IB* 6 (ed. G. A. Buttrick; New York: Abingdon, 1956) 1143-44.

[5] Wilhelm Rudolph, *Haggai-Sacharja-Maleachi* (KAT 13/4; Gütersloh: Gütersloher Verlagshaus Gerd Mohn, 1976) 7.

[6] J. M. P. Smith, 85.

[7] J. M. P. Smith, 85.

[8] Ibid.

[9] Ibid., 82.

the profound changes produced by the incoming of Greek customs and thought, changes eagerly grasped at by the younger generation to the horror of their more orthodox parents.[10]

The considerations urged in support of the late origin of Mal 3:22-24 need to be reexamined, especially the contention that these verses are contextually unrelated to the body of Malachi's prophecy, the claim that the quarrels among family members alluded to in Mal 3:24 can only be understood against the background of the Hellenistic era and the use of linguistic criteria to uphold the thesis of lateness and thus secondary authorship, despite the recognition that such criteria are inconclusive.[11] If it can be demonstrated that Mal 3:22-24 are integrally related to the preceding six oracle units both thematically and linguistically and if familial disharmony may be viewed as a consequence of conditions in the Persian period, the probability that these final verses are the conscious literary product of Malachi himself must be seriously considered.

[3:22] Text and Commentary

זִכְרוּ is a qal m.pl. impv. of זָכַר, "to remember, recall, call to mind."[12] According to J. Pedersen, "When a soul remembers something, it does not mean that it has an objective memory image of some thing or event, but that this image is called forth in the soul and assists in determining its direction, its action. When man remembers God, he lets his being and his actions be determined by him."[13] Malachi uses remember (זכר) in this sense of not only recalling the law, but living in obedience to it. The combination זכר + תּוֹרָה is found only here. More common is the alliance of זָכַר with מִצְוֹת יהוה (Num 15:39f), מִשְׁפָּטִים (Ps 119:52) and פִּקֻּדִים (Ps 103:18).

Those scholars who maintain that Malachi was acquainted with the D Code but not the P consistently refer to this verse to uphold their thesis.[14] Van Hoonacker remarks that זָכַר in the

[10] C. C. Torrey, "The Prophet Malachi," *JBL* 17 (1898) 7. Mason, 160; J. M. P. Smith, 82-83.

[11] Cf. J. M. P. Smith, 85.

[12] BDB, 269.

[13] Johannes Pedersen, *Israel Its Life and Culture* (4 vols.; London: Oxford University, 1973) 1.106.

[14] Cf. van Hoonacker, 740; Sellin and Fohrer, 470; Mason, 159. Ernst Sellin, *Das Zwölfprophetenbuch übersetzt und erklärt* (KAT 12/2; Leipzig: A

imperative is more frequent in Deuteronomy (cf. 9:7, 27; 24:9; 25:17; 32:17) than in P, that the mountain of the law is called חֹרֵב in Deuteronomy (1:6; 4:10, 15; 5:2; 9:8; 18:16) whereas the Priestly writers call it סִינַי and that the phrase חֻקִּים וּמִשְׁפָּטִים is part of the deuteronomic vocabulary (4:1, 5, 8, 14, 45; 5:1, 28; 6:1; 7:11; 11:32; 12:1).[15] Von Bulmerincq contends, however, that in Deuteronomy זָכַר has

> die Bedeutung des Zurückblickens in der Vergangenheit odor der Erinnerung an geschichtliche Tatsachen, und zwar als Motiv für eine bestimmte Handlungsweise, vgl. Deut. 5:15; 7:18; 8:2; 9:7; 15:15; 16:3, 12; 24:9 . . . [16] Dagen findet sich זָכַר im Sinne von זכר לעשות bzw. זכר ועשה als terminus für das Festhalten am Gesetz nur bei P (Num. 15:39f) und im Psalter (Pss. 103:18; 119:52). . . . In diesem Sinne ist der Ausdruck wohl auch an unserer Stelle zu verstehen; vollständig würde er daher lauten: זכרו תורת משה לעשותה . . . d.h. gedenket der Tora Mosis, sei zu beobachten . . . [17]

Characteristic of Deuteronomy is its use of חֹרֵב to designate the mountain at which Moses received the law. The P writers consistently employ סִינַי or הַר סִינַי (cf. Exod 16:1; 24:16; 31:18; 34:29, 32; Lev 7:38; 25:1; 26:46; 27:34; Num 3:1; 28:6). If, however, this datum is used to support the hypothesis that Malachi was acquainted with D but not with P "dann müsste man auch annehmen, dass das Deuteronomium nur E, aber nicht J gekannt haben,"[18] since חֹרֵב is characteristic of the former (cf. Exod 3:1;

Deichertsche, 1930) 617; Otto Eissfeldt, *The Old Testament: An Introduction* (New York: Harper and Row, 1965) 443. It should be noted that these same scholars avow that Mal 3:22-24 are an addition to be dated to the Hellenistic period, cf. above, 243-44. Are we to infer that the P corpus was unknown at that late date?

[15] van Hoonacker, 740 and cf. also Sellin, 617.

[16] von Bulmerincq, also notes: "Jedenfalls ist es auffallend, dass während die elohistische Rezension des Dekalogs die Einschärfung des Sabbatgebots mit dem Ausdruck זכור einleitet (Exod. 20, 8) das Deuteronomium dafür שמור einsetzt (Deut. 5, 12), A. von Bulmerincq, *Der Prophet Maleachi* (2 vols.; Tartu: J. G. Krüger, 1926-1932) 2.551.

[17] von Bulmerincq, 2.551.

[18] Ibid., 557.

17:6; 33:6) and סִינַי of the latter (cf. Exod 19:2, 23; 34:2, 4).[19]
Analogously, should one infer from the Chronicler's use of the
Deuteronomic combination חֻקִּים וּמִשְׁפָּטִים "statutes and ordi-
naces," that he was acquainted solely with the D corpus of
writing?

At issue here is not the preponderance of D terminology in
Mal 3:22 (cf. also תּוֹרַת מֹשֶׁה, Josh 8:31f; 23:6; 1 Kgs 2:3; 2 Kgs 14:6;
21:8; מֹשֶׁה עַבְדִּי, Deut 3:24; 34:5; Joseh 1:1f; 7:13, 15; 8:31, 33; 9:24;
11:12, 15; 12:6; 13:8; 14:7; 18:7; 22:2, 4f; 1 Kgs 8:53, 56; 2 Kgs 18:12;
21:8). What is at issue is the inference drawn from this and other
passages in the prophecy (cf. esp 2:4-5) that Malachi was unfa-
miliar with the Priestly writings. As discussed above, priestly
influence is clearly discernible in the prophet's terminology.[20]
This may indicate that the Priestly tradition was promulgated in
its final form and accepted as authoritative in Malachi's time
although such a supposition is not strictly necessary since we
have to assume that it codified practices which had long been
followed in some quarters. The numerous points of intersection
between Malachi and the Deuteronomic and Priestly traditions
suggest that he was influenced by and drew material from both.
Therefore, the preponderance of D terminology in Mal 3:22
cannot be ascribed to a lack of familiarity with P. Rather, the
language of 3:22 serves as a natural introduction to the figure of
Elijah (3:23-24), whose story is part of the D corpus, whose
theophanic experience occurred at Horeb (1 Kgs 19:4f) and who
spoke to "all Israel" (1 Kgs 18:20) challenging the people to
respond to God by forcing a decision between right and wrong.

תּוֹרַת מֹשֶׁה עַבְדִּי: The combination תּוֹרַת מֹשֶׁה, "law of Moses,"
cf. סֵפֶר תּוֹרַת מֹשֶׁה, "the book of the law of Moses," is also found
in Josh 8:31f; 23:6; 1 Kgs 2:3; 2 Kgs 14:6; 21:8; Dan 9:11, 13;
Ezra 3:2; 2 Chr 23:18; 30:16; Neh 8:1; 8:14; 10:30; Ezra 7:6. Mason
asserts that in Mal 3:22, "the reference is to the Torah as a whole
and so represents a late stage when it had achieved its final form
and gained authority."[21] According to J. M. P. Smith, at the
time when this verse was added, "the tradition of the Mosaic

---

[19] Note that the Chronicler also employs the term חרב (2 Chr. 5:10). Should
one infer from this that he was acquainted with the D writing only?
[20] Cf. above on vv. 2:4-5.
[21] Mason, 159.

origin of the law was evidently well established, though the development of that law and that tradition may not have been completed."[22] Von Bulmerincq considers the תּוֹרַת מֹשֶׁה to be a reference to the law book Ezra brought with him (cf. Neh 8:1; Ezra 7:6).[23]

Malachi lays final emphasis upon the necessity of keeping the Mosaic law. Earlier in his prophecy he had rebuked the priests, who were the custodians and expounders of the law (תּוֹרָה), for having caused many to stumble (2:7-8). He also warned that obedience to the law is the only sure path of blessing, urgently pointing out to them that the reason a curse remained on the nation's labors was because its people had forgotten the law (סָרְתֶּם מֵחֻקַּי וְלֹא שְׁמַרְתֶּם, 2:17-3:12). That the prophet was cognizant of the P tradition is revealed by his reference to the Covenant with Levi (Num 25:12f)[24] and to the tithing provisions found in Lev 27:30f and Num 18:21-31.[25] According to the Deuteronomists, "it is the law, given by Moses, set out and expounded in Deuteronomy, which provides the norm for the people's life and the life of the king, the standard by which they are judged."[26] So too in Malachi, the law functions as the unchanging authority for the whole community. Obedience to it issues in blessing; disobedience calls forth a curse (cf. 2:8-9, 3:7, 9, 10-12; 3:22).[27]

It has been conjectured that in the exilic period, a time of great literary activity, the Torah and the Former Prophets were edited.[28] The fact that the writings just named contain no clear

---

[22] J. M. P. Smith, 81.

[23] von Bulmerincq, 2.553.

[24] Cf. above on vv. 2:5-6.

[25] Cf. above on v. 3:8.

[26] G. von Rad, *Old Testament Theology* (2 vols.; New York: Harper and Row, 1962-1965) 1.336. Note that references to a written form of the תורה of Moses are to be found in 1 Kgs 2:3; 2 Kgs 10:30; 14:16, 17.13; 21:8; 22:8, 11; 23:24f.

[27] Note that there is an assumption in the prophetic literature too that the תּוֹרָה is a fundamental basis of Israel's life. Therefore, much of the prophetic indictment can be summarized as forsaking the תּוֹרָה of Yahweh revealed at Sinai, cf. Amos 2:4; Hos 4:6; 8:1; Isa 5:24. Note too that in Nehemiah, the תורת האלהים (cf. תורת יהוה) is the same as the תורת משה, cf. 10:30—תורת האלהים אשר נתנה ביד משה עבד האלהים.

[28] Donald Gowan, *Bridge Between the Testaments* (Pittsburgh: Pickwick, 1976) 320; Bustenay Oded, "Judah and the Exile," in *Israelite and Judean History* (Philadelphia: Westminster, 1977) 485.

allusions to any event after 540 B.C. makes the conjecture very probable.[29] D. Gowan asserts that "The Chronicler . . . seems to know the Torah in its final form, which means the work was completed no later than 350 B.C. and probably a good deal earlier."[30] To maintain, as is often done, that the Torah was "canonized" by the Chronicler's time (ca. 350 B.C.) is misleading. Its contents had been authoritative long before that as can be seen from Malachi's knowledge of and appeal to both the Deuteronomic and Priestly traditions.

The designation of Moses as עבד יהוה appears once in Deut 34:5 (cf. 3:24 where Moses calls himself עבדך). The expression משה עבד יהוה (cf. also משה עבדו, משה עבדו, משה עבדי) is most common in the books of Joshua and Kings (cf. Josh 1:1f, 7, 13, 15; 8:31, 33; 9:24; 11:12, 15; 12:6; 13:8; 14:7; 18:7; 22:2, 4f; 1 Kgs 8:53, 56; 2 Kgs 18:12; 21:8). It can also be found in Num 12:7f (עבדי משה), in Exod 14:31 (משה עבדו) and in Ps 105:26, 2 Chr 1:3; 24:6; Neh 1:7f; 9:14.[31] Von Bulmerincq remarks that

> von den genannten Stellen dürften die aus dem Nehemia-buch besonders beachtenswert sein . . . wobei hier eberfalls das Ehrenprädikat עבד־יהוה bzw. עבד האלהים Mose beigelegt wird in direktem Zusammenhang mit seiner Tätigkeit als Vermittler der göttlichen Tora (Neh. 9:14; 10:30, vgl. auch Josh. 1:7; 8:31; 22:5; 2 Kön. 21:8; Dan 9:11) bzw. der göttlichen Gebote (Neh. 1:7) odor Worte (Neh. 1:8).[32]

In Malachi the term עבד, "serve," describes man's proper conduct toward God, cf. 1:6 (עֶבֶד); 3:18 (עֹבֵד). The prophet's use of the phrase תּוֹרַת מֹשֶׁה עַבְדִּי demonstrates his awareness of the tradition that Moses was the meditator of Yahweh's instruction and intimates that he sees in Moses' service (עבד) an example of the conduct most pleasing to God. Further, it is possible to infer from Malachi's admonition "to remember the law of Moses my servant," that one consequence of the day of Yahweh will be the

[29] Cf. von Rad, 1.338.

[30] Gowan, 321.

[31] Note the parallel designation עבד האלהים, 1 Chr 6:34; 2 Chr 24:9; Dan 9:11; Neh 10:30.

[32] von Bulmerincq, 2.555.

renewal of the time of Moses, a time when God's laws were upheld and his people served him well (cf. also 3:4; 3:17–18).[33]

Halévy, אֲשֶׁר צִוִּיתִי אוֹתוֹ בְחֹרֵב עַל־כָּל־יִשְׂרָאֵל חֻקִּים וּמִשְׁפָּטִים: J. M. P. Smith and E. Sellin consider אֲשֶׁר to be a relative pronoun referring to תּוֹרַת מֹשֶׁה and translate: "which I commanded him in Horeb for all Israel—statutes and ordinances."[34] Von Bulmerincq however, suggests that אֲשֶׁר be linked with מֹשֶׁה עַבְדִּי and that אוֹתוֹ be understood "als rückbezügliches Pronomen zu אֲשֶׁר."[35] Thus he translates: "to whom I commanded at Horeb statutes and ordinances concerning all Israel."[36] In this way "sind חֻקִּים וּמִשְׁפָּטִים naturgemäss als Akkusative des affizierten sachlichen objekts zu erklären."[37]

The construction צִוָּה + double accusative (one of the person, אוֹתוֹ, and one of the thing, חֻקִּים וּמִשְׁפָּטִים) + עַל can be found elsewhere only in 1 Chr 22:13. צִוָּה + double accusative is more commonly followed by אֶל— (cf. Exod 25:22; Lev 27:34; Deut 1:3). In combination with verbs of saying, narrating, telling and commanding however, both prepositions, אֶל— and עַל—, may be translated "with regard to, concerning."[38]

In Deut 29 Moses mediates a covenant between Yahweh and כָּל־יִשְׂרָאֵל, all Israel (v. 1). The inclusiveness of the expression כָּל־יִשְׂרָאֵל is made explicit in vv. 9f where it is stated that the covenant community embraces ראשיכם שבטיכם זקניכם ושטריכם כל איש ישראל טפכם נשיכם וגרך אשר בקרב מחניך מחטב עציך עד שאב מימיך. Moreover, according to Deut 29:14–15, even those not present for the ceremony are bound by the covenant's stipulations. Similarly, in Mal 3:22 the expression כָּל־יִשְׂרָאֵל describes the covenant community in its totality. No one may exempt himself from obedience to Yahweh's תּוֹרָה mediated by Moses. Indeed, it is through the use of the imperative זִכְרוּ that Malachi reminds his recalcitrant contemporaries (cf. 2:7) that they too are part of כָּל־יִשְׂרָאֵל, the covenant community, and that they too are

[33] That this verse refers to the day of Yahweh is made clear by its association with 3:23.
[34] J. Halévy, "Le prophète Malachi," RS 17 (1909) 34; J. M. P. Smith, 81; Sellin, 615.
[35] von Bulmerincq, 2.556.
[36] Ibid., 556.
[37] Ibid., 560.
[38] BDB, 40, 754.

responsible for the fulfillment of the conditions enjoined on the generation which directly participated in the Mt. Sinai experience. It may be said that for Malachi כָּל־יִשְׂרָאֵל connotes the totality of the covenant community past and present and the mutuality of its responsibility before Yahweh.

The חֻקִּים וּמִשְׁפָּטִים, "statutes and ordinances," make up the body of Yahweh's תּוֹרָה (cf. Deut 4:8, 44-45; Neh 10:30). מִשְׁפָּטִים are primarily legal decisions; their goal is the preservation of God's order. As L. Köhler emphasizes, they express the demanding, imperative nature of the law, God's demands.[39] According to Hertzberg, "the expression of God's will results in a claim being made by God upon those who worship him; mišpāṭ becomes the binding law that contains the demands of Yahweh."[40] As such man must fulfill it in order to live (cf. Ezek 20:11). A חֹק is something prescribed, established, a statute. It became חֹק in Israel that the young women bewailed the fate of Jephthah's daughter (Judg 11:39); the moon, the stars and the sea each has its חֹק (Jer 31:35f). According to J. Pedersen, the terms חֹק and מִשְׁפָּט are synonymous since "every law is a mišpāṭ, because it is a manifestation of right, the right."[41]

The evidence for regarding Mal 3:22 as a late appendix is extremely weak. The theme of this verse is the theme of the prophecy as a whole—the necessity of keeping the law. That Malachi here employs the term תּוֹרַת מֹשֶׁה and not הַתּוֹרָה (cf. 2:8), and that he designates the people as כָּל־יִשְׂרָאֵל instead of כָּל־הָעָם (2:9) or הַגּוֹי כֻּלּוֹ (3:9) cannot be used to support the thesis that this verse is the product of another, later hand.[42] Variety of expression is a characteristic of Israel's literature.[43]

The significance of Mal 3:22 lies in the effect it has on the interpretation of the book as a whole. Indeed, this verse is the

---

[39] L. Köhler, *Old Testament Theology* (Philadelphia: Westminster, 1957) 204f.

[40] W. Hertzberg, "Die Entwicklung des Begriffes *mišpāṭ* im Alten Testament," *ZAW* 40 (1922) 283.

[41] Pedersen, 2.353.

[42] Against J. M. P. Smith, 85.

[43] Note that Ezekiel calls his people כל־העם (45:16), כל־בית ישראל (3:7b; 12:10; 20:40; 45:6), בית ישראל (3:4, 7a: 6:11) and ישראל (14:1; 20:1; 21:17; 44:29), and that the prophet Zephaniah employs six different expressions to designate the day of Yahweh, cf. 254.

prophetic crescendo establishing an important critical perspective in the light of which Malachi's disputation assumes its proper place. The imperative זִכְרוּ forcefully reminds the people that the whole nation of Israel still stands under the law of Moses and that the law of Moses still functions as the unchanging authority for the covenant community.

[3:23–24] Text and Commentary

הנה אנכי שלח לכם את אליה הנביא: This line is parallel to 3:1 (cf. הִנְנִי שֹׁלֵחַ מַלְאָכִי). The construction הִנֵּה + participle affirms that Elijah's arrival is near at hand and sure to happen.

The pronoun אָנֹכִי, I, appears only here; אֲנִי is used elsewhere (cf. 1:4; 1:6 (2x); 1:14; 2:9; 3:6, 17, 21). J. M. P. Smith argues that this use of אָנֹכִי supports the thesis of secondary authorship.[44] Hosea employs both pronouns (cf. אֲנִי 3:3; 4:6; 5:2f, 12, 14b; 7:15; 10:11; 13:5; 14:9; אָנֹכִי 1:9; 2:4, 10; 4:14a; 7:13; 11:3; 12:10f; 13:4) as does Jonah (אֲנִי—1:9b, 12; 2:10; 4:11; אָנֹכִי—1:9a; 3:2), Jeremiah (אֲנִי—1:8, 11ff, 19; 3:12; 4:13; 11:19; 23:3; אָנֹכִי—1:6f, 17; 3:14; 4:6; 23:32) and Isaiah (אֲנִי—43:4, 13b; 44:6; 45:12b; אָנֹכִי—45:13; 49:25). In Ezekiel, however, אָנֹכִי is found only once (36:28); אֲנִי is used elsewhere. In Amos אֲנִי is found once (4:6) while אָנֹכִי is used in 2:9f, 13; 4:7; 5:1; 6:8; 7:14; 9:9. Therefore, the form אָנֹכִי cannot be taken as an *a priori* indication of secondary authorship.[45]

אֵלִיָּה: This form of Elijah's name appears only here and in 2 Kgs 1:3f, 8, 12; אֵלִיָּהוּ is the more common designation (cf. 1 Kgs 17:1; 18:1; 19:1; 2 Kgs 1:10; 2:1). However as a personal name אֵלִיָּה is found in 1 Chr 8:27, a Benjaminite, Ezra 10:21, a priest and Ezra 10:26, a son of Elam.

לפני בוא יום יהוה הגדול והנורא: According to J. M. P. Smith and Böhme the characterization of the day of Yahweh as גָּדוֹל וְנוֹרָא is evidence for the lateness of this verse since Malachi speaks only of הַיּוֹם הַבָּא or הַיּוֹם אֲשֶׁר אֲנִי עֹשֶׂה.[46] Sellin remarks: "v 23b halte ich für späteren Einschub ... weil Jahwe sonst in

---

[44] J. M. P. Smith, 85.

[45] For a discussion of the pronouns אני and אנכי, cf. G. W. Ahlström, *Joel and the Temple Cult of Jerusalem* (SVT 21; Leiden: Brill, 1971) 8–11.

[46] J. M. P. Smith, 85; W. Böhme, "Zu Maleachi und Haggai," *ZAW* 7 (1887) 210–11.

v. 23a and 24 in der I. Person redet, und . . . weil der Satz sich als
aus Jo 3:4b beigeschriebene Randnote verrät, denn dort ist er
sicher original."[47] Similarly, Torrey attacks the genuineness of
this line contending that it is derived from Joel 3:4.[48] Based on
literary and historical criteria, both van Hoonacker and G. W.
Ahlström date the book of Joel to between 515-500 B.C.[49] Therefore, the possibility that Malachi (ca. 475-450 B.C.)[50] had access
to Joel's prophecy cannot be dismissed. It is not strictly necessary
however, to posit borrowing from Joel. Both the expression יוֹם
יהוה, day of Yahweh, and the description of that day as גָּדוֹל,
great, are found in the pre-exilic prophetic texts (cf. Amos 5:18
and Zeph 1:14; Hos 2:2; cf. also Jer 30:7). It is thus likely, as von
Bulmerincq opines, that the expression יוֹם יהוה הַגָּדוֹל "gehört . . .
bereits der vorprophetischen Volkseschatologie an."[51] Its further
development to יוֹם יהוה הַגָּדוֹל וְהַנּוֹרָא may have resulted from the
deuteronomic association of both adjectives (cf. Deut 1:19; 7:21;
8:15; 10:21; 2 Sam 7:23).[52] It is possible therefore "dass der
Prophet den Ausdruck יוֹם יהוה הַגָּדוֹל וְהַנּוֹרָא bereits als festge-
prägten terminus gefunden."[53] The possibility is strengthened
by the fact that this expression which is in the third person,
is found between two Yahweh speeches in the first person
(cf. 3:23a, 24). Indeed, " . . . ein derartigen Übergang von einer
Person zu anderen bei stehenden Formeln leicht eintreten
konnte"[54] (cf. Lev 25:14; Ezek 18:30a; Zech 7:10b).[55]

A comparison of 3:23b with 3:24c (אָבוֹא) clearly shows that
for Malachi, the "great and terrible day of Yahweh" is none
other than the day when Yahweh comes, cf. יוֹם בּוֹאוֹ, 3:2; it is the
day that is coming, הַיּוֹם הַבָּא, 3:19. That the prophet here
describes Yahweh's day as גָּדוֹל וְנוֹרָא and not as הַיּוֹם אֲשֶׁר אֲנִי עֹשֶׂה
(cf. 3:17, 21), or as הַיּוֹם הַבָּא, 3:19 cannot be used to substantiate

---

[47] Sellin, 617.

[48] Torrey, 7, n. 14.

[49] van Hoonacker, 153; Ahlström, *Joel*, 129 and cf. J. M. Myers, "Some
Considerations Bearing on the Date of Joel," *ZAW* 74 (1962) 190.

[50] Cf. above, 14f.

[51] von Bulmerincq, 2.574.

[52] Note that Malachi employs both adjectives in 1:14.

[53] von Bulmerincq, 2.575.

[54] Ibid.

[55] Note that although Yahweh is speaking in Zeph 1:14-17, designations of
his day are in the third person, cf. קוֹל יוֹם יהוה; יוֹם יהוה גדול, v. 14.

the thesis of late origin. Variety of expression appears to be a characteristic of prophetic descriptions of the day of Yahweh. For Amos the day of Yahweh, יום יהוה (5:2), is a יום רע (6:3). Joel employs four different expressions: יום יהוה (1:15b; 2:1; 4:14); יום חשך ואפלה (1:15a) and יום יהוה הגדול והנורא (3:4; cf. 2:11); היום (2:2); Isaiah 13 two: יום יהוה (13:6, 9) and יום חרון (1:14), יום ענן וערפל (13:13); and Zephaniah six: יום יהוה (1:7) יום יהוה הגדול (1:14), יום אף־יהוה (2:3) and יום עברת יהוה (1:18), יום זבח יהוה (1:8), קומי לעד (3:8, LXX), to give but a few examples.

. . . וְהֵשִׁיב לֵב־אָבוֹת עַל־בָּנִים (hiphil pf. of שוב) is usually rendered "zurückfahren,"[56] "faire retourner,"[57] "turn,"[58] and the line translated: "And he will turn the hearts of fathers toward their sons and the hearts of sons toward their fathers."[59] Scholars contend that this line depicts a state of estrangement within families which is the direct consequence of the incoming of Hellenistic thought and influence.[60] According to W. Rudolph, it is the sons who are primarily responsible for the discord. In their desire to adopt Greek attitudes and dress they clash with their parents and so violate the commandment to honor them (Exod 20:12; Deut 5:16; 27:16).[61]

The assertion that the familial disharmony referred to in Mal 3:24 can only be understood as the result of tensions originating in the Hellenistic period is the direct consequence of the affirmation that verses 22–24 are late additions to the prophecy. As has been discussed above, however, the evidence for regarding Mal 3:22 as secondary is extremely weak.[62] Moreover, linguistically, there is nothing in either v. 23 or v. 24 that suggests lateness. If, as is likely, this verse originated with Malachi, the cause of the discord among parents and children must be rooted in the conditions of the prophet's own time. It may be that the precariousness of the economic situation in Judah during the Persian period[63] induced young men to ally

[56] Sellin, 615.
[57] Halévy, 34.
[58] J. M. P. Smith, 83.
[59] Ibid., 83.
[60] Rudolph, 292; Mason, 160–61; J. M. P. Smith, 83.
[61] Rudolph, 293.
[62] Cf. above, 245f.
[63] Cf. above, 11–13.

themselves with rich, influential families through intermarriage. This act was condemned by Malachi because it led to the turning away from Yahweh in favor of the god(s) of the foreign wife (cf. 2:10-16). Further, it is probable that the intermarriage was preceded by divorce from the Judean wife (2:14), a circumstance abhorrent to Yahweh. The young man's deceitful, treacherous behavior (2:14) may have led both to the alienation of father and son and to the creation of tension between his family and that of his former wife. Von Bulmerincq remarks that

> der ganz singuläre Ausdruck הֵשִׁיב לֵב ist vermutlich gebildet nach Analogie des mehrfach gebrauchten הֵשִׁיב נֶפֶשׁ = erquicken, neubeleben (Ps 19:18; Prov. 25:13...), stärken, aufrichten (Ru. 4:15 // כלכל...). Veranlasst wurde diese Analogiebildung möglicherweise durch den ganz ähnlich lautenden Ausdruck in der Eliageschichte הסב לב,[64]

ואתה הסבת את־לבם אחרנית, 1 Kgs 18:37 and cf. Ezra 6:22, והסב לב מלך־אשור עליהם.

The heart (לֵב) is generally considered to be the locus of the emotions. "The heart receives impressions, the heart frames plans, the heart is the seat of religious knowledge."[65] According to J. Pedersen, "The heart . . . designates the whole of the essence and the character. When Saul had been anointed king, God gave him another heart (1 Sam. 10:9). It means that the whole of his essence changed; he was no more a common soul but a royal soul."[66] The prophets look upon the heart as the only thing that counts in life. It is of supreme importance that the heart should serve God (Deut 6:5). In Jer 4:4 (cf. Deut 10:16; 30:6) the demand is made as emphatically as possible, to dedicate one's heart to God before the sanctification of the body by circumcision. Isaiah rebukes the people's mechanical worship; they have removed their heart from God (29:13). According to Ezekiel, when Yahweh gives his people a new heart (לב חדש), they will once again live according to his laws (cf. 11:19f; 36:26f).

---

[64] von Bulmerincq, 2.582-583.

[65] Helmer Ringgren, *Israelite Religion* (Philadelphia: Fortress, 1966) 122.

[66] Pedersen, 2.102-103.

The demand that the people turn to (שׁוּב אל—) Yahweh and the lament that, in spite of Yahweh's actions on their behalf, the people refuse to return to him echoes throughout the biblical literature (cf. Hos 6:1; 14:2-3; Isa 10:21; 31:6; 1 Kgs 8:33, 48 and Hos 5:4; 7:10; Amos 4:6, 8, 10, 11; Isa 9:12; Jer 3:7). According to Jer 3:9-10, it is Israel's eagerness to sin that prohibits her wholehearted (בכל לבה) return to Yahweh. Therefore, Yahweh will give the people a heart (לב) with which to understand that he is the Lord and they will return to him with their whole heart (בכל לבם) (24:7). In his temple dedication speech, Solomon entreats Yahweh to listen to and forgive his people when they turn to him בכל לבם with their whole heart (1 Kgs 8:48f). To turn wholeheartedly to Yahweh (שׁוב בכל לב) is to turn to him totally, unreservedly, to orient (or reorient) the whole of one's essence to him and his will.

It is possible that Mal 3:24a, b . . . וְהֵשִׁיב לֵב־אָבוֹת עַל־בָּנִים should be translated not "to turn the heart of the fathers to the children," but "to turn the hearts of the fathers together with[67] that of the children" to Yahweh (implied). J. M. P. Smith remarks that although it is possible to render the preposition עַל by "with" and to interpret to the effect that fathers and sons together will be urged by Elijah to repent, "this yields an intolerable tautology within the sentence and adds no statement of strength to the thought.[68] To the contrary, it is likely that Malachi juxtaposed לֵב בָּנִים עַל־אֲבוֹתָם and לֵב־אָבוֹת עַל־בָּנִים to emphasize the immensity of the task confronting Elijah (cf. 3:7a, 9). Indeed, in view of the reference to הָאָרֶץ, the land, in 3:24c, the repetition stresses that the entire population of the land, young and old alike, will be the target of the prophet's efforts. According to von Bulmerincq, "bestätigt wird diese Auffassung durch Jer. 6, 31 und 13, 14 wo der gleiche Ausdruck in Parallele zu העם הזה (Jer. 6, 21) bzw. כל־ישבי הארץ (Jer. 13, 13) steht."[69]

The theme of "turning" (שׁוב) to Yahweh is at the heart of Malachi's prophecy. In 3:7b, Yahweh avows that if the people

---

[67] For על, "with," see *Gesenius' Hebrew and Chaldee Lexicon*, (Grand Rapids, Michigan: Wm. B. Eerdmans, 1949) 628-29.

[68] J. M. P. Smith, 83.

[69] von Bulmerincq, 2.583.

turn to him (שׁוּבוּ אֵלַי) he will turn to them (וְאָשׁוּבָה אֲלֵיכֶם) and so lift the curse that has plagued them (3:9) as a result of their failure to follow his laws (3:7a). Therefore, the suggestion that it is Elijah's task to reorient the very essence of man, the heart (לֵב), to God harmonizes well with Malachi's concerns. Significantly, such an interpretation also emphasizes the compatible relationship between the Elijah tradition and the prophetic proclamation. Elijah addressed "all Israel" (1 Kgs 18:20), a people who did not follow the מצות יהוה (1 Kgs 18:18) but instead served Baal (1 Kgs 18:21) and who were thus cursed (1 Kgs 18:1). On Mount Carmel, Elijah challenged his people to respond to God, to reorient their lives to him. When they did so, when they recognized that יהוה הוא האליהים (1 Kgs 18:39), the curse of drought ended, rain fell (1 Kgs 18:45). Finally, this interpretation forges a link between Mal 3:23-34 and Mal 3:22. Turning to Yahweh entails submission to his will through the observance of the חֻקִּים וּמִשְׁפָּטִים enjoined in the תּוֹרַת מֹשֶׁה.

פֶּן־אָבוֹא וְהִכֵּיתִי אֶת־הָאָרֶץ חֵרֶם: Von Bulmerincq remarks that of the two verbs (הִכֵּיתִי, אָבוֹא) in 3:24c,

> וְהִכֵּיתִי den Hauptbegriff ausdrücke, d.h. durch die Bekehrung Israels solle nicht das Kommen Gottes und die Vollstreckung des Bannes abgewandt werden, sondern nur das letztere, da das Kommen Gottes unwiderruflich sei . . . Bei dieser Erklärung wäre אָבוֹא gleichbedeutend mit (Gen. 48, 7; Ezek. 43, 3 vgl. auch das analoge בְּבֹאִי Gen. 33, 18; 35:9; Exod. 28, 29f, 35; 2 Kon. 4, 10). Ähnliche von —פֶּן abhängige Doppelsätze, genauer Doppelsätze, deren zweiter Satz von —פֶּן abhängt, während der erste eine Zeitbestimmung oder eine Voraussetzung des ersten enthält, Deut. 8, 12ff; 25:3; Ps. 28, 1; Prov. 25, 16; 25:9f.[70]

The line should thus be translated: "So that when I come I will not strike the land with utter destruction."[71]

הִכֵּיתִי is a hiphil pf. 1 sg. (waw consecutive) of נָכָה, "to smite, strike."[72] In Mal 3:24c, הִכָּה governs two accusatives: אֶרֶץ, with which it is commonly associated (cf. Num 32:4; Josh 10:40; Isa 11:4; Jer 43:11; 46:13), and חֵרֶם. According to von Bulmerincq,

---

[70] Ibid., 586.
[71] Cf. also Halévy, 34.
[72] BDB, 645.

> ... im Hinblick auf Amos 6, 11 חֵרֶם als akkusativ des,
> Produkts bzw. des konkreten effizierten Objekts aufzufas-
> sen und dementsprechend ... zu übersetzen: zum Banne =
> also dass es Bann wird bzw. dass es zum Ban wird. Doch
> hätte der Prophet in diesem Fall vermutlich והיתה חרם
> bzw. ותהי חרם ... geschrieben.[73]

However that may be, Yahweh is often said to smite a person, a
people or a country with something, e.g., a plague, disease
(cf. Gen 19:11; Num 14:12; 1 Sam 5:6; 2 Kgs 6:18; Amos 4:9;
Hag 2:17, Isa 11:15; Zech 10:11). It is thus possible to translate
Mal 3:24c, וְהִכֵּיתִי אֶת־הָאָרֶץ חֵרֶם, "I will smite the land with a
ban,"[74] i.e., destroy it.

Based on the parallelism between אֶרֶץ, "land" (3:24c) and
אבות / בנים, "fathers, children" (3:24a, b), it is possible that אֶרֶץ
not only circumscribes the territory inhabited by the אבות / בנים
but should be considered "als metonymisch Bezeichnung für
die gesamte Landesbevölkerung"[75] as well. According to Deuteronomy, the land, הארץ, is the proper milieu for the fulfillment
of the law. It is emphasized again and again that the people are
to learn the law "that they should do it in the land Yahweh is
giving them" (Deut 4:5, 14; 5:31; 6:1; 11:31f; 12:1). Significantly,
there is an intimate connection between the nature of the land
and the men who dwell in it. If the people maintain Yahweh's
blessing through obedience to his commands, it penetrates the
land and makes it a land of abundant fertility (cf. Deut 28:2-14;
Lev 26:6; Pss 65:10-14; 72:3; Amos 9:13; Joel 4:18). The negative
transformation of the earth is a consequence of the curse that
comes on the land because of disobedience (cf. Lev 26:19f: "your
land shall not yield its increase, and the trees of the land shall not
yield their fruit"). According to Lev 26:32f, Yahweh will deva-
state the land so that it will be a desolation (cf. also Deut 28:23;
Jer 12:4, 12; Isa 1:7; 6:12; 9:18; Ezek 12:19; Mic 7:13). The intimate
companionship between people and land makes it clear that the
people's disobedience affects the land by violating its sacral
character (cf. Lev 19:29; Num 35:33; Jer 2:7; 3:2, 9). Further,

---

[73] von Bulmerincq, 2.591.

[74] *GKC* #117dd, ff and especially his reference to Mic 7:12, איש את־אחיהו צודו
חרם, "They hunt every man his brother with a net," #117ff, 370-71.

[75] von Bulmerincq, 2.588.

Yahweh's curse, which is a consequence of sin must also invariably react on the land (cf. Isa 24:5-7, 10; Jer 4:23-26). Thus it is
likely that Yahweh's striking action in 3:24c is directed against
both the people who fail to follow his law and the land which
has been defiled by their disobedience.[76]

The noun (m.) חרם means "a devoted thing, devotion,
ban."[77] According to Pedersen, חרם is the Israelite term "for the
sphere which is utterly incompatible with what is sacred, for
that which is hostile and alien, and, because incapable of assimilation must be destroyed . . . To make herem, or to place under
the ban, means to root out of the community of Israel, to
place totally outside the Israelite psychic totality, and as a
natural consequence this usually involves extermination."[78]
Everything connected with that which is חרם is a danger,
cf. Josh 7. R. de Vaux points out that חרם is identical with the
curse in its most potent form. "When Meroz did not obey
the summons to come to battle with Deborah, it was cursed
(Judg 5:23). When Jabesh did not take part in the general campaign against Benjamin, it was made ḥērem (Judg. 21:11). The
two things are identical."[79]

The scholarly concensus is that Mal 3:23-24 are a gloss
upon 3:1-5.[80] As J. M. P. Smith remarks, in 3:1-5 "the conditions
on earth are well defined. Society falls into two classes—the
godly and the ungodly. All that is needed is the overthrow of the
latter and the exultation of the former."[81] In 3:23-24, however,
"all classes seem to be regarded as deserving of destruction.
There are no hard and fast, sharply defined moral and spiritual
lines between classes."[82] Smith concludes that the final verses
"reflect the conditions of a later age when Hellenizing influences
had wrought profound changes throughout all Israel."[83] Such
an analysis is incomplete because it concentrates solely on 3:1-5

---

[76] Note Mal 3:9f. The people are cursed for their failure to follow Yahweh's
laws (3:7); the land is ravaged.

[77] BDB, 356.

[78] Pedersen, 3.273.

[79] Roland de Vaux, *Ancient Israel* (2 vols.; New York: Mc Graw-Hill,
1965) 1.260.

[80] J. M. P. Smith, 82; Mason, 160f; Sellin, 617-18; Torrey, 7.

[81] J. M. P. Smith, 82.

[82] Ibid.

[83] Ibid., 82.

and 3:23–24 failing to take into account the fifth and sixth oracle units (3:6–12; 13–21) with which the final verses are closely linked. According to Mal 3:7f, the people are presently in the grip of a curse (מארה, 3:9a) because of their failure to keep the law (3:7a); their land has been devastated by drought and locusts (3:10–11). To remedy the situation, to change curse into blessing, Yahweh avers that the people need only turn to (שוב אל—) him, 3:7b and cf. 3:12. Significantly, the final verses (3:23–24a) assign to Elijah the task of abetting their return to God and, by implication, to his law (3:22). Should he be unsuccessful, however, Yahweh will place the people and the land they defiled under a ban (חרם) when he comes on his day (3:24b). The movement from present curse (מארה, 3:9) to future destruction (חרם, 3:24b) must be viewed against the background of the sixth oracle unit (3:13–21). To the righteous who lament that they alone are affected by the curse while the wicked so deserving of punishment prosper despite the adverse conditions (3:14–15), Yahweh responds that he will take action against the evildoers on his day. They will be clearly distinguished from the Yahweh fearers (3:18), set ablaze and reduced to ashes (3:19, 21). Although the curse (מארה, 3:9), the fire (cf. 3:19) and the חרם (3:24) are all instruments of Yahweh's judgment and powerful manifestations of his anger, the curse is a punishment placed on a people who still have a chance to reorient their lives (3:7); it is revokable. With Yahweh's arrival on his day, however, no further opportunity will be extended. The punishment for those who have failed to return to God is absolute annihilation (cf. 3:10, 24). It is significant that, according to the sixth oracle unit, Yahweh's judgment of destruction is not indiscriminate. It is for the evildoers alone. Those who fear Yahweh will be reckoned his special possession (3:17a, b) and as a result, will be spared on his day (3:17c, d, 21). It is probable, therefore, that the ban of destruction, חרם, pronounced in 3:24c is similarly restricted to those who have failed to turn to Yahweh, to the wicked. De Vaux remarks that in theory, the חרם admits of no exception whatsoever:

> At Jericho, all living things, men and beasts, had to be put to death, the town and all its movables were burnt, the metal objects consecrated to Yahweh (Josh. 6:18–

24). . . . In Saul's war against the Amalekites (1 Sam.
15), too, the anathema was to admit of no exception. . . .
Elsewhere, however, the ḥērem was more or less restricted:
it applied to all human beings, but the cattle and movable
goods could be kept as booty (Deut 2:34-35; 3:6-7 . . .
Josh. 8:2, 27; 11:14. . .).[84]

According to Joshua 6, the city of Jericho was placed under the
ban but because Rahab, one of the city's inhabitants, had hidden
some Israelite messengers sent by Joshua to reconnoiter the area,
she and her family were spared (6:17, 25). By transgressing the
חֵרֶם on Jericho, Achan brought down a curse upon the Israelites:
they too came under the ban (7:13). Significantly however, only
Achan, the one who had incurred the חֵרֶם, was killed (7:25).[85]
Finally, as 1 Kgs 20:42 elucidates, it was sometimes demanded
that single individuals should be placed under the ban, חֵרֶם,
especially the responsible leader of the hostile army.

The opinion of Smith and others[86] that Mal 3:23-24 describes
a society so totally permeated by wickedness that all must be
destroyed, cannot be sustained. Rather, the division of Israel into
two classes—good and evil—is consistently emphasized by the
prophet, in 3:1-5, in 3:13-21 and in 3:23-24. Significantly, these
three sections all describe the day of Yahweh, the day when
distinctions will be obliterated, the day when the wicked will be
judged and destroyed.

To further buttress the claim that Mal 3:23-24 are a gloss on
3:1f, scholars point out that the messenger's task has been
changed from that which Malachi assigned in 3:1f.[87] He is not to
prepare the temple for Yahweh's coming but to restore peace
and social well-being to the community so as to avert God's
wrath in the impending judgment.[88] Thus, these verses are
commonly characterized as "a bit of speculative exegesis"[89] which

---

[84] De Vaux, 1.260.

[85] The implication is that Achan's family, his possessions and the goods he
had stolen were destroyed but this is not stated explicitly (7:24ff).

[86] Cf. above, 259f.

[87] Mason, 160.

[88] Cf. Mason, 160; Torrey, 7; Rudolph, 299; Sellin, 617; Sigmund Mowinckel,
He That Cometh (New York: Abingdon, 1954) 299.

[89] Dentan, 1143-1144.

offer a secondary attempt to identify the figure promised in
3:1. There are explicit statements indicating that prophecy
had ceased in the intertestamental period and that there were
no more prophets in Israel (cf. 1 Macc 4:46; 14:41; 9:27). There
are also references to indicate that the writers looked forward
to a time when prophecy would return (cf. 1 Macc 4:46; 14:41).
As Mowinckel remarks:

> An age which had no prophets felt the need of men of
> God, filled with the spirit, who could preach penitence
> and conversion with greater power and effect that the
> *epigoni* of the prophets (the learned custodians of the
> law and the 'wise') felt that they could. Therefore, they
> interpreted Malachi's words as a promise of a prophet of
> the old kind, one of the old prophets themselves; and
> whom was it more natural to expect than Elijah, who
> had not died, but had been taken up into heaven alive?[90]

Mason opines that Elijah may have been singled out by the
writer of this addition because "he was the first major prophet
of the Old Testament and he may symbolize the promise of
a renewal of prophecy to prepare the people for the last time,
at a period when the living voice of prophecy had faded."[91]
Further, "he was also remembered in the tradition for saving
the faith of Yahwism at a time of religious apostasy, crisis and
persecution."[92]

The thesis that the functional change in the messenger's
role and his identification with Elijah is the speculative product
of the Hellenistic period must be challenged. Both Mal 3:1f
and 3:23-24 are attempts to assure disgruntled Yahweh fearers
that, in spite of the evident inequalities of life, a just God
does indeed exist (cf. 2:17; 3:13f) and both affirm that the justice
so ardently sought will be established in the coming day of
Yahweh. Mal 3:1-4 are the last words directed to the priests and
are closely linked to the second oracle unit (1:6-2:9) in which
they are severely chastized for their slovenly cultic performance.
Because the maintenance of the covenant relationship is con-

---

[90] Mowinckel, *He That Cometh*, 299.
[91] Mason, 160.
[92] Ibid.

tingent upon a correct Yahweh cult,[93] it should not be surprising that the preparatory efforts of the מַלְאָךְ and the actions of Yahweh will be concentrated on the priests first. On the day of Yahweh, they will be cleansed and so rededicated to God's service. No longer will they permit the people to bring improper, blemished offerings (cf. 1:14) but will ensure that sacrifices are ritually correct and properly offered. They will participate in and oversee a cult that is pleasing to Yahweh, in accordance with his norms (3:4). The final verse of the fourth oracle unit (3:5) is directed to the people at large and indicates clearly that they will be the object of the second stage of Yahweh's purifactory work. For the evildoers among them Yahweh's day will be a day of destruction, of annihilation (3:19f). Yahweh's final words affirm that such a punishment can be averted only by returning to him (3:23–24; cf. 3:7b). It is Elijah's task to instigate that return prior to Yahweh's arrival on his day.

Mal 3:1f and 3:23–24 are clearly directed to different segments of the population. They contain Yahweh's final words to the priests (3:1f) and to the people (3:23–24). Just as Yahweh's judgmental actions on his day differ with respect to each group so too do the preparatory efforts of his messenger. This analysis suggests not only that it is unnecessary to contend that Mal 3:23–24 are secondary because the role of the messenger diverges from that assigned in 3:1, but the possibility that the מַלְאָךְ and Elijah are one and the same as well. A comparison of Mal 3:1 and 3:23–24 shows clearly how closely related the figures of the מַלְאָךְ and Elijah are. Of both it is said that Yahweh will send them (שׁלח), that their arrival is imminent (הִנֵּה) and that their appearance will prepare the way for Yahweh's coming on his day. The task of the מַלְאָךְ is connected with the revitalization of the priesthood and the restoration of the cultus "zu seiner ursprünglichen gottwohlgefälligen Reinheit,"[94] 3:3f. It is Elijah's task to revitalize the cult community, to reorient it to Yahweh, 3:24. In view of the parallelism between Mal 3:1f and 3:23–24, it is highly probable that these verses describe not two figures, a nameless מַלְאָךְ and Elijah, but one, a מַלְאָךְ who is none other than Elijah. Von Bulmerincq remarks that the

[93] Ahlström, *Joel*, 97.
[94] von Bulmerincq, 2.569.

> verschiedenartige Bezeichnung des göttlichen Vorläufers
> zunächst durch ein Apellativum (3, 1) und dann durch
> einen Eigennamen (3, 23) hat übrigens eine Parallele an
> der Art und Weise, wie Deuterojesaia den König Dyros
> einführt: nachdem er anfänglich auf den persischen
> Eroberer nur mit einer umschreibenden Charakteristik
> hingewiesen (Jes. 41, 2. 25), nennt er erst im weiteren Ver-
> lauf der Darstellung seinen Namen (Jes. 44, 28; 45, 1).[95]

Further, as previously mentioned, a prophetic connotation for
messenger is not novel in post-exilic literature, cf. Isa 42:19;
44:26; Hag 1:13.[96] Indeed, the Chronicler explicitly designates
the prophets as Yahweh's messengers (2 Chr 36:15–16). It is
significant that Malachi's announcement that a prophet will
appear prior to Yahweh's judgment is consistent with Israel's
experience.

> Such is the sum and substance of the Chronicler's observa-
> tion on the place of Israel's earlier prophets. They
> had come to warn the nation. Yahweh then appeared
> in judgment, and since Israel had not repented, his
> judgment fell on them. The Chronicler observed that the
> prophets preceded Yahweh's coming, that they had
> attempted to prepare the people for it. Now this memory
> was turned into an expectation for prophecy to precede
> Yahweh's appearance on his day.[97]

In Joel 3:1–5, prophecy is explicitly linked to the Yôm
Yahweh. It is a sign that will precede Yahweh's coming (cf. 3:4).[98]
According to 3:1, Yahweh will pour out his spirit on all flesh,
כל בשר, which suggests that all Israel will receive the gift of
prophecy and will be spared the ravaging effects of the "great
and terrible day of Yahweh." Joel 3:5, however, makes it clear
that כל בשר (3:1) refers to כל אשר־יקרא בשם יהוה. Only those who
call upon the name of Yahweh will be delivered. These are, at
the same time, "all those whom Yahweh has called," (3:5c), "the

---

[95] Ibid., 570–91.

[96] Cf. above on 3:1, p. 133f.

[97] David L. Petersen, *Late Israelite Prophecy: Studies in Deutero-Prophetic Literature and in Chronicles* (SBLMS 23; Missoula: Scholars, 1977) 44.

[98] Hans Walter Wolff, *Joel and Amos* (Philadelphia: Fortress, 1977) 67.

ideal cult congregation."[99] The key to understanding the par-
tiality of salvation is the "calling" theme. According to Zech
13:7-9, on the day of Yahweh only a purified remnant will
survive, those who יקרא בשמי ואני אענה אתו אמרתי עמי הוא והוא
יאמר יהוה אלהי. In both the Joel and Zechariah texts the same
assertion is made—that in the coming day of Yahweh, only
some will be spared. They must call upon Yahweh and they will
be called upon by him. The "calling" theme is implicit in
Malachi as well. Those who will escape judgment and annihilation (cf. חרם, 3:24) are those who fear Yahweh and esteem him
(חֹשְׁבֵי שְׁמוֹ, 3:16); they are the ones designated by Yahweh to be
his סְגֻלָּה, "special possession," 3:17.

Malachi and Joel both describe the coming day of Yahweh,
both use identical phraseology: "the great and terrible day of
Yahweh," (Joel 3:4; Mal 3:24); and both have a pointed concern
for what will precede Yahweh's appearance. Indeed, in both,
prophecy is expected as a necessary sign of the times just prior to
Yahweh's theophany. According to Joel, those who call upon
Yahweh will prophecy. As a result of the outpouring of his
spirit (3:1) they will stand in a relationship of immediacy to God
as did the prophets who were similarly "endowed with speech by
the spirit (2 Chron 15:1; 20:14; 24:20)."[100] Malachi expects the
appearance of a single prophetic figure, a figure whose task it is
to reorient the people to Yahweh (3:24), to restore the relationship
severed by their failure to keep his law (3:7).

What is remarkable in Malachi's presentation is not the
expectation that prophecy will precede Yahweh's coming in
judgment, but the prediction of the return of a particular historic
prophet—Elijah.[101] The juxtaposition of Moses (Mal 3:22) and
Elijah (3:23-24) suggests that Malachi may have been influenced
by two interrelated Deuteronomic passages, Deut 18:15f and
2 Kgs 17:13-14. Deut 15f affirms that Yahweh will send to Israel
a prophet 'like Moses.' "The prophet 'like Moses' means for
Deuteronomy an example of the one outstanding office by means
of which Israel comes into quite direct contact with God."[102]

[99] Ahlström, *Joel*, 61.

[100] Wolff, *Joel and Amos*, 66.

[101] If Mal 3:23-24 are considered part of the prophet's message, these verses
cannot be said to promise the return of prophecy, cf. above, 262.

[102] G. von Rad, *Deuteronomy* (OTL; Philadelphia: Westminster, 1966) 124.

The prophet 'like Moses' will be Yahweh's mouthpiece, imparting all Yahweh's commands. His words are those the people must heed, Deut 18:19. Since Deut 18:9 takes such elaborate trouble to prove the authority of this prophetic office, an office which came into being at Mt. Sinai as the result of Israel's pleas to be spared the necessity of hearing the divine voice directly (Deut 18:16 and cf. Deut 5:24; Exod 20:19f), it is likely that it has in view a quite definite institution. According to R. E. Clements, Deut 18:15f "presents an interpretation of the work of certain unnamed prophets which it views as functioning within the order of the covenant which was inaugurated on Mount Horeb (Sinai) by Moses."[103] This view is strengthened by 2 Kgs 17:13 where the role of the prophets in Israel's history is singularly emphasized and interpreted: ויעד יהוה בישראל וביהודה ביד כל־נביאו כל־חזה לאמר שבו מדרכיכם הרעים ושמרו מצותי חקותי ככל־התורה אשר צויתי את־אבתיכם ואשר שלחתי אליכם ביד עבדי הנביאים.

> This asserts that it was the function of the prophets, who are regarded as a recognizable group, to warn both Israel and Judah to repent and keep the law (torah), which had itself been given to the people by prophets. Thus the prophets are presented as preachers of repentance whose messages was a call to return to the law. In line with the entire History this can only refer to the Mosaic law given at Sinai-Horeb.[104]

Clements concludes that

> the Deuteronomic covenant theology is here being impressed on the prophets, who are almost certainly to be regarded as the same prophets who were in mind in Deut. 18:15ff. Thus these are the great figures like Elijah and Elisha . . . Amos and Hosea . . . and perhaps Isaiah and Micah . . . [105]

These two passages, Deut 18:15f and 2 Kgs 17:13–14, stress that the prophetic role was instituted by Yahweh to be a ministry of

[103] R. E. Clements, *Prophecy and Tradition* (Atlanta: John Knox, 1975) 42.
[104] Clements, *Prophecy*, 50.
[105] Ibid., 51. Cf. also Wolff, *Joel and Amos*, 170.

the covenant inaugurated by Moses. The prophetic message may be summarized as a call to return to the תּוֹרָה which details Israel's covenant responsibilities. Indeed both passages affirm that the law and prophets are not in opposition to each other, but constitute an essential unity within God's purpose.

Cognizant of the Deuteronomic tradition,[106] it is likely that Malachi was influenced by its claim that Yahweh would send another prophet 'like Moses.'[107] Mal 3:22 demands an undivided commitment to the conditions of fellowship with Yahweh; it demands a return to his תּוֹרָה mediated by Moses which implies a return to Yahweh himself. Elijah is to be the agent of this return (3:23). Indeed, 'like Moses,' he functions as the means by which Israel can be assured of the most intimate association with its God.

There are probably several reasons why Elijah was singled out as the prophet to appear before Yahweh came to stand in judgment. Driver remarks that the "mention of Elijah follows naturally on the mention of Horeb"[108] and may indicate a reminiscence of the two theophanies which bound Moses and Elijah on the same mountain. In an age troubled by prophets who "did not always have the right to claim authorization by Yahweh,"[109] Elijah stood out as a recognizable and a proven figure. He was the first of the prophetic champions of Yahweh, as Moses was the first and greatest of Israel's lawgivers. That Elijah was available to reappear prior to the יוֹם יהוה was the natural extension of the belief that he had not died but was whisked up to heaven alive (2 Kgs 2:11).

Mal 3:22–24 comprises the climax of the prophecy. In them Malachi brings together elements from his preaching into a sharper focus. Indeed, all the major themes of the prophecy are found in these final verses: the stress on the law (3:22, cf. 2:6-8; 3:7), the coming prophetic figure whose task it is to prepare for Yahweh's appearance (3:23, cf. 3:1), the day of Yahweh itself (3:23, cf. 3:1f, 17-21) when Yahweh will judge and destroy the evildoers (3:24, cf. 3:5, 18-19, 21). Moreover, in these final verses

[106] Cf. above, 246f.

[107] Rudolph, 292.

[108] S. R. Driver, *The Minor Prophets* (New York: Oxford Univeristy, American Branch, Henry Frowde, 1906) 328.

[109] Von Rad, *Deuteronomy*, 37f and cf. Petersen, 98-99.

Malachi sets his message in a picture which is enriched by Israel's fuller traditions. His claim that Elijah is the precursant messenger serves to equate the hearers of his prophecy with the disobedient, vacillating people of Elijah's time whose allegiance to the God of their fathers was similarly in danger of being dissolved. Implicit in this analogy is the hope that Elijah will be able to elicit from Malachi's contemporaries the same recognition of Yahweh's greatness and power that he did from his own (1 Kgs 18:39) and so avert God's wrath (cf. 3:24).

The concept of Elijah as the forerunner put forward by Malachi underwent a marked development in subsequent literature. In Mal 3:23-24, Elijah's coming precedes that of Yahweh's. He is the agent of repentance and reconciliation, his task being to turn (הֵשִׁיב) the hearts of fathers and sons to Yahweh.[110] In the LXX is to be seen the first stage in the growth of variant interpretations. The rendering throughout is very free: הנביא, "the prophet," is read as τὸν Θεσβίτην, "the Tishbite," and instead of לב בנים על־אבותם, "the heart of the sons together with that of their fathers," the Greek has καρδίαν ἀνθρώπου πρὸς τὸν πλησίον αὐτοῦ, "the heart of a man to his neighbor." The most significant deviation is the translation of הֵשִׁיב not as ἐπιστρέψει (cf. ἐριστρεμμα, "to turn or return")[111] but as ἀποκαταστήσει. Elijah is to serve as the restorer of shattered relationships, working for "reconciliation among men."[112] Although "to restore" is a recognized meaning of the hiphil of שׁוב,[113] it is not the meaning which suits the context of Mal 3:24, especially in view of Yahweh's demand in 3:7b, שׁוּבוּ אֵלַי.

The influence of the LXX ἀποκαταστήσει gave rise to the further expectation that Elijah was to be an agent of restoration, in some sense, as well as repentance. This can be seen in the work of Ben Sira.[114] In his "Praise of the Fathers," he gives one

---

[110] Cf. above, 254-57.

[111] *LSJ*, 661. Note that Luke uses ἐτιστρεφαι to render the הֵשִׁיב of Malachi 3:24, cf. 1:16-17.

[112] Howard M. Teeple, *The Mosaic Eschatological Prophet* (SBLMS 10; Philadelphia: Society of Biblical Literature, 1957) 5.

[113] BDB, 999.

[114] R. H. Charles dates the original Hebrew of Ben Sira to 180-175 B.C. and the Greek translation to between 132-116 B.C., *The Apocrypha and Pseudepigrapha of the Old Testament*, 1 (Oxford: Clarendon [1913], 1973) 293.

section to Elijah (48:1-12). Verses 1-9 are based on 1 Kgs 17f and v. 10 on Mal 3:23-24:

> Who are ready for the time, as it is written,
>> To still wrath before the fierce anger of God,
> To turn the heart of the fathers unto his children,[115]
> And to restore the tribes to Israel.[116]

In Ben Sira 48:10c, d the two explanations of הֵשִׁיב which have been noted in the MT and LXX are found side by side. The Hebrew of Ben Sira retains the הֵשִׁיב of the MT and translates the ἀποκαταστήσει of the Greek back into Hebrew as הֵכִין, "to (re)establish, (re)-constitute, restore."[117] This suggests that the idea of restoration, based on the LXX rendering, is already firmly established.[118]

The two-fold interpretation of הֵשִׁיב is also found in the Synoptics. In Luke 1:16-17, John the Baptist is identified with Elijah. His work as the forerunner is to make ready for the Lord a people prepared for him by bringing back (ἐπιστρέψει) many of the sons of Israel to the Lord and turning (ἐπιστρέψαι) the hearts of fathers to their children. No mention is made of a work of restoration. In Mark 9:12 and its parallel Matt 17:11, however, it is said that Elijah comes first and restores (ἀποκαταστήσει) all things. This is a major enlargement of Elijah's mission. According to the LXX, Elijah will restore the heart of the fathers to his children and the heart of a man to his neighbor. In Ben Sira his task is to restore the tribes of Israel while according to Mark and Matthew, he will restore all things. The next step was for the idea of restoration to pass into that of resurrection which it did in the rabbinic literature, cf. M. Sota IX.15.[119]

---

[115] The Hebrew of Ben Sira, להשיב לב אבות על־בנים may be translated, "to turn the heart of the fathers together with that of the children [to Yahweh]," cf. Mal 3:24.

[116] Charles, 500-1.

[117] BDB, 466; Gesenius' Hebrew and Chaldee Lexicon, 387.

[118] Although the Greek of Ben Sira has a marked resemblance to Isa 49:6, the Hebrew does not so that the inference that the word "restore" comes from the LXX of Malachi still stands.

[119] Morris M. Faierstein, "Why Do the Scribes say that Elijah Must Come First?" JBL 100 (1981) 82.

Finally, in Malachi, Elijah is the forerunner of the יום יהוה;
he will precede Yahweh's coming. In the Synoptics Elijah is the
forerunner of the Messiah. Morris Faierstein remarks that "contrary to the accepted scholarly consensus, almost no evidence has
been preserved which indicates that the concept of Elijah as
forerunner of the Messiah was known or accepted in the first
century C.E."[120] Thus, he suggests that this concept is a *novum*
in the New Testament.[121]

[120] Ibid., 86.
[121] Ibid.

CHAPTER XII

CONCLUDING REMARKS

To be dogmatic about the transmission and writing down of Malachi's oracles would be unwise especially since the prophet provides no information relative to the problem. On the basis of the available information, many scholars conclude that

> the prophets did not commit their own prophecies to writing except in very rare instances and on very rare occasions. Instead they preached orally, and at first their oracles were preserved primarily by oral transmission. This continued until, for one reason or another, these oracles were fixed in written form; but even then, the oral transmission continued alongside the written in all subsequent periods.[1]

Further, it is maintained that the prophetic disciples played an important part in the collection and transmission of the prophets' teaching. Indeed, according to J. Lindblom, "For most of the prophetic literature which has been transmitted to us we are above all indebted to the disciples of the prophets. They learnt from the prophets, they listened to what they said, they stored up in their memory and sometimes put down in writing what they heard."[2] It must be stressed however, that sometimes the prophets themselves made the move from oral proclamation to written record. Using the example of Jer 36, G. W. Ahlström points out that

---

[1] Ivan Engnell, *A Rigid Scrutiny* (Nashville: Vanderbilt University, 1969) 163-64 and cf. also R. E. Clements, *Prophecy and Tradition* (Atlanta: John Knox, 1975) 46; Geo Widengren, "Oral Tradition and Written Literature among the Hebrews in the Light of Arabic Evidence," *Acta Orientalia* 23 (1959) 215.

[2] J. Lindblom, *Prophecy in Ancient Israel* (Philadelphia: Fortress, 1962) 163.

written words can be understood as proof of what the
sender of the message really has to say, and also as a
legitimation of the herald. In this case Jeremiah himself
could not go to the king or to the temple; he was
prevented from doing this, v. 5, and this is the basic
reason for this particular writing. . . . After about two
decades of acting as a prophet Jeremiah still knows what
he has said, and he obviously knows it so well that he
can twice dictate it to his scribe. . . . Therefore we can
say that the oral transmission and in this case the written
transmission starts with the prophet master himself.[3]

Ahlström concludes that "Jer. 36 may indicate this as a possibility
with regard to other prophets."[4] Indeed, Isaiah wrote on a tablet:
"Spoil hastens, Booty hurries" (8:1). The same prophet was
commanded to write down a revelation that it might be a
testimony forever (30:8). Ezekiel was instructed to record in
writing the description of the new temple (43:10–12), and Habakkuk was commanded to write down a certain revelation so that it
might be kept as a witness of the reliability of the prophetic
word, (2:2f). Of course these examples do not rule out oral
transmission and training in memorization but they do suggest
that it is incorrect to say that the prophetic oracles were handed
down orally for many years, and then, at a subsequent period,
recorded in writing. In view of these passages we must allow for
the existence of both oral and written transmission from the
beginning, although it is possible that the former predominated
in the earliest period.

As the oracular messenger-formula, "Thus says Yahweh,"
clearly shows, the words spoken by the prophets were conceived
as Yahweh's words (cf. Jer 1:9). The prophets were his messengers, his mouthpiece. It is likely that the recognition that
their words were the words of Yahweh prompted them to take
measures to preserve the oracles they received. G. W. Ahlström
contends that "the prophetical self-consciousness of being the
messenger of the words of Yahweh" is an indication for reliability
in the transmission of their prophecies whether the message

[3] G. W. Ahlström, "Oral and Written Transmission. Some Considerations,"
HTR 59 (1966) 78–79.
[4] Ibid., 79.

circulated orally for a time or was written down upon receipt.[5]
Further, oracles were preserved because their relevance did not
cease with the original proclamation. Through being written
down and/or repeated orally, they could always perform the task
of influencing their readers or hearers. Finally, the possibility
must be considered that the prophets took steps to ensure that
their messages were preserved in writing as a witness against the
day when the threats would be fulfilled (cf. Isa 8:1; Hab 2:2f).

Of Malachi's contemporaries, some were skeptical, unsure
of Yahweh's concern for them, others were utterly contemptuous
of religious service and thus of God himself. The likelihood that
Malachi took steps to preserve his oracles in writing so that their
truth and the trustworthiness of the prophet could be verified
by the course of events should not be dismissed. Indeed, from
the standpoint of tradition history two possibilities may be
considered—that Malachi wrote his oracles down as a composition which he never delivered orally or, that the prophet
addressed his people and at a later date either he or someone else
committed his words to writing. In view of the form and
character of the message, the latter is most likely. The question
and answer schema employed by the prophet suggests actual
dialogue between Malachi and his contemporaries. He may
even have confronted separately the different segments of the
population—the priests, evildoers and Yahweh fearers. If it is
the case that Malachi's prophecy was not given all at once, but
over a period of time, "one has to reckon with a period of oral
transmission . . . a period of the prophet's own memorization of
his utterances."[6] At some later date, perhaps shortly after he had
delivered his final oracle, either Malachi or a disciple trained by
him, wrote the message down in its entirety. From this point of
view, the whole of the prophecy may be considered the conscious
literary product of Malachi.

Malachi did not live like other Old Testament prophets in a
time of great political events or world shaking revolutions. His
milieu was everyday life in a small political system within the
great Persian realm. We know nothing of his call but we can

---

[5] Ibid., 81.

[6] G. W. Ahlström, *Joel and the Temple Cult of Jerusalem* (SVT 21; Leiden:
Brill, 1971) 137.

recognize it in his appearances and in the frequent use of the messenger formula which legitimized him as a prophet. Malachi may indeed have been a cult prophet. His interest in and knowledge of cultic phenomena suggest as much. His task, which was to strengthen his people's belief in Yahweh and remind them of their responsibilities as members of Yahweh's covenant community, was certainly not an easy one. The prophetic promises of prosperity once the temple was restored had not come true (Hag 2:6-9). The land was under Persian domination and, even if there is no evidence of oppression or abuse of power, the lot of a subject state is never a happy one. Under the most liberal of regimes vassals must bear the cost of occupation and levies for Persian military exploits in the region must have been a drain on the limited manpower of the small community. Nature herself had added her quota of afflictions in the form of drought, locust plagues and blighted vineyards (Mal 3:10-11). Zechariah's pleas for a deeper commitment to Yahweh had been mocked by God's apparent failure to safeguard even the primary needs of the his people (8:4-13). So too in Malachi's day, the priests were perfunctory in their duties (1:6-2:9). Paying little heed to the law, they reckoned that any sacrifice was good enough for Yahweh (1:7-8). Adultery, perjury and victimization of the underprivileged were rife (3:5) as was the refusal to give Yahweh his due in the way of tithes and offerings (3:10-11). It is likely that Yahweh's failure to provide for his people induced them to better themselves through intermarriage with prominent, wealthy families the result of which was not only the divorce of Judean wives but the infiltration of foreign religious practices into Yahwism itself (2:10-16). The law, the heart of the covenant, was neglected (3:7a). Malachi deplores the people's neglect and contempt of their religious duties not because they are important in and of themselves, but because such neglect reveals a lack of reverence, faith and love for Yahweh. Clearly, succinctly, Malachi states that it is precisely the sins of Israel that render it inconceivable that the blessing of Yahweh should rest upon her as she now is and he demands certain definite and tangible actions as a prerequisite to the coming of the desired good. Malachi demands a return to covenant law (3:22), a demand which involves no less than a wholehearted return to Yahweh himself (3:7b). Only then may Yahweh be counted on to fulfill all his promises made through the prophets. Twice the Yahweh fearers question God's justice contending that it is the evildoers who prosper (2:17; 3:14f). Indeed, the facts of life seem to tell against the profitability of godliness. To them Malachi holds out the promise of the imminent day of Yahweh, the day when the priests will be rededicated and so promote offerings in which Yahweh can delight (3:3f), the day when the wicked will be annihilated (3:18f), the day when the righteous, as Yahweh's סְגֻלָּה, special treasure, will experience his protective love (3:17). To them Malachi holds out the promise of Elijah (3:23-24). Known to all, he is the herald of Yahweh's coming in judgment; he is the sign by which the righteous will know that their vindication is at hand.

The very vigor of Malachi's critique makes it clear that for him religion cannot be satisfied with externalities. He does not regard ritual as an end in itself or an *opus operatum;* it is but the outer and visible expression of faith in and devotion to Yahweh. It is this devotion to God that Malachi seeks to instill in his people. His prophecy is a call to return to (שׁוּב אֶל—) Yahweh and the right cult, and his promise is that man's repentance will lead to a responsive turning on God's part; he will pour out upon his people the blessings they so ardently seek.

The significance of Malachi's prophecy should not be underestimated. His name, מַלְאָכִי, which aptly describes his function, may have been assumed at his call to be a prophet. Like Elijah who preceded him and who was soon to reappear, Malachi was Yahweh's מַלְאָךְ, his messenger, his spokesman. It was his task to bring God's words to his people, to his time. In so doing he opens a window on a little-known period of Judean history. Indeed, as R. Pautrel remarked: "Il suffit, pour l'apprécier, de constater combien, en un livre si court et avec des moyens si simples, Malachie nous fait encore penetrer dans le secret des consciences d'un temps si reculé."[7]

---

[7] R. Paultrel, "Malachie," in *Dictionnaire de la Bible, Supplément* (Tome 5; ed. F. G. Vigouroux and L. Pirot; Paris: Librairie Letouzey et Ané, 1957) 745.

SELECTED BIBLIOGRAPHY

Ackroyd, P. R. *Exile and Restoration*. London: S. C. M. Press, 1968.

Ahlström, Gösta W. *Joel and the Temple Cult of Jerusalem*. Supplements to Vetus Testamentum 21. Leiden: E. J. Brill, 1971.

————. "Oral and Written Transmission. Some Considerations." *Harvard Theological Review* 59 (1966): 69-81.

————. *Psalm 89: Eine Liturgie aus dem Ritual des leidenden Königs*. Lund: C. W. K. Gleerup, 1959.

————. "Some Remarks on Prophets and Cult." *Essays in Divinity VI: Transitions in Biblical Scholarship*. Edited by J. C. Rylaarsdam. Chicago: The University of Chicago Press, 1968, pp. 113-30.

Bartlett, J. R. "From Edomites to Nabataeans: A Study in Continuity." *The Palestine Exploration Quarterly* 111 (1979): 53-66.

Begrich, Joachim. "Die priesterliche Tora." *Werden und Wesen des Alten Testaments*. Beihefte zur Zeitschrift für die Alttestamentliche Wissenschaft 66. Berlin: Alfred Töpelmman (1936): 63-88.

Biggs, Robert D. *ŠA.ZI.GA., Ancient Mesopotamian Potency Incantations*. Locust Valley, N.Y.: J. J. Augustin, 1967.

Black, M., ed. *Peake's Commentary on the Bible*. Edinburgh: Thomas Nelson and Sons, Ltd., 1962.

Boecker, Hans Jochen. "Bemerkungen zur formgeschichtlichen Terminologie des Buches Maleachi." *Zeitschrift für die Alttestamentliche Wissenschaft* 78 (1966): 78-81.

Böhme, W. "Zu Maleachi und Haggai." *Zeitschrift für die Alttestamentliche Wissenschaft* 7 (1887): 210-17.

Botterweck, G. Johannes. "Jacob habe ich lieb-Esau hasse ich." *Bibel und Leben* 1 (1960): 28-38.

_____. "Ideal und Wirklichkeit der Jerusalemer Priester." *Bibel und Leben* 1 (1960): 100–9.

_____. "Schelt-und Mehrede gegen Mischehen und Ehescheidung." *Bibel und Leben* 1 (1960): 179–85.

Botterweck, G. Johannes, and Ringgren, Helmer, eds. *Theological Dictionary of the Old Testament*. 3 Vols. Translated by John Willis (Vols. I–II) and John Willis, G. W. Bromiley and D. E. Green (Vol. III). Grand Rapids: William B. Eerdmans Publishing Co., 1974–78.

Brichto, Herbert Chanan. *The Problem of "Curse" in the Hebrew Bible*. Journal of Biblical Literature Monograph Series, Vol. 13. Philadelphia: Society of Biblical Literature and Exegesis, 1963.

Bright, John. *Jeremiah*. The Anchor Bible. New York: Doubleday and Co., 1965.

Brongers, H. A. "La Crainte du Seigneur (Jirᵓat Jhwh, Jirᵓat ᶜElohim)." *Oudtestamentische Studien* 5 (1948): 151–73.

Broome, E. C. "Nabaiati, Nebaioth and the Nabataens: The Linguistic Problem." *Journal of Semitic Studies* 18 (1973): 1–16.

Brown, Francis, Driver, S. R., and Briggs, C. A., eds. *A Hebrew English Lexicon of the Old Testament*. 1907. Reprint ed. Oxford: Clarendon Press, 1974.

Browning, Iain. *Petra*. London: Chatto and Windus, 1974.

von Bulmerincq, Alexander. *Der Prophet Maleachi*. 2 Vols. Tartu: J. G. Krüger, 1926–1932.

Burrows, Millar. *The Basis of Israelite Marriage*. American Oriental Society 15. New Haven: American Oriental Society, 1938.

Busink, Th. A. *Der Tempel von Jerusalem, von Salomo bis Herodes; eine archäologisch historische Studie unter Berücksichtigung des westsemitischen Tempelbaus*. Leiden: E. J. Brill, 1970.

Buttrick, George Arthur, ed. *The Interpreter's Bible*. 12 Vols. New York: Abingdon Press, 1952–1957.

_____. *The Interpreter's Dictionary of the Bible*. 4 Vols. Nashville: Abingdon Press, 1962.

Carroll, Robert P. *When Prophecy Failed*. New York: The Seabury Press, 1979.

Charles, R. H. *The Apocrypha and Pseudepigrapha of the Old Testament*. Vol. 1, 1913. Reprint ed., Oxford: The Clarenden Press, 1973.

Chary, Th. *Les prophètes et le culte à partir de l'exil*. Tournai: Desclée & Cie, 1955.

Childs, Brevard. *The Book of Exodus*. The Old Testament Library. Philadelphia: The Westminster Press, 1974.

Clements, R. E. *Prophecy and Tradition*. Growing Points in Theology. Atlanta: John Knox Press, 1975.

Cody, Aelred. *A History of the Old Testament Priesthood*. Analecta Biblica 35. Rome: Pontifical Biblical Institute, 1969.

Cohen, A. *The Twelve Prophets*. Soncino Books of the Bible. London: The Soncino Press, 1948.

Cowley, A. E., ed. *Aramaic Papyri of the Fifth Century* B.C. Oxford: The Clarendon Press, 1923.

Cross, Frank Moore, and Freedman, David Noel. "The Blessing of Moses." *Journal of Biblical Literature* 67 (1948): 191–210.

Dahood, Mitchell. *Psalms II*. The Anchor Bible. Garden City, N.Y.: Doubleday and Company,

——. *Psalms III*. The Anchor Bible. Garden City, N.Y.: Doubleday and Company, 1970.

Dalman, Gustaf. *Arbeit und Sitte in Palastina*. Vol. 1. Gütersloh: Gütersloher Verlagshaus Gerd Mohn, 1928. Reprint ed., Hildesheim: Georg Olms, 1964.

Danell, G. A. *Studies in the Name of Israel in the Old Testament*. Uppsala: Appelbergs boktryckeri-a.-b., 1946.

Donner, H., and Röllig, W. *Kanaanäische und Aramäische Inschriften*. 3 Vols. Wiesbaden: Otto Harrassowitz, 1966–1969.

Driver, G. R. "Three Technical Terms in the Pentateuch." *Journal of Semitic Studies* 1 (1956): 97–105.

Driver, S. R. *A Critical and Exegetical Commentary on Deuteronomy*. 3rd ed. Edinburgh: T. & T. Clark, 1902.

——. *The Minor Prophets*. The New Century Bible. New York: Oxford University Press, American Branch, Henry Frowde, 1906.

——. *Notes on the Hebrew Text and the Topography of the Books of Samuel*. 2nd ed. Oxford: The Clarendon Press, 1966.

Duhm, B. "Anmerkungen zu den Zwölf Propheten." *Zeitschrift für die Alttestamentliche Wissenschaft* 31 (1911): 1-43; 81-110; 161-204.

Eissfeldt, Otto. *The Old Testament: An Introduction.* Translated by P. R. Ackroyd. New York: Harper and Row, 1965.

Elliger, K. *Das Buch der Zwölf Kleinen Propheten* II. Das Alte Testament Deutsch. Göttingen: Vandenhoeck & Ruprecht, 1951.

Elliger, K., and Rudolph, W., eds. *Biblia Hebraica Stuttgartensia.* Stuttgart: Deutsch Bibelstiftung, 1967-1977.

Engnell, Ivan. *A Rigid Scrutiny.* Translated by John T. Willis. Nashville: Vanderbilt University Press, 1969.

Faierstein, Morris M. "Why do the Scribes Say that Elijah Must Come First?" *Journal of Biblical Literature* 100 (1981): 75-86.

Falk, Z. W. "Hebrew Legal Terms." *Journal of Semitic Studies* 5 (1960): 350-54.

Fensham, F. Charles. "Widow, Orphan and the Poor in Ancient New Eastern Legal and Wisdom Literature." *Journal of Near Eastern Studies* 21 (1962): 129-39.

Fischer, James A. "Notes on the Literary Form and Message of Malachi." *The Catholic Biblical Quarterly* 34 (1972): 315-20.

Fohrer, Georg. *History of Israelite Religion.* Translated by David E. Green. New York: Abingdon Press, 1972.

Foster, Raymond S. *The Restoration of Israel.* London: Darton, Longman and Todd, 1970.

Gehman, Henry S. "The 'Burden' of the Prophets." *The Jewish Quarterly Review* 31 (1940): 107-21.

Geller, Stephen A. *Parallelism in Early Biblical Poetry.* Harvard Semitic Monographs, no. 20. Missoula: Scholars Press, 1979.

Gemser, B. "The Importance of the Motive Clause in Old Testament Law." In Supplements to Vetus Testamentum. Leiden: E. J. Brill, 1 (1953): 50-66.

Gesenius, William. *Gesenius' Hebrew and Chaldee Lexicon.* Translated by Samuel P. Tregelles. Grand Rapids, Michigan: William B. Eerdmans Publishing Company, 1949.

Ghirshman, R. *Iran.* Paris: Payot, 1951. Reprint ed., New York: Penguin Books, 1978.

Giesebrecht, F. *Das Buch Jeremia.* Handkommentar zum Alten Testament. Göttingen: Vandenhoeck & Ruprecht, 1907.

Gluck, J. J. "Assonance in Ancient Hebrew Poetry: Sound Patterns as a Literary Device." In *De Fructu Oris Sui, Essays in Honor of Adrianus van Selms.* Edited by I. H. Eybers, F. C. Fensham, C. J. Labuschagne, et al., Pretoria Oriental Series. Leiden: E. J. Brill 9 (1971): 69–84.

Glueck, Nelson. "Explorations in Eastern Palestine." *Annual of the American Schools of Oriental Research* 15 (1935): 60–75.

Gordis, Robert. *The Word and the Book. Studies in Biblical Language and Literature.* New York: Ktav Publishing House, Inc., 1976.

Gordon, Cyrus. Review of *Phönizisch-punische Grammatik* by Johannes Friedrich. *Orientalia* 21 (1952): 119–23.

Gowan, Donald E. *Bridge Between the Testaments.* Pittsburgh: The Pickwick Press, 1976.

_____. "Prophets, Deuteronomy and the Syncretistic Cult in Israel." In *Essays in Divinity VI: Transitions in Biblical Scholarship.* Edited by J. Coert Rylaarsdam. Chicago: The University of Chicago Press, 1968, pp. 93–112.

Graf, K. H. *Der Prophet Jeremia erklärt.* Leipzig: T. O. Weigel, 1862.

Gray, G. Buchanan. "The Foundation and Extension of the Persian Empire." In *The Cambridge Ancient History.* Edited by J. B. Bury, S. A. Cook and F. E. Adcock, Cambridge: The Cambridge University Press, 4 (1926): 1–24.

Gray, G. Buchanan, and Cary, M. "The Reign of Darius." In *The Cambridge Ancient History.* Edited by J. B. Bury, S. A. Cook and F. E. Adcock. Cambridge: The Cambridge University Press, 4 (1926): 173–228.

Gray, John. "The Day of Yahweh in Cultic Experience and Eschatological Prospect." *Svensk Exegetisk Årsbok* 39 (1974): 5–37.

_____. "The Rephaim." *Palestine Exploration Quarterly* 81 (1949): 127–139.

Greenberg, Moshe. "Hebrew Segullā: Akkadian Sikiltu." *Journal of the American Oriental Society* 71 (1951): 172–74.

Greengus, Samuel. "The Aramaic Marriage Contracts in the Light of the Ancient Near East and the Later Jewish Materials." Master's Thesis, the University of Chicago, 1959.

Halévy, J. "Le prophète Malachie." *Revue Sémitique* 17 (1909): 1–44.

Hammershaimb, E. *Some Aspects of Old Testament Prophecy from Isaiah to Malachi*. Theologiske Skrifter 4. Copenhagen: Rosenkilde og Bagger, 1966.

Hammond, Philip C. *The Nabataeans—Their History, Culture and Archaeology*. Studies in Mediterranean Archaeology, Vol. 37. Gothenberg, Sweden: Paul Åstroms Förlag, 1973.

Hanson, Paul D. *The Dawn of Apocalyptic*. Philadelphia: Fortress Press, 1975.

Haran, M. "Biblical Studies: The Idea of the Divine Presence in the Israelite Cult." *Tarbiz* 38 (1968): 105-19.

Hertzberg, W. "Die Entwicklung des Begriffes *mišpāṭ* im Alten Testament." *Zeitschrift für die Alttestamentliche Wissenschaft* 40 (1922): 256-87.

Holtzmann, O. "Der Prophet Maleachi und der Ursprung des Pharisäerbundes." *Archiv für Religionswissenschaft* 29 (1931): 1-21.

van Hoonacker, A. *Les douze petits prophètes*. Paris: J. Gabalda & Cie., 1908.

_____. "Notes sur l'histoire de la restauration juive après l'exile de Babylone." *Revue Biblique* 10 (1901): 1-26, 175-99.

Horner, T. M. "Changing Concepts of the 'Stranger' in the OT." *American Theological Review* 42 (1960): 49-53.

Horst, Friedrich. *Die Zwölf kleinen Propheten*. Handbuch zum Alten Testament. Tübingen: J. C. B. Mohr, 1938.

_____. *Die Zwölf kleinen Propheten: Nahum bis Maleachi*. Handbuch zum Alten Testament, 3rd Aufl. Tübingen: J. C. B. Mohr, 1964.

Humbert, P. "Le substantif to ᶜēbā et le verb tᶜb dans l'Ancien Testament." *Zeitschrift für die Alttestamentlich Wissenschaft* 72 (1960): 217-37.

Hvidberg, F. F. *Weeping and Laughter in the Old Testament*. Leiden: E. J. Brill, 1962.

Hyatt, J. Philip. "Jeremiah and Deuteronomy." *Journal of Near Eastern Studies* 1 (1942): 156-73.

van Imschoot, P. "Sagesse et esprit dans l'Ancien Testament." *Revue Biblique* 47 (1938): 23-49.

Isaksson, Abel. *Marriage and Ministry in the New Temple*. Lund: C. W. K. Gleerup, 1965.

Janzen, Waldemar. "ᵓAšrê in the Old Testament." *Harvard Theological Review* 58 (1965): 215-26.

Jeremias, J. *Theophanie*. Wissenschaftliche Monographien zum Alten und Neuen Testament, no. 10. Neukirchen-Vluyn: Neukirchener Verlag, 1965.

Jones, Douglas. "The Traditio of the Oracles of Isaiah of Jerusalem." *Zeitschrift für die Alttestamentliche Wissenschaft* 67 (1955): 226–46.

Kaiser, Otto. *Isaiah 1–12*. Translated by R. A. Wilson. The Old Testament Library. Philadelphia: The Westminster Press, 1972.

―――. *Isaiah 13–39*. Translated by R. A. Wilson. The Old Testament Library. Philadelphia: The Westminster Press, 1974.

Kautzsch, E., ed. *Gesenius' Hebrew Grammar*. 2nd rev. ed. Translated by A. E. Cowley. Oxford: The Clarendon Press, 1974.

Keel, Othmar. *The Symbolism of the Biblical World*. Translated by T. J. Hallett. New York: The Seabury Press, 1978.

Kent, Roland G. "A New Inscription of Xerxes." *Language* 9 (1933): 35–46.

Koehler, Ludwig, and Baumgartner, Walter, eds. *Lexicon in Veteris Testamenti Libros*. Leiden: E. J. Brill, 1958.

Köhler, L. *Old Testament Theology*. Translated by A. S. Todd. Philadelphia: Westminster Press, 1957.

König, Franz. "Die Religion Zarathustras." In *Christus und die Religionen der Erde; Handbuch der Religionsgeschichte*, 2 Edited by Franz König. Wien: Herder (1951): 645–58.

Kornfeld, Walter. "L'adultère dans l'Orient antique." *Revue Biblique* 57 (1950): 92–102.

Kutsch, E. *Verheissung und Gesetz. Untersuchungen zum sogenannten 'Bund' im Alten Testament*. Beihefte zur Zeitschrift für die Alttestamentliche Wissenschaft, 131. Berlin: Alfred Töpelmann, 1973.

Lagrange, M.-J. "Notes sur les prophéties messianiques des derniers prophètes." *Revue Biblique* 15 (1906): 67–83.

Liddell, H. G., and Scott, R., comp. *A Greek-English Lexicon*. 1843. Reprint ed., Oxford: Clarendon Press, 1977.

Lindblom, J. *Prophecy in Ancient Israel*. Philadelphia: Fortress Press, 1962.

Lindhagen, C. *The Servant Motif in the Old Testament*. Uppsala: Lundeqvist, 1950.

Lindsay, John. "The Babylonian Kings and Edom, 605–550 B.C." *Palestine Exploration Quarterly* 108 (1976): 23–29.

Lipínski, E. *La royauté de Yahwé dans la poésie et le culte de l'ancien Israël*. Brussels: Paleis der Academiën, 1965.

Long, B. O. "Two Question and Answer Schemata in the Prophets." *Journal of Biblical Literature* 90 (1971): 129-39.

Macintosh, A. A. "A Consideration of Hebrew גער." *Vetus Testamentum* 19 (1969): 471-79.

Mason, Rex. *The Books of Haggai, Zechariah and Malachi*. The Cambridge Bible Commentary. Cambridge: Cambridge University Press, 1977.

Matthews, J. G. "Tammuz Worship in the Book of Malachi." *Journal of the Palestine Oriental Society* II (1931): 42-50.

Meyer, Eduard. *Geschichte des Altertums*. 7 Vols. 2nd ed. Stuttgart: J. G. Cotta'sche Buchhandlung, 1928-1939.

Miller, P. O. "Fire in the Mythology of Canaan and Israel." *The Catholic Biblical Quarterly* 27 (1965): 256-61.

Moran, W. L. "The Scandal of the 'Great Sin' at Ugarit." *Journal of Near Eastern Studies* 18 (1959): 280-88.

Morgenstern, Julian. "Jerusalem—485 B.C." *Hebrew Union College Annual* 28 (1975): 15-47.

Mowinckel, Sigmund. *He That Cometh*. Translated by G. W. Anderson. New York: Abingdon Press, 1954.

———. *The Psalms in Israel's Worship*. 2 Vols. Translated by D. R. Ap-Thomas. New York: Abingdon Press, 1962.

Müller, D. H. "Discours de Malachie sur les rites des sacrifices." *Revue Biblique* 5 (1896): 535-39.

Myers, Jacob M. "Some Considerations Bearing on the Date of Joel." *Zeitschrift für die Alttestamentliche Wissenschaft* 74 (1962): 177-95.

North, Robert, S. J. "Angel-Prophet or Satan-Prophet." *Zeitschrift für die Alttestamentliche Wissenschaft* 82 (1970): 31-67.

Noth, Martin. *Leviticus*. Translated by J. E. Anderson. The Old Testament Library. Philadelphia: The Westminster Press, 1977.

Nötscher, Friedrich. *Altorientalischer und Alttestamentliche Auferstehungsglauben*. Würzburg: C. J. Becker, 1926.

———. *Das Buch Jeremias*. Die Heilige Schrift des Alten Testament. Bonn: Peter Hanstein, 1934.

Oded, Bustenay. "Judah and the Exile." In *Israelite and Judean History*. Edited by John H. Hayes and J. Maxwell Miller. Philadelphia: The Westminster Press, 1977, pp. 435-88.

Olmstead, A. T. *History of the Persian Empire*. Chicago: The University of Chicago Press, 1948.

Oppenheim, A. Leo, and Reiner, Erica, eds. *The Assyrian Dictionary*. Vol. 1/1. Chicago: The Oriental Institute, 1963.

Oppenheim, A. Leo, Reiner, Erica, and Biggs, Robert, D., eds. *The Assyrian Dictionary*. Vol. 1/2. Chicago. The Oriental Institute, 1968.

von Orelli, C. *The Twelve Minor Prophets*. Translated by J. S. Banks. Edinburgh: T. & T. Clark, 1893.

Patai, Raphael. *Sex and Family in the Bible and the Middle East*. Garden City, N.Y.: Doubleday and Company, Inc., 1959.

Payne Smith, R. *A Compendious Syriac Dictionary*. Oxford: The Clarendon Press, 1903.

Pedersen, Johannes. *Israel: Its Life and Culture*. 4 Vols. London: Oxford University Press, 1973.

Perlitt, L. *Bundestheologie im Alten Testament*. Wissenschaftliche Monographien zum Alten und Neuen Testament, no. 36. Neukirchen-Vluyn: Neukirchener Verlag, 1969.

Petersen, David L. *Late Israelite Prophecy: Studies in Deutero-Prophetic Literature and in Chronicles*. Society of Biblical Literature Monograph Series, Vol. 23. Missoula: Scholars Press, 1977.

Pfeiffer, Egon. "Die Disputationsworte im Buche Maleachi (Ein Beitrag zur formgeschichtlichen Struktur)." *Evangelische Theologie* 19 (1959): 546–68.

Pidoux, Georges. *L'homme dans l'Ancien Testament*. Cahiers Theologiques 32. Neuchâtal and Paris: Delachaux & Niestlé, 1953.

Pope, Marvin, H. "Notes on the Rephaim Texts from Ugarit." In *Essays on the Ancient Near East in Memory of Jacob Joel Finkelstein*. Connecticut Academy of Arts and Sciences: Memoires 19. Hamden, CT: Anchor Books, 1977, pp. 163–82.

―――. *Song of Songs*. The Anchor Bible. Garden City, N.Y.: Doubleday and Company, Inc., 1977.

Porteous, Norman. *Daniel*. The Old Testament Library. Philadelphia: The Westminster Press, 1965.

Pritchard, James, B., ed., *Ancient Near Eastern Texts Relating to the Old Testament*. Princeton: Princeton University Press, 1969.

Procksch, O. *Die kleinen prophetischen Schriften nach dem Exil*. Stuttgart: Verlag der Vereinsbuchhandlung, 1916.

Rabin, C. "Hebrew D = Hand." *Journal of Jewish Studies* 6 (1955): 111-15.

Rabinowitz, J. J. "The 'Great Sin' in Ancient Egyptian Marriage Contract." *Journal of Near Eastern Studies* 18 (1959): 73.

von Rad, Gerhard. *Deuteronomy*. The Old Testament Library. Translated by Dorothea Barton. Philadelphia: The Westminster Press, 1966.

———. *Old Testament Theology*. 2 Vols. Translated by D. M. G. Stalker. New York: Harper and Row, 1962-1965.

Rehm, Martin. "Das Opfer der Völker nach Mal. 1.11." In *Lex Tua Veritas: Festschrift für Hurbert Junker*. Trier: Paulinus-Verlag, 1961, pp. 193-208.

Ringgren, Helmer. *Israelite Religion*. Translated by David E. Green. Philadelphia: Fortress Press, 1966.

Robert, A., and Feuillet, A. *Introduction to the Old Testament*. Translated by Msgr. P. W. Skehan. New York: Desclee Company, 1968.

Robinson, Alan. "God, The Refiner of Silver." *The Catholic Biblical Quarterly* 11 (1949): 188-90.

Robinson, G. L. *The Twelve Minor Prophets*. New York: George H. Doran Co., 1926.

Rosenthal, Franz, ed. *An Aramaic Handbook*. 2 Vols. Wiesbaden: Otto Harrassowitz, 1967.

Ross, James F. "The Prophet as Yahweh's Messenger." In *Israel's Prophetic Heritage: Essays in Honor of James Muilenburg*. Edited by Bernhard W. Anderson and Walter Harrelson. New York: Harper and Brothers, 1962, pp. 98-107.

Rost, L. "Die Bezeichnungen für Land und Volk im AT." In *Festschrift Otto Procksch zum sechzigsten Geburtstag am 9. August 1934*. Edited by Albrecht Alt. Leipzig: A. Deichert, 1934, pp. 125-48.

Rowley, H. H. *The Servant of the Lord*. 2nd rev. ed., Oxford: Basil Blackwell, 1965.

Rudolph, Wilhelm. *Der Prophet Jeremia.* Handkommentar zum Alten Testament. Göttingen: Vandenhoeck & Ruprecht, 1958.

———. *Haggai-Sacharja-Maleachi.* Kommentar zum Alten Testament, Band 13, 4. Gütersloh: Gütersloher Verlagshaus Gerd Mohn, 1976.

Russell, D. S. *The Method and Message of Jewish Apocalyptic.* The Old Testament Library. Philadelphia: The Westminster Press, 1976.

Sasson, Jack M. *Ruth.* Baltimore: The Johns Hopkins University Press, 1979.

Saydon, P. P. "Assonance in Hebrew as a Means of Expressing Emphasis." *Biblica* 36 (1955): 36–50; 287–304.

Scharbert, J. "'Fluchen' und 'Segnen' im A.T." *Biblica* 39 (1958): 2–5.

Schnutenhaus, F. "Das Kommen und Erscheinen Gottes." *Zeitschrift für die Alttestamentliche Wissenschaft* 76 (1964): 1–22.

Sellin, Ernst. *Das Zwölfprophetenbuch übersetzt und erklärt.* Kommentar zum Alten Testament, Band XII, zweite Hälfte. Leipzig: A. Deichertsche Verlagsbuchhandlung, 1930.

Sellin, Ernst, and Fohrer, Georg. *Introduction to the Old Testament.* Translated by David E. Green. Nashville: Abingdon Press, 1968.

Smith, G. A. *The Book of the Twelve Prophets,* Vol. 2. The Expositor's Bible, 3rd ed. New York: A. C. Armstrong and Son, 1899.

Smith, John Merlin Powis. *Malachi.* The International Critical Commentary. Edinburgh: T. & T. Clark, 1912.

Speiser, E. A. "'People' and 'Nation' of Israel." *Journal of Biblical Literature* 70 (1960): 157–63.

Stamm, J. J., and Andrew, M. E. *The Ten Commandments in Recent Research.* Studies in Biblical Theology. Second Series, no. 5. London: SCM Press Ltd., 1967.

Starcky, Jean. "The Nabataeans: A Historical Sketch." *The Biblical Archaeologist* 18 (1955): 84–106.

Stummer, Fr. "Einige keilschriftliche Parallelen zu Jes 40–66." *Journal of Biblical Literature* 45 (1926): 171–89.

Swetnam, James. "Malachi I, 11: An Interpretation." *The Catholic Biblical Quarterly* 31 (1969): 200–209.

Teeple, Howard M. *The Mosaic Eschatological Prophet*. Society of Biblical Literature Monograph Series, Vol. 10. Philadelphia: Society of Biblical Literature, 1957.

Torrey, C. C. "The Prophet Malachi." *Journal of Biblical Literature* 17 (1898): 1-15.

Van Seters, John. *Abraham in History and Tradition*. New Haven: Yale University Press, 1975.

de Vaux, Roland. *Ancient Israel*. 2 Vols. New York: McGraw-Hill Book Company, 1965.

_____. "Les décrets de Cyrus et de Darius sur la reconstruction du temple." *Revue Biblique* 46 (1937): 29-57.

Vigouroux, Fulcran G., and Priot, Louis, eds. *Dictionnaire de la Bible, Supplément*. Tome 5. Paris: Librairie Letouzey et Ané, 1957.

Volz, Paul. *Jesaja* II. Kommentar zum Alten Testament. Leipzig: Deichert, 1932.

Vriezen, Th. C. *An Outline of Old Testament Theology*. 2nd ed. Newton, MA.: Charles T. Branford Col., 1970.

Waldman, Nahum. "Some Notes on Malachi 3:6; 3:13 and Psalm 42:11." *Journal of Biblical Literature* 93 (1974): 543-49.

von Waldow, H. E. "Anlass und Hintergrund der Verkündigen des Deuterojesaja." Diss. Theol., Bonn, 1953.

Wallis, Gerhard. "Wesen und Struktur der Botschaft Maleachis." *Das Ferne und Nahe Wort*. Beihefte zur Zeitschrift für die Alttestamentliche Wissenschaft. Berlin: Alfred Töpelmann, 105 (1967): 229-37.

Webster's Third New International Dictionary of the English Language, unabridged. Springfield, MA: G. & C. Merriam Co., 1976.

Webster's New World Dictionary of the American Language. Cleveland and New York: The World Publishing Co., 1968.

Weinfeld, Moshe. *Deuteronomy and the Deuteronomic School*. Oxford: The Clarendon Press, 1972.

Wellhausen, Julius. *Die kleinen Propheten übersetzt und erklärt*. Skizzen und Vorarbeiten 5. Berlin: Georg Reimer, 1892.

_____. *Prolegomena to the History of Ancient Israel*. Reprint ed., Gloucester, MA: Peter Smith, 1973.

Westermann, Claus. "Die Begriffe für Fragen und Suchen im AT." *Kerygma und Dogma* 6 (1960): 2-30.

————. *Isaiah 40–66.* Translated by David M. G. Stalker. The
Old Testament Library. Philadelphia: The Westminster
Press, 1969.

Widengren, Geo. "Oral Tradition and Written Literature among
the Hebrews in the Light of Arabic Evidence with Special
Regard to Prose Narratives." *Acta Orientalia* 23 (1959): 201–62.

————. "The Persian Period." In *Israelite and Judean History.*
Edited by John H. Hayes and J. Maxwell Miller. Philadelphia: The Westminster Press, 1977, pp. 489–538.

Wildberger, H. "Israel und sein Land." *Evangelische Theologie*
16 (1956): 404–22.

Wolff, Hans Walter. "Das Kerygma des deuteronomistischen
Geschichtswerk." *Zeitschrift für die Alttestamentliche Wissenschaft* 73 (1961): 171–83.

————. *Hosea.* Translated by Gary Stansell. Philadelphia: Fortress Press, 1974.

————. *Joel and Amos.* Translated by W. Janzen, S. D. McBride,
Jr., and C. A. Muenchow. Philadelphia: Fortress Press, 1977.

Zimmerli, W. *Gottes Offenbarung: Gesammelte Aufsätze.*
Münich: Kaiser, 1963.